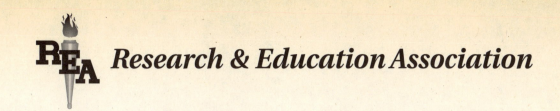

The Best Teachers' Test Preparation for the

NYSTCE®

Mathematics

Content Specialty Test (004)

Mel Friedman
Professor of Mathematics

and the Staff of
Research & Education Association

Visit our Educator Support Center at:
www.REA.com/teacher

The Mathematics Content Specialty Test Objectives presented in this book were created and implemented by the New York State Education Department and National Evaluation Systems, Inc. For further information visit the NYSTCE website at *www.nystce.nesinc.com.*

For all references in this book, New York State Certification Examinations™ and NYSTCE® are trademarks of the New York State Education Department and National Evaluation Systems, Inc.™ NES® is a registered trademark of National Evaluation Systems, Inc.™

Research & Education Association
61 Ethel Road West
Piscataway, New Jersey 08854
E-mail: info@rea.com

The Best Teachers' Test Preparation for the NYSTCE® Mathematics Content Specialty Test (004)

Printed in the United States of America

Library of Congress Control Number 2006930583

International Standard Book Number 0-7386-0243-4

About Research & Education Association

Founded in 1959, Research & Education Association is dedicated to publishing the finest and most effective educational materials—including software, study guides, and test preps—for students in middle school, high school, college, graduate school, and beyond.

REA's Test Preparation series includes books and software for all academic levels in almost all disciplines. Research & Education Association publishes test preps for students who have not yet entered high school, as well as for high school students preparing to enter college. Students from countries around the world seeking to attend college in the United States will find the assistance they need in REA's publications. For college students seeking advanced degrees, REA publishes test preps for many major graduate school admission examinations in a wide variety of disciplines, including engineering, law, and medicine. Students at every level, in every field, with every ambition can find what they are looking for among REA's publications.

REA's practice tests are always based upon the most recently administered exams and include every type of question that you can expect on the actual exams.

REA's publications and educational materials are highly regarded and continually receive an unprecedented amount of praise from professionals, instructors, librarians, parents, and students. Our authors are as diverse as the fields represented in the books we publish. They are well-known in their respective disciplines and serve on the faculties of prestigious high schools, colleges, and universities throughout the United States and Canada.

Today, REA's wide-ranging catalog is a leading resource for teachers, students, and professionals.

We invite you to visit us at *www.rea.com* to find out how "REA is making the world smarter."

Acknowledgments

We would like to thank REA's Carl Fuchs, President, for supervising development; Pam Weston, Vice President, Publishing, for setting the quality standards for production integrity and managing the publication to completion; Larry Kling, Vice President, Editorial, for his editorial direction; Christine Reilley, Senior Editor, for project management and preflight editorial review; Diane Goldschmidt, Senior Editor, for post-production quality assurance; Leanne Wells, Vincent Biancomano and Sandra Rush for their editorial contributions; Christine Saul, Senior Graphic Artist, for cover design; and Jeff LoBalbo, Senior Graphic Artist, for post-production file mapping.

We also gratefully acknowledge the team at Aquent Publishing Services for typesetting and indexing the manuscript.

CONTENTS

CHAPTER 1   1

INTRODUCTION: PASSING THE EXAMINATION 1

About This Book 1

About the Test. 1

How to Use This Book 2

Studying for the NYSTCE Mathematics CST 3

NYSTCE Mathematics CST Study Schedule 3

Format of the NYSTCE 3

About the Review Sections. 4

Scoring the NYSTCE Mathematics CST 4

The Day of the Test 5

DIAGNOSTIC TEST   7

Sample Mathematics Definitions and Formulas 9

Definitions and Formulas for Mathematics 9

Answer Sheet 12

Diagnostic Test 15

Answer Key. 21

Diagnostic Test: Detailed Explanations of Answers. 22

Scoring Guidelines for Constructed Written Assignment 30

Performance Characteristics 30

Scoring Scale 30

CHAPTER 2   33

SUBAREA I: MATHEMATICAL REASONING AND COMMUNICATION 33

Basic Concepts of Logic. 33
Method of Proof 35
Mathematics as Communication 41
Defining Objects and Concepts in Mathematics 41
The Language of Mathematics 42
Beyond Words. 42
Mathematical Connections. 42
Mental Connections 43
Equivalent Representations 43
Relationships Between Mathematical Topics 43
Representations of Arithmetic Operations 44

CHAPTER 3   45

SUBAREA II: ALGEBRA. 45

Real Numbers and Their Components. 45
Algebra Terms. 51
Operations with Polynomials 51
Simplifying Algebraic Expressions. 53
Linear Equations. 55
Slope of the Line. 56
Two Linear Equations 58
Quadratic Equations 61
Absolute Value Equations. 72
Inequalities. 72
Vectors. 74
Ratio, Proportion, and Variation 76
Elementary Functions 87
Properties of Functions 89
Graphing a Function. 90
Polynomial Functions and Their Graphs. 93

CHAPTER 4   97

SUBAREA III: TRIGONOMETRY AND CALCULUS 97

Angles and Trigonometric Functions 97
Calculus 107
Limits 107
The Derivative 112
Application of the Derivative 120
The Definite Integral 133
Applications of the Integral 141

CHAPTER 5   147

SUBAREA IV: MEASUREMENT AND GEOMETRY 147

Points, Lines, and Angles 147
Congruent Angles and Congruent Line Segments 157
Quiz: Method of Proof—Congruent Angles & Line Segments 159
Triangles 164
Quadrilaterals 168
Solid Geometry 174
Coordinate Geometry 179
Conic Sections 181
Quiz: Conic Sections 191

CHAPTER 6   199

SUBAREA V: DATA ANALYSIS, PROBABILITY, STATISTICS & DISCRETE MATHEMATICS 199

Probability 199
Properties of Probabilities 199
Methods of Computing Probabilities 200
Bayesian Decision Analysis 201
Probability Tables 202
Counting Methods 202
Statistics 209
Data Description: Graphs 209
Numerical Methods of Describing Data 213

Contents

Measures of Variability 220

Sampling 223

Simple Linear Regression 226

Experimental Design 228

Discrete Mathematics 231

Sequences and Series. 231

Linear Equations and Matrices 232

Matrices. 235

Matrix Arithmetic. 238

PRACTICE TEST   243

Sample Mathematics Definitions and Formulas 245

Definitions and Formulas for Mathematics 245

Answer Sheet 248

Practice Test. 251

Answer Key. 262

Practice Test: Detailed Explanations of Answers 263

Scoring Guidelines for Constructed Written Assignment 276

Performance Characteristics 276

Scoring Scale 276

INDEX   279

Introduction: Passing the Examination

About This Book

REA's *The Best Teachers' Preparation for the NYSTCE (New York State Teacher Certification Examinations) Mathematics CST* is a comprehensive guide designed to assist you in preparing to take the NYSTCE required for teaching mathematics in New York State. To enhance your chances of success in this important step toward your career as a teacher in New York schools, this test guide:

- presents an accurate and complete overview of the NYSTCE Mathematics
- identifies all of the important information and its representation on the exam
- provides a comprehensive review of every Subarea and objective
- presents sample questions in the actual test format
- suggests tips and strategies for successfully completing standardized tests
- provides a half-length diagnostic test to help pinpoint strengths and weaknesses
- provides a full-length practice test based on the most recently administered NYSTCE
- replicates the format of the official exam, including levels of difficulty
- supplies the correct answer and detailed explanations for each question on the diagnostic and practice

tests, which enables you to identify correct answers and understand why they are correct and, just as important, why the other answers are incorrect.

This guide is the result of studying many resources. The editors considered the most recent test administrations and professional standards. They also researched information from the New York State Education Department, professional journals, textbooks, and educators. This guide includes the best test preparation materials based on the latest information available.

About the Test

Below are the subareas used as the basis for the NYSTCE Mathematics CST, as well as the approximate percentage of the total test that each subarea occupies. These subareas represent the knowledge that teams of teachers, subject area specialists, and district-level educators have determined to be important for beginning teachers. This book contains a thorough review of these subareas, as well as the specific skills that demonstrate each area.

Who Administers the Test?

All the NYSTCE tests are administered by the New York State Education Department.

Subarea	Percentage
I. Mathematical Reasoning and Communication	13%
II. Algebra	26%
III. Trigonometry and Calculus	17%
IV. Measurement and Geometry	17%
V. Data Analysis, Probability, Statistics, and Discrete Mathematics	17%
VI. Algebra: Constructed-Response Assignment	10%

Can I Retake the Test?

Candidates who do not pass a test may retake it as often as necessary until a passing score is achieved. Candidates must reregister each time they retake a test. Candidates who have passed a NYSTCE test have met that part of the testing requirement for certification and, therefore, are not eligible to retake the test.

When Should the NYSTCE Be Taken?

The NYSTCE CST can be taken in either your junior or senior year. This recommended schedule will allow you to prepare for one test at a time and will give you an opportunity to retake any of the tests, if needed, before completing your teacher preparation program.

The New York teacher certification exams are given throughout the year. A current schedule of dates can be found on the Internet at *http://www.nystce.nesinc.com*. Click on "Before You Register" for information about test dates, test sites, and all the information you need. Candidates may register by Internet, postal mail, or telephone for most tests:

NYSTCE
National Evaluation Systems, Inc.
300 Venture Way
Hadley, MA 01035
(413) 256-2882
http://www.nystce.nesinc.com

Is There a Registration Fee?

To take the NYSTCE Mathematics CST there is a fee. A complete summary of the registration fees can be found at the website above, or by calling the number above.

How to Use This Book

How Do I Begin Studying?

Review the organization of this test preparation guide.

1. To best utilize your study time, follow our NYSTCE Independent Study Schedule. The schedule is based on a seven-week program, but can be condensed to four weeks if necessary.
2. Take the diagnostic test, and score it according to directions.
3. Review the format of the NYSTCE.
4. Review the test-taking advice and suggestions presented later in this chapter.
5. Pay attention to the information about subareas and objectives on the test.
6. Spend time reviewing topics that stand out as needing more study.
7. Take the Practice Test, review the explanations to your answers carefully, study the subareas that your scores indicate need further review.
8. Follow the suggestions at the end of this chapter for the day before and the day of the test.

Note: Graphic calculators should be brought for the test. See the website under the topic "The Day of the Test" for what to bring to the test site, including which brands and models of calculators are acceptable.

When Should I Start Studying?

It is never too early to start studying for the NYSTCE. The earlier you begin, the more time you will have to sharpen your skills. Do not procrastinate!

Cramming is not an effective way to study, since it does not allow you the time to think about the content, review the content and the practice test. It is important, however, to review the material one last time the night before the test administration.

Studying for the NYSTCE Mathematics CST

It is very important for you to choose the time and place for studying that works best for you. Some individuals may set aside a certain number of hours every morning to study, while others may choose to study at night before going to sleep. Other people may study during the day, while waiting in line, or even while eating lunch. Only you can determine when and where your study time will be most effective. Be consistent and use your time wisely. Work out a study routine and stick to it.

When you take the practice tests, simulate the conditions of the actual test as closely as possible. Turn your television and radio off, and sit down at a quiet table free from distraction. As you complete each practice test, score your test and thoroughly review the explanations to the questions you answered incorrectly; however, do not review too much at any one time. Concentrate on one problem area at a time by reviewing the question and explanation, and by studying our review until you are confident that you have mastered the material.

Keep track of your scores. By doing so, you will be able to gauge your progress and discover general weaknesses in particular sections. Give extra attention to the reviews that cover your areas of difficulty, as this will build your skills in those areas.

NYSTCE Mathematics CST Study Schedule

The following study schedule allows for thorough preparation for the NYSTCE. The course of study here is seven weeks, but you can condense or expand the timeline to suit your personal schedule. It is vital that you adhere to a structured plan and set aside ample time

each day to study. The more time you devote to studying, the more prepared and confident you will be on the day of the test.

Week 1. Take the diagnostic exam. The score will indicate your strengths and weaknesses. Make sure you simulate real exam conditions when you take the test. Afterwards, score it and review the explanations, especially for questions you answered incorrectly.

Week 2. Review the explanations for the questions you missed, and review the appropriate chapter sections. Useful study techniques include highlighting key terms and information, taking notes as you review the book's sections, and putting new terms and information on note cards to help retain the information.

Weeks 3 and 4. Reread all your note cards, refresh your understanding of the exam's subareas and skills, review your college textbooks, and read over class notes you've previously taken. This is also the time to consider any other supplementary materials that your counselor or the New York State Education Department suggests. Review the Department's website at *http://ohe32.nysed.gov/tcert/*.

Week 5. Begin to condense your notes and findings. A structured list of important facts and concepts, based on your note cards and the book's subareas, will help you thoroughly review for the test. Review the answers and explanations for all missed questions.

Week 6. Have someone quiz you using the index cards you created. Take the practice test, adhering to the time limits and simulated test-day conditions.

Week 7. Review your areas of weakness using all study materials. This is a good time to re-take the practice test.

Format of the NYSTCE

The NYSTCE Mathematics CST addresses 6 main content areas, or subareas, deemed by the New York State Education Department to be foundational to effective teaching. Divided between the 6 subareas are 21 objectives that provide information about the knowledge and skills assessed by the Mathematics test. Individual test questions require a variety of different thinking levels, ranging from simple recall to evaluation and problem solving.

All 90 questions in the first five subareas on the NYSTCE are in multiple-choice format. Each question will have four options, lettered A through D, from which to choose. You should have plenty of time in which to complete the NYSTCE, but be aware of the amount of time you are spending on each question so that you allow yourself time to complete the test. Although speed is not very important, a steady pace should be maintained when answering the questions. Using the practice tests will help you prepare for this task.

The final subarea is a constructed-response (written) assignment. This section requires that you prepare a written response of about one to two pages on the assigned topic. You should plan, write, review, and edit your response in the time allotted. Your response will not be judged on writing ability, but must be communicated clearly and will be scored on a scale of 1 to 4. Your response is evaluated on the basis of the following criteria:

Purpose: Fulfill the charge of the assignment

Application of Content: Accurately and effectively apply the relevant knowledge and skills

Support: Support the response with appropriate examples and/or sound reasoning reflecting an understanding of the relevant knowledge and skills.

About the Review Sections

The reviews in this book are designed to help you sharpen the basic skills needed to approach the NYSTCE, as well as provide strategies for attacking the questions.

Each teaching subarea is examined in a separate chapter. The skills required for all six subareas are extensively discussed to optimize your understanding of what the NYSTCE covers.

Your schooling has taught you most of what you need to answer the questions on the test. The education classes you took should have provided you with the know-how to make important decisions about situations you will face as a teacher. Our review is designed to help you fit the information you have acquired into specific

subarea components. Reviewing your class notes and textbooks together with our subarea reviews will give you an excellent springboard for passing the NYSTCE.

Scoring the NYSTCE Mathematics CST

The approximate percentage of the test corresponding to each subarea is listed near the beginning of this Introduction.

An examinee's performance on a test is evaluated against an established standard. The passing requirement for each test is established by the New York State Commissioner of Education based on the professional judgments and recommendations of New York State educators.

The following characteristics guide the scoring of responses to the constructed-response (written) assignment: (1) Purpose—fulfill the charge of the assignment, (2) Application of Content—accurately and effectively apply the relevant knowledge and skills, (3) Support—support the response with appropriate examples and/or reasoning reflecting an understanding of the relevant knowledge and skills.

The NYSTCE Mathematics CST scores are reported using a 1-through-4 scale, 4 being the best score. The total test score is reported in a range from 100 to 300 and is based on performance on all sections of the test. An examinee's multiple-choice score and scores on any constructed-response assignments are combined to obtain the total test score. A score of 220 represents the minimum passing score. An examinee with a total test score of 220 or above passes the test. An examinee with a total test score below 220 does not pass the test. Candidates who do not pass a test may retake it as often as necessary until a passing score is achieved. Candidates must reregister each time they retake a test. For more information about score reporting, visit the NYSTCE Web site at *http://www.nystce.nesinc.com*.

Score Results

Your test scores will be reported to you, the NYSED (and are automatically added to your certification application file), and, if applicable, the institution that you indicated when you registered. Your score report will be mailed on the score report date published in the Test Dates section of the NYSTCE Web site at *http://www.nystce.nesinc.com.*

Test-Taking Tips

Although you may not be familiar with tests like the NYSTCE, this book will help acquaint you with this type of exam and help alleviate your test-taking anxieties. Listed below are ways to help you become accustomed to the NYSTCE, some of which may be applied to other tests as well.

Tip 1. Become comfortable with the format of the NYSTCE. When you are practicing, stay calm and pace yourself. After simulating the test only once, you will boost your chances of doing well, and you will be able to sit down for the actual NYSTCE with much more confidence.

Tip 2. Read all of the possible answers. Just because you think you have found the correct response, do not automatically assume that it is the best answer. Read through each choice to be sure that you are not making a mistake by jumping to conclusions.

Tip 3. Use the process of elimination. Go through each answer to a question and eliminate as many of the answer choices as possible. By eliminating two answer choices, you have given yourself a better chance of getting the item correct since there will only be two choices left from which to make your guess. Do not leave an answer blank; it is better to guess than to not answer a question on the NYSTCE test.

Tip 4. Place a question mark in your answer booklet next to answers you guessed, then recheck them later if you have time.

Tip 5. Work quickly and steadily. You will have two and one-half hours to complete the test, so work quickly and steadily to avoid focusing on any one problem too long. Taking the practice tests in this book will help you learn to budget your precious time.

Tip 6. Learn the directions and format of the test. Familiarizing yourself with the directions and format of the test will not only save time, but will also help you avoid anxiety (and the mistakes caused by getting anxious).

Tip 7. Be sure that the answer circle you are marking corresponds to the number of the question in the test booklet. Since the test is multiple-choice, it is graded by machine, and marking one wrong answer can throw off your answer key and your score. Be extremely careful.

The Day of the Test

Before the Test

On the day of the test, make sure to dress comfortably, so that you are not distracted by being too hot or too cold while taking the test. Plan to arrive at the test center early. This will allow you to collect your thoughts and relax before the test, and will also spare you the anguish that comes with being late.

You should check your NYSTCE Registration Bulletin to find out what time to arrive at the testing center.

Before you leave for the test center, make sure that you have your admission ticket and two forms of identification, one of which must contain a recent photograph, your name, and signature (i.e., driver's license). You will not be admitted to the test center if you do not have proper identification.

You must bring several sharpened No. 2 pencils with erasers and an approved graphic calculator (see above) as none will be provided at the test center.

If you would like, you may wear a watch to the test center. However, you may not wear one that makes noise, because it may disturb the other test takers. Dictionaries, textbooks, notebooks, briefcases, or packages will not be permitted. Drinking, smoking, and eating are prohibited.

During the Test

The NYSTCE is given in one sitting with no breaks. Procedures will be followed to maintain test security. Once you enter the test center, follow all of the rules and instructions given by the test supervisor. If you do not, you risk being dismissed from the test and having your scores cancelled.

When all of the materials have been distributed, the test instructor will give you directions for filling out your answer sheet. Fill out this sheet carefully since this information will be printed on your score report.

Once the test begins, mark only one answer per question, completely erase unwanted answers and marks, and fill in answers darkly and neatly.

After the Test

When you finish your test, hand in your materials and you will be dismissed. Then, go home and relax—you deserve it!

NYSTCE

New York State Teacher Certification Examinations

Mathematics CST (004)

Diagnostic Test

Sample Mathematics Definitions and Formulas

Definitions and Formulas for Mathematics

LOGIC

$a \rightarrow b$	a implies b
$a \leftrightarrow b$	a if and only if b
$a \wedge b$	a and b
$a \vee b$	a or b
$\sim a$	not a
$A \cup B$	A union B
$A \cap B$	A intersect B
$\overline{A}$	complement of A
U	universal set
$\{\}$	empty set

ALGEBRA

$i = \sqrt{-1}$	imaginary unit
$\overline{z}$	complex conjugate of z
A^{-1}	inverse of matrix A
$\vec{v}$	vector v

GEOMETRY

surface area of a sphere	$S = 4\pi r^2$	$\sim$	is similar to
volume of a sphere	$V = \dfrac{4}{3}\pi r^3$	$\cong$	is congruent to

GEOMETRY (*Continued*)

Congruent Angles

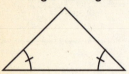

Parallel Lines

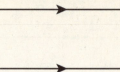

Congruent Sides

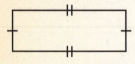

Heron's Formula

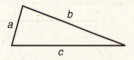

$$\text{Area} = \sqrt{s(s-a)(s-b)(s-c)}$$

$$\text{where } s = \frac{a+b+c}{2}$$

Ellipse

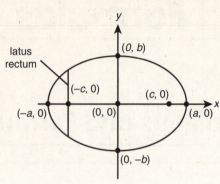

$$\frac{(x-h)^2}{a^2} + \frac{(y-k)^2}{b^2} = 1$$

$$\text{where } c^2 = a^2 - b^2$$

Parabola

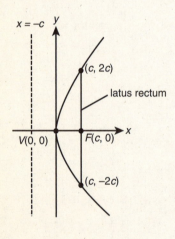

$$(y-k)^2 = 4c(x-h)$$

Hyperbola

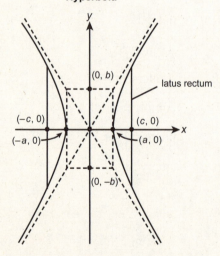

$$\frac{(x-h)^2}{a^2} - \frac{(y-k)^2}{b^2} = 1 \text{ where } b^2 = c^2 - a^2$$

Directrices of a Conic

$$x = \pm\frac{a}{e} = \pm\frac{a^2}{c}$$

Eccentricity of a Conic

$$e = \frac{c}{a}$$

TRIGONOMETRY

$$\sin(\theta_1 \pm \theta_2) = \sin\theta_1 \cos\theta_2 \pm \cos\theta_1 \sin\theta_2$$

$$\cos(\theta_1 \pm \theta_2) = \cos\theta_1 \cos\theta_2 \pm \sin\theta_1 \sin\theta_2$$

$$\tan(\theta_1 \pm \theta_2) = \frac{\tan\theta_1 \pm \tan\theta_2}{1 \pm \tan\theta_1 \tan\theta_2}$$

$$\sin\frac{\theta}{2} = \pm\sqrt{\frac{1-\cos\theta}{2}}$$

$$\cos\frac{\theta}{2} = \pm\sqrt{\frac{1+\cos\theta}{2}}$$

$$\tan\frac{\theta}{2} = \pm\sqrt{\frac{1-\cos\theta}{1+\cos\theta}}$$

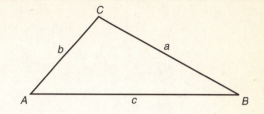

Law of Sines

$$\frac{\sin A}{a} = \frac{\sin B}{b} = \frac{\sin C}{c}$$

Law of Cosines

$$c^2 = a^2 + b^2 - 2ab\cos C$$

STATISTICS

$$\text{standard deviation of a sample mean} = \frac{\sigma}{\sqrt{N}}$$

NOTES FOR MATHEMATICS TEST

Assume all functions are real-valued functions unless otherwise noted.

Diagrams may not be drawn to scale.

Answer Sheet

1. Ⓐ Ⓑ Ⓒ Ⓓ
2. Ⓐ Ⓑ Ⓒ Ⓓ
3. Ⓐ Ⓑ Ⓒ Ⓓ
4. Ⓐ Ⓑ Ⓒ Ⓓ
5. Ⓐ Ⓑ Ⓒ Ⓓ
6. Ⓐ Ⓑ Ⓒ Ⓓ
7. Ⓐ Ⓑ Ⓒ Ⓓ
8. Ⓐ Ⓑ Ⓒ Ⓓ
9. Ⓐ Ⓑ Ⓒ Ⓓ
10. Ⓐ Ⓑ Ⓒ Ⓓ
11. Ⓐ Ⓑ Ⓒ Ⓓ
12. Ⓐ Ⓑ Ⓒ Ⓓ
13. Ⓐ Ⓑ Ⓒ Ⓓ
14. Ⓐ Ⓑ Ⓒ Ⓓ
15. Ⓐ Ⓑ Ⓒ Ⓓ
16. Ⓐ Ⓑ Ⓒ Ⓓ
17. Ⓐ Ⓑ Ⓒ Ⓓ
18. Ⓐ Ⓑ Ⓒ Ⓓ
19. Ⓐ Ⓑ Ⓒ Ⓓ
20. Ⓐ Ⓑ Ⓒ Ⓓ
21. Ⓐ Ⓑ Ⓒ Ⓓ
22. Ⓐ Ⓑ Ⓒ Ⓓ
23. Ⓐ Ⓑ Ⓒ Ⓓ

24. Ⓐ Ⓑ Ⓒ Ⓓ
25. Ⓐ Ⓑ Ⓒ Ⓓ
26. Ⓐ Ⓑ Ⓒ Ⓓ
27. Ⓐ Ⓑ Ⓒ Ⓓ
28. Ⓐ Ⓑ Ⓒ Ⓓ
29. Ⓐ Ⓑ Ⓒ Ⓓ
30. Ⓐ Ⓑ Ⓒ Ⓓ
31. Ⓐ Ⓑ Ⓒ Ⓓ
32. Ⓐ Ⓑ Ⓒ Ⓓ
33. Ⓐ Ⓑ Ⓒ Ⓓ
34. Ⓐ Ⓑ Ⓒ Ⓓ
35. Ⓐ Ⓑ Ⓒ Ⓓ
36. Ⓐ Ⓑ Ⓒ Ⓓ
37. Ⓐ Ⓑ Ⓒ Ⓓ
38. Ⓐ Ⓑ Ⓒ Ⓓ
39. Ⓐ Ⓑ Ⓒ Ⓓ
40. Ⓐ Ⓑ Ⓒ Ⓓ
41. Ⓐ Ⓑ Ⓒ Ⓓ
42. Ⓐ Ⓑ Ⓒ Ⓓ
43. Ⓐ Ⓑ Ⓒ Ⓓ
44. Ⓐ Ⓑ Ⓒ Ⓓ
45. Ⓐ Ⓑ Ⓒ Ⓓ

46. Constructed Written Assignment

Continue on Next Page

Constructed Written Assignment *(Continued)*

NYSTCE Mathematics CST (004) Diagnostic Test

Note: This diagnostic test is half the length of the actual test. There is a full-length practice test following the review.

TIME: 2 hours
45 multiple-choice questions and 1 constructed-response assignment.

> **Directions:** Read each item and select the best answer.

1. What is (are) the value(s) of x in the following equation?

$$\sqrt{37 - 3x} = 3 + \sqrt{x + 20}$$

   (A) 10.25 only   (C) −4 only

   (B) 10.25 and −4   (D) −10.25 and 4

2.

x	1	2	3	4
y	24	17	−2	−39

In the table shown above, which expression best represents the relationship between x and y?

   (A) $y = -13x + 37$ (C) $y = -x^3 + 25$

   (B) $y = -7x + 31$ (D) $y = -7x^2 + 14x + 17$

3. Exclusive of the numbers 1 and 1176, how many factors are there for the number 1176?

   (A) 20   (C) 24

   (B) 22   (D) 26

4. A windshield wiper of a car is 12 inches long. If it takes 1/4 second to trace out 1/6 revolution, what is the approximate speed, in inches per second, of the tip of the wiper?

   (A) 18   (C) 38

   (B) 26   (D) 50

5.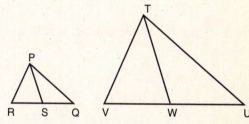

In the figures above, $\Delta PQR \sim \Delta TUV$. Point S is the midpoint of $\overline{QR}$ and point W is the midpoint of $\overline{UV}$. If PR/TV = 3/5, what is the value of the following ratio?

(Area of ΔPSR)/(Area of ΔTUV)

   (A) .18   (C) .36

   (B) .30   (D) .40

6. The graph of $y = 3x^2 - 19$ is translated 4 units horizontally to the right and 6 units vertically downward. Which of the following represents the x value

of a point on the translated graph in which the y value is 2?

(A) 9

(C) 5

(B) 7

(D) 3

7. Which of the following is a geometric representation of a rational number between 6 and 7?

(A) The length of the hypotenuse of a right triangle whose two legs are 4 and 5

(B) The length of the altitude of an equilateral triangle with a side of 4

(C) The length of the arc of a circle formed by two radii and a central angle of 90°, in which the diameter is 22/π

(D) The length of the circumference of a circle whose radius is 3.2/π

8. What is the sum, in radians, of the solutions for x in the following equation?

$\text{Tan}^2 x = (3/2)(\sec x), 0 \leq x \leq 2\pi$

(A) π/3

(C) 2π

(B) 4π/3

(D) 8π/3

9. Which of the following groups of data has two modes?

(A) 2, 2, 3, 3, 4, 4, 5, 6, 7

(B) 2, 2, 2, 3, 3, 4, 4, 4, 5

(C) 2, 3, 3, 4, 4, 4, 5, 5, 6

(D) 2, 3, 3, 3, 3, 4, 5, 6, 6

10. Look at the following summary of the students in a small college.

	Freshmen	Sophomores	Juniors	Seniors
Males	75	90	150	125
Females	105	170	200	85

The name of each student is put on a slip of paper and put into a jar. One slip of paper is randomly drawn. Given that the name drawn is that of a female student, what is the probability that the individual is a sophomore or a junior?

(A) .71

(C) .61

(B) .66

(D) .56

11. The cost of a cab ride with the Built-Rite Taxi Company is as follows: An initial cost of $2.50, plus $0.15 for each 1/4 mile. If Mike takes a cab ride for a distance of 20 miles, which equation could be used to calculate his total cost?

(A) T = ($2.50 + $0.15)(20)

(B) T = ($2.50 + $0.60)(20)

(C) T = $2.50 + ($0.15)(20)

(D) T = $2.50 + ($0.60)(20)

12. The position of a particle moving along a straight line at any time t is given by $S(t) = 2t^3 - 4t^2 + 2t - 1$. The least velocity during the time interval [0, 2] is

(A) 4.25

(C) −0.67

(B) 0.5

(D) −1.5

13.

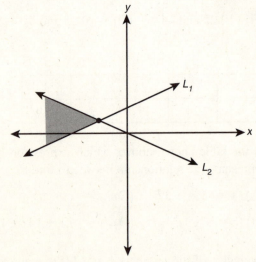

The above graph shows the intersection of two lines L_1 and L_2, and a shaded region. The solution to which of the following systems of inequalities could represent the shaded region?

(A) $x + 2y \geq 0$

$x - 2y \leq -4$

(B) $x + 2y \leq 0$

$x - 2y \geq -4$

(C) $x + 2y \le 0$
$\qquad x - 2y \le -4$

(D) $x + 2y \ge 0$
$\qquad x - 2y \ge -4$

14. Solve for x.

$$5x + 2y = -5$$
$$-3x + y = 3$$

(A) 0

(C) 1

(B) $-\frac{1}{11}$

(D) -1

15. If $f'(c) = 0$ for $f(x) = 3x^2 - 12x + 9$, where $0 \le x \le 4$, then $c =$

(A) 2

(C) 0

(B) 3

(D) 1

16. For the graph of $(x + 1)^2 / 9 + (y - 2)^2 / 4 = 1$, which of the following is <u>completely</u> accurate?

(A) The center is located at $(-1, 2)$ and the length of the minor axis is 6

(B) The center is located at $(1, -2)$ and the length of the minor axis is 4

(C) The center is located at $(1, -2)$ and the length of the major axis is 2

(D) The center is located at $(-1, 2)$ and the length of the major axis is 6

17. Use this graph to answer the question.

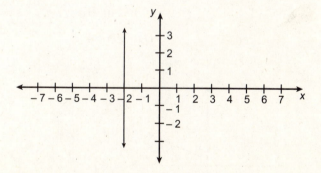

Which equation is represented above?

(A) $x = 2$

(C) $y = 2$

(B) $x = -2$

(D) $y = -2$

18. The distance between the point $(2, 4)$ and the line $y + 2x - 3 = 0$ is

(A) 1.9

(C) 2.24

(B) 3.24

(D) 3.8

19. In an apartment building there are 9 apartments having terraces for every 16 apartments. If the apartment building has a total of 144 apartments, how many apartments have terraces?

(A) 137

(C) 63

(B) 81

(D) 102

20.

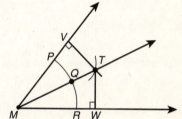

In the diagram above, $\angle PMR$ is acute. At point M, an arc PR is drawn so that $MR = MP$. Arc $\overset{\frown}{PR}$ is then bisected at point Q by the construction shown at point T. The ray joining M, Q, and T is drawn and a perpendicular segment is drawn from T so that $\overline{TV} \perp \overline{MV}$ and $\overline{TW} \perp \overline{MW}$. Which of the following may be <u>false</u>?

(A) $TV = TW$

(B) $m\angle VMW > m\angle VTM$

(C) $m\angle VTM = m\angle WTM$

(D) $MW > MP$

21. The area between the line $y = x$ and the curve $y = \frac{1}{2}x^2$ is

(A) 1

(C) $\frac{2}{3}$

(B) $\frac{1}{2}$

(D) $\frac{3}{2}$

22. If m $\overset{\frown}{ABC}$ is $\frac{3}{2}\pi$ radians, then y is equal to

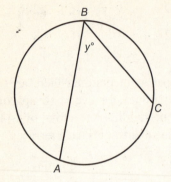

(A) 90°.   (C) 45°.

(B) 72°.   (D) 36°.

23. Consider the following identities:

$1 + 3 = 2^2$, $1 + 3 + 5 = 3^2$, $1 + 3 + 5 + 7 = 4^2$. Which of the following statements best describes this pattern?

(A) The sum of n odd numbers, beginning with 1, is equal to n^2

(B) The sum of any n odd numbers is equal to n^2

(C) The sum of n numbers, beginning with 1, is equal to n^2

(D) The sum of any n numbers is equal to n^2

24. What is the value of $(\log_2 5)(\log_5 8)(\log_8 16)$?

(A) 5   (C) 3

(B) 4   (D) 2

25. Events A and B are dependent, where $P(B) = .20$, $P(B \mid A) = .40$, and $P(A \cup B) = .29$. What is the value of $P(A)$? Note: $P(A)$ means the probability of event A.

(A) .09   (C) .29

(B) .15   (D) .31

26. Select the statement that is the negation of the statement "If I am hungry, then I will have a snack."

(A) If I am not hungry, then I will not have a snack.

(B) I am not hungry and I will have a snack.

(C) I am hungry or I will not have a snack.

(D) I am hungry and I will not have a snack.

27. Which of the following inequalities has no solution?

(A) $|9 - x| < 0$ (C) $|9 - x| > 0$

(B) $|9 - x| \le 0$ (D) $|9 - x| \ge 0$

28. Read the graph and answer the question.

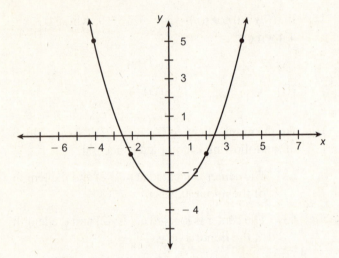

Which equation could be represented by the graph?

(A) $y = \frac{1}{2}x^2 + 3$ (C) $y = \frac{1}{2}x^2 - 3$

(B) $y = -\frac{1}{2}x^2 - 3$ (D) $y = -\frac{1}{2}x^2 + 3$

29. $(\sin\theta \times \cot\theta)^2 + (\cos\theta \times \tan\theta)^2 =$

(A) 1   (C) $2\sin^2\theta$

(B) $2\cos^2\theta$ (D) $2\cot^2\theta$

30.

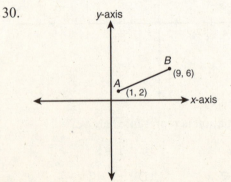

In the graph shown on the previous page, if $\overline{AB}$ is reflected about the x-axis, what will be the reflected coordinates of the midpoint of $\overline{AB}$?

(A) (5, 4)　　　　(C) (5, –4)

(B) (–5, –4)　　　(D) (–5, 4)

31. A zoo has eight elephants. On any given day three of the elephants are selected and lined up to give rides to the visitors. How many different arrangements of any three selected elephants are there?

(A) 21　　　　(C) 336

(B) 24　　　　(D) 6

32. Which of the following has the highest value?

(A) The number of distinct ways of arranging nine people in a line

(B) The number of distinct ways of selecting four different letters from the alphabet

(C) The number of distinct committees of five people chosen from a list of 33 people

(D) The number of distinct sequences of heads and tails when an ordinary coin is flipped 18 times

33. $\sin(x + y) = 0.9659$, $\sin(x) = 0.5$. Find $\cos(y)$.

(A) 0.425　　　　(C) 0.707

(B) 0.034　　　　(D) 0.816

34. What is the slope of the tangent to the curve $y = x^2 + 11x - 2$ at the point where $x = -3$?

(A) –44　　　　(C) 3

(B) –36　　　　(D) 5

35. An amount of N dollars was placed into an account 6 months ago. This account pays compound interest at the annual rate of 16% compounded quarterly. Currently, this account has $2000. Assuming that no money has been withdrawn from or added to this account, what is the value of N? (Nearest dollar)

(A) $1843　　　　(C) $1847

(B) $1845　　　　(D) $1849

36. Look at the following problem:

Lorraine can take any one of three roads to go from city A to city B, any one of five roads to go from city B to city C, and any one of six roads to go from city C to city D. How many different routes are possible for Lorraine to travel from city A to city D, by way of cities B and C?

Which of the following would be the best way to solve the above problem?

(A) Tree diagram　　(C) Frequency curve

(B) Pie graph　　　(D) Probability table

37. Which of the following is the position vector for $\overrightarrow{P_1P_2}$ if $P_1 = (1, -2)$ and $P_2 = (6, 4)$?

(A) $5i - 6j$　　　　(C) $6i - 5j$

(B) $5i + 6j$　　　　(D) $6i + 5j$

38. Which of the following sentences below concerning the equation of an ellipse

$$\frac{x^2}{a^2} + \frac{y^2}{b^2} = 1,$$

is true when $a = b = r$?

I. The equation reduces to $x^2 + y^2 = r^2$.

II. The equation reduces to an equation of a circle with center at (0, 0) and radius r.

III. The equation reduces to an equation of a circle, center (0, r).

(A) I only.　　　　(C) II and III only.

(B) I and II only.　(D) III only.

39. If the period of $y = (A)(\cos Bx)$ is $2\pi/5$ and its amplitude is 3, what is the value of A/B?

(A) 5/2　　　　(C) 3/5

(B) 5/3　　　　(D) 2/5

40. In a Normal Distribution of data with a mean of 80 and a standard deviation of 4, approximately what percent of the data lies between 74 and 86?

(A) 86.64 (C) 49.72

(B) 74.98 (D) 43.32

41. If $\int_a^b f(x)\,dx = 8$, $a = 2$, f is continuous, and the average value of f on $[a, b]$ is 4, then $b =$

(A) 0 (C) 4

(B) 2 (D) 3

42. Representatives to a student group are being selected to fill vacancies. Two of five freshmen will be selected and three of four sophomores will be selected. In how many different ways can these students be selected?

(A) 480 (C) 80

(B) 120 (D) 40

43. What is the solution for x in the following inequality?

$$x^2 - 5x < 6$$

(A) $-2 < x < 3$ (C) $-1 < x < 6$

(B) $-3 < x < 2$ (D) $-6 < x < 1$

44. The mean of a group of 20 numbers is 9. If one number is removed, the mean of the remaining numbers is 7. What is the value of the removed number?

(A) 16 (C) 40

(B) 25 (D) 47

45. In Pascal's triangle, the top row is 1, the second row is 1 1, the third row is 1 2 1, etc. What is the sum of the numbers in the 20th row?

(A) 131,072 (C) 524,288

(B) 262,144 (D) 1,048,576

46. **Constructed Written Assignment**

Directions: Prepare a legibly written response of one to two pages on the problem below. Plan, write,

review, and edit your response. Your response will not be judged on writing ability, but must be communicated clearly and will be scored on a scale of 1 to 4. It will be evaluated on the following:

Purpose: Fulfill the charge of the assignment.

Application of Content: Accurately and effectively apply the relevant knowledge and skills.

Support: Support the response with appropriate examples and/or sound reasoning reflecting an understanding of the relevant knowledge and skills.

A small housing community consists of three dwellings, as shown below.

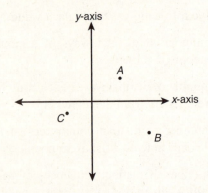

The town planner wants to construct a clubhouse which is equidistant from each dwelling.

• If you had only a straight edge and a compass, how would you determine the exact location of the clubhouse?

• If the coordinates of the dwellings are (4, 3), (−3, −1), and (7, −6), what are the coordinates of the clubhouse?

• A direct walkway will be built between the clubhouse and each dwelling. Each walkway is rectangular in shape and will be 4 feet wide. The length of each walkway is 20 feet times the distance in units on the graph from each dwelling to the clubhouse. If the cost of the walkway is $15 per square foot, what is the total cost of all three walkways?

1. (C)	16. (D)	31. (C)
2. (C)	17. (B)	32. (A)
3. (B)	18. (C)	33. (C)
4. (D)	19. (B)	34. (D)
5. (A)	20. (B)	35. (D)
6. (B)	21. (C)	36. (A)
7. (D)	22. (C)	37. (B)
8. (C)	23. (A)	38. (B)
9. (B)	24. (B)	39. (C)
10. (B)	25. (B)	40. (A)
11. (D)	26. (D)	41. (C)
12. (C)	27. (A)	42. (D)
13. (C)	28. (C)	43. (C)
14. (D)	29. (A)	44. (D)
15. (A)	30. (C)	45. (C)

Detailed Explanations of Answers

1. (C)

−4 only

Square each side of the equation to get $37 - 3x = 9 + 6\sqrt{x + 20} + x + 20$. Simplify this to $8 - 4x = 6\sqrt{x + 20}$. Square each side to get $64 - 64x + 16x^2 = 36(x + 20)$. Simplify this to $16x^2 - 100x - 656 = 0$ or reduced to $4x^2 - 25x - 164 = 0$. Using either the Quadratic Formula or by factoring as $(x + 4)(4x - 41) = 0$, the results are $x = -4$ and $x = 10.25$. However, only −4 checks the equation.

2. (C)

$y = -x^3 + 25$

Each pair of values in the table will check this equation. Answer Choice (A) is wrong since (2, 17) and (4, −39) do not check the equation. Answer Choice (B) is wrong since (3, −2) and (4, −39) do not check the equation. Answer Choice (D) is wrong since (3, −2) does not check the equation.

3. (B)

22

The number 1176 can be written as $2^3 \cdot 3^1 \cdot 7^2$. The total number of factors is given by the product of the value of the exponents increased by 1, which becomes (4)(2)(3) = 24. However, this number includes the factors of 1 and 1176. Remove these two numbers to get 22 factors.

4. (D)

50

The wiper will make (1/6)(4) = 2/3 of a revolution in one second. A revolution is equivalent to the circumference, which is 24π inches. So, 2/3 of a revolution = $(2/3)(24\pi) = 16\pi$, which is approximately 50 in.

5. (A)

.18

The ratio of the area of ΔPQR to the area of ΔTUV must be the square of the ratio of corresponding sides = (3/5)(3/5) = 9/25. However, we note that the area of ΔPSR is one-half of the area of ΔPQR. Thus, the correct ratio = (1/2)(9/25) = 9/50 = .18.

6. (B)

7

Given the directions of the translation, the equation of the new graph is $y = 3(x - 4)^2 - 25$. Substitute 2 for y to get $2 = 3(x - 4)^2 - 25$. This simplifies to $3x^2 - 24x + 21 = 0$. Further simplification to $x^2 - 8x + 7 = 0$, and then factoring as $(x - 7)(x - 1) = 0$, we get $x = 7$ and $x = 1$. Note that 1 does not appear as an answer choice.

7. (D)

The length of the circumference of a circle whose radius is $3.2/\pi$

The circumference = $(2\pi)(3.2/\pi) = 6.4$, which is rational and between 6 and 7. Answer Choice (A) is wrong since the length is $\sqrt{41}$, which is irrational. Answer Choice (B) is wrong since the length is $4\sqrt{3}$, which is irrational. Answer Choice (C) is wrong since the arc's length is one-fourth the circumference, which is (1/4)(22) = 5.5.

8. (C)

2π

Substitute $\sec^2 x - 1$ for $\tan^2 x$ to get $\sec^2 x - 1 = (3/2)\sec x$. Rewrite as $2\sec^2 x - 3\sec x - 2 = 0$. Factor as $(2\sec x + 1)(\sec x - 2) = 0$. $2\sec x + 1 = 0$ has no solution, but $\sec x - 2 = 0$ has the solutions $\pi/3$ and $5\pi/3$, so their sum is 2π.

9. (B)

2, 2, 2, 3, 3, 4, 4, 4, 5

The two modes are 2 and 4. Answer Choice (A) is wrong since it has three modes. Answer Choice (C) is wrong since 4 is the only mode. Answer Choice (D) is wrong since 3 is the only mode.

10. (B)

.66

There are a total of 560 female students. Of that total, 370 are either sophomores or juniors. Then 370/560 = .66 (nearest hundredth).

11. (D)

T = $2.50 + ($0.60)(20)

$0.15 per one-fourth mile is equivalent to $0.60 per mile. Since Mike is traveling 20 miles, his total cost would be $2.50 + ($0.60)(20).

12. (C)

The rate of movement of the particle is the velocity $s'(t)$. Use your graphic calculator to draw both $s(t)$ and $s'(t)$.

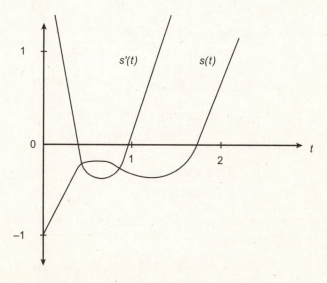

The velocity is given by $v(t) = 6t^2 - 8t + 2$.

The acceleration $a(t) = 12t - 8$ vanishes at $t = \frac{2}{3}$;

at this time the velocity has reached its minimum. This occurs during the interval [0, 2]

Therefore, the minimum velocity of $v = -\frac{2}{3}$ occurs at $t = \frac{2}{3}$.

13. (C)

$$x + 2y \leq 0$$
$$x - 2y \leq -4$$

The equation $x + 2y = 0$ has a slope of $-1/2$, so it must correspond to line L_2. Likewise, the equation $x - 2y = -4$ has a slope of $1/2$, so it must correspond to line L_1. The shaded area lies below L_2 but above L_1.

14. (D)

$$5x + 2y = -5$$
$$-3x + y = 3$$

Multiply the bottom equation by -2 so that the terms in the y-column will cancel as follows (in this way if the y-terms cancel you will be solving for x).

$$5x + 2y = -5$$
$$-2(-3x + y) = -2(3) \implies$$

$$5x + 2y = -5$$
$$6x - 2y = -6$$

$$\frac{11x}{11} = \frac{-11}{11}$$
$$x = -1$$

Add the coefficients/terms in the x-column and the constants on the right side. Then divide both sides by 11, the coefficient of the x-term.

Answer choice (A) is incorrect because it solved for the variable y.

$$3(\ 5x + 2y = -5) = 15x + 6y = -15$$
$$5(-3x + y = \ 3) = -15x + 5y = \ 15$$
$$11y = \ 0$$
$$y = \ 0$$

Answer choice (B) is incorrect because of an error in adding 2 negative numbers.

$$5x + 2y = -5$$
$$6x - 2y = -6$$
$$11x = -1, \ x = -\frac{1}{11}$$

Answer choice (C) is incorrect because of an error in signs.

$$5x + 2y = -5$$
$$\underline{-6x - 2y = -6}$$
$$x \quad\quad = 1$$

15. **(A)**

$$f'(x) = 6x - 12$$
$$f'(c) = 0$$
$$6c - 12 = 0$$
$$c = 2$$

16. **(D)**

The center is located at $(-1, 2)$ and the length of the major axis is 6.

This equation represents an ellipse, for which the general equation is, $a > b$, $(x - h)^2 / a^2 + (y - k)^2 / b^2 = 1$. In this format, the center is located at (h, k) and its major axis is $2a$. Substitute $a = 3$, $b = 2$, $h = -1$, and $k = 2$.

17. **(B)**

The graphs of the equations represented by the other choices are as follows.

Answer choice (A): $x = 2$

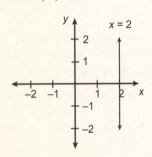

Answer choice (C): $y = 2$

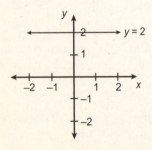

Answer choice (D): $y = -2$

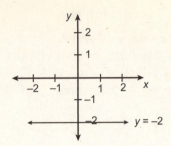

The graph of $x = -2$ is parallel to the y-axis and passes through the point $(-2, 0)$.

18. **(C)**

The distance d of a point (x_0, y_0) to the line

$$Ax + By + C = 0$$

is $d = \dfrac{|Ax_0 + By_0 + C|}{\sqrt{A^2 + B^2}}$

For the problem given here, we therefore have

$$d = \frac{|2 \times 2 + 1 \times 4 - 3|}{\sqrt{2^2 + 1^2}} = \sqrt{5} = 2.236$$

19. **(B)**

$$\frac{9 \text{ apartments with terraces}}{16 \text{ apartments}} = \frac{?}{144 \text{ apartments}}$$

Solving this proportion for the "?"

$$? = \frac{9 \text{ apartments} \times 144 \text{ apartments}}{16 \text{ apartments}}$$

$$= \frac{1296 \text{ apartments}}{16 \text{ apartments}} = 81 \text{ apartments}$$

Answer (A) is incorrect because the apartments were subtracted.

$$144 - (16 - 9) = 144 - 7 = 137 \text{ apartments}$$

Answer (C) is incorrect because the number of apartments with terraces is 9, not $16 - 9$.

$$(144 \div 16) \times (16 - 9) = 9 \times 7 = 63$$

Answer (D) is incorrect due to a multiplication factor guess of 6.

$$144 - [(16 - 9) \times 6] = 102$$

20. (B)

$$m \angle VMW > m \angle VTM$$

By the construction, $m\angle VMT = m\angle WMT$. We already have a right angle in each of triangles VMT and WMT. So, $m\angle VTM = m\angle WTM$. Since $\overline{MT}$ is an angle bisector, $TV = TW$. By the construction of the arc $\overset{\frown}{PR}$, we also know that $MP = MR$. Since $MW > MR$, it follows that $MW > MP$. Although it may appear that $m\angle VMW$ is greater than $m\angle VTM$, there are no numerical values to verify this statement. We would need to know the relationship between $m\angle VMT$ and $m\angle VTM$. We only know that $m\angle VMT + m\angle VTM = 90°$.

21. (C)

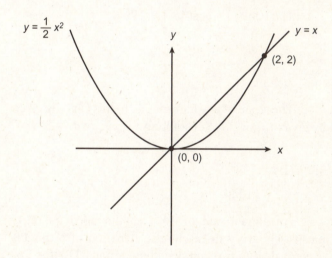

The curve is below the line, so

$$\text{Area} = \int_0^2 \left(x - \frac{1}{2}x^2 \right) dx = \left(\frac{x^2}{2} - \frac{x^3}{6} \right)\Bigg|_0^2 = 2 - \frac{8}{6} = \frac{2}{3}.$$

22. (C)

From a theorem we know that the measure of an inscribed angle is equal to $\frac{1}{2}$ the intercepted arc.

We are told that $m\,\overset{\frown}{ABC}$ is $\frac{3}{2}\pi$ radians. There are 2π radians in a circle. Therefore, the intercepted arc is the remaining $\frac{\pi}{2}$ radians.

Converting to degrees:

$$\left(\frac{\pi}{2} \right)\left(\frac{180}{\pi} \right) = 90°.$$

The angle y is half of this:

$$y = \frac{90°}{2} = 45°.$$

23. (A)

The sum of n odd numbers, beginning with 1, is equal to n^2.

Note that the sum of the first two odd numbers, beginning with 1, is equal to 2 squared; the sum of the first three odd numbers, beginning with 1, is equal to 3 squared; the sum of the first four odd numbers, beginning with 1, is equal to 4 squared. This pattern works for any value of n.

24. (B)

4

Let $x = \log_2 5$, so that $2^x = 5$. Let $y = \log_5 8$, so that $5^y = 8$. By substitution, we have $2^{xy} = 8$. Let $z = \log_8 16$, so that $8^z = 16$. Again by substitution, $2^{xyz} = 16$, so $xyz = 4$.

25. (B)

.15

Using the formula $P(A \cup B) = P(A) + P(B) - P(A \cap B)$, and replacing $P(A \cap B)$ with $P(A) \cdot P(B \mid A)$, we get $.29 = P(A) + .20 - P(A) \cdot .40$. This equation simplifies to $.09 = .60 \cdot P(A)$ So $P(A) = .09/.60 = .15$.

26. (D)

Let p = if I am hungry.

Let q = I will have a snack.

Then the original statement is: If p, then q.

The negation is: ~ (if p, then q) = p and not q.

To negate a conditional: If p, then q, the result is p and not q. Therefore, the negation of the original statement is: "I am hungry and I will not have a snack."

27. (A)

$$|9 - x| < 0$$

The lowest value of any absolute value quantity is zero.

28. (C)

The graph passes through the points $(0, -3)$, $(2, -1)$, $(-2, -1)$, $(4, 5)$, and $(-4, +5)$. Also, the graph is a parabola which faces upward and, therefore, the coefficient of the x^2-term must be positive. These conditions are only satisfied by

$$y = \tfrac{1}{2}x^2 - 3$$

and, therefore, answer choices (A), (B), and (D) are incorrect.

29. (A)

$$(\sin\theta \times \cot\theta)^2 + (\cos\theta\tan\theta)^2$$

$$= \left(\sin\theta\left(\frac{\cos\theta}{\sin\theta}\right)\right)^2 + \left(\cos\theta\left(\frac{\sin\theta}{\cos\theta}\right)\right)^2$$
$$= \cos^2\theta + \sin^2\theta = 1$$

30. (C)

$$(5, -4)$$

The midpoint of $\overline{AB}$ is located at $(5, 4)$, which represents the average of the x and y coordinated of the endpoints. When a point is reflected about the x-axis, its x value remains unchanged and its y value simply changes sign.

31. (C)

336

Eight elephants are available to be selected for the first position. Given that the first elephant has been selected, only 7 elephants are left to be selected for the second position. The first and second positions have been selected, leaving 6 for the third position. Thus $8 \times 7 \times 6 = 336$. (A), (B), and (D) are incorrect because they do not illustrate the fundamental counting principle for this example.

32. (A)

The number of distinct ways of arranging nine people in a line.

The actual numerical value of this answer choice is given by 9 factorial, which equals 362,880. The answers for Answer Choices (B), (C), and (D), respectively are 358,800; 324,632; and 262,144

33. (C)

$$x = \sin^{-1}(0.5) = 30°.$$
$$x + y = \sin^{-1}(0.9659) = 75°.$$

Then find y to be

$$y = 75° - 30° = 45°.$$
Then $\cos(y) = \cos(45°) = 0.707$.

34. (D)

5

The slope of any tangent line to this curve is given by $dy/dx = 2x + 11$. Substituting $x = -3$, $dy/dx = 5$.

35. (D)

$1849

An annual rate of 16% compounded quarterly means 4% every three months. A period of 6 months is equivalent to two compounding periods. Use the formula $(N)(1.04)^2 = \$2000$. Solving, $N \approx \$1849.11$, which rounds off to $1849.

36. (A)

Tree diagram

We can illustrate three selections in going from city A to city B, five selections in going from city B to city C, and six selections in going from city C to city D. The actual answer is $(3)(5)(6) = 90$. The diagram would appear as follows:

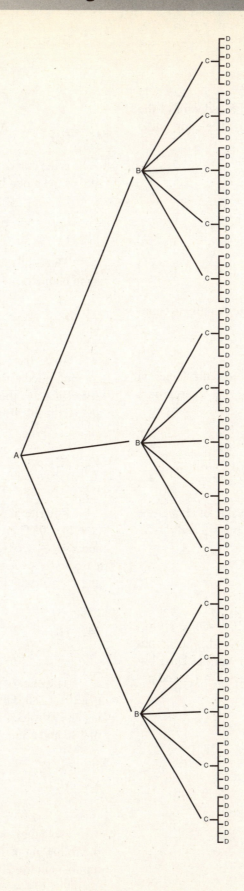

37. (B)

$5i + 6j$

The position vector is given by $ai + bj$, where the values of i and j correspond to the endpoint of the equivalent vector that begins at (0, 0). The endpoint is given by $(6 - 1, 4 - [-2]) = (5, 6)$.

38. (B)

If $a = b = r$, the given equation becomes

$$\frac{x^2}{a^2} + \frac{y^2}{b^2} = \frac{x^2}{r^2} + \frac{y^2}{r^2} = 1. \quad (1)$$

Multiplying the last branch of the equality in equation (1) by r^2 yields

$$x^2 + y^2 = r^2. \quad (2)$$

This is the equation of a circle with center at $C(0, 0)$ and radius r. Hence, we see that a circle is a special case of an ellipse.

39. (C)

3/5

The amplitude is given by the value of A, and the period is given by the value of $2\pi/B$. So $A = 3$ and $B = 5$.

40. (A)

86.64

Convert 74 and 86 to standard (z) scores as follows: 74 becomes $(74 - 80)/4 = -1.5$ and 86 becomes $(86 - 80)/4 = 1.5$. Using a Standard Normal Distribution Table, the amount of data between $z = 1.5$ and $z = 1.5$ is $.8664 = 86.64\%$.

41. (C)

Average value of f in

$$[a, b] = \frac{1}{b-a} \int_a^b f(x)dx$$
$$\Leftrightarrow 4 = \frac{1}{b-2} \times 8$$

substituting the given values

$$\Leftrightarrow 4(b - 2) = 8$$
$$\Leftrightarrow b = 4.$$

42. (D)

is the correct response. In how many ways can two of five freshmen be selected:

$$5C_2 \text{ or } \frac{5!}{2!3!} = \frac{5 \times 4 \times 3 \times 2 \times 1}{2 \times 1 \times 3 \times 2 \times 1} = 10$$

Three of four sophomores can be selected in the same manner.

$$4C_3 \text{ or } \frac{4!}{3!1!} = \frac{4 \times 3 \times 2 \times 1}{3 \times 2 \times 1 \times 1} = 4$$

Since the two events are independent, the values are multiplied (10×4 or 40) to determine the number of different ways these students can be selected. (A), (B), and (C) result from the use of inappropriate formulas.

43. (C)

$-1 < x < 6$

Rewrite as $x^2 - 5x - 6 < 0$, then factor as $(x - 6)(x + 1) < 0$. There are two possible cases: (1) $x - 6 > 0$ and $x + 1 < 0$, or (2) $x - 6 < 0$ and $x + 1 > 0$ For case (1), $x > 6$ and $x < -1$, which is impossible. For case (2), $x < 6$ and $x > -1$, which can be written as $-1 < x < 6$.

44. (D)

47

The sum of the original group of 20 numbers was $(9)(20) = 180$. The sum of the new group of 19 numbers is $(7)(19) = 133$. The removed number is the difference of 180 and 133.

45. (C)

524,288

Note that the sum in each row is a power of 2, with the following pattern: 2^0, 2^1, 2^2, 2^3, etc. Thus the sum of numbers in the 20th row would be $2^{19} = 524,288$.

46.

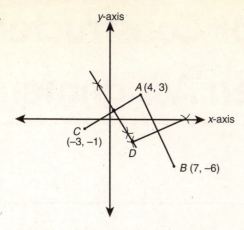

- Draw line segments $\overline{AC}$ and $\overline{AB}$. Construct the perpendicular bisector of each of these segments, as shown above. The point of intersection, D, of these perpendicular bisectors is equidistant from A, B, and C. Point D is the center of the circle which contains points A, B, and C.

- The equation of $\overline{AC}$ can be determined as $y = (4/7)x + 5/7$. The perpendicular bisector of $\overline{AC}$ would have a slope of $-7/4$ and would pass through the midpoint of $\overline{AC}$, which is $(0.5, 1)$; its equation would be given by $y = (-7/4)x + 15/8$.

  Likewise, the equation of $\overline{AB}$ can be determined as $y = -3x + 15$. The perpendicular bisector of $\overline{AB}$ would have a slope of $1/3$ and would pass thru the midpoint of $\overline{AB}$, which is $(5.5, -1.5)$; its equation would be given by $y = (1/3)x - 10/3$.

  We need to find the intersection of these two perpendicular bisectors. We can write $(-7/4)x + 15/8 =$

$(1/3)x - 10/3$. Multiplying this equation by 24, we get $-42x + 45 = 8x - 80$. Solving, $x = 2.5$. We can now determine that using either of these two equations $y = -2.5$ The clubhouse is located at $(2.5, -2.5)$.

- We need to find the distance between D and any of A, B, or C. The distance between A and D equals $\sqrt{(4-2.5)^2 + (3+2.5)^2} = \sqrt{32.5} \approx 5.7$. So, the length of the walkway between A and D is $(20)(5.7) = 114$ feet, and its area is $(114)(4) = 456$ square feet. The cost of this walkway is $(\$15)(456) = \$6840$. Since three walkways will be constructed, the total cost is $\$20,520$.

Another possible solution for the second bullet.

Let (x, y) represent the point which is equidistant from points A, B, and C. The distance from A to $D = \sqrt{(x-4)^2 + (y-3)^2}$ and the distance from B to $D = \sqrt{(x-7)^2 + (y+6)^2}$. Equating these distances and squaring both sides, we get $x^2 - 8x + 16 + y^2 - 6y + 9 = x^2 - 14x + 49 + y^2 + 12y + 36$. This simplifies to $6x - 18y = 60$, or $x - 3y = 10$. The distance from C to $D = \sqrt{(x+3)^2 + (y+1)^2}$. Equating this distance with the distance from A to D and squaring both sides, we get $x^2 - 8x + 16 + y^2 - 6y + 9 = x^2 + 6x + 9 + y^2 + 12y + 36$. This simplifies to $14x + 8y = 15$. Solving the equations $x - 3y = 10$ and $14x + 8y = 15$ simultaneously, we get $x = 2.5$ and $y = -2.5$. Thus, the clubhouse is located at $(2.5, -2.5)$.

See Next Page for Scoring Guidelines for Constructed Written Assignment

Scoring Guidelines for Constructed Written Assignment

Performance Characteristics

The following characteristics guide the scoring of responses to the written assignment.

Purpose:	Fulfill the charge of the assignment.
Application of Content:	Accurately and effectively apply the relevant knowledge and skills.
Support:	Support the response with appropriate examples and/or sound reasoning reflecting an understanding of the relevant knowledge and skills.

Scoring Scale

Scores will be assigned to each response to the written assignment according to the following scoring scale.

Score Point	Score Point Description
4	**The "4" response reflects a thorough command of the relevant knowledge and skills.** • The response completely fulfills the purpose of the assignment by responding fully to the given task. • The response demonstrates an accurate and highly effective application of the relevant knowledge and skills. • The response provides strong support with high-quality, relevant examples and/or sound reasoning.
3	**The "3" response reflects a general command of the relevant knowledge and skills.** • The response generally fulfills the purpose of the assignment by responding to the given task. • The response demonstrates a generally accurate and effective application of the relevant knowledge and skills. • The response provides support with some relevant examples and/or generally sound reasoning.

2	**The "2" response reflects a partial command of the relevant knowledge and skills.** • The response partially fulfills the purpose of the assignment by responding in a limited way to the given task. • The response demonstrates a limited, partially accurate and partially effective application of the relevant knowledge and skills. • The response provides limited support with few examples and/or some flawed reasoning.
1	**The "1" response reflects little or no command of the relevant knowledge and skills.** • The response fails to fulfill the purpose of the assignment. • The response demonstrates a largely inaccurate and/or ineffective application of the relevant knowledge and skills. • The response provides little or no support with few, if any, examples and/or seriously flawed reasoning.

SUBAREA I: Mathematical Reasoning and Communication

Basic Concepts of Logic

Sentences

Logic is concerned with declarative sentences that are unambiguous and definite, and either true or false (though we may not know which).

Truth Values

There are two truth values: Truth and Falsity.

Every sentence to which standard logic applies has exactly one of the two truth values (that is, is either true or false, but not both). No sentence can be both true and false.

Arguments

An *argument* is a set of sentences, one of which is the *conclusion*. The remaining sentences are the *premises* of the argument, where the *premises* are taken to present evidence or reasons in support of the *conclusion*.

Conclusion-Indicator Words

To identify arguments in a text or conversation, it is important to understand what function each sentence in the discourse is performing. English offers some "indicator words" as clues to help identify what function sentences are serving. These serve only as a guide and do not guarantee that an argument is present. (This is because these words, like most words of English, have several different meanings.)

Conclusion-indicator words include: *therefore, thus, hence, so, consequently, it follows that.*

Premise-Indicator words

Premise-indicator words include: *since, because, for, given that, inasmuch as, for the reason that, on account of.*

Evaluating Arguments

Arguments may be evaluated according to a variety of criteria or standards.

One such standard is the FACT standard: are all of the premises true? Is the data (evidence) offered in the premises actually, as a matter of fact, true? Are the reasons offered correct? Logic generally offers no help regarding the question of the truth or falsity of premises.

Logic is concerned with the LOGIC question: the evaluation of arguments in terms of the strength of support the premises provide for the conclusion. That is, logic develops standards for determining how strongly the premises, if all true, support the conclusion. This is an evaluation of how relevant the evidence or reasons given in the premises is to the claim made by the conclusion. Deductive logic formulates the most demanding standards by which to evaluate arguments.

Deductive Validity and Invalidity

An argument is (deductively) valid if and only if it is *impossible* that all its premises be true while its conclusion is false. That is, the premises of a valid argument, if they were all true, *guarantee* the truth of the conclusion; to accept all the premises and deny the conclusion would be inconsistent.

An argument is invalid if and only if it is not valid. That is, even if the premises are or were assumed (imagined) to be all true, the conclusion could still be false.

The relationship of evidential strength that premises lend to a conclusion can be seen in the following table:

The premises of a valid argument are said to entail its conclusion.

The table below summarizes these relationships between truth values of premises and conclusion and the validity and invalidity of arguments.

Premises	Conclusion	Validity
all true	true	can't tell
all true	false	invalid
one or more false	true	can't tell
one or more false	false	can't tell

Inductive Strength and Weakness

Invalid arguments may still be good arguments when evaluated by other acceptable standards. Inductive logic develops different standards by which arguments are evaluated.

An argument is *inductively strong* if and only if it is *improbable* that all its premises be true while its conclusion is false. Inductive strength is typically measured as a real number value from zero (false) to one (certain).

An argument is inductively weak if and only if it is not inductively strong.

Examples:

The following argument is invalid, but inductively strong:

Evidential Strength between Premises and Conclusion		
Example of an argument that . . .	**Valid** (The truth of the premises guarantees the truth of the conclusion.)	**Invalid** (The truth of the premises does not guarantee the truth of the conclusion.)
All true premises, true conclusion	If Chicago is in Illinois, then it is in the USA. Chicago is in Illinois. Therefore, Chicago is in the USA.	Clinton was President in 1995. Therefore, Washington was the 1st US President.
All true premises, false conclusion	**By definition of "valid," none exist**	Either Bush or Clinton have been presidents. Bush was a president. Therefore, Clinton has not been President.
One or more false premises, true conclusion	Either Reagan was a President or Bush was a Vice-President. Reagan was not a President. Therefore, Bush was a Vice President.	Bush was not a President. Therefore, Bush was a Vice President.
One or more false premises, false conclusion	Clinton was a President and Dukakis was a President. Therefore, Dukakis was a President.	Bush was not a President. Therefore, Bush was not a Vice President.

Ninety percent of restaurants in Chicago are owned by Greeks.

Lou Mitchell's is a restaurant in Chicago.
Therefore, Lou Mitchell's is owned by Greeks.

This argument is inductively strong, because given the truth of the premises, the chances are that Lou Mitchell's will be among the 90 percent of restaurants that are Greek-owned. The argument is invalid because there is some chance that Lou Mitchell's may be among the 10 percent that are not Greek-owned; so it is not *impossible* that even should the premises be true, the conclusion may still be false.

The following argument is valid:

100 percent (that is, all) of restaurants in Chicago are owned by Greeks.

Lou Mitchell's is a restaurant in Chicago.

Therefore, Lou Mitchell's is owned by Greeks.

Note that while the premises in fact are not true, if they were, the conclusion would have to be true. Also note that any percentage in the first premise less than 100 percent would give an invalid argument; as long as the percentage is greater than 0 percent, the argument has some inductive strength; as the percentage approaches 0 percent, the reason to accept the conclusion, given the evidence supplied by the premises, approaches no reason at all.

Symbolic logic is concerned only with deductive standards for evaluating arguments and with matters related to these standards.

Logical Properties of Sentences

Consistency

A sentence is *consistent* if and only if it is *possible* that it is true.

A sentence is *inconsistent* if and only if it is not consistent; that is, if and only if it is *impossible* that it is true.

Example: At least one odd number is not odd.

Logical Truth

A sentence is *logically true* if and only if it is *impossible* for it to be false; that is, the denial of the sentence is inconsistent.

Example: Either Mars is a planet or Mars is not a planet.

Logical Falsity

A sentence is *logically false* if and only if it is *impossible* for it to be true; that is, the sentence is inconsistent.

Example: Mars is a planet and Mars is not a planet.

Logical Indeterminacy (Contingency)

A sentence is *logically indeterminate* (*contingent*) if and only if it is neither logically true nor logically false.

Example: Einstein was a physicist and Pauling was a chemist.

Logical Equivalence of Sentences

Two sentences are *logically equivalent* if and only if it is *impossible* for one of the sentences to be true while the other sentence is false; that is, if and only if it is impossible for the two sentences to have different truth values.

Example: "Chicago is in Illinois and Pittsburgh is in Pennsylvania" is logically equivalent to "Pittsburgh is in Pennsylvania and Chicago is in Illinois."

Method of Proof

Logic

Definition 1

A statement is a sentence which is either true or false, but not both.

Definition 2

If a and b are statements, then a statement of the form "a and b" is called the conjunction of a and b, denoted by $a \wedge b$.

Definition 3

The disjunction of two statements *a* and *b* is shown by the compound statement "*a* or *b*," denoted by $a \lor b$.

Definition 4

The negation of a statement *q* is the statement "not *q*," denoted by $\sim q$.

Definition 5

The compound statement "if *a*, then *b*," denoted by $a \rightarrow b$, is called a conditional statement or an implication.

"If *a*" is called the hypothesis or premise of the implication, "then *b*" is called the conclusion of the implication.

Further, statement *a* is called the antecedent of the implication, and statement *b* is called the consequent of the implication.

Definition 6

The converse of $a \rightarrow b$ is $b \rightarrow a$.

Definition 7

The contrapositive of $a \rightarrow b$ is $\sim b \rightarrow \sim a$.

Definition 8

The inverse of $a \rightarrow b$ is $\sim a \rightarrow \sim b$.

Definition 9

The statement of the form "*p* if and only if *q*," denoted by $p \leftrightarrow q$, is called a biconditional statement.

Definition 10

An argument is valid if the truth of the premises means that the conclusion must also be true.

Definition 11

Intuition is the process of making generalizations on insight.

PROBLEM

Write the inverse for each of the following statements. Determine whether the inverse is true or false. (a) If a person is stealing, he is breaking the law. (b) If a line is perpendicular to a segment at its midpoint, it is the perpendicular bisector of the segment. (c) Dead men tell no tales.

SOLUTION

The inverse of a given conditional statement is formed by negating both the hypothesis and conclusion of the conditional statement.

(a) The hypothesis of this statement is "a person is stealing;" the conclusion is "he is breaking the law." The negation of the hypothesis is "a person is not stealing." The inverse is "if a person is not stealing, he is not breaking the law."

The inverse is false, since there are more ways to break the law than by stealing. Clearly, a murderer may not be stealing but he is surely breaking the law.

(b) In this statement, the hypothesis contains two conditions: (1) the line is perpendicular to the segment; and (2) the line intersects the segment at the midpoint. The negation of (statement a *and* statement b) is (not statement a *or* not statement b). Thus, the negation of the hypothesis is "The line is not perpendicular to the segment or it doesn't intersect the segment at the midpoint." The negation of the conclusion is "the line is not the perpendicular bisector of a segment."

The inverse is "if a line is not perpendicular to the segment or does not intersect the segment at the midpoint, then the line is not the perpendicular bisector of the segment."

In this case, the inverse is true. If either of the conditions holds (the line is not perpendicular; the line does not intersect at the midpoint), then the line cannot be a perpendicular bisector.

(c) This statement is not written in if-then form, which makes its hypothesis and conclusion more difficult to see. The hypothesis is implied to be "the man is dead"; the conclusion is implied to be "the man tells no tales." The inverse is, therefore, "If a man is not dead, then he will tell tales."

The inverse is false. Many witnesses to crimes are still alive but they have never told their stories to the police, either out of fear or because they didn't want to get involved.

Basic Principles, Laws, and Theorems

1. Any statement is either true or false. (The law of the Excluded Middle)

2. A statement cannot be both true and false. (The Law of Contradiction)

3. The converse of a true statement is not necessarily true.

4. The converse of a definition is always true.

5. For a theorem to be true, it must be true for all cases.

6. A statement is false if one false instance of the statement exists.

7. The inverse of a true statement is not necessarily true.

8. The contrapositive of a true statement is true and the contrapositive of a false statement is false.

9. If the converse of a true statement is true, then the inverse is true. Likewise, if the converse is false, the inverse is false.

10. Statements which are either both true or false are said to be logically equivalent.

11. If a given statement and its converse are both true, then the conditions in the hypothesis of the statement are both necessary and sufficient for the conclusion of the statement.

    If a given statement is true but its converse is false, then the conditions are sufficient but not necessary for the conclusion of the statement.

    If a given statement and its converse are both false, then the conditions are neither sufficient nor necessary for the statement's conclusion.

Deductive Reasoning

An arrangement of statements that would allow you to deduce the third one from the preceding two is called a syllogism. A syllogism has three parts:

The first part is a general statement concerning a whole group. This is called the major premise.

The second part is a specific statement which indicates that a certain individual is a member of that group. This is called the minor premise.

The last part of a syllogism is a statement to the effect that the general statement which applies to the group also applies to the individual. This third statement of a syllogism is called a deduction.

Example A: Properly Deduced Argument

A) Major Premise: All birds have feathers.

B) Minor Premise: An eagle is a bird.

C) Deduction: An eagle has feathers.

The technique of employing a syllogism to arrive at a conclusion is called deductive reasoning.

If a major premise which is true is followed by an appropriate minor premise which is true, a conclusion can be deduced which must be true, and the reasoning is valid. However, if a major premise which is true is followed by an inappropriate minor premise which is also true, a conclusion cannot be deduced.

Example B: Improperly Deduced Argument

A) Major Premise: All people who vote are at least 18 years old.

B) Improper Minor Premise: Jane is at least 18.

C) Illogical Deduction: Jane votes.

The flaw in example B is that the major premise stated in A makes a condition on people who vote, not on a person's age. If statements B and C are interchanged, the resulting three-part deduction would be logical.

Indirect Proof

Indirect proofs involve considering two possible outcomes—the result we would like to prove and its negative—and then showing, under the given hypothesis, that a contradiction of prior known theorems, postulates, or definitions is reached when the negative is assumed.

Postulate 1

A proposition contradicting a true proposition is false.

Postulate 2

If one of a given set of propositions must be true, and all except one of those propositions have been proved to be false, then this one remaining proposition must be true.

The method of indirect proof may be summarized as follows:

Step 1. List all the possible conclusions.

Step 2. Prove all but one of those possible conclusions to be false (use Postulate 1 given).

Step 3. The only remaining possible conclusion is proved true according to Postulate 2.

- **EXAMPLE**

When attempting to prove that in a scalene triangle the bisector of an angle cannot be perpendicular to the opposite side, one method of solution could be to consider the two possible conclusions:

1) the bisector can be perpendicular to the opposite side, or

2) the bisector cannot be perpendicular to the opposite side.

Obviously, one and only one of these conclusions can be true; therefore, if we can prove that all of the possibilities, except one, are false, then the remaining possibility must be a valid conclusion. In this example, it can be proven that, for all cases, the statement which asserts that the bisector of an angle of a scalene triangle can be perpendicular to the opposite side is false. Therefore, the contradicting possibility—the bisector cannot be perpendicular to the opposite side—is in fact true.

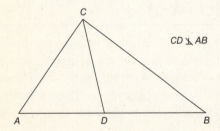

$CD \perp AB$

PROBLEM

Prove, by indirect method, that if two angles are not congruent, then they are not both right angles.

SOLUTION

Indirect proofs involve considering two possible outcomes, the result we would like to prove and its negative, and then showing, under the given hypothesis, that a contradiction of prior known theorems, postulates, or definitions is reached when the negative is assumed.

In this case, the outcomes can be that the two angles are not right angles or that the two angles are right angles. Assume the negative of what we want to prove— that the two angles are right angles.

The given hypothesis in this problem is that the two angles are not congruent. A previous theorem states that all right angles are congruent. Therefore, the conclusion we have assumed true leads to a logical contradiction. As such, the alternative conclusion must be true. Therefore, if two angles are not congruent, then they are not both right angles.

Inductive Reasoning

Inductive reasoning is a method of reasoning by which one draws a conclusion or generalization based on a pattern of specific cases. Observing a well-defined pattern can lead us to predict an answer for the unknown portion of the pattern.

For example, observing the numbers 2, 5, 8, 11, . . ., we find that a pattern is defined based on a difference of 3 between each two consecutive numbers. Extrapolating this pattern, we can conclude that the number immediately following 11 is $11 + 3 = 14$.

In mathematics, we use the following steps as the general method of inductive reasoning.

Let $P(n)$ be a statement or proposition, where n is a positive integer.

Try to verify that $P(1)$ is a true statement. That is, replace n with 1 in the given statement or proposition to see whether the statement is true or false. If the statement is true, assume that it is also true for all the following values of n, up to k. That is, assume that $P(n)$ is true for $n = k$.

Next, using the true statements $P(1)$ and $P(k)$, try to verify that $P(n)$ is true for $n = k + 1$ as well. If you succeed in verifying this step, you can claim that the statement or proposition $P(n)$ is true for all integer values of n.

PROBLEM

Prove by mathematical induction that

$1 + 7 + 13 + \ldots + (6n - 5) = n(3n - 2)$.

SOLUTION

Denote $1 + 7 + 13 + \ldots + (6n - 5)$ by $P(n)$.

So, (1) $P(n) = 1 + 7 + 13 + \ldots + (6n - 5)$

Step 1. Check the statement to see whether it is true for $n = 1$. To do so, simply replace n with 1 in the given statement.

(2) $P(1) = [6(1) - 5] = 1[3(1) - 2]$

Computing both sides of (2) indicates the statement is true for $n = 1$.

Step 2. Assume that the statement is true for $n = k$. This means that

(3) $P(k) = 1 + 7 + 13 + \ldots + (6k - 5) = k(3k - 2)$.

Step 3. Now, try to prove that the statement is true for $n = k + 1$ as well. To do so, add $6k + 1$ to the right side equation in (3).

(4) $1 + 7 + 13 + \ldots + (6k - 5) + 6k + 1 = k(3k - 2) + 6k + 1$

We know that

(5) $(6k - 5) + 6k + 1 = 6k - 5 + 6k + 1 - 6 + 6$

$= (6k - 5) + (6k + 6) - 5$

$= (6k - 5) + [6(k + 1) - 5]$

Next, simplify and rearrange the right side of (4) as follows

(6) $k(3k - 2) + 6k + 1 = 3k^2 - 2k + 6k + 1$

$= 3k^2 + 4k + 1$

$= 3k^2 + 3k + k + 1$

$= 3k(k + 1) + (k + 1)$

$= (k + 1)(3k + 1)$

$= (k + 1)[3(k + 1) - 2]$

$= (k + 1)(3k + 3 - 2)$

$= (k + 1)[3(k + 1) - 2]$

Placing the final results obtained through (5) and (6) into (4), we get

(7) $1 + 7 + 13 + \ldots + (6k - 5) + [6(k + 1) - 5]$

$= k(3k - 2) + (k + 1)[3(k + 1) - 2]$.

That is, $P(n)$ is true for $n = k + 1$.

Defined and Undefined Terms: Axioms, Postulates, and Assumptions; Theorems and Corollaries

To build a logical system of mathematics, the first step is to take a known and then move to what is not known. The terms which we will accept as known are called undefined terms. We accept certain basic terms as undefined, since their definition would of necessity include other undefined terms. Examples of some important undefined terms with characteristics that you must know are:

A) Set: The sets we will be concerned with will have clearly defined characteristics.

B) Point: Although we represent points on paper with small dots, a point has no size, thickness, or width. A point is denoted by a capital letter.

C) Line: A line is a series of adjacent points which extends indefinitely. A line can be either curved or straight; however, unless otherwise stated, the term "line" refers to a straight line. A line is denoted by listing two points on the line and drawing a line with arrows on top, i.e., $\overleftrightarrow{AB}$.

D) Plane: A plane is the collection of all points lying on a flat surface which extends indefinitely in all directions. Imagine holding a record cover in a room and imagine that the record cover divides the entire room. Remember that a plane has no thickness.

We use these undefined terms to construct defined terms so we can describe more sophisticated expressions.

Necessary characteristics of a good definition are:

A) It names the term being defined.

B) It uses only known terms or accepted undefined terms.

C) It places the term into the smallest set to which it belongs.

D) It states the characteristics of the defined term which distinguish it from the other members of the set.

E) It contains the least possible amount of information.

F) It is always reversible.

Axioms, postulates, and assumptions are the statements in geometry which are accepted as true without proof, whereas theorems are the statements in geometry which are proven to be true.

A corollary is a theorem that can be deduced easily from another theorem or from a postulate.

In this text, the term postulate is used exclusively, instead of axiom or assumption.

Postulate 1

A quantity is equal to itself (reflexive law).

Postulate 2

If two quantities are equal to the same quantity, they are equal to each other (transitive law).

Postulate 3

If a & b are any quantities, and $a = b$, then $b = a$ (symmetric law).

Postulate 4

The whole is equal to the sum of its parts.

Postulates 5

If equal quantities are added to equal quantities, the sums are equal quantities.

Postulate 6

If equal quantities are subtracted from equal quantities, the differences are equal quantities.

Postulate 7

If equal quantities are multiplied by equal quantities, the products are equal quantities.

Postulate 8

If equal quantities are divided by equal quantities (not 0), the quotients are equal quantities.

Postulates 9

There exists one and only one straight line through any two distinct points.

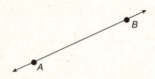

Postulate 10

Two straight lines can intersect at only one point.

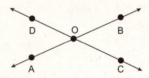

PROBLEM

In the figure shown, the measure of ∡*DAC* equals the measure of ∡*ECA* and the measure of ∡1 equals the measure of ∡2. Show that the measure of ∡3 equals the measure of ∡4.

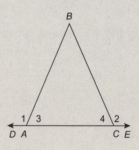

SOLUTION

This proof will require the subtraction postulate, which states that if equal quantities are subtracted from equal quantities, the differences are equal.

Given: $\angle DAC \cong \angle ECA$, $\angle 1 \cong \angle 2$

Prove: $\angle 3 \cong \angle 4$

Statement	Reason
1. $m\angle DAC = m\angle ECA$ $m\angle 1 = m\angle 2$	1. Given.
2. $m\angle DAC - m\angle 1 = m\angle ECA - m\angle 2$	2. Subtraction Postulate.
3. $m\angle 3 = m\angle 4$	3. Substitution Postulate.

Mathematics as Communication

The teacher has knowledge of the nature of mathematics as a form of communication and is able to apply this knowledge to provide meaningful instruction to the student.

• Identify statements that correctly communicate mathematical definitions or concepts.

• Interpret written presentations of mathematics.

• Select or interpret appropriate concrete examples, pictorial illustrations, and symbolic representations in developing mathematical concepts.

It is necessary for students, parents, and teachers to understand that mathematics is a means of communication, complete with its own syntax, grammar, dialects, and slang. A simple and common rule that many math teachers share is the translation of the word 'is' into '=' when teaching students to decode word problems. This is a useful piece of information but it is just a very small example of what it means to communicate using mathematics. Although mathematics is indeed a language in which symbols can be translated into nouns and verbs and equations into sentences, it is also pictures, graphs, proofs, diagrams, and abstractions. Teachers must appreciate and understand the complexity and importance of mathematical language and language about mathematics. Moreover, being able to effectively communicate about and communicate with mathematics allows teachers to reach more students in more meaningful ways.

Defining Objects and Concepts in Mathematics

One of the most attractive and yet daunting characteristics of mathematics is that the rules and objects used in doing math in Moscow are the same as in Singapore or in Kigali or in Miami. The emphases in curricula may differ and the styles of teaching may reflect different cultural norms but a *square* in London must also be a *square* in New Delhi. Therefore, a mathematics teacher should be knowledgeable of the necessary and sufficient conditions required to define mathematical objects and concepts and be careful in the sharing of this knowledge with students.

Of key importance is the difference between descriptions and definitions. A description may in its fullness accidentally include enough information to define a mathematical object but will likely contain information that is not essential and may lack information that is. A good definition in mathematics provides the information that is necessary to distinguish one object or concept from another—no more and no less. In the table below are some likely 'definitions' of a square along with an evaluation of each.

Many advocates of education reform, including the *National Council of Teachers of Mathematics*, suggest that teachers introduce content-related jargon after students have developed a need for the term in order to make communication about the problem that they are solving or the idea that they are exploring more coherent. This is quite different from the tradition of providing students with a list of terms and definitions at the start of each chapter or section. However, regardless of instructional strategy, mathematics teachers need to ensure that the definitions students develop or work with are good ones.

Possible Definition of a Square

Definitions	Comments
A shape with four right angles.	Does not contain sufficient information to determine that the shape is a quadrilateral or the necessary information to distinguish the shape from a rectangle. This is not an adequate definition.
A four-sided quadrilateral with opposite sides parallel, all sides congruent, and four right angles.	Although accurate the definition is unwieldy and contains redundant and, therefore, unnecessary information. This is not a good definition.
A quadrilateral with congruent sides and four right angles.	Contains the necessary and sufficient information to distinguish a shape as square or not a square. This is a good definition.

The Language of Mathematics

Along with a careful approach to defining terms and concepts, teachers of mathematics should be accurate and precise in their understanding and use of language when talking or writing about math. Beyond being able to recite definitions, axioms, and formulas, teachers need to have a working knowledge of mathematical jargon. Teachers need to understand and be able to use terms like *at least one, direct variation, rate of change, if and only if, or mutually exclusive*. It is this ability that will help tie one mathematical concept to another. Also, teachers need to recognize the difference between mathematical terminology, like *rate of change*, and mathematical slang, such as *rise over run*. The use of mathematical slang is not necessarily a bad thing but meaning and understanding are more important than expedient turns of phrase.

Beyond Words

In addition to using concise mathematical language, a skilled mathematics teacher often uses analogies and concrete examples to illustrate ideas or to help students make connections. Physical representations, even if they are approximations to the mathematical ideal, are a powerful tool in engaging minds. A good example is the concept of *slope*. Math teachers commonly use a hill or a flight of stairs as a model and then equate the slope of a line with the *steepness* of the model. Physical experiences of doing mathematics or observing mathematical constructs afford students with an immediacy of experience that often goes beyond words. The same is true for pictorial representations of an idea. For example, Leonardo da Vinci's anatomical sketch *Vitruvian Man* is great for the study of proportions or a guided discovery of the golden mean.

Although an effective mathematics teacher will choose appropriate physical and pictorial examples, the careful teacher should ensure that student understanding is rooted in the mathematics. The teacher needs to be sure that the learner can go beyond the model or representation to use his or her mathematical knowledge of the concept in a meaningful way. Being able to compare slope to steepness is valuable but if the student can not calculate the slope of a line—or the steepness of a flight of stairs—then the mathematics has been lost.

Finally, it is important that teachers foster this attention to the language of mathematics among their students. Carelessness or ambiguity in language is a good indicator of insufficient understanding.

Mathematical Connections

The teacher understands the connections within the structure of mathematics and is able to use those connections to further student understanding as well as provide more avenues of access to mathematics ideas.

- Identify equivalent representations of the same concept or procedure (e.g., graphical, algebraic, verbal, numeric).

- Interpret relationships between mathematical topics (e.g., multiplication as repeated addition, powers as repeated multiplication).

- Interpret descriptions, diagrams, and representations of arithmetic operations.

Mental Connections

The study of mathematics has developed over several millennia into ever more specialized fields. In our public schools, the distinctions are being made even at the middle and elementary school levels but are most pronounced in high schools where students receive mathematics instruction in year-long doses of algebra, geometry, or calculus. This is advantageous with regard to course scheduling and high mobility rates among students but it neglects the interconnectedness of mathematics as a whole and limits student exploration of the field. An effective mathematics teacher should have knowledge of these connections and use them to give students a more comprehensive picture of mathematics.

Using these *mathematical* connections, teachers will be able to give students more chances to make mental connections to multiple ideas resulting in an increase in retention and more depth in understanding. Furthermore, teachers that understand these links in the underlying structure of mathematics are better able to make meaningful long-term instructional and curricular plans by using already mastered concepts to develop new ones.

Equivalent Representations

A good test for depth of understanding of any topic is a person's ability to communicate about the subject in multiple ways. Teachers should use several different but equivalent representations of a concept or procedure to build mathematical understanding and encourage flexible thinking. For example, in creating a lesson on linear relationships, a teacher can have students a) collect and organize data using a chart or table, b) explore the data using graphs or pictograms, c) analyze the graphs for more information, d) develop a symbolic model for the phenomenon and e) write an evaluation of the experiment and a summary of conclusions. Throughout the process, the teacher needs to reinforce the concept of linearity as it manifests in each of the representations.

It is also essential that students learn how each representation highlights different aspects of the same idea. Numeric information draws our attention to patterns within data and the degree of the relationship between variables. Tables and charts allow us to organize data in ways that make looking for patterns easier. Graphs or pictograms afford us with a way to see trends in data as well as provide visual information that can sometimes match the actual physical behavior of objects. Written or verbal communications offer the opportunity for providing explanations or setting conditions. Symbolic representations allow us to make generalizations and explore the phenomenon under different conditions. Students should be able to determine what representation is best to highlight the periodic behavior in a pendulum or the possible permutations of a 5-letter combination.

Finally, the teacher needs to use multiple representations often enough that students become competent in selecting and constructing the most appropriate representation or representations for their needs. Students should come to see the multitude of representations as tools that they can create and then use to explore and solve concrete, real-world problems.

Relationships Between Mathematical Topics

In addition to being able to represent one idea or procedure in multiple ways, teachers must understand that topics within and between fields of mathematical study are connected. The seemingly disjointed courses of algebra and geometry are rife with connections such as the concept of linearity, the usefulness of co-ordinate systems, number sequences and the properties of geometric shapes, etc. Sometimes the connections are so important that one concept is actually defined by the other. A good example is the relationship between addition and multiplication. At the elementary level, the fact that multiplication is simply *multiple* additions helps students construct an understanding of what multiplication is and does. However, at more advanced levels this understanding can help students simplify or manipulate complex expressions.

It is also important for teachers to recognize themes and behaviors that extend throughout mathematics. For example, dilation and translation are concepts that appear in Algebra I, Geometry, and Algebra II again and again. Teachers should plan for and take advantage of the repetition.

The idea of building models from collected data is another important, ongoing theme that becomes increasingly important in the study of mathematics and its applications. Furthermore, mathematics teachers should be aware of the connections between mathematics and other fields of study. The vast majority of our students will not become theoretical mathematicians. They will become users of mathematics in the social, life, and physical sciences as well as in business, marketing, and service industries.

Representations of Arithmetic Operations

Teachers of elementary mathematics have long used base ten blocks, multiplication rectangles, and pictograms to help students learn the basic add, subtract, multiply, and divide operations. These diagrams and representations of the basic operations can be directly transferred to the teaching of algebra.

Teachers should be able to interpret and use these models to develop procedures such as distributing through a quantity or factoring an equation. Algebra tiles can take the place of base ten blocks and the multiplication rectangles can be set up in similar fashion to provide a model for the multiplication problem $(x + 3)(x + 1)$ or the factoring problem $3x^2 - 4x - 4$. Understanding these connections to the elementary models can help demystify many of these algebra procedures.

For in depth explanations of the base ten blocks and multiplication rectangles see J. A. Van de Walle's *Elementary and Middle School Mathematics: Teaching Developmentally* and for information on the use of algebra tiles see the manuals accompanying the tiles or visit one of the many dedicated sites on the internet.

SUBAREA II:
Algebra

Real Numbers and Their Components

The set of all real numbers has various components. These components are the set of all natural numbers, N, the set of all whole numbers, W, the set of all integers, I, the set of all rational numbers, Q, and the set of all irrational numbers, S. Then,

$N = \{1, 2, 3, \ldots\}$,

$W = \{0, 1, 2, 3, \ldots\}$,

$I = \{\ldots, -3, -2, -1, 0, 1, 2, 3, \ldots\}$,

$Q = \left\{ \dfrac{a}{b} \mid a, b \in I \text{ and } b \neq 0 \right\}$;

and $S = \{x \mid x$ has a decimal name which is nonterminating and does not have a repeating block$\}$.

It is obvious that $N \subseteq W$, $W \subseteq I$, and $I \subseteq Q$, but a similar relationship does not hold between Q and S. More specifically, the decimal names for elements of Q are

(1) terminating or

(2) nonterminating with a repeating block.

For example, $\dfrac{1}{2} = .5$ and $\dfrac{1}{3} = .333\ldots$ This means that Q and S have no common elements. Examples of irrational numbers include $.101001000\ldots$, π and $\sqrt{2}$.

All real numbers are normally represented by R and $R = Q \cup S$. This means that every real number is either rational or irrational. A nice way to visualize real numbers geometrically is that real numbers can be put in a one-to-one correspondence with the set of all points on a line.

Real Number Properties of Equality

The standard properties of equality involving real numbers are:

Reflexive Property of Equality

For each real number a,

$a = a$

Symmetric Property of Equality

For each real number a, for each real number b,

if $a = b$, then $b = a$

Transitive Property of Equality

For each real number a, for each real number b, for each real number c,

if $a = b$ and $b = c$, then $a = c$

Real Number Operations and Their Properties

The operations of addition and multiplication are of particular importance. As a result, many properties concerning those operations have been determined and named. Here is a list of the most important of these properties.

Closure Property of Addition

For every real number a, for every real number b,

$a + b$

is a real number.

Closure Property of Multiplication

For every real number a, for every real number b,

ab

is a real number.

Commutative Property of Addition

For every real number a, for every real number b,

$a + b = b + a$.

Commutative Property of Multiplication

For every real number a, for every real number b,

$ab = ba$.

Associative Property of Addition

For every real number a, for every real number b, for every real number c,

$(a + b) + c = a + (b + c)$.

Associative Property of Multiplication

For every real number a, for every real number b, for every real number c,

$(ab)c = a(bc)$.

Identity Property of Addition

For every real number a,

$a + 0 = 0 + a = a$.

Identity Property of Multiplication

For every real number a,

$a \times 1 = 1 \times a = a$.

Inverse Property of Addition

For every real number a, there is a real number $-a$ such that

$a + -a = -a + a = 0$.

Inverse Property of Multiplication

For every real number a, $a \neq 0$, there is a real number a^{-1} such that

$a \times a^{-1} = a^{-1} \times a = 1$.

Distributive Property

For every real number a, for every real number b, for every real number c,

$a(b + c) = ab + ac$.

The operations of subtraction and division are also important, but less important than addition and multiplication. Here are the definitions for these operations.

For every real number a, for every real number b, for every real number c,

$a - b = c$ if and only if $b + c = a$.

For every real number a, for every real number b, for every real number c,

$a \div b = c$ if and only if c is the unique real number such that $bc = a$.

The definition of division eliminates division *by* 0. Thus, for example, $4 \div 0$ is undefined, $0 \div 0$ is undefined, but $0 \div 4 = 0$.

In many instances, it is possible to perform subtraction by first converting a subtraction statement to an addition statement. This is illustrated below.

For every real number *a*, for every real number *b*,

$$a - b = a + (-b).$$

In a similar way, every division statement can be converted to a multiplication statement. Use the following model:

For every real number *a*, for every real number *b*, $b \neq 0$,

$$a \div b = a \times b^{-1}$$

Complex Numbers

A **complex number** is a number that can be written in the form $a + bi$, where *a* and *b* are real numbers and $i = \sqrt{-1}$. The number *a* is the **real part,** and the number *b* is the **imaginary part** of the complex number.

Returning momentarily to real numbers, the square of a real number cannot be negative. More specifically, the square of a positive real number is positive, the square of a negative real number is positive, and the square of 0 is 0. Then *i* is defined to be a number with a property that

$$i^2 = -1.$$

Obviously *i* is not a real number. *C* is then used to represent the set of all complex numbers and

$$C = \{a + bi \mid a \text{ and } b \text{ are real numbers}\}.$$

Here are the definitions of addition, subtraction, and multiplication of complex numbers.

Suppose $x + yi$ and $z + wi$ are complex numbers. Then

$$(x + yi) + (z + wi) = (x + z) + (y + w)i$$
$$(x + yi) - (z + wi) = (x - z) + (y - w)i$$
$$(x + yi) \times (z + wi) = (xz - y) + (xw + yz)i.$$

To add, subtract, or multiply complex numbers, compute in the usual way, replace i^2 with -1, and simplify.

$$(a + bi) + (c + di) = (a + c) + (b + d)i$$
$$(a + bi) - (c + di) = (a - c) + (b - d)i$$
$$(a + bi)(c + di) = ac + adi + bci + bdi^2$$
$$= ac - bd + (ad + bc)i$$

PROBLEM

Simplify the following: $(3 + i)(2 + i)$.

SOLUTION

$$\begin{aligned}(3 + i)(2 + i) &= 3(2 + i) + i(2 + i) \\ &= 6 + 3i + 2i + i^2 \\ &= 6 + (3 + 2)i + (-1) \\ &= 5 + 5i\end{aligned}$$

Complex numbers, $a + bi$, may be obtained when using the quadratic formula to solve quadratic equations.

PROBLEM

Solve the equation $x^2 - x + 1 = 0$.

SOLUTION

In this equation, $a = 1$, $b = -1$ and $c = 1$. Substitute into the quadratic formula.

$$\begin{aligned}x &= \frac{-(-1) \pm \sqrt{(-1)^2 - 4(1)(1)}}{2(1)} \\ &= \frac{1 \pm \sqrt{1 - 4}}{2} \\ &= \frac{1 \pm \sqrt{-3}}{2} \\ &= \frac{1 \pm \sqrt{3}i}{2} \\ x &= \frac{1 + \sqrt{3}i}{2} \text{ or } x = \frac{1 - \sqrt{3}i}{2}\end{aligned}$$

Division of two complex numbers is usually accomplished with a special procedure that involves the conjugate of a complex number. The conjugate of $a + bi$ is denoted by

$$\overline{a + bi} \text{ and } \overline{a + bi} = a - bi.$$

Also, $(a + bi)(a - bi) = a^2 + b^2$.

The usual procedure for division is illustrated below.

$$\frac{x + yi}{z + wi} = \frac{x + yi}{z + wi} \times \frac{z - wi}{z - wi}$$

$$= \frac{(xz + yw) + (-xw + yz)i}{z^2 + w^2}$$

$$= \frac{xz + yw}{z^2 + w^2} + \frac{-xw + yz}{z^2 + w^2}i$$

All the properties of real numbers described in the previous section carry over to complex numbers, however, those properties will not be stated again.

If a is a real number, then a can be expressed in the form $a = a + 0i$. Hence, every real number is a complex number and $R \subseteq C$.

Drill: Real and Complex Numbers

DIRECTIONS: Solve the following equations.

1. $3i^3 =$

   (A) $-3i$ (C) $9i$

   (B) $3i$ (D) $-i$

2. $2i^7 =$

   (A) $-128i$ (C) $14i$

   (B) $2i$ (D) $-2i$

3. $-4i^4 =$

   (A) 4 (C) $4i$

   (B) -4 (D) $-4i$

4. $-5i^6 =$

   (A) -5 (C) $-i$

   (B) $-5i$ (D) 5

5. $(3 + 2i)(2 + 3i) =$

   (A) $12 + 13i$ (C) $13i$

   (B) $-12 - 13i$ (D) $-13i$

6. $(2 - i)(2 + i) =$

   (A) -5 (C) $-5i$

   (B) $5i$ (D) 5

7. $(5 - 4i)^2 =$

   (A) $9 - 40i$ (C) $41 - 40i$

   (B) $-9 - 40i$ (D) $9 + 40i$

8. $x^2 + 16 = 0$

   (A) ± 4 (C) $4 \pm i$

   (B) $\pm 4i$ (D) $-4 \pm i$

9. $4y^2 + 1 = 0$

   (A) $\pm \dfrac{1}{2}$ (C) $-i \pm \dfrac{1}{2}$

   (B) $i \pm \dfrac{1}{2}$ (D) $\pm \dfrac{1}{2}i$

10. $x^2 - 4x + 13 = 0$

    (A) $3 \pm 2i$ (C) $\pm 5i$

    (B) $\pm 6i$ (D) $2 \pm 3i$

ANSWER KEY

1. (A)
2. (D)
3. (B)
4. (D)
5. (C)
6. (D)
7. (A)
8. (B)
9. (D)
10. (D)

Detailed Explanations of Answers

1. (A)

$$3i^3 = 3i(i)^2 = 3i(-1) = -3i$$

2. (D)

$$2i^7 = 2i(i^2)(i^2)(i^2) = 2i(-1)(-1)(-1) = -2i$$

3. (B)

$$-4i^4 = -4(i^2)(i^2) = -4(-1)(-1) = -4$$

4. (D)

$$-5i^6 = -5(i^2)(i^2)(i^2) = -5(-1)(-1)(-1) = 5$$

5. (C)

$$(3+2i)(2+3i) = 6 + \underbrace{9i + 4i}_{} + 6i^2$$
$$= 6 + \;\; 13i \;\; -6$$
$$= 13i$$

6. (D)

$$(2-i)(2+i) = 4 + 2i - 2i - i^2$$
$$= 4 + 0 - (-1)$$
$$= 5$$

7. (A)

$$(5-4i)^2 = (5-4i)(5-4i)$$
$$= (25 - 20i - 20i + 16i^2)$$
$$= 25 - 40i + 16(-1)$$
$$= 9 - 40i$$

8. (B)

$$x^2 + 16 = 0$$
$$x^2 = -16$$
$$x^2 = (16)(-1)$$
$$x = \pm 4i$$

9. (D)

$$4y^2 + 1 = 0$$
$$4y^2 = -1 \Rightarrow y^2 = -\frac{1}{4} \quad y = \pm\frac{1}{2}i$$

10. (D)

$$x^2 - 4x + 13 = 0$$

by the quadratic formula

$$\frac{-b \pm \sqrt{b^2 - 4ac}}{2a} = \frac{4 \pm \sqrt{16 - 4(1)(13)}}{2}$$
$$= \frac{4 \pm \sqrt[2]{16 - 52}}{2}$$
$$= \frac{4 \pm \sqrt[2]{-36}}{2}$$
$$= \frac{4 \pm 6i}{2}$$
$$= 2 \pm 3i$$

Algebra Terms

In algebra, letters or variables are used to represent numbers. A **variable** is defined as a placeholder, which can take on any of several values at a given time. A **constant,** on the other hand, is a symbol which takes on only one value at a given time. A **term** is a constant, a variable, or a combination of constants and variables. For example: 7.76, $3x$, xyz, $\dfrac{5z}{x}$, $(0.99)x^2$ are terms. If a term is a combination of constants and variables, the constant part of the term is referred to as the **coefficient** of the variable. If a variable is written without a coefficient, the coefficient is assumed to be 1.

- **EXAMPLES**

    $3x^2$ y^3

    coefficient: 3   coefficient: 1

    variable: x variable: y

An **expression** is a collection of one or more terms. If the number of terms is greater than 1, the expression is said to be the sum of the terms.

- **EXAMPLES**

    $9, 9xy, 6x + \dfrac{x}{3}, 8yz - 2x$

An algebraic expression consisting of only one term is called a **monomial**; of two terms is called a **binomial**; of three terms is called a **trinomial**. In general, an algebraic expression consisting of two or more terms is called a **polynomial**.

Operations with Polynomials

A) **Addition of polynomials** is achieved by combining like terms, terms which differ only in their numerical coefficients, e.g.,

$$P(x) = (x^2 - 3x + 5) + (4x^2 + 6x - 3)$$

Note that the parentheses are used to distinguish the polynomials.

By using the commutative and associative laws, we can rewrite $P(x)$ as:

$$P(x) = (x^2 + 4x^2) + (6x - 3x) + (5 - 3)$$

Using the distributive law, $ab + ac = a(b + c)$, yields:

$$(1 + 4)x^2 + (6 - 3)x + (5 - 3) = 5x^2 + 3x + 2$$

B) **Subtraction of two polynomials** is achieved by first changing the sign of all terms in the expression which are being subtracted and then adding this result to the other expression, e.g.,

$$(5x^2 + 4y^2 + 3z^2) - (4xy + 7y^2 - 3z^2 + 1)$$
$$= 5x^2 + 4y^2 + 3z^2 - 4xy - 7y^2 + 3z^2 - 1$$
$$= 5x^2 + (4y^2 - 7y^2) + (3z^2 + 3z^2) - 4xy - 1$$
$$= 5x^2 + (-3y^2) + 6z^2 - 4xy - 1$$

C) **Multiplication of two or more polynomials** is achieved by using the laws of exponents, the rules of signs, and the commutative and associative laws of multiplication. Begin by multiplying the coefficients and then multiply the variables according to the laws of exponents, e.g.,

$$(y^2)\,(5)\,(6y^2)\,(yz)\,(2z^2)$$
$$= (1)\,(5)\,(6)\,(1)\,(2)\,(y^2)\,(y^2)\,(yz)\,(z^2)$$
$$= 60[(y^2)\,(y^2)\,(y)]\,[(z)\,(z^2)]$$
$$= 60(y^5)\,(z^3)$$
$$= 60y^5z^3$$

D) **Multiplication of a polynomial by a monomial** is achieved by multiplying each term of the polynomial by the monomial and combining the results, e.g.,

$$(4x^2 + 3y)\,(6xz^2)$$
$$= (4x^2)\,(6xz^2) + (3y)\,(6xz^2)$$
$$= 24x^3z^2 + 18xyz^2$$

E) **Multiplication of a polynomial by a polynomial** is achieved by multiplying each of the terms of one polynomial by each of the terms of the other polynomial and combining the result, e.g.,

$$(5y + z + 1)\,(y^2 + 2y)$$
$$[(5y)\,(y^2) + (5y)\,(2y)] + [(z)\,(y^2) + (z)\,(2y)] +$$

$[(1)\,(y^2) + (1)\,(2y)]$

$= (5y^3 + 10y^2) + (y^2z + 2yz) + (y^2 + 2y)$

$= (5y^3) + (10y^2 + y^2) + (y^2z) + (2yz) + (2y)$

$= 5y^3 + 11y^2 + y^2z + 2yz + 2y$

F) **Division of a monomial by a monomial** is achieved by first dividing the constant coefficients and the variable factors separately, and then multiplying these quotients, e.g.,

$6xyz^2 \div 2y^2z$

$= \left(\dfrac{6}{2}\right)\left(\dfrac{x}{1}\right)\left(\dfrac{y}{y^2}\right)\left(\dfrac{z^2}{z}\right)$

$= 3xy^{-1}z$

$= \dfrac{3xz}{y}$

G) **Division of a polynomial by a polynomial** is achieved by following the given procedure, called long division.

Step 1: The terms of both the polynomials are arranged in order of ascending or descending powers of one variable.

Step 2: The first term of the dividend is divided by the first term of the divisor which gives the first term of the quotient.

Step 3: This first term of the quotient is multiplied by the entire divisor and the result is subtracted from the dividend.

Step 4: Using the remainder obtained from Step 3 as the new dividend, Steps 2 and 3 are repeated until the remainder is zero or the degree of the remainder is less than the degree of the divisor.

Step 5: The result is written as follows:

$$\frac{\text{dividend}}{\text{divisor}} = \text{quotient} + \frac{\text{remainder}}{\text{divisor}}$$

divisor $\neq 0$

e.g., $(2x^2 + x + 6) \div (x + 1)$

$$
\begin{array}{r}
2x - 1 \\
(x+1)\overline{)2x^2 + x + 6} \\
-(2x^2 + 2x) \\
\hline
-x + 6 \\
-(-x - 1) \\
\hline
7
\end{array}
$$

The result is $(2x^2 + x + 6) \div (x + 1) = 2x - 1 + \dfrac{7}{x + 1}$

Drill: Operations with Polynomials

Addition

DIRECTIONS: Add the following polynomials.

1. $9a^2b + 3c + 2a^2b + 5c =$

    (A) $19a^2bc$ (C) $11a^4b^2 + 8c^2$

    (B) $11a^2b + 8c$ (D) $19a^4b^2c^2$

2. $14m^2n^3 + 6m^2n^3 + 3m^2n^3 =$

    (A) $20m^2n^3$ (C) $23m^2n^3$

    (B) $23m^6n^9$ (D) $32m^6n^9$

3. $3x + 2y + 16x + 3z + 6y =$

    (A) $19x + 8y$ (C) $19x + 8y + 3z$

    (B) $19x + 11yz$ (D) $11xy + 19xz$

4. $(4d^2 + 7e^3 + 12f) + (3d^2 + 6e^3 + 2f) =$

    (A) $23d^2e^3f$ (C) $33d^4e^6f^2$

    (B) $33d^2e^2f$ (D) $7d^2 + 13e^3 + 14f$

5. $3ac^2 + 2b^2c + 7ac^2 + 2ac^2 + b^2c =$

    (A) $12ac^2 + 3b^2c$ (C) $11ac^2 + 4ab^2c$

    (B) $14ab^2c^2$ (D) $15ab^2c^2$

Subtraction

DIRECTIONS: Subtract the following polynomials.

6. $14m^2n - 6m^2n =$

    (A) $20m^2n$ (C) $8m$

    (B) $8m^2n$ (D) 8

7. $3x^3y^2 - 4xz - 6x^3y^2 =$

    (A) $-7x^2y^2z$ (C) $-3x^3y^2 - 4xz$

    (B) $3x^3y^2 - 10x^4y^2z$ (D) $-x^2y^2z - 6x^3y^2$

8. $9g^2 + 6h - 2g^2 - 5h =$

    (A) $15g^2h - 7g^2h$ (C) $11g^2 + 7h$

    (B) $7g^4h^2$ (D) $7g^2 + h$

9. $7b^3 - 4c^2 - 6b^3 + 3c^2 =$

    (A) $b^3 - c^2$ (C) $13b^3 - c$

    (B) $-11b^2 - 3c^2$ (D) $7b - c$

10. $11q^2r - 4q^2r - 8q^2r =$

    (A) $22q^2r$ (C) $-2q^2r$

    (B) q^2r (D) $-q^2r$

Multiplication

DIRECTIONS: Multiply the following polynomials.

11. $5p^2t \times 3p^2t =$

    (A) $15p^2t$ (C) $15p^4t^2$

    (B) $15p^4t$ (D) $8p^2t$

12. $(2r + s)\,14r =$

    (A) $28rs$ (C) $16r^2 + 14rs$

    (B) $28r^2 + 14sr$ (D) $28r + 14sr$

13. $(4m + p)\,(3m - 2p) =$

    (A) $12m^2 + 5mp + 2p^2$

    (B) $12m^2 - 2mp + 2p^2$

    (C) $7m - p$

    (D) $12m^2 - 5mp - 2p^2$

14. $(2a + b)\,(3a^2 + ab + b^2) =$

    (A) $6a^3 + 5a^2b + 3ab^2 + b^3$

    (B) $5a^3 + 3ab + b^3$

    (C) $6a^3 + 2a^2b + 2ab^2$

    (D) $3a^2 + 2a + ab + b + b^2$

15. $(6t^2 + 2t + 1)\,3t =$

    (A) $9t^2 + 5t + 3$ (C) $9t^3 + 6t^2 + 3t$

    (B) $18t^2 + 6t + 3$ (D) $18t^3 + 6t^2 + 3t$

Division

DIRECTIONS: Divide the following polynomials.

16. $(x^2 + x - 6) \div (x - 2) =$

    (A) $x - 3$ (C) $x + 3$

    (B) $x + 2$ (D) $x - 2$

17. $24b^4c^3 \div 6b^2c =$

    (A) $3b^2c^2$ (C) $4b^3c^2$

    (B) $4b^4c^3$ (D) $4b^2c^2$

18. $(3p^2 + pq - 2q^2) \div (p + q) =$

    (A) $3p + 2q$ (C) $3p - q$

    (B) $2q - 3p$ (D) $3p - 2q$

19. $(y^3 - 2y^2 - y + 2) \div (y - 2) =$

    (A) $(y - 1)^2$

    (B) $y^2 - 1$

    (C) $(y + 2)\,(y - 1)$

    (D) $(y + 1)^2$

20. $(m^2 + m - 14) \div (m + 4) =$

    (A) $m - 2$ (C) $m - 3 + \dfrac{4}{m + 4}$

    (B) $m - 3 + \dfrac{-2}{m + 4}$ (D) $m - 3$

Simplifying Algebraic Expressions

To factor a polynomial completely is to find the prime factors of the polynomial with respect to a specified set of numbers.

The following concepts are important while factoring or simplifying expressions.

A) The factors of an algebraic expression consist of two or more algebraic expressions which, when multiplied together, produce the given algebraic expression.

B) A **prime factor** is a polynomial with no factors other than itself and 1. The **least common multiple (LCM)** for a set of numbers is the smallest quantity divisible by every number of the set. For algebraic expressions, the least common numerical coefficients for each of the given expressions will be a factor.

C) The **greatest common factor (GCF)** for a set of numbers is the largest factor that is common to all members of the set.

D) For algebraic expressions, the greatest common factor is the polynomial of highest degree and the largest numerical coefficient which is a factor of all the given expressions.

Some important formulas, useful for the factoring of polynomials, are listed below.

$a(c + d) = ac + ad$

$(a + b)(a - b) = a^2 - b^2$

$(a + b)(a + b) = (a + b)^2 = a^2 + 2ab + b^2$

$(a - b)(a - b) = (a - b)^2 = a^2 - 2ab + b^2$

$(x + a)(x + b) = x^2 + (a + b)x + ab$

$(ax + b)(cx + d) = acx^2 + (ad + bc)x + bd$

$(a + b)(c + d) = ac + bc + ad + bd$

$(a + b)(a + b)(a + b) = (a + b)^3 = a^3 + 3a^2b + 3ab^2 + b^3$

$(a - b)(a - b)(a - b) = (a - b)^3 = a^3 - 3a^2b + 3ab^2 - b^3$

$(a - b)(a^2 + ab + b^2) = a^3 - b^3$

$(a + b)(a^2 - ab + b^2) = a^3 + b^3$

$(a + b + c)^2 = a^2 + b^2 + c^2 + 2ab + 2ac + 2bc$

$(a - b)(a^3 + a^2b + ab^2 + b^3) = a^4 - b^4$

$(a - b)(a^4 + a^3b + a^2b^2 + ab^3 + b^4) = a^5 - b^5$

$(a - b)(a^5 + a^4b + a^3b^2 + a^2b^3 + ab^4 + b^5) = a^6 - b^6$

$(a - b)(a^{n-1} + a^{n-2}b + a^{n-3}b^2 + \ldots + ab^{n-2} + b^{n-1}) = a^n - b^n$

where n is any positive integer (1, 2, 3, 4, …).

$(a + b)(a^{n-1} - a^{n-2}b + a^{n-3}b^2 - \ldots - ab^{n-2} + b^{n-1}) = a^n + b^n$

where n is any positive odd integer (1, 3, 5, 7, …).

The procedure for factoring an algebraic expression completely is as follows:

Step 1: First find the greatest common factor if there is any. Then examine each factor remaining for greatest common factors.

Step 2: Continue factoring the factors obtained in Step 1 until all factors other than monomial factors are prime.

• **EXAMPLE**

Factoring $4 - 16x^2$,

$4 - 16x^2 = 4(1 - 4x^2) = 4(1 + 2x)(1 - 2x)$

PROBLEM

Express each of the following as a single term.

(1) $3x^2 + 2x^2 - 4x^2$

(2) $5axy^2 - 7axy^2 - 3xy^2$

SOLUTION

(1) Factor x^2 in the expression.

$3x^2 + 2x^2 - 4x^2 = (3 + 2 - 4)x^2 = 1x^2 = x^2$

(2) Factor xy^2 in the expression and then factor a.

$$5axy^2 - 7axy^2 - 3xy^2 = (5a - 7a - 3)xy^2$$
$$= [(5 - 7)a - 3]xy^2$$
$$= (-2a - 3)xy^2$$

PROBLEM

Simplify $\dfrac{\dfrac{1}{x-1} - \dfrac{1}{x-2}}{\dfrac{1}{x-2} - \dfrac{1}{x-3}}$.

SOLUTION

Simplify the expression in the numerator by using the addition rule:

$$\frac{a}{b} + \frac{c}{d} = \frac{ad + bc}{bd}$$

Notice *bd* is the Least Common Denominator, LCD. We obtain

$$\frac{x-2-(x-1)}{(x-1)(x-2)} = \frac{-1}{(x-1)(x-2)}$$

in the numerator.

Repeat this procedure for the expression in the denominator:

$$\frac{x-3-(x-2)}{(x-2)(x-3)} = \frac{-1}{(x-2)(x-3)}$$

We now have

$$\frac{\dfrac{-1}{(x-1)(x-2)}}{\dfrac{-1}{(x-2)(x-3)}}$$

which is simplified by inverting the fraction in the denominator and multiplying it by the numerator and cancelling like terms

$$\frac{-1}{(x-1)(x-2)} \times \frac{(x-2)(x-3)}{-1} = \frac{x-3}{x-1}$$

Drill: Simplifying Algebraic Expressions

DIRECTIONS: Simplify the following expressions.

1. $16b^2 - 25z^2 =$

    (A) $(4b-5z)^2$ (C) $(4b-5z)(4b+5z)$

    (B) $(4b+5z)^2$ (D) $(16b-25z)^2$

2. $x^2 - 2x - 8 =$

    (A) $(x-4)^2$ (C) $(x+4)(x-2)$

    (B) $(x-6)(x-2)$ (D) $(x-4)(x+2)$

3. $2c^2 + 5cd - 3d^2 =$

    (A) $(c-3d)(c+2d)$

    (B) $(2c-d)(c+3d)$

    (C) $(c-d)(2c+3d)$

    (D) $(2c+d)(c+3d)$

4. $4t^3 - 20t =$

    (A) $4t(t^2-5)$ (C) $4t(t+4)(t-5)$

    (B) $4t^2(t-20)$ (D) $2t(2t^2-10)$

5. $x^2 + xy - 2y^2 =$

    (A) $(x-2y)(x+y)$ (C) $(x+2y)(x+y)$

    (B) $(x-2y)(x-y)$ (D) $(x+2y)(x-y)$

Linear Equations

A linear equation with one unknown is one that can be put into the form $ax + b = 0$, where a and b are constants, $a \neq 0$.

To solve a linear equation means to transform it in the form $x = \dfrac{-b}{a}$.

A) If the equation has unknowns on both sides of the equality, it is convenient to put similar terms on the same sides. Refer to the following example.

$$4x + 3 = 2x + 9$$
$$4x + 3 - 2x = 2x + 9 - 2x$$
$$(4x - 2x) + 3 = (2x - 2x) + 9$$
$$2x + 3 = 0 + 9$$
$$2x + 3 - 3 = 0 + 9 - 3$$
$$2x = 6$$
$$\frac{2x}{2} = \frac{6}{2}$$
$$x = 3$$

B) If the equation appears in fractional form, it is necessary to transform it, using cross-multiplication, and then repeat the same procedure as in A. We obtain:

$$\frac{3x+4}{3} \quad\diagdown\!\!\!\!\diagup\quad \frac{7x+2}{5}$$

By using cross-multiplication we would obtain:

$3(7x + 2) = 5(3x + 4)$.

This is equivalent to:

$21x + 6 = 15x + 20$,

which can be solved as in A.

$$21x + 6 = 15x + 20$$
$$21x - 15x + 6 = 15x - 15x + 20$$
$$6x + 6 - 6 = 20 - 6$$
$$6x = 14$$
$$x = \frac{14}{6}$$
$$x = \frac{7}{3}$$

C) If there are radicals in the equation, it is necessary to square both sides and then apply A.

$$\sqrt{3x + 1} = 5$$
$$(\sqrt{3x + 1})^2 = 5^2$$
$$3x + 1 = 25$$
$$3x + 1 - 1 = 25 - 1$$
$$3x = 24$$
$$x = \frac{24}{3}$$
$$x = 8$$

Slope of the Line

The slope of the line containing two points (x_1, y_1) and (x_2, y_2) is given by:

$$\text{Slope} = m = \frac{y_2 - y_1}{x_2 - x_1}$$

Horizontal lines have a slope of zero, and the slope of vertical lines is undefined. Parallel lines have equal slopes and perpendicular lines have slopes that are negative reciprocals of each other.

The equation of a line with slope m passing through a point $Q(x_0, y_0)$ is of the form:

$$y - y_0 = m(x - x_0)$$

This is called the *point-slope form* of a linear equation.

The equation of a line passing through $Q(x_1, y_1)$ and $P(x_2, y_2)$ is given by:

$$\frac{y - y_1}{x - x_1} = \frac{y_2 - y_1}{x_2 - x_1}$$

This is the *two-point form* of a linear equation.

The equation of a line intersecting the x-axis at $(x_0, 0)$ and the y-axis at $(0, y_0)$ is given by:

$$\frac{x}{x_0} + \frac{y}{y_0} = 1$$

This is the *intercept form* of a linear equation.

The equation of a line with slope m intersecting the y-axis at $(0, b)$ is given by:

$$y = mx + b$$

This is the *slope-intercept* form of a linear equation.

PROBLEMS ON LINEAR EQUATIONS:

A) Find the slope, the y-intercept, and the x-intercept of the equation $2x - 3y - 18 = 0$.

Solution: The equation $2x - 3y - 18 = 0$ can be written in the form of the general linear equation, $ax + by = c$.

$$2x - 3y - 18 = 0$$
$$2x - 3y = 18$$

To find the slope and y-intercept, we derive them from the formula of the general linear equation $ax + by = c$. Dividing by b and solving for y, we obtain:

$$\frac{a}{b}x + y = \frac{c}{b}$$
$$y = \frac{c}{b} - \frac{a}{b}x$$

where $\frac{-a}{b}$ = slope and $\frac{c}{b}$ = y-intercept

To find the x-intercept, solve for x and let $y = 0$:

$$x = \frac{c}{a} - \frac{b}{a}y$$
$$x = \frac{c}{a}$$

In this form we have $a = 2$, $b = -3$, and $c = 18$. Thus,

$$\text{slope} = -\frac{a}{b} = -\frac{2}{-3} = \frac{2}{3}$$
$$y\text{-intercept} = \frac{c}{b} = \frac{18}{-3} = -6$$
$$x\text{-intercept} = \frac{c}{a} = \frac{18}{2} = 9$$

B) Find the equation for the line passing through $(3, 5)$ and $(-1, 2)$.

Solution A): We use the two-point form with $(x_1, y_1) =$ (3, 5) and $(x_2, y_2) = (-1, 2)$. Then

$$\frac{y - y_1}{x - x_1} = \frac{y_2 - y_1}{x_2 - x_1}$$

$$\frac{y_2 - y_1}{x_2 - x_1} = \frac{2 - 5}{-1 - 3} \quad \text{thus} \quad \frac{y - 5}{x - 3} = \frac{-3}{-4}$$

Cross multiply, $\qquad -4(y - 5) = -3(x - 3)$.

Distribute, $\qquad\quad -4y + 20 = -3x + 9$

Place in general form, $\quad 3x - 4y = -11$.

Solution B): Does the same equation result if we let $(x_1, y_1) = (-1, 2)$ and $(x_2, y_2) = (3, 5)$?

$$\frac{y_2 - y_1}{x_2 - x_1} = \frac{5 - 2}{3 - (-1)} \quad \text{thus} \quad \frac{y - 2}{x + 1} = \frac{3}{4}$$

Cross multiply, $4(y - 2) = 3(x + 1)$

Distribute $3x - 4y = -11$

Place in general form, $3x - 4y = -11$.

Hence, either replacement results in the same equation. Keep in mind that the coefficient of the x-term should always be positive.

C) (a) Find the equation of the line passing through (2, 5) with slope 3.

(b) Suppose a line passes through the y-axis at (0,b). How can we write the equation if the point-slope form is used?

Solution C): (a) In the point-slope form, let $x_1 = 2$, $y_1 = 5$, $m = 3$.

The point-slope form of a line is:

$$y - y_1 = m(x - x_1)$$
$$y - 5 = 3(x - 2)$$
$$y - 5 = 3x - 6 \qquad \text{Distributive property}$$
$$y = 3x - 1 \qquad \text{Transposition}$$

(b) $y - b = m(x - 0)$
$$y = mx + b.$$

Notice that this is the slope-intercept form for the equation of a line.

PROBLEM

Construct the graph of the function defined by $y = 3x - 9$.

SOLUTION

This linear equation is in the slope-intercept form, $y = mx + b$.

A line can be determined by two points. Let us choose the intercepts. The x-intercept lies on the x-axis and the y-intercept is on the y-axis.

We can find the y-intercept by assigning 0 to x in the given equation and then find the x-intercept by assigning 0 to y. It is helpful to have a third point. We find a third point by assigning 4 to x and solving for y. Thus, we get the following table of corresponding numbers:

x	$y = 3x - 9$	y
0	$y = 3(0) - 9$	-9
3	$0 = 3x - 9,\ x = 9/3 = 3$	0
4	$y = 3(4) - 9$	3

The three points are (0, −9), (3, 0), and (4, 3). Draw a line through them as in Figure below.

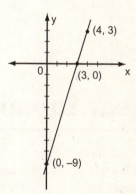

PROBLEM

Graph the function defined by $3x - 4y = 12$.

SOLUTION

Solve for y:

$$3x - 4y = 12$$
$$-4y = 12 - 3x$$
$$y = -3 + \frac{3}{4}x$$
$$y = \frac{3}{4}x - 3$$

The graph of this function is a straight line since it is of the form $y = mx + b$. The y-intercept crosses (intersects) the y-axis at the point $(0, -3)$ since for $x = 0$, $y = b = -3$. The x-intercept crosses (intersects) the x-axis at the point $(4, 0)$ since for $y = 0$, $x = (y + 3) \times \frac{4}{3} = (0 + 3) \times \frac{4}{3} = 4$. These two points, $(0, -3)$ and $(4, 0)$ are sufficient to determine the graph (see Figure below). A third point, $(8, 3)$, satisfying the equation of the function is plotted as a partial check of the intercepts. Note that the slope of the line is $m = \frac{3}{4}$. This means that y increases three units as x increases four units anywhere along the line.

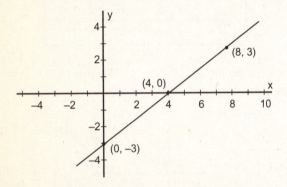

Two Linear Equations

Equations of the form $ax + by = c$, where a, b, c are constants and $a, b \neq 0$ are called **linear equations** with two unknown variables.

There are several ways to solve systems of linear equations with two variables.

Method 1:   **Addition or subtraction**—If necessary, multiply the equations by numbers that will make the coefficients of one unknown in the resulting equations numerically equal. If the signs of equal coefficients are the same, subtract the equation; otherwise, add.

The result is one equation with one unknown; we solve it and substitute the value into the other equations to find the unknown that we first eliminated.

Method 2:   **Substitution**—Find the value of one unknown in terms of the other. Substitute this value in the other equation and solve.

Method 3:   **Graph**—Graph both equations. The point of intersection of the drawn lines is a simultaneous solution for the equations, and its coordinates correspond to the answer that would be found analytically.

If the lines are parallel they have no simultaneous solution.

Dependent equations are equations that represent the same line; therefore, every point on the line of a dependent equation represents a solution. Since there is an infinite number of points on a line, there is an infinite number of simultaneous solutions. For example,

$$\begin{cases} 2x + y = 8 \\ 4x + 2y = 16 \end{cases}$$

These equations are dependent. Since they represent the same line, all points that satisfy either of the equations are solutions of the system.

A system of linear equations is consistent if there is only one solution for the system.

A system of linear equations is inconsistent if it does not have any solutions.

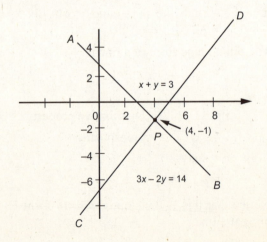

• **EXAMPLE**

Find the point of intersection of the graphs of the equations as shown in the previous figure.

$$x + y = 3$$
$$3x - 2y = 14$$

To solve these linear equations, solve for y in terms of x. The equations will be in the form $y = mx + b$, where m is the slope and b is the intercept on the y-axis.

$$x + y = 3$$

Subtract x from both sides: $y = 3 - x$

Subtract $3x$ from both sides: $3x - 2y = 14$

Divide by -2: $\qquad -2y = 14 - 3x$

$$y = -7 + \frac{3}{2}x$$

The graphs of the linear functions, $y = 3 - x$ and $y = 7 + \frac{3}{2}x$ can be determined by plotting only two points. For example, for $y = 3 - x$, let $x = 0$, then $y = 3$. Let $x = 1$, then $y = 2$. The two points on this first line are $(0,3)$ and $(1,2)$. For $y = -7 + \frac{3}{2}x$ let $x = 0$, then $y = -7$. Let $x = 1$, then $y = -5\frac{1}{2}$. The two points on this second line are $(0,-7)$ and $(1,-5\frac{1}{2})$.

To find the point of intersection P of

$$x + y = 3 \text{ and } 3x - 2y = 14,$$

solve them algebraically. Multiply the first equation by 2. Add these two equations to eliminate the variable y.

$$\begin{array}{r} 2x + 2y = 6 \\ 3x - 2y = 14 \\ \hline 5x \qquad = 20 \end{array}$$

Solve for x to obtain $x = 4$. Substitute this into $y = 3 - x$ to get $y = 3 - 4 = -1$. P is $(4,-1)$. AB is the graph of the first equation, and CD is the graph of the second equation. The point of intersection P of the two graphs is the only point on both lines. The coordinates of P satisfy both equations and represent the desired solution of the problem. From the graph, P seems to be the point $(4,-1)$. These coordinates satisfy both equations, and hence are the exact coordinates of the point of intersection of the two lines.

To show that $(4,-1)$ satisfies both equations, substitute this point into both equations.

$$\begin{array}{ll} x + y = 3 & 3x - 2y = 14 \\ 4 + (-1) = 3 & 3(4) - 2(-1) = 14 \\ 4 - 1 = 3 & 12 + 2 = 14 \\ 3 = 3 & 14 = 14 \end{array}$$

• **EXAMPLE**

Solve the equations $2x + 3y = 6$ and $4x + 6y = 7$ simultaneously.

We have two equations and two unknowns,
$$2x + 3y = 6 \qquad\qquad (1)$$
and
$$4x + 6y = 7 \qquad\qquad (2)$$

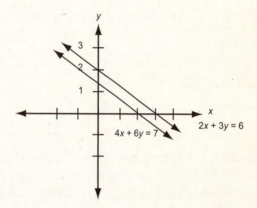

There are several methods to solve this problem. We have chosen to multiply each equation by a different number so that when the two equations are added, one of the variables drops out. Thus,

Multiply equation (1) by 2: $\quad 4x + 6y = 12 \quad$ (3)

Multiply equation (2) by -1: $\underline{-4x - 6y = -7} \quad$ (4)

Add equations (3) and (4): $\qquad\qquad 0 = 5$

We obtain a peculiar result!

Actually, what we have shown in this case is that if there were a simultaneous solution to the given equations, then 0 would equal 5. But the conclusion is impossible; therefore, there can be no simultaneous solution to these two equations, hence no point satisfying both.

The straight lines which are the graphs of these equations must be parallel if they never intersect, but not identical, which can be seen from the graph of these equations (see the figure).

- ### EXAMPLE

Solve the equations $2x + 3y = 6$ and $y = -\left(\dfrac{2x}{3}\right) + 2$ simultaneously.

We have two equations and two unknowns.

$$2x + 3y = 6 \tag{1}$$

and

$$y = -\left(\dfrac{2x}{3}\right) + 2 \tag{2}$$

There are several methods of solution for this problem. Since equation (2) already gives us an expression for y, we use the method of substitution.

Substitute $-\left(\dfrac{2x}{3}\right) + 2$ for y in the first equation:

$$2x + 3\left(-\dfrac{2x}{3} + 2\right) = 6$$

Distribute: $\qquad 2x - 2x + 6 = 6$

$$6 = 6$$

The result $6 = 6$ is true, but indicates no solution. Actually, our work shows that no matter what real number x is, if y is determined by the second equation, then the first equation will always be satisfied.

The reason for this peculiarity may be seen if we take a closer look at the equation $y = -\left(\dfrac{2x}{3}\right) + 2$. It is equivalent to $3y = -2x + 6$, or $2x + 3y = 6$.

In other words, the two equations are equivalent. Any pair of values of x and y which satisfies one satisfies the other.

It is hardly necessary to verify that in this case the graphs of the given equations are identical lines, and that there are an infinite number of simultaneous solutions to these equations.

A system of three linear equations in three unknowns is solved by eliminating one unknown from any two of the three equations and solving them. After finding two unknowns substitute them in any of the equations to find the third unknown.

PROBLEM

Solve the system

$$2x + 3y - 4z = -8 \tag{1}$$
$$x + y - 2z = -5 \tag{2}$$
$$7x - 2y + 5z = 4 \tag{3}$$

SOLUTION

We cannot eliminate any variable from two pairs of equations by a single multiplication. However, both x and z may be eliminated from equations (1) and (2) by multiplying equation (2) by -2. Then

$$2x + 3y - 4z = -8 \tag{1}$$
$$-2x - 2y + 4z = 10 \tag{4}$$

By addition, we have $y = 2$. Although we may now eliminate either x or z from another pair of equations, we can more conveniently substitute $y = 2$ in equations (2) and (3) to get two equations in two variables. Thus, making the substitution $y = 2$ in equations (2) and (3), we have

$$x - 2z = -7 \tag{5}$$
$$7x + 5z = 8 \tag{6}$$

Multiply equation (5) by 5 and multiply (6) by 2. Then add the two new equations. Then $x = -1$. Substitute x in either equation (5) or (6) to find z.

The solution of the system is $x = -1$, $y = 2$, and $z = 3$. Check by substitution.

A system of equations, as shown below, that has all constant terms $b_1, b_2, \ldots, b_n$ equal to zero is said to be a homogeneous system.

$$\begin{cases} a_{11}x_1 + a_{12}x_2 + \ldots + a_{1n}x_m = b_1 \\ a_{21}x_1 + a_{22}x_2 + \ldots + a_{2n}x_m = b_2 \\ \vdots \qquad \vdots \qquad \qquad \vdots \qquad \vdots \\ a_{n1}x_1 + a_{n2}x_2 + \ldots + a_{nn}x_m = b_n \end{cases}$$

A homogeneous system (one in which each variable can be replaced by a constant and the constant can be factored out) always has at least one solution which is called the trivial solution that is $x_1 = 0$, $x_2 = 0$, $\ldots$, $x_m = 0$.

For any given homogeneous system of equations, in which the number of variables is greater than or equal to the number of equations, there are non-trivial solutions.

Two systems of linear equations are said to be equivalent if and only if they have the same solution set.

Drill: Two Linear Equations

<u>DIRECTIONS</u>: **Find the solution set for each pair of equations.**

1. $3x + 4y = -2$
    $x - 6y = -8$

    (A) $(2, -1)$ (C) $(-2, -1)$

    (B) $(1, -2)$ (D) $(-2, 1)$

2. $2x + y = -10$
    $-2x - 4y = 4$

    (A) $(6, -2)$ (C) $(-2, 6)$

    (B) $(-6, 2)$ (D) $(2, 6)$

3. $6x + 5y = -4$
    $3x - 3y = 9$

    (A) $(1, -2)$ (C) $(2, -1)$

    (B) $(1, 2)$ (D) $(-2, 1)$

4. $4x + 3y = 9$
    $2x - 2y = 8$

    (A) $(-3, 1)$ (C) $(3, 1)$

    (B) $(1, -3)$ (D) $(3, -1)$

5. $x + y = 7$
    $x = y - 3$

    (A) $(5, 2)$ (C) $(2, 5)$

    (B) $(-5, 2)$ (D) $(-2, 5)$

Quadratic Equations

A second-degree equation in x of the type $ax^2 + bx + c = 0$, $a \neq 0$, a, b, and c are real numbers, is called a quadratic equation.

To solve a quadratic equation is to find values of x which satisfy $ax^2 + bx + c = 0$. These values of x are called solutions, or roots, of the equation.

A quadratic equation has a maximum of two roots. Methods of solving quadratic equations:

A) Direct solution: Given $x^2 - 9 = 0$.

   We can solve directly by isolating the variable x:

   $x^2 = 9$

   $x = \pm 3$

B) Factoring: Given a quadratic equation $ax^2 + bx + c = 0$, a, b, $c \neq 0$, to factor means to express it as the product $a(x - r_1)(x - r_2) = 0$, where r_1 and r_2 are the two roots.

   Some helpful hints to remember are:

   (a) $r_1 + r_2 = -\dfrac{b}{a}$.

   (b) $r_1 + r_2 = \dfrac{c}{a}$.

   Given $x^2 - 5x + 5 = 0$.

   Since $r_1 + r_2 = \dfrac{-b}{a} = \dfrac{-(-5)}{1} = 5$, so the possible solutions are $(3, 2)$, $(4, 1)$, and $(5, 0)$. Also $r_1 r_2 = \dfrac{c}{a} = \dfrac{4}{1} = 4$; this equation is satisfied only by the second pair, so $r_1 = 4$, $r_2 = 1$ and the factored form is $(x - 4)(x - 1) = 0$.

   If the coefficient of x^2 is not 1, it is necessary to divide the equation by this coefficient and then factor.

   Given $2x^2 - 12x + 16 = 0$.

   Dividing by 2, we obtain:

   $x^2 - 6x + 8 = 0$

   Since $r_1 + r_2 = \dfrac{-b}{a} = 6$, the possible solutions are $(6, 0)$, $(5, 1)$, $(4, 2)$, $(3, 3)$. Also $r_1 r_2 = 8$, so the only possible answer is $(4, 2)$ and the expression $x^2 - 6x + 8 = 0$ can be factored as $(x - 4)(x - 2)$.

C) Completing the square: If it is difficult to factor the quadratic equation using the previous method, we can complete the square.

   Given $x^2 - 12x + 8 = 0$.

We know that the two roots added up should be 12 because $r_1 + r_2 = \dfrac{-b}{a} = \dfrac{-(-12)}{1} = 12$. The possible roots are (12, 0), (11, 1), (10, 2), (9,3), (8, 4), (7, 5), (6, 6).

But none of these satisfy $r_1 r_2 = 8$, so we cannot use (B).

To complete the square it is necessary to isolate the constant term,

$x^2 - 12x = -8$.

Then take $\dfrac{1}{2}$ coefficient of the x term, square it and add to both sides

$$x^2 - 12x + \left(\dfrac{-12}{2}\right)^2 = -8 + \left(\dfrac{-12}{2}\right)^2$$
$$x^2 - 12x + 36 = -8 + 36 = 28$$

Now we can use the previous method to factor the left side: $r_1 + r_2 = 12$, $r_1 r_2 = 36$ is satisfied by the pair (6, 6), so we have:

$(x - 6)(x - 6) = (x - 6)^2 = 28$.

Now take the square root of both sides and solve for x. Remember when taking a square root that the solution can be positive or negative.

$$(x - 6) = \pm\sqrt{28} = \pm 2\sqrt{7}$$
$$x = \pm 2\sqrt{7} + 6$$

So the roots are: $x = 2\sqrt{7} + 6$, $x = -2\sqrt{7} + 6$

PROBLEM

> Solve $2x^2 + 8x + 4 = 0$ by completing the square.

SOLUTION

Divide both members by 2, the coefficient of x^2.

$x^2 + 4x + 2 = 0$

Subtract the constant term, 2, from both members.

$x^2 + 4x = -2$

Add to each member the square of one-half the coefficient of the x-term.

$x^2 + 4x + 4 = -2 + 4$

Factor

$(x + 2)(x + 2) = (x + 2)^2 = 2$

Set the square root of the left member (a perfect square) equal to $\pm$ the square root of the right member and solve for x.

$x + 2 = \sqrt{2}$ or $x + 2 = -\sqrt{2}$

The roots are $\sqrt{2} - 2$ and $\sqrt{2} - 2$. Check each solution.

$$2\left(\sqrt{2} - 2\right)^2 + 8\left(\sqrt{2} - 2\right) + 4$$
$$= 2\left(2 - 4\sqrt{2} + 4\right) + 8\sqrt{2} - 16 + 4$$
$$= 4 - 8\sqrt{2} + 8 + 8\sqrt{2} - 16 + 4$$
$$= 0$$

$$2\left(-\sqrt{2} - 2\right)^2 + 8\left(-\sqrt{2} - 2\right) + 4$$
$$= 2\left(2 + 4\sqrt{2} + 4\right) - 8\sqrt{2} - 16 + 4$$
$$= 4 + 8\sqrt{2} + 8 - 8\sqrt{2} - 16 + 4$$
$$= 0$$

Quadratic Formula

Consider the polynomial:

$ax^2 + bx + c = 0$, where $a \neq 0$.

The roots of this equation can be determined in terms of the coefficients a, b, and c as shown below:

$$x = \dfrac{-b \pm \sqrt{b^2 - 4ac}}{2a}$$

where $(b^2 - 4ac)$ is called the discriminant of the quadratic equation.

Note that if the discriminant is less than zero ($b^2 - 4ac < 0$), the roots are complex numbers, since the discriminant appears under a radical and square roots of negatives are complex numbers, and a real number added to an imaginary number yields a complex number.

If the discriminant is equal to zero ($b^2 - 4ac = 0$), the result is one real root.

If the discriminant is greater than zero ($b^2 - 4ac > 0$), then the roots are real and unequal. Further, the roots are rational if and only if a and b are rational and ($b^2 - 4ac$) is a perfect square, otherwise the roots are irrational.

Example: Compute the value of the discriminant and then determine the nature of the roots of each of the following four equations:

A) $4x^2 - 12x + 9 = 0$

B) $3x^2 - 7x - 6 = 0$

C) $5x^2 + 2x - 9 = 0$

D) $x^2 + 3x + 5 = 0$

A) $4x^2 - 12x + 9 = 0$,

Here a, b, and c are integers,

$$a = 4, b = -12, \text{ and } c = 9.$$

Therefore,

$$b^2 - 4ac = (-12)^2 - 4(4)(9) = 144 - 144 = 0.$$

Since the discriminant is 0, the roots are rational and equal.

B) $3x^2 - 7x - 6 = 0$

Here a, b, and c are integers,

$$a = 3, b = -7, \text{ and } c = -6.$$

Therefore,

$$b^2 - 4ac = (-7)^2 - 4(3)(-6) = 49 + 72 = 121 = 11^2.$$

Since the discriminant is a perfect square, the roots are rational and unequal.

C) $5x^2 + 2x - 9 = 0$

Here a, b, and c are integers,

$$a = 5, b = 2, \text{ and } c = -9.$$

Therefore,

$$b^2 - 4ac = 2^2 - 4(5)(-9) = 4 + 180 = 184.$$

Since the discriminant is greater than zero, but not a perfect square, the roots are irrational and unequal.

D) $x^2 + 3x + 5 = 0$

Here a, b, and c are integers,

$$a = 1, b = 3, \text{ and } c = 5.$$

Therefore,

$$b^2 - 4ac = 3^2 - 4(1)(5) = 9 - 20 = -11.$$

Since the discriminant is negative, the roots are imaginary.

Example: Find the equation whose roots are $\dfrac{\alpha}{\beta}, \dfrac{\beta}{\alpha}$.

Solution: The roots of the equation are $x = \dfrac{\alpha}{\beta}$ and $x = \dfrac{\beta}{\alpha}$.

Subtract $\dfrac{\alpha}{\beta}$ from both sides of the first equation:

$$x - \frac{\alpha}{\beta} = \frac{\alpha}{\beta} - \frac{\alpha}{\beta} = 0$$

or

$$x - \frac{\alpha}{\beta} = 0$$

Subtract $\dfrac{\beta}{\alpha}$ from both sides of the second equation:

$$x - \frac{\beta}{\alpha} = \frac{\beta}{\alpha} - \frac{\beta}{\alpha} = 0$$

or

$$x - \frac{\beta}{\alpha} = 0$$

Therefore:

$$\left(x - \frac{\alpha}{\beta} \right)\left(x - \frac{\beta}{\alpha} \right) = (0)(0),$$

or

$$\left(x - \frac{\alpha}{\beta} \right)\left(x - \frac{\beta}{\alpha} \right) = 0. \tag{1}$$

Equation (1) is of the form:

$$(x - c)(x - d) = 0, \text{ or}$$
$$x^2 - cx - dx + cd = 0, \text{ or}$$
$$x^2 - (c + d)x + cd = 0. \tag{2}$$

Note that c corresponds to the root $\dfrac{\alpha}{\beta}$ and d corresponds to the root $\dfrac{\beta}{\alpha}$. The sum of the roots is:

$$c + d = \frac{\alpha}{\beta} + \frac{\beta}{\alpha} = \frac{\alpha(\alpha)}{\alpha(\beta)} + \frac{\beta(\beta)}{\beta(\alpha)} = \frac{\alpha^2}{\alpha\beta} + \frac{\beta^2}{\alpha\beta}$$

$$= \frac{\alpha^2 + \beta^2}{\alpha\beta}$$

The product of the roots is:

$$c \times d = \frac{\alpha}{\beta} \times \frac{\beta}{\alpha} = \frac{\alpha\beta}{\beta\alpha} = \frac{\alpha\beta}{\alpha\beta} = 1$$

Using the form of Equation (2):

$$\left(x - \frac{\alpha}{\beta}\right)\left(x - \frac{\beta}{\alpha}\right) = x^2 - \left(\frac{\alpha^2 + \beta^2}{\alpha\beta}\right)x + 1 = 0.$$

Hence,

$$x^2 - \left(\frac{\alpha^2 + \beta^2}{\alpha\beta}\right)x + 1 = 0. \tag{3}$$

Multiply both sides of Equation (3) by $\alpha\beta$

$$\alpha\beta\left[x^2 - \left(\frac{\alpha^2 + \beta^2}{\alpha\beta}\right)x + 1\right] = \alpha\beta(0)$$

Distributing,

$$\alpha\beta x^2 - (\alpha^2 + \beta^2)x + \alpha\beta = 0,$$

which is the equation whose roots are $\dfrac{\alpha}{\beta}, \dfrac{\beta}{\alpha}$.

Radical Equation

An equation that has one or more unknowns under a radical is called a radical equation.

To solve a radical equation, isolate the radical term on one side of the equation and move all the other terms to the other side. Then both members of the equation are raised to a power equal to the index of the isolated radical.

After solving the resulting equation, the roots obtained must be checked, since this method often introduces extraneous roots.

These introduced roots must be excluded if they are not solutions.

$$\text{Given } \sqrt{x^2 + 2} + 6x = x - 4$$
$$\sqrt{x^2 + 2} = x - 4 - 6x = -5x - 4$$
$$\left(\sqrt{x^2 + 2}\right)^2 = (-(5x + 4))^2$$
$$x^2 + 2 = (5x + 4)^2$$

$$x^2 + 2 = 25x^2 + 40x + 16$$
$$24x^2 + 40x + 14 = 0$$

Applying the quadratic formula, we obtain:

$$x = \frac{-40 \pm \sqrt{1600 - 4(24)(14)}}{2(24)} = \frac{-40 \pm 16}{48}$$

$$x_1 = \frac{-7}{6}, \quad x_2 = \frac{-1}{2}$$

Checking roots:

$$\sqrt{\left(\frac{-7}{6}\right)^2 + 2} + 6\left(\frac{-7}{6}\right) \overset{?}{=} \left(\frac{-7}{6}\right) - 4$$

$$\frac{11}{6} - 7 \overset{?}{=} \frac{-31}{6}$$

$$\frac{-31}{6} = \frac{-31}{6}$$

$$\sqrt{\left(\frac{-1}{2}\right)^2 + 2} + 6\left(\frac{-1}{2}\right) \overset{?}{=} \left(\frac{-1}{2}\right) - 4$$

$$\frac{3}{2} - 3 \overset{?}{=} \frac{-9}{2}$$

$$\frac{-3}{2} \neq \frac{-9}{2}$$

Hence, $-\dfrac{1}{2}$ is not a root of the equation, but $\dfrac{-7}{6}$ is a root.

PROBLEM

Solve for x: $4x^2 - 7 = 0$.

SOLUTION

This quadratic equation can be solved for x using the quadratic formula, which applies to equations in the form $ax^2 + bx + c = 0$ (in our equation $b = 0$). There is, however, an easier method that we can use:

Adding 7 to both sides, $4x^2 = 7$

Dividing both sides by 4, $x^2 = \dfrac{7}{4}$

Taking the square root of both sides, $x = \pm\sqrt{\dfrac{7}{4}} = \pm\dfrac{\sqrt{7}}{2}$.

The double sign $\pm$ (read "plus or minus") indicates that the two roots of the equation are $+\dfrac{\sqrt{7}}{2}$ and $-\dfrac{\sqrt{7}}{2}$.

PROBLEM

Solve the equation $2x^2 - 5x + 3 = 0$.

SOLUTION

$2x^2 - 5x + 3 = 0$

The equation is a quadratic equation of the form $ax^2 + bx + c = 0$ in which $a = 2$, $b = -5$, and $c = 3$. Therefore, the quadratic formula $x = \dfrac{-b \pm \sqrt{b^2 - 4ac}}{2a}$ may be used to find the solutions of the given equation. Substituting the values for a, b, and c in the quadratic formula:

$$x = \frac{-(-5) \pm \sqrt{(-5)^2 - 4(2)(3)}}{2(2)}$$

$$x = \frac{5 \pm \sqrt{1}}{4}$$

$$x = \frac{5+1}{4} = \frac{3}{2} \text{ and } x = \frac{5-1}{4} = 1$$

Check: Substituting $x = \dfrac{3}{2}$ in the given equation,

$$2\left(\frac{3}{2}\right)^2 - 5\left(\frac{3}{2}\right) + 3 = 0$$

$$0 = 0$$

Substituting $x = 1$ in the given equation,

$$2(1)^2 - 5(1) + 3 = 0$$

$$0 = 0$$

So the roots of $2x^2 - 5x + 3 = 0$ are $x = \dfrac{3}{2}$ and $x = 1$.

Quadratic Functions

The function $f(x) = ax^2 + bx + c$, $a \pm 0$, where a, b, and c are real numbers, is called a quadratic function (or a function of second degree) in one unknown.

The graph of $y = ax^2 + bx + c$ is a curve known as a parabola.

The vertex of the parabola is the point $v\left(\dfrac{-b}{2a}, \dfrac{4ac - b^2}{4a}\right)$. The parabola's axis is the line $x = \dfrac{-b}{2a}$.

The graph of the parabola opens upward if $a > 0$ and downward if $a < 0$. If $a = 0$ the quadratic is reduced to a linear function whose graph is a straight line.

Figures below show parabolas with $a > 0$, and $a < 0$, respectively.

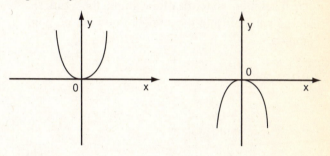

PROBLEM

Solve the system

$$y = -x^2 + 7x - 5 \qquad (1)$$

$$y - 2x = 2 \qquad (2)$$

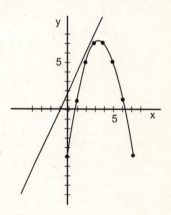

SOLUTION

Solving Equation (2) for y yields an expression for y in terms of x. Substituting this expression in Equation (1),

$$2x + 2 = -x^2 + 7x - 5 \qquad (3)$$

We have a single equation, in terms of a single variable, to be solved. Writing Equation (3) in standard quadratic form,

$$x^2 - 5x + 7 = 0 \qquad (4)$$

Since the equation is not factorable, the roots are not found in this manner. Evaluating the discriminant will indicate whether Equation (4) has real roots. The discriminant, $b^2 - 4ac$, of Equation (4) equals $(-5)^2 - 4(1)(7)$ $= 25 - 28 = -3$. Since the discriminant is negative, equation (4) has no real roots, and therefore the system has no real solution. In terms of the graph, the figure shows that the parabola and the straight line have no point in common.

PROBLEM

Solve the system

$$y = 3x^2 - 2x + 5 \qquad (1)$$
$$y = 4x + 2 \qquad (2)$$

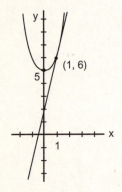

SOLUTION

To obtain a single equation with one unknown variable, x, substitute the value of y from Equation (2) in Equation (1),

$$4x + 2 = 3x^2 - 2x + 5. \qquad (3)$$

Writing Equation (3) in standard quadratic form,

$$3x^2 - 6x + 3 = 0. \qquad (4)$$

We may simplify equation (4) by dividing both members by 3, which is a factor common to each term:

$$x^2 - 2x + 1 = 0. \qquad (5)$$

To find the roots, factor and set each factor = 0. This may be done since a product = 0 implies one or all of the factors must = 0.

$$(x - 1)(x - 1) = 0$$
$$x - 1 = 0 \mid x - 1 = 0$$
$$x = 1 \mid x = 1$$

Equation (5) has two equal roots, each equal to 1. For $x = 1$, from Equation (2), we have $y = 4(1) + 2 = 6$. Therefore, the system has but one common solution:

$$x = 1, \quad y = 6.$$

The figure indicates that our solution is probably correct. We may also check to see if our values satisfy Equation (1) as well:

Substituting in:
$$y = 3x^2 - 2x + 5$$
$$6 \overset{?}{=} 3(1)^2 - 2(1) + 5$$
$$6 \overset{?}{=} 3 - 2 + 5$$
$$6 = 6$$

Quadratic Equations in Two Unknowns and Systems of Equations

A quadratic equation in two unknowns has the general form:

$$ax^2 + bxy + cy^2 + dx + ey + f = 0$$

where a, b, and c are not all zero and a, b, c, d, e, and f are constants.

Graphing: If $b^2 - 4ac < 0$, $b \neq 0$ and $a \neq c$, the graph of $ax^2 + bxy + cy^2 + dx + ey + f$ is a closed curve called an ellipse. If $b = 0$ and $a = c$, the graph $ax^2 + bxy + cy^2 + dx + ey + f$ is a point or a circle, or else it does not exist.

If $b^2 - 4ac > 0$, the graph of $ax^2 + bxy + cy^2 + dx + ey + f = 0$ is a curve called a hyperbola.

If $b^2 - 4ac = 0$, the graph of $ax^2 + bxy + cy^2 + dx + ey + f = 0$ is a parabola or a pair of parallel lines which may be coincident, or else it does not exist.

Solving Systems of Equations Involving Quadratics

Some methods for solving systems of equations involving quadratics are given below:

A) One linear and one quadratic equation

Solve the linear equation for one of the two unknowns, then substitute this value into the quadratic equation.

B) Two quadratic equations

Eliminate one of the unknowns using the method given for solving systems of linear equations.

Example:

$$\begin{cases} x^2 + y^2 = 9 & (1) \\ x^2 + 2y^2 = 18 & (2) \end{cases}$$

Subtracting Equation (1) from (2), we obtain:

$y^2 = 9, y = \pm 3$

By substituting the values of y into (1) or (2), we obtain:

$x_1 = 0$ and $x_2 = 0$

So the solutions are:

$x = 0, y = 3$ and $x = 0, y = -3$

C) Two quadratic equations, one homogeneous

An equation is said to be homogeneous if it is of the form

$ax^2 + bxy + cy^2 + dx + ey = 0.$

Consider the system

$$\begin{cases} x^2 + 3xy + 2y^2 = 0 & (1) \\ x^2 - 3xy + 2y^2 = 12 & (2) \end{cases}$$

Equation (1) can be factored into the product of two linear equations:

$x^2 + 3xy + 2y^2 = (x + 2y)(x + y) = 0$

From this we determine that:

$x + 2y = 0 \Rightarrow x = -2y$
$x + y = 0 \Rightarrow x = -y$

Substituting $x = -2y$ into Equation (2), we find:

$$(-2y)^2 - 3(-2y)y + 2y^2 = 12$$
$$4y^2 + 6y^2 + 2y^2 = 12$$
$$12y^2 = 12$$
$$y^2 = 1$$
$$y = \pm 1, \text{ so } x = \pm 2$$

Substituting $x = -y$ into Equation (2) yields:

$$(-y)^2 - 3(-y)y + 2y^2 = 12$$
$$y^2 + 3y^2 + 2y^2 = 12$$
$$6y^2 = 12$$
$$y^2 = 2$$
$$y = \pm\sqrt{2}, \text{ so } x = \pm\sqrt{2}$$

So the solutions of Equations (1) and (2) are:

$x = 2, y = -1, x = -2, y = 1, x = \sqrt{2}, y = -\sqrt{2},$
and $x = -\sqrt{2}, y = \sqrt{2}$

D) Two quadratic equations of the form

$ax^2 + bxy + cy^2 = d$

Combine the two equations to obtain a homogeneous quadratic equation then solve the equations by the third method.

E) Two quadratic equations, each symmetrical in x and y

Note: An equation is said to be symmetrical in x and y if by exchanging the coefficients of x and y we obtain the same equation.

Example: $x^2 + y^2 = 9$.

To solve systems involving this type of equations, substitute $u + v$ for x and $u - v$ for y and solve the resulting equations for u and v.

Example: Given the system below:

$$\begin{cases} x^2 + y^2 = 25 & (1) \\ x^2 + xy + y^2 = 37 & (2) \end{cases}$$

Substitute:

$x = u + v$

$y = u - v$

If we substitute the new values for x and y into Equation (2) we obtain:

$$(u + v)^2 + (u + v)(u - v) + (u - v)^2 = 37$$
$$u^2 + 2uv + v^2 + u^2 - v^2 + u^2 - 2uv + v^2 = 37$$
$$3u^2 + v^2 = 37.$$

If we substitute for x and y into Equation (1), we obtain:

$$(u + v)^2 + (u - v)^2 = 25$$
$$u^2 + 2uv + v^2 + u^2 - 2uv + v^2 = 25$$
$$2u^2 + 2v^2 = 25.$$

The "new" system is:

$$\begin{cases} 3u^2 + v^2 = 37 \\ 2u^2 + 2v^2 = 25 \end{cases}$$

By substituting $a = u^2$ and $b = v^2$, these equations become:

$$\begin{cases} 3a + b = 37 \\ 2a + 2b = 25 \end{cases}$$
and

$$a = \frac{49}{4}, \quad b = \frac{1}{4}$$

So

$$u^2 = \frac{49}{4} \quad \text{and} \quad v^2 = \frac{1}{4}$$

$$u = \pm\frac{7}{2}$$

$$v = \pm\frac{1}{2}$$

$$x = \frac{7}{2} + \frac{1}{2} = 4 \quad \text{or} \quad \frac{-7}{2} - \frac{1}{2} = -4$$

$$y = \frac{7}{2} - \frac{1}{2} = 3 \quad \text{or} \quad \frac{-7}{2} + \frac{1}{2} = -3$$

Since x and y are symmetrical, the possible solutions are (4, 3), (–4, –3), (3, 4), (–3, –4).

Note that if the equation is symmetrical it is possible to interchange the solutions too. If $x = 3$, then $y = 4$ or vice-versa.

PROBLEM

Solve the system

$$2x^2 - 3xy - 4y^2 + x + y - 1 = 0$$
$$2x - y = 3.$$

SOLUTION

A system of equations consisting of one linear and one quadratic is solved by expressing one of the unknowns in the linear equation in terms of the other, and substituting the result in the quadratic equation. From the second equation, $y = 2x - 3$. Replacing y by this linear function of x in the first equation, we find

$$2x^2 - 3x(2x - 3) - 4(2x - 3)^2 + x + 2x - 3 - 1 = 0$$
$$2x^2 - 3x(2x - 3) - 4(4x^2 - 12x + 9) + x + 2x - 3 - 1 = 0$$

Distribute,

$$2x^2 - 6x^2 + 9x - 16x^2 + 48x - 36 + x + 2x - 3 - 1 = 0$$

Combine terms, $\qquad -20x^2 + 60x - 40 = 0$

Divide both sides by –20, $\quad \dfrac{-20x^2}{-20} + \dfrac{60x}{-20} - \dfrac{40}{-20} = \dfrac{0}{-20}$

$$x^2 - 3x + 2 = 0$$

Factoring, $\qquad\qquad\qquad (x - 2)(x - 1) = 0$

Setting each factor equal to zero, we obtain:

$$x - 2 = 0 \qquad\qquad x - 1 = 0$$
$$x = 2 \qquad\qquad\quad x = 1$$

To find the corresponding y-values, substitute the x-values in $y = 2x - 3$:

when $x = 1$, $\qquad\qquad$ when $x = 2$,
$$y = 2(1) - 3 \qquad\qquad y = 2(2) - 3$$
$$y = 2 - 3 \qquad\qquad\quad y = 4 - 3$$
$$y = -1 \qquad\qquad\qquad y = 1$$

Therefore, the two solutions of the system are

$$(1, -1), \qquad\qquad\qquad (2, 1),$$

and the solution set is $\{(1, -1), (2, 1)\}$.

PROBLEM

Solve the system
$$2x^2 - 3xy + 4y^2 = 3 \qquad (1)$$
$$x^2 + xy - 8y^2 = -6 \qquad (2)$$

SOLUTION

Multiply both sides of the first equation by 2.

$$2(2x^2 - 3xy + 4y^2) = 2(3)$$
$$4x^2 - 6xy + 8y^2 = 6 \qquad\qquad (3)$$

Add Equation (3) to Equation (2):

$$x^2 + xy - 8y^2 = -6$$
$$\underline{4x^2 - 6xy + 8y^2 = 6}$$
$$5x^2 - 5xy = 0 \qquad (4)$$

Factoring out the common factor, $5x$, from the left side of Equation (4):

$$5x(x - y) = 0$$

Whenever a product $ab = 0$, where a and b are any two numbers, either $a = 0$ or $b = 0$ or both. Hence, either

$$5x = 0 \qquad \text{or} \qquad x - y = 0$$
$$x = 0/5 \qquad\qquad\qquad x = y$$
$$x = 0$$

Substituting $x = 0$ in Equation (1):

$$2(0)^2 - 3(0)y + 4y^2 = 3$$
$$0 - 0 + 4y^2 = 3$$
$$4y^2 = 3$$
$$y^2 = \frac{3}{4}$$

$$y = \pm\sqrt{\frac{3}{4}}$$
$$= \pm\frac{\sqrt{3}}{\sqrt{4}}$$
$$= \pm\frac{\sqrt{3}}{2}$$

Hence, two solutions are: $\left(0, \frac{\sqrt{3}}{2}\right), \left(0, -\frac{\sqrt{3}}{2}\right)$

Substituting x for y ($x = y$) in equation (1):

$$2x^2 - 3x(x) + 4(x)^2 = 3$$
$$2x^2 - 3x^2 + 4x^2 = 3$$
$$-x^2 + 4x^2 = 3$$
$$3x^2 = 3$$
$$x^2 = 3/3$$
$$x^2 = 1$$
$$x = \pm\sqrt{1} = \pm 1$$

Therefore, when $x = 1$, $y = x = 1$. Also, when $x = -1$, $y = x = -1$. Hence, two other solutions are: (1, 1) and (-1, -1). Thus the four solutions of the system are

$$\left(0, \frac{\sqrt{3}}{2}\right), \left(0, -\frac{\sqrt{3}}{2}\right), (1,1), \text{ and } (-1,-1)$$

Drill: Quadratic Equations

Solve for all values of x.

1. $x^2 - 2x - 8 = 0$
   (A) 4 and -2   (D) -2 and 8
   (B) 4 and 8   (E) -2
   (C) 4

2. $x^2 + 2x - 3 = 0$
   (A) -3 and 2   (D) -3 and 1
   (B) 2 and 1   (E) -3
   (C) 3 and 1

3. $x^2 - 7x = -10$
   (A) -3 and 5   (D) -2 and -5
   (B) 2 and 5   (E) 5
   (C) 2

4. $x^2 - 8x + 16 = 0$
   (A) 8 and 2   (D) -2 and 4
   (B) 1 and 16   (E) 4 and -4
   (C) 4

5. $3x^2 + 3x = 6$
   (A) 3 and -6   (D) 1 and -3
   (B) 2 and 3   (E) 1 and -2
   (C) -3 and 2

6. $x^2 + 7x = 0$
   (A) 7   (D) 0 and 7
   (B) 0 and -7   (E) 0
   (C) -7

7. $x^2 - 25 = 0$

    (A) 5   (D) −5 and 10

    (B) 5 and −5   (E) −5

    (C) 15 and 10

8. $2x^2 + 4x = 16$

    (A) 2 and −2   (D) 2 and −4

    (B) 8 and −2   (E) 2 and 4

    (C) 4 and 8

9. $2x^2 - 11x - 6 = 0$

    (A) 1 and −3   (D) −4

    (B) 0 and 4   (E) −½ and 6

    (C) 1

10. $x^2 - 2x - 3 = 0$

    (A) 0   (D) 2

    (B) −1 and 3   (E) 1 and −2

    (C) 5 and −3

ANSWER KEY

1. (A)   6. (B)
2. (D)   7. (B)
3. (B)   8. (D)
4. (C)   9. (E)
5. (E)   10. (B)

Absolute Value Equations

The absolute value of a, $|a|$, is defined as

$|a| = a$ when $a > 0$,

$|a| = -a$ when $a < 0$,

$|a| = 0$ when $a = 0$.

When the definition of absolute value is applied to an equation, the quantity within the absolute value symbol is considered to have two values. This value can be either positive or negative before the absolute value is taken. As a result, each absolute value equation actually contains two separate equations.

When evaluating equations containing absolute values, proceed as follows:

- **EXAMPLE**

$|5 - 3x| = 7$ is valid if either

$$5 - 3x = 7 \qquad \text{or} \qquad 5 - 3x = -7$$
$$-3x = 2 \qquad\qquad\qquad -3x = -12$$
$$x = -\frac{2}{3} \qquad\qquad\qquad x = 4$$

The solution set is therefore $x = \left(-\frac{2}{3}, 4\right)$.

Remember, the absolute value of a number cannot be negative. So, for the equation $|5x + 4| = -3$, there would be no solution.

Drill: Absolute Value Equations

DIRECTIONS: Find the appropriate solutions.

1. $|4x - 2| = 6$

   (A) -2 and -1 (C) 2

   (B) -1 and 2   (D) No solution

2. $\left| 3 - \frac{1}{2}y \right| = -7$

   (A) -8 and 20   (C) 2 and -5

   (B) 8 and -20 (D) No solution

3. $2|x + 7| = 12$

   (A) -13 and -1 (C) -1 and 13

   (B) -6 and 6   (D) No solution

4. $|5x| - 7 = 3$

   (A) 2 and 4   (C) -2 and 2

   (B) $\frac{4}{5}$ and 3   (D) No solution

5. $\left| \frac{3}{4}m \right| = 9$

   (A) 24 and -16 (C) -12 and 12

   (B) $\frac{4}{27}$ and $-\frac{4}{3}$ (D) No solution

Inequalities

An inequality is a statement where the value of one quantity or expression is greater than ($>$), less than ($<$), greater than or equal to ($\geq$), less than or equal to ($\leq$), or not equal to ($\neq$) that of another.

- **EXAMPLE**

$5 > 4$

The expression above means that the value of 5 is greater than the value of 4.

A **conditional inequality** is an inequality whose validity depends on the values of the variables in the expression. That is, certain values of the variables will make the expression true, and others will make it false.

$3 - y > 3 + y$

is a conditional inequality for the set of real numbers, since it is true for any replacement less than zero and false for all others.

$x + 5 > x + 2$

is an **absolute inequality** for the set of real numbers, meaning that for any real value x, the expression on the left is greater than the expression on the right.

$5y < 2y + y$

is inconsistent for the set of non-negative real numbers. For any y greater than 0 the sentence is always false.

An expression is inconsistent if it is always false when its variables assume allowable values.

The solution of a given inequality in one variable x consists of all values of x for which the inequality is true.

The graph of an inequality in one variable is represented by either a ray or a line segment on the real number line.

The endpoint is not a solution if the variable is strictly less than or greater than a particular value.

• **EXAMPLE**

$x > 2$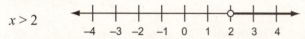

2 is not a solution and should be represented as shown.

The endpoint is a solution if the variable is either (1) less than or equal to or (2) greater than or equal to a particular value.

• **EXAMPLE**

$5 > x \geq 2$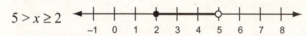

In this case 2 is a solution and should be represented as shown.

Properties of Inequalities

If x and y are real numbers, then one and only one of the following statements is true.

$x > y$, $x = y$, or $x < y$.

This is the order property of real numbers.

If a, b, and c are real numbers, the following statements are true:

    A) If $a < b$ and $b < c$ then $a < c$.

    B) If $a > b$ and $b > c$ then $a > c$.

This is the transitive property of inequalities.

If a, b, and c are real numbers and $a > b$, then $a + c > b + c$ and $a - c > b - c$. This is the **addition property of inequality.**

Two inequalities are said to have the same **sense** if their signs of inequality point in the same direction.

The sense of an inequality remains the same if both sides are multiplied or divided by the same positive real number.

• **EXAMPLE**

$4 > 3$

If we multiply both sides by 5, we will obtain

$4 \times 5 > 3 \times 5$

$20 > 15$

The sense of the inequality does not change.

The sense of an inequality becomes opposite if each side is multiplied or divided by the same negative real number.

• **EXAMPLE**

$4 > 3$

If we multiply both sides by -5, we would obtain

$4 \times -5 < 3 \times -5$

$-20 < -15$

The sense of the inequality becomes opposite.

If $a > b$ and a, b, and n are positive real numbers, then

$a^n > b^n$ and $a^{-n} < b^{-n}$

If $x > y$ and $q > p$, then $x + q > y + p$.

If $x > y > 0$ and $q > p > 0$, then $xq > yp$.

Inequalities that have the same solution set are called **equivalent inequalities.**

PROBLEM

Solve the inequality $2x + 5 > 9$.

SOLUTION

Add -5 to both sides: $2x + 5 + (-5) > 9 + (-5)$

Additive inverse property: $2x + 0 > 9 + (-5)$

Additive identity property: $2x > 9 + (-5)$

Combine terms: $2x > 4$

Multiply both sides by $\frac{1}{2}$: $\frac{1}{2}(2x) > \frac{1}{2} \times 4$

$$x > 2$$

The solution set is

$$X = \{x \mid 2x + 5 > 9\}$$
$$= \{x \mid x > 2\}$$

(that is all x, such that x is greater than 2).

Drill: Inequalities

DIRECTIONS: **Find the solution set for each inequality.**

1. $3m + 2 < 7$

   (A) $m \geq \dfrac{5}{3}$ (C) $m < 2$

   (B) $m > 2$ (D) $m < \dfrac{5}{3}$

2. $\dfrac{1}{2}x - 3 \leq 1$

   (A) $-4 \leq x \leq 8$ (C) $x \leq 8$

   (B) $x \geq -8$ (D) $2 \leq x \leq 8$

3. $-3p + 1 \geq 16$

   (A) $p \geq -5$ (C) $p \leq \dfrac{-17}{3}$

   (B) $p \geq \dfrac{-17}{3}$ (D) $p \leq 5$

4. $-6 < \dfrac{2}{3}r + 6 \leq 2$

   (A) $-6 < r \leq -3$ (C) $r \geq -6$

   (B) $-18 < r \leq -6$ (D) $-2 < r \leq -\dfrac{4}{3}$

5. $0 < 2 - y < 6$

   (A) $-4 < y < 2$ (C) $-4 < y < -2$

   (B) $-4 < y < 0$ (D) $-2 < y < 4$

Vectors

Definition 1:

A scalar is a quantity that can be specified by a real number. It has only magnitude.

Definition 2:

A vector is a quantity that has both magnitude and direction. Velocity is an example of a vector quantity.

A vector (AB) is denoted by $\overrightarrow{AB}$, where B represents the head and A represents the tail. This is illustrated in the figure.

The length of a line segment is the magnitude of a vector.

If the magnitude and direction of two vectors are the same, then they are equal.

Definition 3:

Vectors that can be translated from one position to another without any change in their magnitude or direction are called free vectors.

Definition 4:

The unit vector is a vector with a length (magnitude) of one.

Definition 5:

The zero vector has a magnitude of zero.

Definition 6:

The unit vector $\bar{i}$ is a vector with magnitude of one in the direction of the x-axis.

Definition 7:

The unit vector $\vec{J}$ is a vector with magnitude of one in the direction of the y-axis.

Vector Properties

When two vectors are added together, the resultant force of the two vectors produces the same effect as the two combined forces. This is illustrated in the Figures.

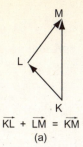

$\overrightarrow{KL} + \overrightarrow{LM} = \overrightarrow{KM}$

(a)

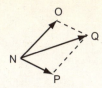

$\overrightarrow{NO} + \overrightarrow{NP} = \overrightarrow{NQ}$

(b)

In these diagrams, the vectors $\overrightarrow{KM}$ and $\overrightarrow{NQ}$ are the resultant forces.

Addition of Two Vectors

Let vector A be $<a_1, a_2>$ and vector B be $<b_1, b_2>$. Then

$$A + B = \left(a_1 + b_1\right)\vec{i} + \left(a_2 + b_2\right)\vec{j}$$

Multiplication of Vector by a Scalar

Let vector A be $\vec{ai} + \vec{bj}$ and let c be a constant. Then,

$$cA = c\left(\vec{ai} + \vec{bj}\right) = c\vec{ai} + c\vec{bj}$$

Additive and Multiplicative Properties of Vectors

Let s, t and u represent vectors and d and c represent real constants. All of the following are true:

1. $s + t = t + s$

2. $(s + t) + u = s + (t + u)$

3. $s + 0 = s$

4. $s + (-s) = 0$

5. $(c+d)s = cs + sd$

6. $c(s+u) = cs + cu$

7. $c(st) = (cs)\,t$

8. $1 \cdot s = s$

9. $0 \cdot s = 0$

10. $s \cdot s = |s|^2$

11. $c(ds) = (cd)s$

The magnitude $|s|$ of a vector $\bar{s} = a_1 i + a_2 j$ is

$$|s| = \sqrt{a_1^{\,2} + a_2^{\,2}}$$

The difference between vectors $\bar{a}$ and $\bar{b}$ is given by the formula

$$\bar{a} - \bar{b} = \bar{a} + (-\bar{b})$$

Scalar (DOT) Product

Two vectors are parallel if (a) one is a scalar multiple of the other; and (b) neither is zero.

Definition:

If vector $A = <a_1, a_2>$ and vector $B = <b_1, b_2>$, then the scalar product of A and B is given by the formula

$$A \cdot B = a_1 b_1 + a_2 b_2$$

Theorem:

If θ is the angle between the vectors $A = a_1\vec{i} + a_2\vec{j}$ and $B = b_1\vec{i} + b_2\vec{j}$ then

$$\cos\theta = \frac{a_1 b_1 + a_2 b_2}{|A||B|}$$

Definition:

Let vector $A = a_1\vec{i} + a_2\vec{j}$ and vector $B = b_1\vec{i} + b_2\vec{j}$ The projection of vector A on B ($\text{Proj}_B A$) is given by the quantity $|A|\cos\theta$, where θ is the angle between the two vectors.

Therefore,

$$\text{Proj}_B A = |A|\cos\theta = \frac{a_1 b_1 + a_2 b_2}{|B|} = \frac{A \cdot B}{|B|}$$

If the angle θ is acute, then $|A|\cos\theta$ is positive; if θ is obtuse, then $|A|\cos\theta$ is negative.

The scalar product of two non-zero vectors A and B is now redefined by the formula

$$A \cdot B = |A||B|\cos\theta = a_1 b_1 + a_2 b_2$$

PROBLEM

Which of the following vectors are equal to $\overrightarrow{MN}$ if M = (2, 1) and N = (3, –4)?

(a) $\overrightarrow{AB}$, where A = (1, –1) and B = (2, 3)

(b) $\overrightarrow{CD}$, where C = (–4, 5) and D = (–3, 10)

(c) $\overrightarrow{EF}$, where E = (3, –2) and F = (4, –7).

SOLUTION

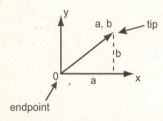

(a-0, b-0) represents the vector.

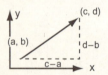

(c-a, d-b) represents the vector.

With each ordered pair in the plane there can be associated a vector from the origin to that point.

The vector is determined by subtracting the coordinates of the endpoint from the corresponding coordinates of the tip. As for $\overrightarrow{MN}$, the tip is the point corresponding to the second letter of the alphabetical notation, N, while the endpoint is the point corresponding to the first, M. In this problem the vectors are of a general nature wherein their endpoints do not lie at the origin.

We first find the ordered pair which represents MN.

$$\overrightarrow{MN} = (3-2, -4-1) = (1, -5)$$

Now, we find the ordered pair representing each vector.

(a) $\overrightarrow{AB} = (2-1, 3-(-1)) = (1, 4)$

(b) $\overrightarrow{CD} = ((-3)-(-4), 10-5) = (1, 5)$

(c) $\overrightarrow{EF} = (4-3, -7-(-2)) = (1, -5)$

Only $\overrightarrow{EF}$ and $\overrightarrow{MN}$ are equal.

Ratio, Proportion, and Variation

The ratio of two numbers x and y written $x{:}y$ is the fraction $\dfrac{x}{y}$ where $y \neq 0$. A proportion is an equality of two ratios. The laws of proportion are listed below:

If $\dfrac{a}{b} = \dfrac{c}{d}$, then:

A) $ad = bc$

B) $\dfrac{b}{a} = \dfrac{d}{c}$

C) $\dfrac{a}{c} = \dfrac{b}{d}$

D) $\dfrac{a+b}{b} = \dfrac{c+d}{d}$

E) $\dfrac{a-b}{b} = \dfrac{c-d}{d}$

Given a proportion $a{:}b = c{:}d$, then a and d are called the extremes, b and c are called the means, and d is called the fourth proportional to a, b, and c.

Problem Solving Examples:

PROBLEM

Solve the proportion $\dfrac{x+1}{4} = \dfrac{15}{12}$.

SOLUTION

Cross multiply to determine x; that is, multiply the numerator of the first fraction by the denominator of the second, and equate this to the product of the numerator of the second and the denominator of the first.

$$(x + 1)12 = 4 \times 15$$
$$12x + 12 = 60$$
$$x = 4$$

PROBLEM

If $a/b = c/d$, $a + b = 60$, $c = 3$, and $d = 2$, find b.

SOLUTION

We are given $\dfrac{a}{b} = \dfrac{c}{d}$. Cross multiplying, we obtain $ad = bc$.

Adding bd to both sides, we have $ad + bd = bc + bd$, which is equivalent to $d(a + b) = b(c + d)$ or

$$\frac{a+b}{b} = \frac{c+d}{d}$$

Replacing $(a + b)$ by 60, c by 3, and d by 2, we obtain

$$\frac{60}{b} = \frac{3+2}{2}$$
$$\frac{60}{b} = \frac{5}{2}$$

Cross multiplying, $5b = 120$
$$b = 24.$$

Variation

A) If x is directly proportional to y written $x\alpha y$, then $x = ky$ or $\dfrac{x}{y} = k$, where k is called the constant of proportionality or the constant of variation.

B) If x varies inversely as y, then $x = \dfrac{k}{y}$.

C) If x varies jointly as y and z, then $x = kyz$.

Example: If y varies jointly as x and z, and $3x:1 = y:z$, find the constant of variation.

Solution: A variable s is said to vary jointly as t and v if s varies directly as the product tv, that is, if $s = ktv$ where k is called the constant of variation.

Here the variable y varies jointly as x and z with k as the constant of variation.

$$y = kxz$$
$$3x:1 = y:z$$

Expressing these ratios as fractions,

$$\frac{3x}{1} = \frac{y}{z}$$

Solving for y by cross-multiplying,

$$y = 3xz$$

Equating both relations for y, we have:

$$kxz = 3xz$$

Solving for the constant of variation, k, we divide both sides by xz,

$$k = 3.$$

PROBLEM

If y varies directly with respect to x and $y = 3$ when $x = -2$, find y when $x = 8$.

SOLUTION

If y varies directly as x, then y is equal to some constant k times x; that is, $y = kx$ where k is a constant. We can now say $y_1 = kx_1$ and $y_2 = kx_2$ or $\dfrac{y_1}{x_1} = k$, $\dfrac{y_2}{x_2} = k$ which implies $\dfrac{y_1}{x_1} = \dfrac{y_2}{x_2}$ which is a proportion. We use the proportion $\dfrac{y_1}{x_1} = \dfrac{y_2}{x_2}$. Thus $\dfrac{3}{-2} = \dfrac{y_2}{8}$. Now solve for y_2:

$$8\left(\frac{3}{-2}\right) = 8\left(\frac{y_2}{8}\right)$$
$$-12 = y_2$$

When $x = 8$, $y = -12$.

PROBLEM

If y varies inversely as the cube of x, and $y = 7$ when $x = 2$, express y as a function of x.

SOLUTION

The relationship "y varies inversely with respect to x" is expressed as,

$$y = \frac{k}{x}$$

The inverse variation is now with respect to the cube of x, x^3, and we have,

$$y = \frac{k}{x^3}$$

Since $y = 7$ and $x = 2$ must satisfy this relation, we replace x and y by these values,

$$7 = \frac{k}{2^3} = \frac{k}{8}$$

and we find $k = 7 \times 8 = 56$. Substitution of this value of k in the general relation gives,

$$y = \frac{56}{x^3}$$

Which expresses y as a function of x. We may now, in addition, find the value of y corresponding to any value of x. If we had the added requirement to find the value of y when $x = 1.2$, $x = 1.2$ would be substituted in the function to give

$$y = \frac{56}{(1.2)^3} = \frac{56}{1.728} = 32.41$$

Other expressions in use are "is proportional to" for "varies directly," and "is inversely proportional to" for "varies inversely."

Drill: Ratios and Proportions

DIRECTIONS: Find the appropriate solutions.

1. Solve for n: $\dfrac{4}{n} = \dfrac{8}{5}$.

   (A) 10   (C) 6

   (B) 8   (D) 2.5

2. Solve for n: $\dfrac{2}{3} = \dfrac{n}{72}$.

   (A) 12   (C) 64

   (B) 48   (D) 56

3. Solve for n: n : 12 = 3 : 4.

   (A) 8   (C) 9

   (B) 1   (D) 4

4. Four out of every five students at West High take a mathematics course. If the enrollment at West is 785, how many students take mathematics?

   (A) 628   (C) 705

   (B) 157   (D) 655

5. At a factory, three out of every 1,000 parts produced are defective. In a day, the factory can produce 25,000 parts. How many of these parts would be defective?

   (A) 7   (C) 750

   (B) 75   (D) 7,500

6. A summer league softball team won 28 out of the 32 games they played. What is the ratio of games won to games played?

   (A) 4 : 5   (C) 7 : 8

   (B) 3 : 4   (D) 2 : 3

Real-World Problems Involving Proportion

PROBLEM

A chemist is preparing a chemical solution. She needs to add 3 parts sodium and 2 parts zinc to a flask of chlorine. If she has already placed 300 grams of sodium into the flask, how much zinc must she now add?

SOLUTION

Step 1 is to determine the ratio of sodium and zinc.

3 parts sodium, 2 parts zinc = 3:2

Step 2 is to write the problem as a proportion.

$$\frac{3}{2} = \frac{300}{?}$$

Step 3 is to put the proportion in the following format:

$AD = BC$ $\qquad$ $3(?) = 2(300)$

Step 4 is to solve the right side of the proportion.

$2(300) = 600$

Step 5 is to rewrite the proportion.

$3(?) = 600$

Step 6 is to find the missing integer that solves the proportion. To do this, divide both sides by the known extreme, 3.

$$\frac{3(?)}{3} = ?$$ $\qquad$ $$\frac{600}{3} = 200$$

Step 7 is to rewrite the proportion.

$? = 200$

The solution is 200 grams of zinc.

PROBLEM

An automobile dealer has to sell 3.5 cars for every 1 truck to achieve the optimum profit. This year, it is estimated that 3,500 cars will be sold. How many trucks must he sell to achieve the optimum profit?

SOLUTION

Step 1 is to determine the ratio of cars to trucks.

3.5 cars, 1 truck = 3.5:1

Make both sides of the ratio an integer. To do this, multiply both sides of the ratio by 2.

2(3.5):2(1) = 7:2

Step 2 is to write the problem as a proportion.

$$\frac{7}{2} = \frac{3,500}{?}$$

Step 3 is to put the proportion in the following format:

$AD = BC$ $\qquad$ $7(?) = 2(3,500)$

Step 4 is to solve the right side of the proportion.

$2(3,500) = 7,000$

Step 5 is to rewrite the proportion.

$7(?) = 7,000$

Step 6 is to find the missing integer that solves the proportion. To do this, divide both sides by the known extreme, 7.

$$\frac{7(?)}{7} = ?$$ $\qquad$ $$\frac{7,000}{7} = 1,000$$

Step 7 is to rewrite the proportion.

$? = 1,000$

The solution is 1,000 trucks.

PROBLEM

A baker is making a new recipe for chocolate chip cookies. He decides that for every 6 cups of flour, he needs to add 1 cup of sugar. He puts 30 cups of flour and 2 cups of sugar into the batter. How much more sugar does he need?

SOLUTION

Step 1 is to determine the ratio of flour to sugar.

6 cups flour, 1 cup sugar = 6:1

Step 2 is to write the problem as a proportion.

$$\frac{6}{1} = \frac{30}{?}$$

Step 3 is to put the proportion in the following format:

$AD = BC$ $\qquad$ $6(?) = 1(30)$

Step 4 is to solve the right side of the proportion.

$1(30) = 30$

Step 5 is to rewrite the proportion.

$6(?) = 30$

Step 6 is to find the missing integer that solves the proportion.

To do this, divide both sides by the known extreme, 6.

$$\frac{6(?)}{6} = ? \qquad\qquad \frac{30}{6} = 5$$

Step 7 is to rewrite the proportion.

$? = 5$

The solution is that 5 cups of sugar must be added to the batter.

Step 8 is to determine how many more cups of sugar are needed.

$5 - 2 = 3$

Since only 2 cups have been added so far, the baker must still add 3 cups.

Algebra

Answer Key

Drill: Operations with Polynomials

1. (B)	6. (B)	11. (C)	16. (C)
2. (C)	7. (C)	12. (B)	17. (D)
3. (C)	8. (D)	13. (D)	18. (D)
4. (D)	9. (A)	14. (A)	19. (B)
5. (A)	10. (D)	15. (D)	20. (B)

Drill: Simplifying Algebraic Expressions

1. (C)	3. (B)	5. (D)
2. (D)	4. (A)	

Drill: Two Linear Equations

1. (D)	3. (A)	5. (C)
2. (B)	4. (D)	

Drill: Absolute Value Equations

1. (B)	3. (A)	5. (C)
2. (D)	4. (C)	

Drill: Inequalities

1. (D)	3. (D)	5. (A)
2. (C)	4. (B)	

Drill: Ratios and Proportions

1. (D)	3. (C)	5. (B)
2. (B)	4. (A)	6. (C)

Detailed Explanations of Answers

Drill: Operations with Polynomials

1. (B)

$$9a^2b + 3c + 2a^2b + 5c = (9a^2b + 2a^2b) + (3c + 5c)$$
$$= 11a^2b + 8c$$

2. (C)

$$14m^2n^3 + 6m^2n^3 + 3m^2n^3 = 23m^2n^3$$

3. (C)

$$3x + 2y + 16x + 3z + 6y = (3x + 16x) + (2y + 6y) + 3z$$
$$= 19x + 8y + 3z$$

4. (D)

$$(4d^2 + 7e^3 + 12f) + (3d^2 + 6e^3 + 2f) =$$
$$(4d^2 + 3d^2) + (7e^3 + 6e^3) + (12f + 2f) =$$
$$7d^2 + 13e^3 + 14f$$

5. (A)

$$3ac^2 = +2b^2c + 7ac^2 + 2ac^2 + b^2c =$$
$$(3ac^2 + 7ac^2 + 2ac^2) + (2b^2c + b^2c) =$$
$$12ac^2 + 3b^2c$$

6. (B)

$$14m^2n - 6m^2n = 8m^2n$$

7. (C)

$$3x^3y^2 - 4xz - 6x^3y^2 = (3x^3y^2 - 6x^3y^2) - 4xz$$
$$= -3x^3y^2 - 4xz$$

8. (D)

$$9g^2 + 6h - 2g^2 - 5h = (9g^2 - 2g^2) + (6h - 5h)$$
$$= 7g^2 + h$$

9. (A)

$$7b^3 - 4c^2 - 6b^3 + 3c^2 = (7b^3 - 6b^3) + (-4c^2 + 3c^2)$$
$$= b^3 - c^2$$

10. (D)

$$11q^2r - 4q^2r - 8q^2r = (11q^2r - 4q^2r) - 8q^2r$$
$$= 7q^2r - 8q^2r$$
$$= -q^2r$$

11. (C)

$$5p^2t \times 3p^2t = (5 \times 3)(p^2 \times p^2)(t \times t)$$
$$= 15p^4t^2$$

12. (B)

$$(2r + s)14r = (2r)(14r) + (s)(14r)$$
$$= 28r^2 + 14sr$$

13. (D)

$$(4m + p)(3m - 2p) = (4m)(3m) + (4m)(-2p)$$
$$+ (p)(3m) + (p)(-2p)$$
$$= 12m^2 [(-8mp) + 3mp] +$$
$$(-2p^2)$$
$$= 12m^2 - 5mp - 2p^2$$

14. (A)

$$(2a + b)(3a^2 + ab + b^2) = (2a)(3a^2) + (2a)(ab) +$$
$$(2a)(b^2) + (b)(3a^2) + (b)(ab) + (b)(b^2)$$
$$= 6a^3 + 2a^2b + 2ab^2 + 3a^2b$$
$$+ ab^2 + b^3 = 6a^3 + 5a^2b + 3ab^2 + b^3$$

15. (D)

$$(6t^2 + 2t + 1)(3t) = (6t^2)(3t) + (2t)(3t) + (1)(3t)$$
$$= 18t^3 + 6t^2 + 3t$$

16. (C)

$$(x^2 + x - 6) \div (x - 2) = \frac{x^2 + x - 6}{(x - 2)} = \frac{(x + 3)(x - 2)}{(x - 2)} = x + 3$$

17. (D)

$$24b^4c^3 \div 6b^2c = \frac{\overset{4}{\cancel{24}} \, \overset{b^2}{\cancel{b^4}} \, \overset{c^2}{\cancel{c^3}}}{\cancel{6} \, \cancel{b^2} \, \cancel{c}} = 4b^2c^2$$

18. (D)

$$(3p^2 + pq - 2q^2) \div (p + q) = \frac{3p^2 + pq - 2q^2}{(p + q)}$$

$$= \frac{(3p - 2q)\cancel{(p + q)}}{\cancel{(p + q)}}$$

$$= 3p - 2q$$

19. (B)

$$(y^3 - 2y^2 - y + 2) \div (y - 2) = y - 2 \overline{)y^3 - 2y^2 - y + 2}$$
$$\underline{- (y^3 - 2y^2)}$$
$$0 - y + 2$$
$$\underline{-(-y + 2)}$$
$$0$$

quotient: $y^2 - 1$

20. (B)

$$(m^2 + m - 14) \div (m + 4) = m + 4 \overline{)m^2 + m - 14}$$
$$\underline{- (m^2 + 4m)}$$
$$-3m - 14$$
$$\underline{-(-3m - 12)}$$
$$-2$$

quotient: $m - 3$

$$= \frac{-2}{m + 4}$$

$$m - 3 + \frac{-2}{m + 4}$$

Drill: Simplifying Algebraic Expressions

1. (C)

$$16b^2 - 25z^2 = (4b + 5z)(4b - 5z)$$

2. (D)

$$x^2 - 2x - 8 = (x - 4)(x + 2)$$

3. (B)

$$2c^2 + 5cd - 3d^2 = (2c - d)(c + 3d)$$

4. (A)

$$4t^3 - 20t = 4t(t^2 - 5)$$

5. (D)

$$x^2 + xy - 2y^2 = (x - y)(x + 2y)$$

Drill: Two Linear Equations

1. (D)

$$3x + 4y = -2 \quad = \quad 3x + 4y = -2$$
$$-3(x - 6y = -8) \quad = \quad \underline{+ \; -3x + 18y = 24}$$
$$0 + 22y = 22$$
$$y = 1$$

Substitute $y = 1$ in $x - 6y = -8$ to get

$$x - 6 = -8$$
$$\underline{+6 \quad +6}$$
$$x = 2$$

$$(-2, 1)$$

2. (B)

$$2x + y = -10$$
$$\underline{-2x - 4y = \; 4}$$
$$0 \; -3y = -6$$

$$\frac{-3y}{-3} = \frac{-6}{-3}$$

$y = 2$ substitute in first equation to get

$$2x + 2 = -10$$
$$\underline{-2 = -2}$$
$$\frac{2x}{2} = \frac{-12}{2}$$

$(-6, 2)$

3. (A)

$$\begin{array}{ll} 6x + 5y = -4 & = \quad 6x + 5y = -4 \\ (3x - 3y = 9)(-2) & = \quad \underline{-6x + 6y = -18} \\ & \qquad\quad 0 + 11y = -22 \\ & \qquad\quad \frac{11y}{11} = \frac{-22}{11} \\ & \qquad\qquad\quad y = -2 \end{array}$$

substitute in the second equation to get

$$3x - 3(-2) = 9$$
$$3x + 6 = 9$$
$$\underline{-6 \quad -6}$$
$$\frac{3x}{3} = \frac{3}{3}$$
$$x = 1$$

$(1, -2)$

4. (D)

$$\begin{array}{ll} 4x + 3y = 9 & = \quad 4x + 3y = 9 \\ (2x - 2y = 8)(-2) & = \quad \underline{-4x + 4y = -16} \\ & \qquad\quad 0 + 7y = -7 \\ & \qquad\qquad\quad y = -1 \end{array}$$

substitute in the first equation to get

$$4x + 3(-1) = 9$$
$$4x - 3 = 9$$
$$\underline{+3 \quad = +3}$$
$$\frac{4x}{4} = \frac{12}{4}$$
$$x = 3$$

$(3, -1)$

5. (C)

$$\begin{array}{lll} x + y = 7 & = & x + y = 7 \\ x = y - 3 & = & \underline{x - y = 3} \\ & & \quad 2x = 4 \\ & & \quad\quad x = 2 \end{array}$$

substitute in the first equation

$$2 + y = 7$$
$$y = 5$$

$(2, 5)$

Drill: Quadratic Equations

1. (A)

$$(x^2 - 2x - 8) = 0$$
$$(x - 4)(x + 2) = 0$$

The values of x are 4 and -2.

2. (D)

$$x^2 + 2x - 3 = 0$$
$$(x + 3)(x - 1) = 0$$

The values of x are -3 and 1.

3. (B)

$$x^2 - 7x = -10$$
$$x^2 - 7x + 10 = 0$$
$$(x - 5)(x - 2) = 0$$

The values of x are 5 and 2.

4. (C)

$$x^2 - 8x + 16 = 0$$
$$(x - 4)(x - 4) = 0$$
$$(x - 4)^2 = 0$$

The value of x is 4.

5. (E)

$$3x^2 + 3x = 6$$
$$3x^2 + 3x - 6 = 0$$
$$3(x^2 + x - 2) = 0$$
$$3(x + 2)(x - 1) = 0$$

The values of x are -2 and 1.

Drill: Absolute Value Equations

1. (B)

$$|4x - 2| = 6 \quad 4x - 2 = 6 \quad \text{or} \quad 4x - 2 = -6$$
$$4x = 8 \qquad\qquad 4x = -4$$
$$x = 2 \quad \text{or} \qquad x = -1$$

2. (D)

$$\left| 3 - \frac{1}{2}y \right| = -7$$

No solution. Absolute value must equal a positive number.

3. (A)

$$2|x + 7| = 12$$
$$|x + 7| = 6 \quad x + 7 = 6 \quad \text{or} \quad x + 7 = -6$$
$$x = -1 \quad \text{or} \qquad x = -13$$

4. (C)

$$|5x| - 7 = 3$$
$$|5x| = 10 \quad 5x = 10 \quad \text{or} \quad 5x = -10$$
$$x = 2 \quad \text{or} \quad x = -2$$

5. (C)

$$\left| \frac{3}{4}m \right| = 9 \qquad \frac{3}{4}m = 9 \qquad\qquad \frac{3}{4}m = -9$$
$$\frac{4}{3}\left(\frac{3}{4}m\right) = 9\left(\frac{4}{3}\right) \quad \frac{4}{3}\left(\frac{3}{4}m\right) = (-9)\left(\frac{4}{3}\right)$$
$$m = 12 \qquad\qquad m = -12$$

Drill: Inequalities

1. (D)

$$3m + 2 < 7$$
$$\underline{-2 \quad -2}$$
$$\left(\frac{1}{3}\right)3m < 5\left(\frac{1}{3}\right)$$
$$m < \frac{5}{3}$$

2. (C)

$$\frac{1}{2}x - 3 \le 1$$
$$\underline{+3 \quad +3}$$
$$\frac{1}{2}x \le 4$$
$$(2)\frac{1}{2}x \le 4(2)$$
$$x \le 8$$

3. (D)

$$-3p + 1 \ge 16$$
$$\underline{-1 \quad -1}$$
$$-3p \ge 15$$
$$\left(-\frac{1}{3}\right)-3p \ge 15\left(-\frac{1}{3}\right)$$
$$p \le 5$$

4. (B)

$$-6 < \frac{2}{3}r + 6 \le 2$$
$$\underline{-6 \qquad -6 \quad -6}$$
$$-12 < \frac{2}{3}r \le -4$$
$$\frac{3}{2}\left(-12 < \frac{2}{3}r \le -4\right)$$
$$-18 < r \le -6$$

5. (A)

$$0 < 2 - y < 6$$
$$\frac{-2 - 2 \quad -2}{-2 < \ \ y < 4}$$
$$-1(-2 < -y < 4)$$
$$-4 < y < 2$$

Drill: Ratios and Proportions

1. (D)

$$\frac{4}{n} = \frac{8}{5} \qquad 5(4) = 8n$$
$$\left(\frac{1}{8}\right)20 = 8n\left(\frac{1}{8}\right)$$
$$\frac{20}{8} = n \Rightarrow 2.5 = n$$

2. (B)

$$\frac{2}{3} = \frac{n}{72} \qquad 2(72) = 3n$$
$$\frac{1}{3}(144) = (3n)\frac{1}{3}$$
$$(2)(24) = n$$
$$48 = n$$

3. (C)

$$n : 12 = 3 : 4 \Rightarrow \quad \frac{n}{12} = \frac{3}{4}$$
$$4n = (12)(3)$$
$$4n = 36$$
$$n = 9$$

4. (A)

$$4 : 5 = x : 785 \Rightarrow \qquad \frac{4}{5} = \frac{x}{785}$$
$$(785)(4) = 5x$$
$$\left(\frac{1}{5}\right)(785)(4) = (5x)\frac{1}{5}$$
$$(157)(4) = x$$
$$628 = x$$

5. (B)

$$3 : 1000 = y : 25000 \Rightarrow \qquad \frac{3}{1000} = \frac{y}{25000}$$
$$(3)(25,000) = y(1000)$$
$$\frac{(3)(25,000)}{1000} = y$$
$$75 = y$$

6. (C)

$$28 : 32 \Rightarrow \frac{28}{32} = \frac{7}{8} \Rightarrow 7 : 8$$

Elementary Functions

A **function** is any process that assigns a single value of y to each number of x. Because the value of x determines the value of y, y is called the **dependent variable** and x is called the **independent variable**. The set of all the values of x by which the function is defined is called the **domain** of the function. The set of corresponding values of y is called the **range** of the function.

PROBLEM

Is $y^2 = x$ a function?

SOLUTION

Graph the equation. Note that x can have two values of y. Therefore, $y^2 = x$ is not a function.

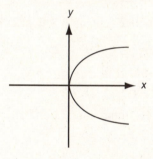

PROBLEM

Find the domain and range for $y = 5 - x^2$.

SOLUTION

First determine if there are any values that would make the function undefined (i.e., dividing by 0). There are none. The domain is the set of real numbers. The range can be found by putting some values in for x.

x	2	1	0	-1	-2
y	1	4	5	4	1

The range is the set of real numbers less than or equal to 5.

PROBLEM

Evaluate $f(1)$ for $y = f(x) = 5x + 2$.

SOLUTION

$$f(x) = 5x + 2$$
$$f(1) = 5(1) + 2$$
$$= 5 + 2$$
$$= 7$$

Functions can be added, subtracted, multiplied, or divided to form new functions.

a. $(f + g)(x) = f(x) + g(x)$

b. $(f - g)(x) = f(x) - g(x)$

c. $(f \times g)(x) = f(x)\, g(x)$

d. $(f / g)(x) = f(x) / g(x)$

PROBLEM

Let $f(x) = 2x^2 - 1$ and $g(x) = 5x + 3$. Determine the following functions:

(1) $f + g$ (2) $f - g$

(3) $f \times g$ (4) f / g

SOLUTION

(1) $(f + g)(x) = f(x) + g(x) = 2x^2 - 1 + 5x + 3$
$$= 2x^2 + 5x + 2$$

(2) $(f - g)(x) = f(x) - g(x) = 2x^2 - 1 - (5x + 3)$
$$= 2x^2 - 1 - 5x - 3$$
$$= 2x^2 - 5x - 4$$

(3) $(f \times g)(x) = f(x)\, g(x) = (2x^2 - 1)\,(5x + 3)$
$$= 10x^3 + 6x^2 - 5x - 3$$

(4) $(f / g)(x) = f(x) / g(x) = (2x^2 - 1) / (5x + 3)$

Note the domain of (4) is for all real numbers except $-\dfrac{3}{5}$.

The **composite function** $f \circ g$ is defined $(f \circ g)(x) = f(g(x))$.

PROBLEM

> Given $f(x) = 3x$ and $g(x) = 4x + 2$.
>
> Find $(f \circ g)(x)$ and $(g \circ f)(x)$.

SOLUTION

$$(f \circ g)(x) = f(g(x)) = 3(4x + 2)$$
$$= 12x + 6$$
$$(g \circ f)(x) = g(f(x)) = 4(3x) + 2$$
$$= 12x + 2$$

Note that $(f \circ g)(x) \neq (g \circ f)(x)$.

PROBLEM

> Find $(f \circ g)(2)$ if
>
> $f(x) = x^2 - 3$ and $g(x) = 3x + 1$

SOLUTION

$$(f \circ g)(2) = f(g(2))$$
$$g(x) = 3x + 1$$

Substitute the value of x.

$$g(2) = 3(2) + 1$$
$$= 7$$
$$f(x) = x^2 - 3$$

Substitute the value of $g(2)$ in $f(x)$.

$$f(7) = (7)^2 - 3$$
$$= 49 - 3$$
$$= 46$$

The **inverse** of a function, f^{-1}, is obtained from f by interchanging the x and y and then solving for y.

Two functions f and g are inverses of one another if $g \circ f = x$ and $f \circ g = x$. To find g when f is given, interchange x and y in the equation $y = f(x)$ and solve for $y = g(x)$. Then replace y with $f^{-1}(x)$.

PROBLEM

> Find the inverse of the functions
>
> (1) $f(x) = 3x + 2$
>
> (2) $f(x) = x^2 - 3$

SOLUTION

(1) $f(x) = y = 3x + 2$

To find $f^{-1}(x)$, interchange x and y.

$$x = 3y + 2$$
$$3y = x - 2$$

Solve for y, then replace y with $f^{-1}(x)$.

$$f^{-1}(x) = \frac{x - 2}{3}$$

(2) $f(x) = y = x^2 - 3$.

To find $f^{-1}(x)$, interchange x and y.

$$x = y^2 - 3$$
$$y^2 = x + 3$$

Solve for y, then replace y with $f^{-1}(x)$.

$$f^{-1}(x) = \sqrt{x + 3}$$

Logarithms and Exponential Functions and Equations

An equation

$$y = b^x$$

(with $b > 0$ and $b \neq 1$) is called an **exponential function**. The exponential function with base b can be written as

$$y = f(x) = b^x.$$

The inverse of an exponential function is the **logarithmic function**,

$$f^{-1}(x) = \log_b x.$$

PROBLEM

Write the following equations in logarithmic form:

$3^4 = 81$ and $M^k = 5$.

SOLUTION

The expression $y = b^x$ is equivalent to the logarithmic expression $\log_b y = x$. Therefore, $3^4 = 81$ is equivalent to the logarithmic expression

$$\log_3 81 = 4$$

and $M^k = 5$ is equivalent to the logarithmic expression

$$\log_M 5 = k.$$

PROBLEM

Find the value of $\log_5 25$ and $\log_4 x = 2$.

SOLUTION

$\log_5 25$ is equivalent to $5^x = 25$. Thus $x = 2$, since $5^2 = 25$.

$\log_4 x = 2$ is equivalent to $4^2 = x \times x = 16$.

Logarithm Properties

If M, N, p, and b are positive numbers and $b = 1$, then

   a. $\log_b 1 = 0$

   b. $\log_b b = 1$

   c. $\log_b b^x = x$

   d. $\log_b M N = \log_b M + \log_b N$

   e. $\log_b M / N = \log_b M - \log_b N$

   f. $\log_b M^p = p \log_b M$

PROBLEM

If $\log_{10} 3 = .4771$ and $\log_{10} 4 = .6021$, find $\log_{10} 12$.

SOLUTION

Since $12 = 4(3)$, $\log_{10} 12 = \log_{10}(4)(3)$

Remember

$$\log_b M N = \log_b M + \log_b N.$$

Therefore,

$$\log_{10} 12 = \log_{10} 4 + \log_{10} 3$$
$$= .6021 + .4771$$
$$= 1.0792$$

Properties of Functions

A) A function F is one to one if for every range value there corresponds exactly one domain value of x.

B) A function is even if $f(-x) = f(x)$ or

$$f(x) + f(-x) = 2f(x).$$

C) A function is said to be odd if $f(-x) = -f(x)$ or $f(x) + f(-x) = 0$.

D) Periodicity

A function f with domain X is periodic if there exists a positive real number p such that $f(x + p) = f(x)$ for all $x \in X$.

The smallest number p with this property is called the period of f.

Over any interval of length p, the behavior of a periodic function can be completely described.

E) Inverse of function

Assuming that f is a one-to-one function with domain X and range Y, then a function g having domain Y and range X is called the inverse function of f if:

$$f(g(y)) = y \text{ for every } y \in Y \text{ and}$$

$$g(f(x)) = x \text{ for every } x \in X.$$

The inverse of the function f is denoted f^{-1}.

To find the inverse function f^{-1}, you must solve the equation $y = f(x)$ for x in terms of y.

Be careful: This solution must be a function.

F) The identity function $f(x) = x$ maps every x to itself.

G) The constant function $f(x) = c$ for all $x \in R$.

The "zeros" of an arbitrary function $f(x)$ are particular values of x for which $f(x) = 0$.

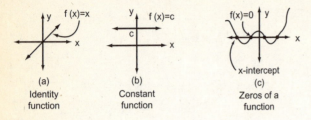

(a)
Identity function

(b)
Constant function

(c)
Zeros of a function

PROBLEM

Find the domain D and range R of the function

$$\left(x, \frac{x}{|x|} \right).$$

SOLUTION

Note that the y-value of any coordinate pair (x,y) is $\frac{x}{|x|}$. We can replace X in the formula $\frac{x}{|x|}$ with any number except 0, since the denominator, $|x|$, cannot equal 0. This is because division by 0 is undefined. Therefore, the domain D is the set of all real numbers except 0. If x is negative, i.e., $x < 0$, then $|x| = -x$ by definition. Hence, if x is negative, then $\frac{x}{|x|} = \frac{x}{-x} = -1$. If x is positive, i.e. $x > 0$, then $|x| = x$ by definition. Hence, if x is positive, then $\frac{x}{|x|} = \frac{x}{x} = 1$. (The case where $x = 0$ has already been found to be undefined). Thus, there are only two numbers -1 and 1 in the range R of the function; that is, $R = \{-1,1\}$.

PROBLEM

If $f(x) = 3x + 4$ and $D = \{x \mid -1 \le x \le 3\}$, find the range of $f(x)$.

SOLUTION

We first prove that the value of $3x + 4$ increases when x increases. If $X > x$, then we may multiply both sides of the inequality by a positive number to obtain an equivalent inequality. Thus, $3X > 3x$. We may also add a number to both sides of the inequality to obtain an equivalent inequality. Thus,

$$3X + 4 > 3x + 4.$$

Hence, if x belongs to D, the function value $f(x) = 3x + 4$ is least when $x = -1$ and greatest when $x = 3$. Consequently, since $f(-1) = -3 + 4 = 1$ and $f(3) = 9 + 4 = 13$, the range is all y from 1 to 13; that is,

$$R = \{y \mid 1 \le y \le 13\}.$$

Graphing a Function

The Cartesian Coordinate System

Consider two lines x and y drawn on a plane region called R.

Let the intersection of x and y be the origin and let us impose a coordinate system on each of the lines.

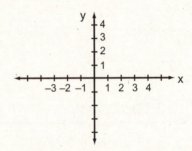

If (x, y) is a point or ordered pair on the coordinate plane R then x is the first coordinate and y is the second coordinate.

To locate an ordered pair on the coordinate plane simply measure the distance of x units along the x-axis, then measure vertically (parallel to the y-axis) y units.

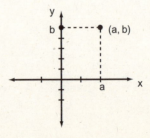

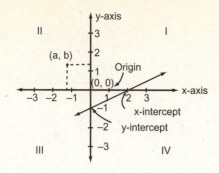

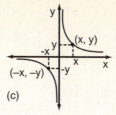

I, II, III, IV are called quadrants in the coordinate plane.

(a,b) is an ordered pair with x-coordinate a and y-coordinate b.

Drawing the Graph

There are several ways to plot the graph of a function. The process of computing and plotting points on the graph is always an aid in this endeavor. The more points we locate on the graph, the more accurate our drawing will be.

It is also helpful if we consider the symmetry of the function. That is,

a) A graph is symmetric with respect to the x-axis if whenever a point (x,y) is on the graph, then $(x,-y)$ is also on the graph.

b) Symmetry with respect to the y-axis occurs when both points $(-x,y)$ and (x,y) appear on the graph for every x and y in the graph.

c) When the simultaneous substitution of $-x$ for x and $-y$ for y does not change the solution of the equation, the graph is said to be symmetric about the origin.

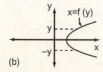

Symmetric about the y-axis

Symmetric about the x-axis
Note: This is not a function of x.

Another aid in drawing a graph is locating any vertical asymptotes.

A vertical asymptote is a vertical line $x = a$, such that the functional value $|f(x)|$ grows indefinitely large as x approaches the fixed value a.

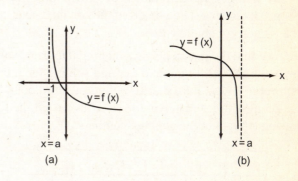

$x = a$ is a vertical asymptote for these functions

The following steps encapsulate the procedure for drawing a graph:

a) Determine the domain and range of the function.

b) Find the intercepts of the graph and plot them.

c) Determine the symmetries of the graph.

d) Locate the vertical asymptotes and plot a few points on the graph near each asymptote.

e) Plot additional points as needed.

PROBLEM

Construct the graph of the function defined by $y = 3x - 9$.

SOLUTION

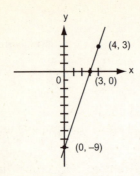

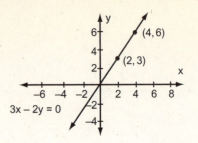

An equation of the form $y = mx + b$ is a linear equation; that is, the equation of a line.

A line can be determined by two points. Let us choose intercepts. The x-intercept lies on the x-axis and the y-intercept on the y-axis.

We find the intercepts by assigning 0 to x and solving for y and by assigning 0 to y and solving for x. It is helpful to have a third point. We find the third point by assigning 4 to x and solving for y. Thus we get the following table of corresponding numbers:

x	$y = 3x - 9$	y
0	$y = 3(0) - 9 = 0 - 9 =$	-9
4	$y = 3(4) - 9 = 12 - 9 =$	3

Solving for x to get the x-intercept:

$$y = 3x - 9$$
$$y + 9 = 3x$$
$$x = \frac{y + 9}{3}$$

When $y = 0$, $x = \frac{9}{3} = 3$. The three points are $(0,-9)$, $(4,3)$, and $(3,0)$. Draw a line through them (see sketch).

PROBLEM

Are the following points on the graph of the equation $3x - 2y = 0$?

a) point $(2,3)$?

b) point $(3,2)$?

c) point $(4,6)$?

SOLUTION

The point (a,b) lies on the graph of the equation $3x - 2y = 0$ if replacement of x and y by a and b, respectively, in the given equation results in an equation which is true.

a) Replacing (x,y) by $(2,3)$:

$$3x - 2y = 0$$
$$3(2) - 2(3) = 0$$
$$6 - 6 = 0$$
$$0 = 0, \text{ which is true.}$$

Therefore $(2,3)$ is a point on the graph.

b) Replacing (x,y) by $(3,2)$:

$$3x - 2y = 0$$
$$3(4) - 2(6) = 0$$
$$9 - 4 = 0$$
$$5 = 0, \text{ which is not true.}$$

Therefore $(3,2)$ is not a point on the graph.

c) Replacing (x,y) by $(4,6)$:

$$3x - 2y = 0$$
$$3(4) - 2(6) = 0$$
$$12 - 12 = 0$$
$$0 = 0, \text{ which is true.}$$

Therefore $(4,6)$ is a point on the graph.

This problem may also be solved geometrically as follows: draw the graph of the line $3x - 2 = 0$ on the coordinate axes. This can be done by solving for y and plotting the points shown in the following table:

x	$y = \dfrac{3}{2}x$
0	0
1	$\dfrac{3}{2} = 1\dfrac{1}{2}$
2	3
-2	-3

(See accompanying figure.)

Observe that we obtain the same result as in our algebraic solution. The points $(2,3)$ and $(4,6)$ lie on the line $3x - 2y = 0$, whereas $(3,2)$ does not.

Polynomial Functions and Their Graphs

A polynomial in x is an expression of the form
$$a_n x^n + a_{n-1} x^{n-1} + \ldots + a_1 x + a_0,$$
where a_1, a_2, $\ldots$ and a_n are real numbers and where all the exponents are positive integers. When $a_n \neq 0$, this polynomial is said to be of degree n. It is common to let $P(x)$ represent
$$a_n x^n + a_{n-1} x^{n-1} + \ldots + a_1 x + a_0.$$

Then $y = P(x)$ is a polynomial function. A function with the property that
$$P(-x) = P(x)$$
is an even function, while a function with the property
$$P(-x) = -P(x)$$
is an odd function. Even functions are symmetric with respect to the y-axis, while odd functions are symmetric with respect to the origin.

It would be possible to obtain the graph of a polynomial function $y = P(x)$ by simply setting up a table and plotting a large number of points; this is how a computer or a graphing calculator operates. However, it is often desirable to have some basic information about the graph prior to plotting points. The graph of the polynomial function, $y = a_0$ is a line which is parallel to the x-axis and $|a_0|$ units above or below the x-axis, depending on whether a_0 is positive or negative. A function of this type is called a constant function. The graph of the polynomial function
$$y = a_1 x + a_0$$
is a line with slope a_1 and with a_0 as the y-intercept. The graph of the polynomial function
$$y = a_2 x^2 + a_1 x + a_0$$
is a parabola.

It is much more difficult to graph a polynomial function with degree greater than two. However, here are three items which should be investigated.

(1) Find lines (x-axis and y-axis) of symmetry and find out whether the origin is a point of symmetry.

(2) Find out about intercepts. The y-intercept is easy to find but the x-intercepts are usually much more difficult to identify. If possible, factor $P(x)$.

(3) Find out what happens to $P(x)$ when $|x|$ is large. This procedure is illustrated in the following example.

• **EXAMPLE**

Graph
$$y = x^4 - 5x^2 + 4$$

(1) The graph has symmetry with respect to the y-axis.

(2) The y-intercept is at 4. Since
$$x^4 - 5x^2 + 4 = (x^2 - 4)(x^2 - 1)$$
$$= (x - 2)(x + 2)(x - 1)(x + 1),$$
the x-intercepts are at 1, 2, -1, and -2.

(3) As $|x|$ gets large, $P(x)$ gets large.

Here is a sketch of the graph.

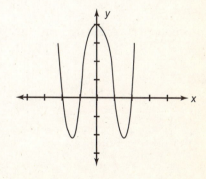

Rational Functions and Their Graphs

When $P(x)$ and $Q(x)$ are polynomials,

$$y = \frac{P(x)}{Q(x)}$$

is called a rational function. The domain of this function is the set of all real numbers x with the property that $Q(x) \neq 0$.

Graphing rational functions is rather difficult. As is the case for polynomial functions, it is desirable to have a general procedure for graphing rational functions. Here is the suggested method for

$$y = \frac{P(x)}{Q(x)}$$

where
$$P(x) = a_n x^n + a_{n-1} x^{n-1} + \ldots + a_1 x + a_0 \text{ and}$$
$$Q(x) = b_m x^m + b_{m-1} x^{m-1} + \ldots + b_1 x + b_0.$$

(1) Find lines (x-axis and y-axis) of symmetry and determine whether the origin is a point of symmetry.

(2) Find out about intercepts. The y-intercept is at $\frac{a_0}{b_0}$ and the x-intercepts will be at values of x where $P(x) = 0$.

(3) Find vertical asymptotes. A line $x = c$ is a vertical asymptote whenever $Q(c) = 0$ and $P(c) \neq 0$.

(4) Find horizontal asymptotes

   (a) If $m = n$, then $y = \frac{a_n}{b_m}$ is the horizontal asymptote.

   (b) If $m > n$, then $y = 0$ is the horizontal asymptote.

   (c) If $m < n$, then there is no horizontal asymptote.

This procedure is illustrated in the following example

• **EXAMPLE**

Graph

$$y = \frac{x}{(x-1)(x+3)}$$

(1) The axes are not lines of symmetry, nor is the origin a point of symmetry.

(2) The x-intercept and the y-intercept are both at the origin.

(3) The lines $x = 1$ and $x = -3$ are both vertical asymptotes.

(4) The line $y = 0$ is the horizontal asymptote.

Here is a sketch of the graph.

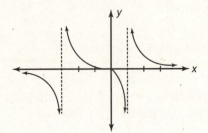

Special Functions and Their Graphs

It is possible to define a function by using different rules for different portions of the domain. The graphs of such functions are determined by graphing the different portions separately. Here is an example.

• **EXAMPLE**

Graph

$$f(x) = \begin{cases} x \text{ if } x \leq 1 \\ 2x \text{ if } x > 1 \end{cases}$$

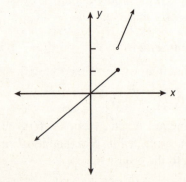

Notice that point $(1,1)$ is part of the graph, but $(1, 2)$ is not.

Functions which involve absolute value can often be completed by translating them to a two-rule form. Consider this example.

• **EXAMPLE**

Graph

$$f(x) = |x| - 1$$

Since $|x| = \begin{cases} x \text{ if } x \geq 0 \\ -x \text{ if } x < 0 \end{cases}$

$f(x)$ can be translated to the following form.

$$f(x) = \begin{cases} x - 1 \text{ if } x \geq 0 \\ -x - 1 \text{ if } x < 0 \end{cases}$$

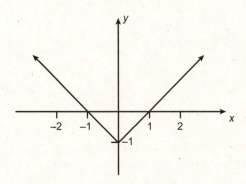

The greatest integer function, denoted by $f(x) = \left[|x| \right]$, is defined by $f(x) = j$, where j is the integer with the property that $j \leq x < j + 1$. The graph of this function follows.

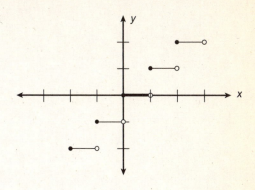

Chapter 4

SUBAREA III: Trigonometry and Calculus

Trigonometry is a field of mathematics that basically is used to solve triangles. With trigonometry, you can find the missing measures (lengths of sides and angles) in a triangle if you have some information about the triangle. Extensions of the use of trigonometry include astronomy, geography, and even medical imaging. The values of trigonometric functions for any angle are available in "trig" tables or on most calculators.

Angles and Trigonometric Functions

The basic trigonometric functions are based on the right triangle, such as $\triangle ABC$, shown in the figure below:

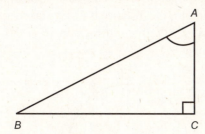

Definition 1: Sine

$$\sin \angle A = \frac{BC}{AB}$$

$$= \frac{\text{measure of side opposite } \angle A}{\text{measure of hypotenuse}}$$

Definition 2: Cosine

$$\cos \angle A = \frac{AC}{AB}$$

$$= \frac{\text{measure of side adjacent to } \angle A}{\text{measure of hypotenuse}}$$

Definition 3: Tangent

$$\tan \angle A = \frac{BC}{AC}$$

$$= \frac{\text{measure of side opposite } \angle A}{\text{measure of side adjacent to } \angle A}$$

Definition 4: Cotangent

$$\cot \angle A = \frac{AC}{BC}$$

$$= \frac{\text{measure of side adjacent to } \angle A}{\text{measure of side opposite } \angle A}$$

Definition 5: Secant

$$\sec \angle A = \frac{AB}{AC}$$

$$= \frac{\text{measure of hypotenuse}}{\text{measure of side adjacent to } \angle A}$$

Definition 6: Cosecant

$$\csc \angle A = \frac{AB}{BC}$$

$$= \frac{\text{measure of hypotenuse}}{\text{measure of side opposite } \angle A}$$

The following table gives the values of sine, cosine, tangent, and cotangent for some special angles. The angles are given in radians and in degrees. A radian is a measure of the central angle in a circle and is usually expressed in terms of π. A full circle has 360°, or 2π radians.

α	$\operatorname{Sin} \alpha$	$\operatorname{Cos} \alpha$	$\operatorname{Tan} \alpha$	$\operatorname{Cot} \alpha$
0°	0	1	0	∞
$\frac{\pi}{6} = 30°$	$\frac{1}{2}$	$\frac{\sqrt{3}}{2}$	$\frac{1}{\sqrt{3}}$	$\sqrt{3}$
$\frac{\pi}{4} = 45°$	$\frac{1}{\sqrt{2}}$	$\frac{1}{\sqrt{2}}$	1	1
$\frac{\pi}{3} = 60°$	$\frac{\sqrt{3}}{2}$	$\frac{1}{2}$	$\sqrt{3}$	$\frac{1}{\sqrt{3}}$
$\frac{\pi}{2} = 90°$	1	0	∞	0

A circle with center located at the origin of the rectangular coordinate axes with radius equal to one unit length is called a unit circle.

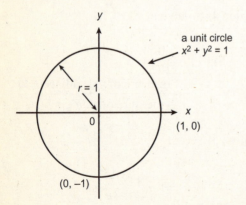

An angle whose vertex is at the origin of a rectangular coordinate system and whose initial side coincides with the positive x-axis is said to be in standard position with respect to the coordinate system.

A quadrant angle is an angle in standard position whose terminal side lies on one of the axes of a Cartesian coordinate system.

An angle in standard position with respect to a Cartesian coordinate system whose terminal side lies in the first (or second or third or fourth) quadrant is called a first (or second or third or fourth) quadrant angle.

If θ is a non-quadrantal angle in standard position and $P(x, y)$ is any point, distinct from the origin, on the terminal side of θ, then the six trigonometric functions of θ are defined in terms of the abscissa (x-coordinate), ordinate (y-coordinate), and distance $\overline{OP}$ as follows:

$$\text{sine } \theta = \sin\theta = \frac{\text{ordinate}}{\text{distance}} = \frac{y}{r}$$

$$\text{cosine } \theta = \cos\theta = \frac{\text{abscissa}}{\text{distance}} = \frac{x}{r}$$

$$\text{tangent } \theta = \tan\theta = \frac{\text{ordinate}}{\text{abscissa}} = \frac{y}{x}$$

$$\text{cotangent } \theta = \cot\theta = \frac{\text{abscissa}}{\text{ordinate}} = \frac{x}{y}$$

$$\text{secant } \theta = \sec\theta = \frac{\text{distance}}{\text{abscissa}} = \frac{r}{x}$$

$$\text{cosecant } \theta = \csc\theta = \frac{\text{distance}}{\text{ordinate}} = \frac{r}{y}$$

The signs of the functions in the quadrants depend on whether the ordinate or abscissa is positive or negative in that quadrant (the distance is always taken as positive). Thus, for $x < 90°$, if $\sin x = \underline{A}$, $\sin (x + 180) = -A$, or $\sin x = -\sin (x + 180)$.

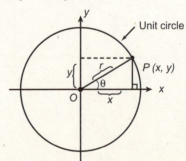

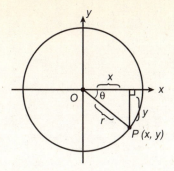

The value of trigonometric functions of quadrantal angles are given in the table.

θ	sin θ	cos θ	tan θ	cot θ	sec θ	csc θ
0°	0	1	0	±∞	1	±∞
90°	1	0	±∞	0	±∞	1
180°	0	−1	0	±∞	−1	±∞
270°	−1	0	±∞	0	±∞	−1

• EXAMPLES

1. Find $\sin\theta$ given $A = 30°$.

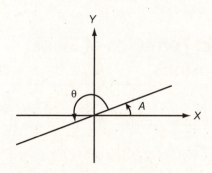

Obviously, $\theta = 180° + A = 210°$. Since sine is negative in the third quadrant, we have

$$\sin\theta = \sin 210° = -|\sin(210° - 180°)| = -\sin 30° = -\frac{1}{2}.$$

2. If $\sin 2x = -\cos(-x + 9°)$, find x.

$\sin 2x = -\cos(-x + 9°) = \cos(-x + 9° + 180°)$

But $2x - x + 9° + 180° = 90°$

$$x = -99°$$

Basic Identities

$$\sin^2\alpha + \cos^2\alpha = 1$$

$$\tan\alpha = \frac{\sin\alpha}{\cos\alpha}$$

$$\cot\alpha = \frac{\cos\alpha}{\sin\alpha} = \frac{1}{\tan\alpha}$$

$$\csc\alpha = \frac{1}{\sin\alpha}$$

$$\sec\alpha = \frac{1}{\cos\alpha}$$

$$1 + \tan^2\alpha = \sec^2\alpha$$

$$1 + \cot^2\alpha = \csc^2\alpha$$

One can find all the trigonometric functions of an acute angle when the value of any one of them is known.

• EXAMPLES

Given α is an acute angle and $\csc\alpha = 2$, then

$$\sin\alpha = \frac{1}{\csc\alpha} = \frac{1}{2}$$

$$\cos^2\alpha + \sin^2\alpha = 1, \ \cos\alpha = \sqrt{1 - \sin^2\alpha}$$

$$= \sqrt{1 - \left(\tfrac{1}{2}\right)^2}$$

$$= \sqrt{1 - \tfrac{1}{4}}$$

$$= \frac{\sqrt{3}}{2}$$

$$\tan\alpha = \frac{\sin\alpha}{\cos\alpha} = \frac{\tfrac{1}{2}}{\tfrac{\sqrt{3}}{2}} = \frac{1}{\sqrt{3}} = \frac{\sqrt{3}}{3}$$

$$\cot\alpha = \frac{1}{\tan\alpha} = \sqrt{3}$$

$$\sec\alpha = \frac{1}{\cos\alpha} = \frac{1}{\tfrac{\sqrt{3}}{2}} = \frac{2}{\sqrt{3}} = \frac{2\sqrt{3}}{3}$$

i) If θ is a first quadrant angle, and ϕ is in standard position, then

   a) $\sin\theta = \sin\phi$ d) $\cot\theta = \cot\phi$
   b) $\cos\theta = \cos\phi$ e) $\sec\theta = \sec\phi$
   c) $\tan\theta = \tan\phi$ f) $\csc\theta = \csc\phi$

ii) If θ is a second quadrant angle:

   a) $\sin\theta = \sin\phi$ d) $\cot\theta = -\cot\phi$
   b) $\cos\theta = -\cos\phi$ e) $\sec\theta = -\sec\phi$
   c) $\tan\theta = -\tan\phi$ f) $\csc\theta = \csc\phi$

iii) If θ is a third quadrant angle, then

   a) $\sin\theta = -\sin\phi$ d) $\cot\theta = \cot\phi$
   b) $\cos\theta = -\cos\phi$ e) $\sec\theta = -\sec\phi$
   c) $\tan\theta = \tan\phi$ f) $\csc\theta = -\csc\phi$

iv) If θ is a fourth quadrant angle, then

   a) $\sin\theta = -\sin\phi$ d) $\cot\theta = -\cot\phi$
   b) $\cos\theta = \cos\phi$ e) $\sec\theta = \sec\phi$
   c) $\tan\theta = -\tan\phi$ f) $\csc\theta = -\csc\phi$

Addition and Subtraction Formulas

$$\sin(A \pm B) = \sin A \cos B \pm \cos A \sin B$$
$$\cos(A \pm B) = \cos A \cos B \pm \sin A \sin B$$
$$\tan(A \pm B) = \frac{\tan A \pm \tan B}{1 \pm \tan A \tan B}$$
$$\cot(A \pm B) = \frac{\cot A \cot B \pm 1}{\cot B \pm \cot A}$$

Double-Angle Formulas

$$\sin 2A = 2\sin A \cos A$$
$$\cos 2A = 2\cos^2 A - 1$$
$$= 1 - 2\sin^2 A$$
$$= \cos^2 A - \sin^2 A$$
$$\tan 2A = \frac{2\tan A}{1 - \tan^2 A}$$

Half-Angle Formulas

$$\sin\frac{A}{2} = \pm\frac{\sqrt{1-\cos A}}{2}$$
$$\cos\frac{A}{2} = \pm\frac{\sqrt{1+\cos A}}{2}$$

$$\tan\frac{A}{2} = \pm\sqrt{\frac{1-\cos A}{1+\cos A}} = \frac{1-\cos A}{\sin A} = \frac{\sin A}{1+\cos A}$$
$$\cot\frac{A}{2} = \pm\sqrt{\frac{1+\cos A}{1-\cos A}} = \frac{1+\cos A}{\sin A} = \frac{\sin A}{1-\cos A}$$

Sum and Difference Formulas

$$\sin\alpha + \sin\beta = 2\sin\left(\frac{\alpha+\beta}{2}\right)\cos\left(\frac{\alpha-\beta}{2}\right)$$
$$\sin\alpha - \sin\beta = 2\cos\left(\frac{\alpha+\beta}{2}\right)\sin\left(\frac{\alpha-\beta}{2}\right)$$
$$\cos\alpha + \cos\beta = 2\cos\left(\frac{\alpha+\beta}{2}\right)\cos\left(\frac{\alpha-\beta}{2}\right)$$
$$\cos\alpha - \cos\beta = -2\sin\left(\frac{\alpha+\beta}{2}\right)\sin\left(\frac{\alpha-\beta}{2}\right)$$

$$\tan\alpha + \tan\beta = \frac{\sin(\alpha+\beta)}{\cos\alpha\cos\beta}$$
$$\tan\alpha \times \tan\beta = \frac{\sin(\alpha-\beta)}{\cos\alpha\cos\beta}$$

Product Formulas of Sines and Cosines

$$\sin A \sin B = \frac{1}{2}[\cos(A-B) - \cos(A+B)]$$
$$\cos A \cos B = \frac{1}{2}[\cos(A+B) + \cos(A-B)]$$
$$\sin A \cos B = \frac{1}{2}[\sin(A+B) + \sin(A-B)]$$
$$\cos A \sin B = \frac{1}{2}[\sin(A+B) + \sin(B-A)]$$

- **EXAMPLE**

If $\sin\alpha = \frac{3}{5}$ and $\cos\beta = \frac{3}{5}$, find $\cos(\alpha+\beta)$.

Since $\cos(\alpha+\beta) = \cos\alpha\cos\beta - \sin\alpha\sin\beta$, we need to find $\cos\alpha$ and $\sin\beta$. But,

$$\cos\alpha = \sqrt{1-\sin^2\alpha} = \sqrt{1-\tfrac{9}{25}} = \sqrt{\tfrac{16}{25}} = \tfrac{4}{5}$$

$$\sin\beta = \sqrt{1-\cos^2\beta} = \sqrt{1-\tfrac{9}{25}} = \sqrt{\tfrac{16}{25}} = \tfrac{4}{5}$$

So,

$$\cos(\alpha+\beta) = \frac{4}{5}\times\frac{3}{5} - \frac{3}{5}\times\frac{4}{5} = 0$$

Properties and Graphs of Trigonometric Functions

The **sine function** is the graph of $y = \sin x$. Other trigonometric functions are defined similarly.

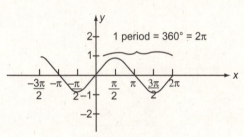

Sine Function

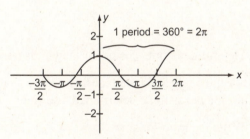

Cosine Function

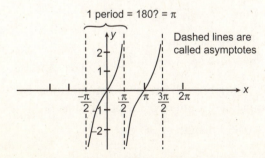

Tangent Function

• EXAMPLE

Draw one period of the graph for the function $y = 0.5\sin(4x + \dfrac{\pi}{6})$ and indicate its amplitude, period, and phase shift.

$$x = 0, y = 0.5\sin\frac{\pi}{6}$$

$$x = \frac{\pi}{4}, y = 0.5\sin(\pi + \frac{\pi}{6}) = -0.5\sin\frac{\pi}{6}$$

$$x = \frac{\pi}{2}, y = 0.5\sin(2\pi + \frac{\pi}{6}) = 0.5\sin\frac{\pi}{6}$$

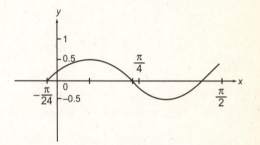

So, amplitude $= \dfrac{1}{2}$

period $= \dfrac{\pi}{2}$

phase shift $= -\dfrac{\pi}{24}$

Inverse Trigonometric Functions

If $-1 < x < 1$, then there are infinitely many angles whose sine is x, as we can see by looking at the graph of the sine function.

Definition:

$\arcsin x =$ the angle between $-\dfrac{\pi}{2}$ and $\dfrac{\pi}{2}$ whose sine is x.

$\mathrm{arccsc}\, x =$ the angle between $-\dfrac{\pi}{2}$ and $\dfrac{\pi}{2}$ whose cosecant is x.

$\arctan x =$ the angle between $-\dfrac{\pi}{2}$ and $\dfrac{\pi}{2}$ whose tangent is x.

arccos x = the angle between θ and π whose cosine is x.

arcsec x = the angle between θ and π whose secant is x.

arccot x = the angle between θ and π whose cotangent is x.

PROBLEM

Evaluate arcsin $\dfrac{1}{2}$.

SOLUTION

Since $\sin\dfrac{\pi}{6}=\dfrac{1}{2}$, $\arcsin\dfrac{1}{2}=\dfrac{\pi}{6}$. The sine function and the arcsine function (abbreviated arcsin or $\sin^{-1}$) are inverses of each other in the sense that the composition of the two functions is the identity function (that is the function that takes x back to x).

$\sin(\arcsin x) = x$

$\arcsin (\sin x) = x$

Periodicity

The **period** of a (repeating) function, f, is the smallest positive number p such that $f(x) = f(x + p)$ for all x.

The period of the tangent and cotangent function is π. This fact is clear from the graphs of the tangent and cotangent functions. Pick any angle, x, on the x-axis, and notice $x + \pi$ has the same tangent as x. The period of the other trigonometric functions is 2π.

If the period of a function f is p, and $g(x) = f(nx)$, then the period of g is p/n.

PROBLEM

What is the period of sin $3x$?

SOLUTION

Since the period of sin x is 2π, the period of sin $3x$ is $\dfrac{2\pi}{3}$.

Use Trigonometry to Solve Right-Triangle Problems

PROBLEM

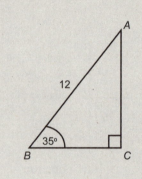

Determine length of side AC in the figure below.

SOLUTION

1. Determine if sine, cosine, or tangent is needed.

Since the angle and hypotenuse are known, and the opposite side needs to be determined, use sine.

2. Write the ratio for sine.

   sin $\angle B$ = opposite side/hypotenuse

3. Using a calculator, find the sine of $\angle B$.

   sin $\angle B$ = sin(35°) = 0.574

4. Rewrite the ratio.

   0.574 = opposite side/12

5. Multiply both sides of the equation by 12 to determine the length of the opposite side.

   6.88 = length of AC

The correct answer is that the length of AC is 6.88.

PROBLEM

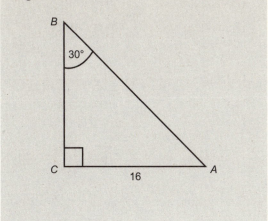

Determine the length of side *AB* in the figure below.

SOLUTION

1. Determine if sine, cosine, or tangent is needed. Since the angle and opposite side are known, and the hypotenuse needs to be determined, use sine.

2. Write the ratio for sine.

sin ∠*B* = opposite side/hypotenuse

3. Using a calculator, find the sine of ∠*B*.

sin ∠*B* = sin(30) = 0.50

4. Rewrite the ratio.

0.50 = 16/hypotenuse

5. Multiply both sides of the equation by the hypotenuse.

hypotenuse(0.50) = 16

6. Divide both sides of the equation by 0.50 to determine the length of the hypotenuse.

hypotenuse = 32

The correct answer is that the length of *AB* is 32.

PROBLEM

A carpenter is trying to determine the height of a flagpole so she can build a new flagpole. The distance from the flagpole to the carpenter is 30 feet. The angle of inclination (the line of sight from where the carpenter is standing to the top of the flagpole) is 30°. See the figure below.

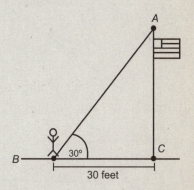

What is the height of the flagpole?

SOLUTION

1. Determine if sine, cosine, or tangent is needed. Since the angle and adjacent side are known, and the opposite side needs to be determined, use tangent.

2. Write the ratio for tangent.

tan ∠*B* = opposite side/adjacent side

3. Using a calculator, find the tangent of ∠*B*.

tan ∠*B* = tan(30) = 0.577

4. Rewrite the ratio. 0.577 = opposite side/30 feet

5. Multiply both sides of the equation by 30 to determine the length of *AC*.

17.31 = length of *AC*.

The correct answer is that the height of the flagpole is 17.31 feet.

PROBLEM

A man is playing billiards with his friend. The cue ball hits the 7 ball at point *C*. The ball travels to point *B* and is deflected toward point *A* (the pocket). If the distance of *CB* is 14 inches, angle *C* is 60°, and ∠*B* is 90°, what is the length of *AB*? See the figure below.

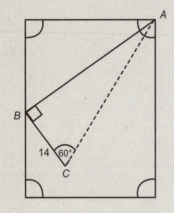

SOLUTION

1. Determine if sine, cosine, or tangent is needed. Since the angle and adjacent side are known, and the opposite side needs to be determined, use tangent.

2. Write the ratio for tangent.

tan ∠*C* = opposite side/adjacent side

3. Using a calculator, find the tangent of ∠*C*.

tan ∠*C* = tan(60) = 1.73

4. Rewrite the ratio.

1.73 = opposite side/14 inches

5. Multiply both sides of the equation by 14 to determine the length of *AB*.

24.22 = length of *AB*

The correct answer is that the distance to the pocket is 24.22 inches.

Drill: Trigonometry

1. $\tan^{-1}(-\sqrt{3}) =$

    (A) −60°   (C) 30°

    (B) 60°   (D) −30°

2. Calculate $\dfrac{\sin^{-1}\frac{1}{2}}{\tan^{-1}1}$.

    (A) $\dfrac{1}{2}$ (C) 45°

    (B) 30°   (D) $\dfrac{2}{3}$

3. Find cos[arcsin(−1)].

    (A) $\dfrac{1}{2}$ (C) 0

    (B) $\dfrac{\sqrt{3}}{2}$ (D) $-\dfrac{\sqrt{3}}{2}$

4. If *x* is inside [0, 2π], one solution for the equation $\sqrt{1+\sin^2 x} = \sqrt{2}\sin x$ is

    (A) $\dfrac{5}{2}\pi$.   (C) $\dfrac{3}{2}\pi$.

    (B) $\dfrac{\pi}{6}$.   (D) $\dfrac{\pi}{2}$.

5. $\sec^2\theta - \tan^2\theta =$

    (A) $\dfrac{4}{5}$ (C) −1

    (B) $\dfrac{1}{2}$ (D) 1

6. $\dfrac{\sin(45°+x)+\sin(45°-x)}{\cos x} =$

    (A) $\sqrt{2}$ (C) $\dfrac{\sqrt{2}}{2}$

    (B) tan *x*   (D) $\dfrac{\sqrt{2}}{2}\cos x$

7. The amplitude of $y = \dfrac{\sqrt{3}}{3}\sin x + \cos x$ is

(A) $\dfrac{\sqrt{3}}{2}$.

(C) $\dfrac{\sqrt{3}}{4}$.

(B) $\dfrac{\sqrt{2}}{2}$.

(D) $\dfrac{2\sqrt{3}}{3}$.

8. $\dfrac{\csc x}{2\cos x} =$

(A) $\cos 3x$

(C) $\sin 2x$

(B) $\tan 2x$

(D) $\csc 2x$

Detailed Explanations of Answers

1. (A)

Using the table, you will find $\tan^{-1}\left(-\sqrt{3}\right) = -60°$ in the 2nd or 4th quadrant.

2. (D)

$$\frac{\sin^{-1}\frac{1}{2}}{\tan^{-1}1} = \frac{30}{45} = \frac{2}{3}$$

3. (C)

$$\cos[\arcsin(-1)] = \cos(-90) = 0$$

4. (D)

$$\left[\sqrt{1+\sin^2 x}\right]^2 = \left[\sqrt{2}\sin x\right]^2 \Rightarrow 1 + \sin^2 x = 2\sin^2 x$$

Subtract $-2\sin^2 x$:

$$\begin{array}{rcl} -2\sin^2 x & & -2\sin^2 x \\ \hline 1-\sin^2 x & = & 0 \\ \cos^2 x & = & 0 \end{array}$$

$\cos x = 0$ at $\frac{\pi}{2}$ or $\frac{3}{2}\pi$

$\frac{3}{2}\pi$ won't satisfy the original equation

So $\frac{\pi}{2}$ is the answer.

5. (D)

$$\sec^2\theta - \tan^2\theta = (\tan^2\theta + 1) - \tan^2\theta = 1$$

6. (A)

$$\frac{\sin(45° + x) + \sin(45° - x)}{\cos x}$$

$$= \frac{\sin 45\cos x + \cos 45\sin x + \sin 45\cos x - \cos 45\sin x}{\cos x}$$

$$= \frac{2\sin 45\cos x}{\cos x}$$

$$= 2\sin 45$$

$$= 2\left(\frac{\sqrt{2}}{2}\right)$$

$$= \sqrt{2}$$

7. (D)

$$y = \frac{\sqrt{3}}{3}\sin x + \cos x$$

Test reference angles 0, 30, 45, 60, and 90 to determine that 30 is the greatest

$$\frac{\sqrt{3}}{3}\sin(30) + \cos(30) = \frac{\sqrt{3}}{3}\left(\frac{1}{2}\right) + \left(\frac{\sqrt{3}}{2}\right)$$

$$= \frac{\sqrt{3}}{6} + \frac{\sqrt{3}}{2}$$

$$= \frac{\sqrt{3}}{6} + \frac{3\sqrt{3}}{6}$$

$$= \frac{4\sqrt{3}}{6}$$

$$= \frac{2\sqrt{3}}{3}$$

8. (D)

$$\frac{\csc x}{2\cos x} = \frac{\frac{1}{\sin x}}{2\cos x} = \frac{1}{2\sin x\cos x} = \frac{1}{\sin 2x} = \csc 2x$$

Calculus

Limits

Definition

Let f be a function that is defined on an open interval containing a, but possibly not defined at a itself. Let L be a real number. The statement

$$\lim_{x \to a} f(x) = L$$

defines the limit of the function $f(x)$ at the point a. Very simply, L is the value that the function has as the point a is approached.

Problem Solving Examples:

PROBLEM

$$\lim_{x \to 2} f(x) = 2x + 1$$

SOLUTION

As x $\to$ 2, f(x) $\to$ 5. Therefore, $\lim_{x \to 2} (2x + 1) = 5$

PROBLEM

Find $\lim_{x \to 3} f(x) = \dfrac{x^2 - 9}{x + 1}$

SOLUTION

$$\lim_{x \to 3} = \frac{x^2 - 9}{x + 1} = \frac{0}{4} = 0.$$

Theorems on Limits

The following are important properties of limits:

Consider $\lim_{x \to a} f(x) = L$ and $\lim_{x \to a} g(x) = K$, then

A) Uniqueness – If $\lim_{x \to a} f(x)$ exists, then it is unique.

B) $\lim_{x \to a} [f(x) + g(x)] = \lim_{x \to a} f(x) + \lim_{x \to a} g(x) = L + K$

C) $\lim_{x \to a} [f(x) - g(x)] = \lim_{x \to a} f(x) - \lim_{x \to a} g(x) = L - K$

D) $\lim_{x \to a} [f(x) \cdot g(x)] = \lim_{x \to a} f(x) \cdot \lim_{x \to a} g(x) = L \cdot K$

E) $\lim_{x \to a} \dfrac{f(x)}{g(x)} = \dfrac{\lim_{x \to a} f(x)}{\lim_{x \to a} g(x)} = \dfrac{L}{K}$ provided $K \neq 0$

F) $\lim_{x \to a} \dfrac{1}{g(x)} = \dfrac{1}{K}, K \neq 0$

G) $\lim_{x \to a} [f(x)]^n = [\lim_{x \to a} f(x)]^n$ for $n > 0$

H) $\lim_{x \to a} [cf(x)] = c[\lim_{x \to a} f(x)], c \in R$

I) $\lim_{x \to a} cx^n = c \lim_{x \to a} x^n = ca^n, c \in R$

J) If f is a polynomial function then $\lim_{x \to a} f(x) = f(a)$ for all $a \in R$.

K) $\lim_{x \to a} \sqrt[n]{x} = \sqrt[n]{a}$ when $a \geq 0$ and n is a positive integer or when $a \leq 0$ and n is an odd positive integer.

L) $\lim_{x \to a} \sqrt[n]{f(x)} = \sqrt[n]{\lim_{x \to a} f(x)}$ when n is a positive integer

M) If $f(x) \leq h(x) \leq g(x)$ for all x in an open interval containing a, except possibly at a, and if $\lim_{x \to a} f(x) = L = \lim_{x \to a} g(x)$ then $\lim_{x \to a} h(x) = L$.

PROBLEM

Find $\lim_{x \to 0} (x\sqrt{x - 3})$

SOLUTION

In checking the function by simple substitution, we see that:

$$x\sqrt{x - 3} = 0$$

if $x = 0.$

However, this function does not have real values for values of x less than 3. Therefore, since x cannot approach 0, $f(x)$ does not approach 0 and the limit does not exist. This example illustrates that we cannot properly find

$$\lim_{x \to a} f(x)$$

by finding $f(a)$, even though they are equal in many cases. We must consider values of x near a, but not equal to a.

One-Sided Limits

Suppose f is a function such that it is not defined for all values of x. Rather, it is defined in such a way that it "jumps" from one y value to the next instead of smoothly going from one y value to the next. Examples are shown in the figures below.

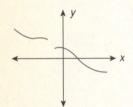

**$y = f(x)$ is not
defined for all x values.**

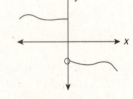

**$y = f(x)$ "jumps"
from a positive value
to a negative one.**

The statement $\lim\limits_{x \to a^+} f(x) = R$ tells us that as x approaches "a" from the right or from positive infinity, the function f has the limit R.

Similarly, the statement $\lim\limits_{x \to a^-} f(x) = L$ says that as x approaches "a" from the left-hand side or from negative infinity, the function f has the limit L.

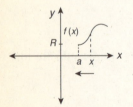

Right-hand limit   **Left-hand limit**

If f is defined in an open interval containing a, except possibly at a, then

$$\lim_{x \to a} f(x) = L \text{ if and only if}$$

$$\lim_{x \to a^+} f(x) = L = \lim_{x \to a^-} f(x)$$

Notice that in the figure below, the right-hand limit is not the same as the left-hand limit,

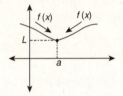

PROBLEM

Let $f(x)$ and $g(x)$ be defined by:

$$f(x) = \begin{cases} x^2 + 2x, & x \leqq 1, \\ 2x, & x > 1, \end{cases}$$

$$g(x) = \begin{cases} 2x^3, & x \leqq 1, \\ 3, & x > 1. \end{cases}$$

Find $\lim\limits_{x \to 1} [f(x) \cdot g(x)]$ if it exists.

SOLUTION

Neither $f(x)$ nor $g(x)$ have limits as $x \to 1$, but one-sided limits exist for both functions. It is possible that the product of two functions may have a limit, even though the two functions do not have limits individually.

$$\lim_{x \to 1^-} f(x) = 3, \qquad \lim_{x \to 1^+} f(x) = 2,$$

$$\lim_{x \to 1^-} g(x) = 2, \qquad \lim_{x \to 1^+} g(x) = 3.$$

Therefore,

$$\lim_{x \to 1^-} [f(x) \cdot g(x)] = 6$$

and

$$\lim_{x \to 1^+} [f(x) \cdot g(x)] = 6$$

Consequently,

$$\lim_{x \to 1} [f(x) \cdot g(x)] = 6$$

PROBLEM

Given that f is the function defined by:

$$f(x) = \begin{cases} x - 3 & \text{if } x \neq 4 \\ 5 & \text{if } x = 4, \end{cases}$$

Find $\lim_{x \to 4} f(x)$.

SOLUTION

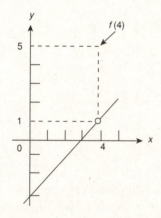

When plotting $f(x)$ to obtain a visual representation, it is seen that $f(x) = x - 3$ is a straight line which has a break or discontinuity at the point $x = 4$. At $x = 4$, the value of $f(x)$ is given as 5, and not as 1 - the value that $f(x)$ would assume if the line were continuous. However, when evaluating $\lim_{x \to 4} f(x)$, we are considering values of x close to 4 but not equal to 4. Thus we have

$$\lim_{x \to 4} f(x) = \lim_{x \to 4}(x - 3)$$
$$= 1.$$

In this example,

$\lim_{x \to 4} f(x) = 1$ but $f(4) = 5$; therefore,

$$\lim_{x \to 4} f(x) \neq f(4).$$

Special Limits

A) $\lim_{x \to 0} \dfrac{\sin x}{x} = 1$, $\lim_{x \to 0} \dfrac{1 - \cos x}{x} = 0$

B) $\lim_{n \to \infty} (1 + \dfrac{1}{n})^n = e$, $\lim_{n \to 0} (1 + n)^{1/n} = e$

C)   For $a > 1$ $\lim_{x \to +\infty} a^x = +\infty$, $\lim_{x \to -\infty} a^x = 0$
$\lim_{x \to +\infty} \log_a x = +\infty$, $\lim_{x \to 0} \log_a x = -\infty$

D)   For $0 < a < 1$, $\lim_{x \to +\infty} a^x = 0$, $\lim_{x \to -\infty} a^x = +\infty$
$\lim_{x \to +\infty} \log_a x = -\infty$, $\lim_{x \to 0} \log_a x = +\infty$

Some nonexistent limits which are frequently encountered are:

A) $\lim_{x \to 0} \dfrac{1}{x^2}$, as x approaches zero, x^2 gets very small and also becomes zero therefore $\dfrac{1}{0}$ is undefined and the limit does not exist.

B) $\lim_{x \to 0} \dfrac{|x|}{x}$ does not exist.

Proof:

If $x > 0$, then $\dfrac{|x|}{x} = \dfrac{x}{x} = 1$ and hence lies to the right of the y-axis, the graph of f coincides with the line $y = 1$. If $x < 0$ then $\dfrac{-x}{x} = -1$ and the graph of f coincides with the line $y = -1$ to the left of the y-axis.

If it were true that $\lim_{x \to 0} \dfrac{|x|}{x} = L$ for some L, then the preceding remarks imply that $-1 \leq L \leq 1$.

If we consider any pair of horizontal lines $y = L \pm \theta$, where $0 < \theta < 1$, then there exists points on the graph which are not between these lines for some non-zero x in every interval $(-\theta, \theta)$ containing 0. It follows that the limit does not exist.

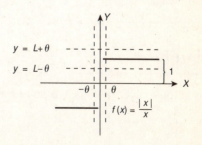

PROBLEM

$$\text{Find } \lim_{x \to 3} f(x) = \frac{1}{(x-3)^2}, \; x \neq 3$$

SOLUTION

Sketching the graph of this function about $x = 3$, we see that it increases without bound as x tends to 3.

Using the method of simple substitution, we find that $\lim_{x \to 3} f(x) = \infty$. There is no limit.

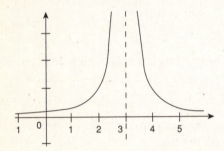

PROBLEM

$$\text{Find } \lim_{x \to 3} \frac{5x}{6-2x}.$$

SOLUTION

$$\lim_{x \to 3} 5x = 15$$

and

$$\lim_{x \to 3} [6-2x] = 0$$

Therefore,

$$\lim_{x \to 3} \frac{5x}{6-2x} = \frac{15}{0} = \infty.$$

The function has no limit.

Continuity

A function f is continuous at a point a if

$$\lim_{x \to a} f(x) = f(a).$$

This implies that three conditions are satisfied:

a) $f(a)$ exists, that is, f is defined at a

b) $\lim_{x \to a} f(x)$ exists, and

c) the two numbers are equal.

To test continuity at a point $x = a$ we test whether

$$\lim_{x \to a^+} F(x) = \lim_{x \to a^-} F(x) = F(a)$$

PROBLEM

Investigate the continuity of the function:

$$h(x) = \begin{cases} 3+x & \text{if } x \leq 1 \\ 3-x & \text{if } 1 < x. \end{cases}$$

SOLUTION

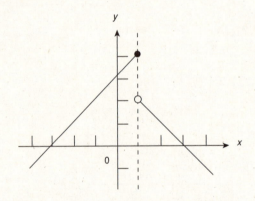

Because there is a break in the graph at the point $x = 1$, we investigate the three conditions for continuity at the point $x = 1$. The three conditions are: (1) $f(x_0)$ is defined, (2) $\lim_{x \to x_0} f(x)$ exists, (3) $\lim_{x \to x_0} f(x) = f(x_0)$. At $x = 1$, $h(1) = 4$; therefore, condition (1) is satisfied.

$$\lim_{x \to 1^-} h(x) = \lim_{x \to 1^-} (3+x) = 4$$
$$\lim_{x \to 1^+} h(x) = \lim_{x \to 1^+} (3-x) = 2.$$

Because $\lim_{x \to 1^-} h(x) \neq \lim_{x \to 1^+} h(x)$, we conclude that $\lim_{x \to 1} h(x)$ does not exist. Therefore, condition (2) fails to hold at 1.

Hence, h is discontinuous at 1.

PROBLEM

Investigate continuity of:

$$F(x) = \begin{cases} |x-3| & \text{if } x \neq 3 \\ 2 & \text{if } x = 3. \end{cases}$$

SOLUTION

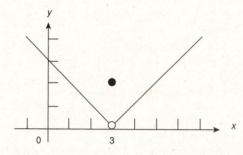

We investigate the three conditions for continuity at the point $x = 3$. The three conditions are: (1) $f(x_0)$ is defined,

(2) $\lim\limits_{x \to x_0} f(x)$ exists, (3) $\lim\limits_{x \to x_0} f(x) = f(x_0)$. At $x = 3$ we have $F(3) = 2$; therefore, condition (1) is satisfied.

$\lim\limits_{x \to 3^-} F(x) = 0$ and $\lim\limits_{x \to 3^+} F(x) = 0$. Therefore, $\lim\limits_{x \to 3} F(x)$ exists and is 0; therefore, condition (2) is satisfied.

$\lim\limits_{x \to 3} F(x) = 0$ but $F(3) = 2$. Therefore, condition (3) is not satisfied. F is thus discontinuous at 3.

Theorems of Continuity

A) A function defined in a closed interval $[a,b]$ is continuous in $[a,b]$ if and only if it is continuous in the open interval (a,b), as well as continuous from the right at "a" and from the left at "b".

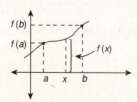

B) If f and g are continuous functions at a, then so are the functions $f + g$, $f - g$, fg and f/g where $g(a) \neq 0$.

C) If $\lim\limits_{x \to a} g(x) = b$ and f is continuous at b,

then $\lim\limits_{x \to a} f(g(x)) = f(b) = f[\lim\limits_{x \to a} g(x)]$.

D) If g is continuous at a and f is continuous at $b = g(a)$, then

$$\lim\limits_{x \to a} f(g(x)) = f[\lim\limits_{x \to a} g(x)] = f(g(a)).$$

E) Intermediate Value Theorem. If f is continuous on a closed interval $[a, b]$ and if $f(a) \neq f(b)$, then f takes on every value between $f(a)$ and $f(b)$ in the interval $[a, b]$.

F) $f(x) = k$, $k \in R$ is continuous everywhere.

G) $f(x) = x$, the identity function is continuous everywhere.

H) If f is continuous at a, then $\lim\limits_{n \to \infty} f(a + \frac{1}{n}) = f(a)$.

I) If f is continuous on an interval containing a and b, $a < b$, and if $f(a) \cdot f(b) < 0$ then there exists at least one point c, $a < c < b$ such that $f(c) = 0$.

PROBLEM

Let h be defined by:

$$h(x) = \begin{cases} 4 - x^2 & \text{if } x < 1 \\ 2 + x^2 & \text{if } 1 < x \end{cases}$$

Find each of the following limits if they exist:

$$\lim\limits_{x \to 1^-} h(x), \lim\limits_{x \to 1^+} h(x), \lim\limits_{x \to 1} h(x).$$

SOLUTION

It is desirable to sketch the given function to aid in visualizing the problem.

Now,

$$\lim\limits_{x \to 1^-} h(x) = \lim\limits_{x \to 1^-} - (4 - x^2) = 3$$

$$\lim\limits_{x \to 1^+} h(x) = \lim\limits_{x \to 1^+} + (2 + x^2) = 3$$

Therefore, $\lim_{x \to 1} h(x)$ exists and is equal to 3. Note that $h(1) = 3$. This holds because the function is continuous.

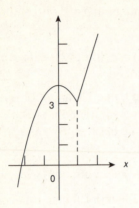

PROBLEM

> If $h(x) = \sqrt{4 - x^2}$, prove that $h(x)$ is continuous in the closed interval $[-2, 2]$.

SOLUTION

To prove continuity we employ the following definition: A function defined in the closed interval $[a,b]$ is said to be continuous in $[a,b]$ if and only if it is continuous in the open interval (a,b), as well as continuous from the right at a and continuous from the left at b. The function h is continuous in the open interval $(-2,2)$. We must show that the function is continuous from the right at -2 and from the left at 2. Therefore, we must show that $f(-2)$ is defined and $\lim_{x \to -2^+} f(x)$ exists and that these are equal. Also, we must show that $f(2) = \lim_{x \to 2^-} f(x)$. We have:

$$\lim_{x \to -2^+} \sqrt{4 - x^2} = 0 = h(-2),$$

and

$$\lim_{x \to 2^-} \sqrt{4 - x^2} = 0 = h(2).$$

Thus, h is continuous in the closed interval $[-2,2]$.

The Derivative

The Definition and △-Method

The derivative of a function expresses its rate of change with respect to an independent variable. The derivative is also the slope of the tangent line to the curve.

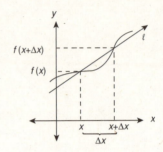

Consider the graph of the function f in the figure. Choosing a point x and a point $x + \Delta x$ (where Δx denotes a small distance on the x-axis) we can obtain both, $f(x)$ and $f(x + \Delta x)$. Drawing a tangent line, l, of the curve through the points $f(x)$ and $f(x + \Delta x)$, we can measure the rate of change of this line. As we let the distance, Δx, approach zero, then

$$\lim_{\Delta x \to 0} \frac{f(x + \Delta x) - f(x)}{\Delta x}$$

becomes the instantaneous rate of change of the function or the derivative.

We denote the derivative of the function f to be f'. So we have

$$f'(x) = \lim_{\Delta x \to 0} \frac{f(x + \Delta x) - f(x)}{\Delta x}$$

If $y = f(x)$, some common notations for the derivative are

$$y' = f'(x)$$
$$\frac{dy}{dx} = f'(x)$$
$$D_x y = f'(x) \text{ or } Df = f'$$

PROBLEM

Find the slope of each of the following curves at the given point, using the Δ-method.

a) $y = 3x^2 - 2x + 4$ at (1,5)

b) $y = x^3 - 3x + 5$ at (−2,3).

SOLUTION

The slope of a given curve at a specified point is the derivative, in this case $\frac{\Delta y}{\Delta x}$, evaluated at that point.

a) From the Δ-method we know that:

$$\frac{\Delta y}{\Delta x} = \frac{f(x + \Delta x) - f(x)}{\Delta x}.$$

For the curve $y = 3x^2 - 2x + 4$, we find:

$$\frac{\Delta y}{\Delta x} = \frac{3(x + \Delta x)^2 - 2(x + \Delta x) + 4 - (3x^2 - 2x + 4)}{\Delta x}$$

$$= \frac{3x^2 + 6x\Delta x + 3(\Delta x)^2 - 2x - 2\Delta x + 4 - 3x^2 + 2x - 4}{\Delta x}$$

$$= \frac{6x\Delta x + 3(\Delta x)^2 - 2\Delta x}{\Delta x}$$

$$= 6x + 3\Delta x - 2.$$

$$\lim_{\Delta x \to 0} \frac{\Delta y}{\Delta x} = \lim_{\Delta x \to 0} 6x + 3\Delta x - 2 = 6x - 2.$$

At (1,5) $\frac{\Delta y}{\Delta x} = 4$ is the required slope.

b) Again using the Δ-method, $\frac{\Delta y}{\Delta x}$ for the curve:

$y = x^3 - 3x + 5$, can be found as follows:

$$\frac{\Delta y}{\Delta x} = \frac{f(x + \Delta x) - f(x)}{\Delta x}.$$

$$\frac{\Delta y}{\Delta x} = \frac{(x + \Delta x)^3 - 3(x \, \Delta x) + 5 - (x^3 - 3x + 5)}{\Delta x}.$$

$$\frac{\Delta y}{\Delta x} = \frac{(x + \Delta x)^3 - 3(x + \Delta x) + 5 - (x^3 - 3x + 5)}{\Delta x}$$

$$= \frac{x^3 + 3x^2\Delta x + 3x(\Delta x)^2 + (\Delta x)^3 - 3x - 3\Delta x + 5 - x^3 + 3x - 5}{\Delta x}$$

$$= \frac{3x^2\Delta x + 3x(\Delta x)^2 + (\Delta x)^3 - 3\Delta x}{\Delta x}$$

$$= 3x^2 + 3x\Delta x + (\Delta x)^2 - 3.$$

$$\lim_{\Delta x \to 0} \frac{\Delta y}{\Delta x} = \lim_{\Delta x \to 0} 3x^2 + 3x\Delta x + (\Delta x)^2 - 3 = 3x^2 - 3.$$

At (−2,3), $\frac{\Delta y}{\Delta x} = 9$ is the required slope.

PROBLEM

Find the average rate of change, by the Δ process, for:

$$y = \frac{1}{x}.$$

SOLUTION

$$y = f(x) = \frac{1}{x}$$

The average rate of change is defined to be

$\frac{\Delta y}{\Delta x}$ with $\Delta y = f(x + \Delta x) - f(x)$.

Since

$$f(x) = \frac{1}{x}, f(x + \Delta x) = \frac{1}{x + \Delta x},$$

and

$$\Delta y = \frac{1}{x + \Delta x} - \frac{1}{x} = \frac{x - (x + \Delta x)}{x(x + \Delta x)}$$

$$= \frac{-\Delta x}{x(x + \Delta x)}.$$

Now,

$$\frac{\Delta y}{\Delta x} = \frac{-\Delta x}{x(x + \Delta x)\Delta x} = -\frac{1}{x(x + \Delta x)}.$$

Therefore, the average rate of change is $\frac{-1}{x(x + \Delta x)}$.

The Derivative at a point

If f is defined on an open interval containing "a", then

$$f'(a) = \lim_{x \to a} \frac{f(x) - f(a)}{x - a},$$

provided the limit exists.

PROBLEM

Find the instantaneous rate of the function:

$$y = \frac{2x}{x+1}$$

for any value of x and for $x = 2$.

SOLUTION

The instantaneous rate of change of a function is defined as,

$$\lim_{\Delta x \to 0} \frac{\Delta y}{\Delta x} = \lim_{\Delta x \to 0} \frac{f(x + \Delta x) - f(x)}{\Delta x}$$

Therefore,

$\Delta y = f(x + \Delta x) - f(x).$

In this case,

$f(x) = \dfrac{2x}{x+1}$, therefore,

$$f(x + \Delta x) = \frac{2(x + \Delta x)}{x + \Delta x + 1}$$

Substituting, we have:

$$\Delta y = \frac{2x + 2 \cdot \Delta x}{x + \Delta x + 1} - \frac{2x}{x + 1}$$

$$= \frac{(2x + 2 \cdot \Delta x)(x+1) - 2x(x + \Delta x + 1)}{(x + \Delta x + 1)(x + 1)}$$

$$= \frac{2x^2 + 2x \cdot \Delta x + 2x + 2 \cdot \Delta x - 2x^2 - 2x \cdot \Delta x - 2x}{(x + \Delta x + 1)(x + 1)}$$

$$= \frac{2 \cdot \Delta x}{(x + \Delta x + 1)(x + 1)}.$$

$$\frac{\Delta y}{\Delta x} = \frac{2 \cdot \Delta x}{(x + \Delta x + 1)(x + 1)(\Delta x)}$$

$$= \frac{2}{(x + \Delta x + 1)(x + 1)}.$$

Now,

$$\lim_{\Delta x \to 0} \frac{\Delta y}{\Delta x} = \lim_{\Delta x \to 0} \frac{2}{(x + \Delta x + 1)(x + 1)}.$$

Substituting 0 for Δx we have,

$$\lim_{\Delta x \to 0} \frac{\Delta y}{\Delta x} = \frac{2}{(x + 1)^2},$$

the instantaneous rate of change for any value of x. For $x = 2$, we have,

$$\frac{2}{(x + 1)^2} = \frac{2}{(2 + 1)^2} = \frac{2}{9}.$$

PROBLEM

Find the rate of change of y with respect to x at the point $x = 5$, if
$$2y = x^2 + 3x - 1.$$

SOLUTION

Rate of change is defined as

$$\lim_{\Delta x \to 0} \frac{\Delta y}{\Delta x}, \text{ with}$$

$\Delta y = f(x + \Delta x) - f(x).$

We have:

$2\Delta y = (x + \Delta x)^2 + 3(x + \Delta x) - 1 - (x^2 + 3x - 1)$

$= x^2 + 2x \cdot \Delta x + (\Delta x)^2 + 3x + 3\Delta x - 1 - x^2 - 3x + 1$

$= 2x \cdot \Delta x + (\Delta x)^2 + 3\Delta x.$

Dividing by Δx,

$$\frac{2\Delta y}{\Delta x} = \frac{2x \cdot \Delta x}{\Delta x} + \frac{(\Delta x)^2}{\Delta x} + \frac{3\Delta x}{\Delta x}$$

$$= 2x + \Delta x + 3$$

and

$$\frac{\Delta y}{\Delta x} = x + \frac{\Delta x}{2} + \frac{3}{2}.$$

Now,

$$\lim_{\Delta x \to 0} \frac{\Delta y}{\Delta x} = \lim_{\Delta x \to 0} x + \frac{\Delta x}{2} + \frac{3}{2} = x + \frac{3}{2}.$$

For $x = 5$,

$$\lim_{\Delta x \to 0} \frac{\Delta y}{\Delta x} = 5 + \frac{3}{2} = 6\frac{1}{2}.$$

Rules for Finding the Derivatives

General rule:

A) If f is a constant function, $f(x) = c$, then $f'(x) = 0$.

B) If $\boxed{f(x) = x, \text{ then } f'(x) = 1.}$

C) If f is differentiable, then $\boxed{(cf(x))' = cf'(x)}$

D) Power Rule: If $f(x) = x^n$, $n \in z$, then $f'(x) = nx^{n-1}$; if $n < 0$ then x^n is not defined at $x = 0$.

E) If f and g are differentiable on the interval (a,b) then:

a) $\boxed{(f + g)'(x) = f'(x) + g'(x)}$

b)   Product Rule: $\boxed{(fg)'(x) = f(x)g'(x) + g(x)f'(x)}$

Example: Find $f'(x)$ if $f(x) = (x^3 + 1)(2x^2 + 8x - 5)$.

$f'(x) = (x^3 + 1)(4x + 8) + (2x^2 + 8x - 5)(3x^2)$

$= 4x^4 + 8x^3 + 4x + 8 + 6x^4 + 24x^3 - 15x^2$

$= 10x^4 + 32x^3 - 15x^2 + 4x + 8$

c)   Quotient Rule:

$$\boxed{\left(\frac{f'}{g}\right)(x) = \frac{g(x)f'(x) - f(x)g'(x)}{[g(x)]^2}}$$

Example: Find $f'(x)$ if $f(x) = \dfrac{3x^2 - x + 2}{4x^2 + 5}$

$$f'(x) = \frac{-(3x^2 - x + 2)(8x) + (4x^2 + 5)(6x - 1)}{(4x^2 + 5)^2}$$

$$= \frac{-(24x^3 - 8x^2 + 16x) + (24x^3 - 4x^2 + 30x - 5)}{(4x^2 + 5)^2}$$

$$= \frac{4x^2 + 14x - 5}{(4x^2 + 5)^2}$$

F)   If $f(x) = x^{m/n}$, then $f'(x) = \dfrac{m}{n} x^{\frac{m}{n} - 1}$ where $m, n \in Z$ and $n \neq 0$

G)   Polynomials. If $f(x) = (a_0 + a_1x + a_2x^2 + ... + a_nx^n)$ then $f'(x) = a_1 + 2a_2x + 3a_3x^2 + ... + na_nx^{n-1}$

This employs the power rule and rules concerning constants.

H)   Chain Rule. Let $f(u)$ be a composite function, where $u = g(x)$.

Then $f'(u) = f'(u)g'(x)$ or if $y = f(u)$ and $u = g(x)$ then $D_x y = (D_u y)(D_x u) = f'(u)g'(x)$

PROBLEM

Find the derivative of: $y = x^{3b}$.

SOLUTION

Applying the theorem for $d(u^n)$,

$$\frac{dy}{dx} = 3b \cdot x^{3b-1}.$$

PROBLEM

Find the derivative of: $y = (x^2 + 2)^3$.

SOLUTION

Method 1. We may expand the cube and write:

$$\frac{dy}{dx} = \frac{d}{dx}[(x^2 + 2)^3] = \frac{d}{dx}(x^6 + 6x^4 + 12x^2 + 8)$$

$$= 6x^5 + 24x^3 + 24x.$$

Method 2. Let $u = x^2 + 2$, then $y = (x^2 + 2)^3 = u^3$;

Using the chain rule we have:

$$\frac{dy}{dx} = \frac{dy}{du} \cdot \frac{du}{dx} = \frac{d(u^3)}{du} \cdot \frac{d(x^2 + 2)}{dx} = 3u^2(2x)$$
$$= 3(x^2 + 2)^2 \cdot (2x) = 3(x^4 + 4x^2 + 4) \cdot (2x)$$
$$= 6x^5 + 24x^3 + 24x.$$

Implicit Differentiation

An implicit function of x and y is a function in which one of the variables is not directly expressed in terms of the other. If these variables are not easily or practically separable, we can still differentiate the expression.

Apply the normal rules of differentiation such as the product rule, the power rule, etc. Remember also the chain rule which states $\frac{du}{dx} \times \frac{dx}{dt} = \frac{du}{dt}$.

Once the rules have been properly applied we will be left with as in the example of x and y, some factors of $\frac{dy}{dx}$.

We can then algebraically solve for the derivative $\frac{dy}{dx}$ and obtain the desired result.

PROBLEM

If $x^2 + y^2 = 16$, find $\frac{dy}{dx}$ as an implicit function of x and y.

SOLUTION

Since y is a function of x, we differentiate the equation implicitly in terms of x and y. We have:

$$2x + 2y \cdot \frac{dy}{dx} = 0 \quad \text{or} \quad 2y \frac{dy}{dx} = -2x.$$
$$\frac{dy}{dx} = -\frac{x}{y}.$$

PROBLEM

Find $\frac{dy}{dx}$ for the expression:
$2x^4 - 3x^2y^2 + y^4 = 0$.

SOLUTION

The equation $2x^4 - 3x^2y^2 + y^4 = 0$, could be solved for y and then differentiated to obtain $\frac{dy}{dx}$, but an easier method is to differentiate implicitly and then solve for $\frac{dy}{dx}$.

Hence, from $2x^4 - 3x^2y^2 + y^4 = 0$ we obtain:

$$8x^3 - 6x^2y\frac{dy}{dx} - 6xy^2 + 4y^3\frac{dy}{dx} = 0.$$

Solving for $\frac{dy}{dx}$,

$$4y^3 \frac{dy}{dx} - 6x^2y \frac{dy}{dx} = 6xy^2 - 8x^3.$$
$$(4y^3 - 6x^2y) \frac{dy}{dx} = 6xy^2 - 8x^3.$$

$$\frac{dy}{dx} = \frac{6xy^2 - 8x^3}{4y^3 - 6x^2y}$$
$$= \frac{3xy^2 - 4x^3}{2y^3 - 3x^2y}.$$

Trigonometric Differentiation

The three most basic trigonometric derivatives are:

$$\frac{d}{dx}(\sin x) = \cos x,$$
$$\frac{d}{dx}(\cos x) = -\sin x,$$
$$\frac{d}{dx}(\tan x) = \sec^2 x,$$

Given any trigonometric function, it can be differentiated by applying these basics in combination with the general rules for differentiating algebraic expressions.

The following will be most useful if committed to memory:

$$D_x \sin u = \cos u \, D_x u$$

$$D_x \cos u = -\sin u \, D_x u$$

$$D_x \tan u = \sec^2 u \, D_x u$$

$$D_x \sec u = \tan u \sec u \, D_x u$$

$$D_x \cot u = -\csc^2 u \, D_x u$$

$$D_x \csc u = -\csc u \cot u \, D_x u$$

PROBLEM

Find the derivative of: $y = \sin ax^2$.

SOLUTION

Applying the theorem for the derivative of the sine of a function,

$$\frac{dy}{dx} = \cos ax^2 \cdot \frac{d}{dx}(ax^2)$$

$$= 2 \, ax \cos ax^2.$$

PROBLEM

Find the derivative of: $y \tan 3\theta$.

SOLUTION

Let $u = 3\theta$

Then, $y = \tan u$, and

$$\frac{dy}{d\theta} = \frac{dy}{du} \cdot \frac{du}{d\theta}$$

$$\frac{du}{d\theta} = 3,$$

and $\dfrac{dy}{du} = \sec^2 u.$

Therefore,

$$\frac{dy}{d\theta} = \frac{dy}{du} \cdot \frac{du}{d\theta} = \sec^2 u \cdot 3 = 3\sec^2(3\theta).$$

Inverse Trigonometric Differentiation

Here are the derivatives for the inverse trigonometric functions which can be found in a manner similar to the above function. If u is a differentiable function of x, then:

$$D_x \sin^{-1} u = \frac{1}{\sqrt{1-u^2}} D_x u \quad , \quad |u| < 1$$

$$D_x \cos^{-1} u = \frac{-1}{\sqrt{1-u^2}} D_x u \quad , \quad |u| < 1$$

$$D_x \tan^{-1} u = \frac{1}{1+u^2} D_x u \quad ,$$

$$D_x \sec^{-1} u = \frac{1}{|u|\sqrt{u^2-1}} D_x u \, , u = f(x), \, |f(x)| > 1$$

$$D_x \cot^{-1} u = \frac{-1}{1+u^2} D_x u \quad ,$$

$$D_x \csc^{-1} u = \frac{-1}{|u|\sqrt{u^2-1}} D_x u \, , u = f(x), \, |f(x)| > 1$$

PROBLEM

Find the derivative of $y = $ arc sin $4x$.

SOLUTION

We use the formula for differentiation of the $\sin^{-1}$ or arc sin function, which states:

$$\frac{d}{dx} \sin^{-1} u = \frac{1}{\sqrt{1-u^2}}.$$

Hence

$$\frac{dy}{dx} = \frac{1}{\sqrt{1-16x^2}}(4) = \frac{4}{\sqrt{1-16x^2}}$$

PROBLEM

Given: $y = \text{arc } \tan \dfrac{3}{x}$, find $\dfrac{dy}{dx}$.

SOLUTION

In this example, we use the formula:

$$\frac{d(\text{arc } \tan u)}{dx} = \frac{1}{1+u^2} \cdot \frac{du}{dx}.$$

For

$$y = \text{arc } \tan \frac{3}{x}, \quad u = \frac{3}{x}, \quad \text{and} \quad du = \frac{-3}{x^2}.$$

Therefore,

$$\frac{dy}{dx} = \frac{1\left(\dfrac{-3}{x^2}\right)}{1+\left(\dfrac{3}{x}\right)^2} = \frac{\dfrac{-3}{x^2}}{\dfrac{x^2+9}{x^2}} = \frac{-3}{x^2+9}.$$

Exponential and Logarithmic Differentiation

The exponential function e^x has the simplest of all derivatives. Its derivative is itself.

$$\boxed{\frac{d}{dx} e^x = e^x}$$

and

$$\boxed{\frac{d}{dx} e^u = e^u \frac{du}{dx}}$$

Since the natural logarithmic function is the inverse of $y = e^x$ and $\ln e = 1$, it follows that

$$\boxed{\frac{d}{dx} \ln y = \frac{1}{y} \frac{dy}{dx}}$$

and

$$\boxed{\frac{d}{dx} \ln u = \frac{1}{u} \frac{du}{dx}}$$

If x is any real number and a is any positive real number, then

$$\boxed{a^x = e^{x \ln a}}$$

From this definition we can obtain the following:

a) $\dfrac{d}{dx} a^x = a^x \ln a$ and $\dfrac{d}{dx} a^u = a^u \ln a \dfrac{du}{dx}$

b) $\dfrac{d}{dx}(\log_a x) = \dfrac{1}{x \ln a}$ and $\dfrac{d}{dx}\log_a |u| = \dfrac{1}{u \ln a}\dfrac{du}{dx}$

where $u \neq 0$

Sometimes it is useful to take the logs of a function and then differentiate since the computation becomes easier (as in the case of a product).

PROBLEM

If $y = e^{\frac{1}{x^2}}$, find $D_x y$.

SOLUTION

To find $D_x y = \dfrac{dy}{dx}$, we use the differentiation formula:

$$\frac{d}{dx} e^u = e^u \frac{du}{dx}, \text{ with } u = \frac{1}{x^2}. \text{ We obtain:}$$

$$D_x y = e^{\frac{1}{x^2}}\left(-\frac{2x}{x^4}\right)$$

$$= e^{\frac{1}{x^2}}\left(-\frac{2}{x^3}\right) = -\frac{2e^{\frac{1}{x^2}}}{x^3}.$$

PROBLEM

Find the derivative of:

$$y = \left(e^{\frac{1}{x}}\right)^2.$$

SOLUTION

We can first rewrite the function as:

$$y = e^{\frac{2}{x}}.$$

Now we use the formula:

$$\frac{d}{dx} e^u = e^u \frac{du}{dx},$$

letting $u = \frac{2}{x}$. Then,

$$\frac{du}{dx} = \frac{(x)(0)-(2)(1)}{x^2} = -\frac{2}{x^2}.$$

Applying the formula, we obtain:

$$\frac{dy}{dx} = e^{\frac{2}{x}} \cdot -\frac{2}{x^2}$$

$$= -\frac{2e^{\frac{2}{x}}}{x^2}.$$

Steps in Logarithmic Differentiation

1. $y = f(x)$ given
2. $\ln y = \ln f(x)$ take logs and simplify
3. $D_x (\ln y) = D_x (\ln f(x))$ differentiate implicitly
4. $\frac{1}{y} D_x y = D_x (\ln f(x))$
5. $D_x y = f(x) D_x (\ln f(x))$ multiply by $y = f(x)$

To complete the solution it is necessary to differentiate $\ln f(x)$. If $f(x) < 0$ for some x then step 2 is invalid and we should replace step 1 by $|y| = |f(x)|$, and then proceed.

Example: $y = (x+5)(x^4+1)$

$$\ln y = \ln[(x+5)(x^4+1)] = \ln(x+5)+\ln(x^4+1)$$

$$\frac{d}{dx} \ln y = \frac{d}{dx} \ln(x+5) + \frac{d}{dx} \ln(x^4+1)$$

$$\frac{1}{y} \frac{dy}{dx} = \frac{1}{x+5} + \frac{4x^3}{x^4+1}$$

$$\frac{dy}{dx} = (x+5)(x^4+1) \left[\frac{1}{x+5} + \frac{4x^3}{x^4+1} \right]$$

$$= (x^4+1) + 4x^3(x+5)$$

This is the same result as obtained by using the product rule.

PROBLEM

Find the derivative of $y = \ln(1 - 2x)^3$

SOLUTION

It is best to rewrite the equation as:

$$y = 3 \ln(1 - 2x).$$

Then we apply the formula:

$$\frac{d}{dx} \ln u = \frac{1}{u} \frac{du}{dx},$$

letting $u = (1 - 2x)$. Then $\frac{du}{dx} = -2$. We obtain:

$$\frac{dy}{dx} = 3 \left(\frac{1}{1-2x} \right) (-2) = \frac{-6}{1-2x}.$$

High-Order Derivatives

The derivative of any function is also a legitimate function which we can differentiate. The second derivative can be obtained by:

$$\frac{d}{dx} \left[\frac{d}{dx} u \right] = \frac{d^2}{dx^2} u = u'' = D^2 u,$$

where $u = g(x)$ is differentiable.

The general formula for higher orders and the nth derivative of u is,

$$\underbrace{\frac{d}{dx} \frac{d}{dx} \cdots \frac{d}{dx}}_{n \text{ times}} u = \frac{d^{(n)}}{dx^n} u = u^{(n)} = D_x^{(n)} u.$$

The rules for first-order derivatives apply at each stage of higher-order differentiation (e.g., sums, products, chain rule).

A function which satisfies the condition that its nth derivative is zero, is the general polynomial

$$p_{n-1}(x) = a_{n-1} x^{n-1} + a_{n-2} x^{n-2} + \dots + a_0.$$

PROBLEM

> Find the sixth derivative of $y = x^6$.

SOLUTION

First derivative $= 6x^{6-1} = 6x^5$

Second derivative $= 5 \cdot 6x^{5-1} = 30x^4$

Third derivative $= 4 \cdot 30x^{4-1} = 120x^3$

Fourth derivative $= 3 \cdot 120x^{3-1} = 360x^2$

Fifth derivative $= 2 \cdot 360x^{2-1} = 720x^1 = 720x$

Sixth derivative $= 1 \cdot 720x^{1-1} = 720x^0 = 720$

The seventh derivative is seen to be zero, and therefore the function $y = x^6$ has seven derivatives.

PROBLEM

> Find y'' for the expression $xy^3 = 1$.

SOLUTION

To find the second derivative, y'', we must first find the first derivative and then differentiate that to obtain the second derivative. We could solve for y and then differentiate to obtain y', but an alternative is implicit differentiation,

$$xy^3 = 1.$$

Differentiating implicitly,

$$3xy^2 \cdot y' + y^3 = 0.$$
$$3xy^2 \cdot y' = -y^3.$$
$$y' = \frac{-y^3}{3xy^2}$$

$$= -\frac{y}{3x}.$$

Now we take the derivative of y' to find y''.

$$y'' = -\frac{1}{3}\left[\frac{x \cdot y' - y}{x^2}\right].$$

Substituting $y' = -\dfrac{y}{3x}$ in the expression for y'' and simplifying

$$y'' = -\frac{1}{3}\left[\frac{-x\left(\dfrac{-y}{3x}\right) - y}{x^2}\right]$$

$$= -\frac{1}{3}\left[\frac{-\dfrac{y}{3} - y}{x^2}\right]$$

$$= -\frac{1}{3}\left[\frac{-\dfrac{4}{3}y}{x^2}\right]$$

$$= \frac{4y}{9x^2}.$$

Application of the Derivative

Rolle's Theorem

Let f be continuous on a closed interval $[a,b]$. Assume $f'(x)$ exists at each point in the open interval (a,b).

If $f(a) = f(b) = 0$ then there is at least one point (x_0) in (a,b) such that $f'(x_0) = 0$.

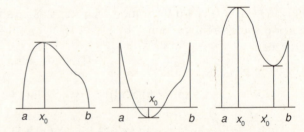

Three functions which satisfy the hypotheses, hence the conclusion, of Rolle's theorem.

The Mean Value Theorem

If f is continuous on $[a,b]$ and has a derivative at every point in the interval (a,b), then there is at least one number c in (a,b) such that

$$f'(c) = \frac{f(b) - f(a)}{b - a}$$

Notice in the Figure that the secant has slope

$$\frac{f(b) - f(a)}{b - a}$$

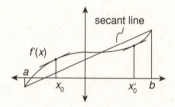

and $f'(x)$ has slope of the tangent to the point $(x, f(x))$. For some x_0 in (a,b) these slopes are equal.

PROBLEM

a) State and prove the Mean Value Theorem for the derivative of a real valued function of a single real variable.

b) Give a geometrical interpretation to this result.

SOLUTION

a) Let f be a real valued function of a real variable, x, which is continuous on a closed interval $[a,b]$ and has a derivative in the open interval (a,b). Then the Mean Value Theorem states that there exists a point c in (a,b) such that

$$f(b) - f(a) = f'(c)(b - a).$$

To prove this theorem, consider the function

$$\phi(x) = f'(x) - \left(f(a) + \frac{f(b) - f(a)}{b - a}(x - a) \right).$$

As can be seen from the Figure, θ is the difference of f and the linear function whose graph consists of the line segment passing through the points $(a, f(a))$ and $(b, f(b))$. Since f is continous on $[a,b]$, so is θ and since f

has a derivative at all points in (a, b), so does θ. Furthermore, $\theta(a) = \theta(b) = 0$ so that all the conditions of Rolle's Theorem are satisfied for the function $\theta(x)$. Hence the conclusion of that theorem holds; i.e., there is a point $c \in (a, b)$ such that

$$\phi(c) = f'(c) - \frac{f(b) - f(a)}{b - a} = 0$$

or

$$f'(c) = \frac{f(b) - f(a)}{b - a}.$$

Thus, the theorem is proved.

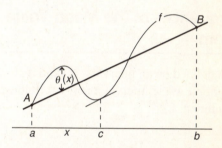

b) The geometrical interpretation of the equation can be seen in the Figure. The equation states that there is a point c whose tangent line has the same slope as (i.e., is parallel to) the line connecting A and B.

PROBLEM

If $f(x) = 3x^2 - x + 1$, find the point x_0 at which $f'(x)$ assumes its mean value in the interval $[2,4]$.

SOLUTION

Recall the Mean Value Theorem. Given a function $f(x)$ which is continuous in $[a,b]$ and differentiable in (a, b), there exists a point x_0 where $a < x_0 < b$ such that:

$$\frac{f(b) - f(a)}{b - a} = f'(x_0).$$

Where x_0 is the mean point in the interval.

In our problem, $3x^2 - x + 1$ is continuous, and the derivative exists in the interval $(2,4)$. We have:

$$\frac{f(4) - f(2)}{4 - 2} = \frac{[3(4)^2 - 4 + 1] - [3(2)^2 - 2 + 1]}{4 - 2}$$
$$= f'(x_0),$$

or

$$\frac{45 - 11}{2} = 17 = f'(x_0) = 6x_0 - 1.$$
$$6x_0 = 18$$
$$x_0 = 3.$$

$x_0 = 3$ is the point where $f'(x)$ assumes its mean value.

Consequences of the Mean Value Theorem

A) If f is defined on an interval (a,b) and if $f'(x) = 0$ for each point in the interval, then $f(x)$ is constant over the interval.

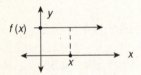

B) Let f and g be differentiable on an interval (a,b). If, for each point x in the interval, $f'(x)$ and $g'(x)$ are equal, then there is a constant, c, such that

$f(x) + c = g(x)$ for all x.

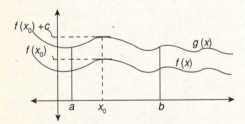

$f(x) + C = g(x)$ for all x

C) The Extended Mean Value Theorem. Assume that the function f and its derivative f' are continuous on $[a,b]$ and that f'' exists at each point x in (a,b), then there exists at least one point x_0, $a < x_0 < b$, such that

$$f(b) = f(a) + (b - a)f'(a) + \tfrac{1}{2}(b - a)^2 f''(x_0).$$

PROBLEM

Show: $e^x \geq 1 + x$ for all real numbers x.

SOLUTION

Divide the problem into 3 cases; $x = 0$, $x > 0$, $x < 0$.

Case 1. $x = 0$

For $x = 0$, we have $e^0 \geq 1 + 0$, or $1 = 1$.

Case 2. $x > 0$

For this case, we apply the Mean Value Theorem. We let

$f(x) = e^x$

and the interval will be $[0, x]$. Applying the theorem, we have

$$\frac{f(x) - f(0)}{x - 0} = \frac{e^x - e^0}{x - 0} = f'(x_0) = e^{x_0},$$

where $0 < x_0 < x$.

Simplifying, we have:

$$e^x = e^{x_0} \cdot x + e^0 = xe^{x_0} + 1$$

since $x_0 > 0$, $e^{x_0} > 1$. Therefore

$e^x > x + 1$

Case 3. $x < 0$

Solution is similar to Case 2 and will be left to the reader as an exercise.

Combining the three results, we have the desired inequality.

The Mean Value Theorem for the integral has a very simple geometric interpretation.

The Mean Value Theorem says that for a continuous function on the closed interval $[a, b]$, there exists a point x_0, where $a < x_0 < b$, such that:

$$f(x_0) = \frac{1}{b - a} \int_a^b f(x)\, dx.$$

If we multiply both sides by $(b - a)$ we have

$$(b - a)\, f(x_0) = \int_a^b f(x)\, dx,$$

which states that the integral from a to b is equal to the area of a rectangle of length $(b-a)$ and height $f(x_0)$. In the diagram, it means that the area in region 1 can be put in region 2, thus forming a rectangle.

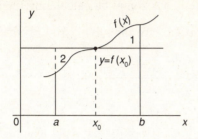

PROBLEM

What is the mean value or mean ordinate of the positive part of the curve $y = 2x - x^2$?

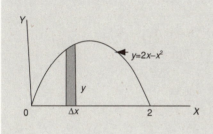

SOLUTION

First determine the length of the base to fix the limits of integration for the area by setting y equal to zero, or:

$0 = 2x - x^2 = x(2-x)$.

Then, $x_1 = 0$, and $x_2 = 2$.

Now,

$$\bar{y}_x = \frac{1}{x_2 - x_1} \int y \cdot dx$$

$$= \frac{1}{2-0} \int_0^2 (2x - x^2)\, dx$$

$$= \int_0^2 \left(x - \frac{x^2}{2} \right) dx$$

$$= \frac{x^2}{2} - \frac{x^3}{6} \Big|_0^2 = \frac{4}{2} - \frac{8}{6} = \frac{2}{3},$$

the mean ordinate.

L'Hôpital's Rule

An application of the Mean Value Theorem is in the evaluation of

$$\lim_{x \to a} \frac{f(x)}{g(x)} \text{ where } f(a)=0 \text{ and } g(a)=0.$$

L'Hôpital's rule states that if the $\lim_{x \to a} \frac{f(x)}{g(x)}$ is an indeterminate form (i.e., $\frac{0}{0}$ or $\frac{\infty}{\infty}$), then we can differentiate the numerator and the denominator separately and arrive at an expression that has the same limit as the original problem.

Thus, $\lim_{x \to a} \frac{f(x)}{g(x)} = \lim_{x \to a} \frac{f'(x)}{g'(x)}$

In general, if $f(x)$ and $g(x)$ have properties

1) $f(a) = g(a) = 0$

2) $f^{(k)}(a) = g^{(k)}(a) = 0$ for $k = 1, 2, \ldots n$

but 3) $f^{(n+1)}(a)$ or $g^{(n+1)}(a)$ is not equal to zero, then

$$\lim_{x \to a} \frac{f(x)}{g(x)} = \frac{f^{(n+1)}(x)}{g^{(n+1)}(x)}$$

PROBLEM

Evaluate $\lim_{x \to 2} \dfrac{(2x^2 - 4x)}{x - 2}$.

SOLUTION

The function takes the form $\frac{0}{0}$ and therefore we can apply L'Hôpital's rule to obtain:

$$\lim_{x \to 2} \frac{4x - 4}{1} = 4$$

We can also solve the problem in a different way by noting that the numerator can be factored.

$$\lim_{x \to 2} \frac{2x^2 - 4x}{x - 2} = \lim_{x \to 2} \frac{2x(x-2)}{x-2}$$

$$= \lim_{x \to 2} 2x$$

$$= 4.$$

PROBLEM

$$\text{Find } \lim_{x \to 3} \frac{x^2 - x - 6}{x - 3}$$

SOLUTION

This limit may be found by writing

$$\frac{x^2 - x - 6}{x - 3} = \frac{(x + 2)(x - 3)}{x - 3} = x + 2.$$

Hence $\lim_{x \to 3} (x + 2) = 5.$

Since $\frac{0}{0}$ (indeterminate) is obtained by substitution in the original function, the limit may also be obtained by L'Hôpital's rule by differentiating separately the numerator and denominator. Thus

$$\lim_{x \to 3} \frac{x^2 - x - 6}{x - 3} = \lim_{x \to 3} \frac{2x - 1}{1} = 5.$$

The application of L'Hôpital's rule is the more systematic approach and should generally be tried first, if another method is not immediately apparent.

Tangents and Normals

Tangents

A line which is tangent to a curve at a point "*a*", must have the same slope as the curve. That is, the slope of the tangent is simply

$$m = \lim_{h \to 0} \frac{f(a + h) - f(a)}{h}$$

Therefore, if we find the derivative of a curve and evaluate for a specific point, we obtain the slope of the curve and the tangent line to the curve at that point.

A curve is said to have a vertical tangent at a point $(a, f(a))$ if f is continuous at a and $\lim_{x \to a} |f'(x)| = \infty.$

PROBLEM

Using the Δ-method, find the points on the curve:
$y = \frac{x}{3} + \frac{3}{x}$, at which the tangent line is horizontal.

SOLUTION

When the slope of a curve equals zero, the curve has a horizontal tangent. We can find the points at which the tangent line is horizontal by calculating the slope $\frac{dy}{dx}$, setting it equal to zero and solving for x. By the Δ-method,

$$\frac{\Delta y}{\Delta x} = \frac{f(x + \Delta x) - f(x)}{\Delta x}$$

$$\frac{\Delta y}{\Delta x} = \frac{\dfrac{(x + \Delta x)}{3} + \dfrac{3}{(x + \Delta x)} - \left(\dfrac{x}{3} - \dfrac{3}{x} \right)}{\Delta x}$$

$$= \frac{\dfrac{x}{3} + \dfrac{\Delta x}{3} + \dfrac{3}{x + \Delta x} - \dfrac{x}{3} - \dfrac{3}{x}}{\Delta x}$$

$$= \frac{\dfrac{\Delta x}{3} + \dfrac{3}{x + \Delta x} - \dfrac{3}{x}}{\Delta x}.$$

$$\frac{\Delta y}{\Delta x} = \frac{\dfrac{x^2 \Delta x + x(\Delta x)^2 - 9 \Delta x}{3(x + \Delta x)x}}{\Delta x}$$

$$= \frac{x^2 + x \Delta x - 9}{3x^2 + 3x \Delta x}.$$

$$\frac{dy}{dx} = \lim_{\Delta x \to 0} \frac{\Delta y}{\Delta x} = \lim_{\Delta x \to 0} \frac{x^2 + x \Delta x - 9}{3x^2 + 3x \Delta x} = \frac{x^2 - 9}{3x^2}.$$

We can set this value, which is the slope, equal to zero and solve for x.

$$\frac{x^2 - 9}{3x^2} = 0$$

$$\frac{(x - 3)(x + 3)}{x(3x)} = 0$$

$$x = 3, \ x = -3.$$

(Remember that x cannot be zero, for that would give an infinite slope.)

Substituting these values for x back into $y = \frac{x}{3} + \frac{3}{x}$, we can obtain the y coordinates. We find $(3, 2)$ and $(-3, -2)$ to be the required points.

Normals

A line normal to a curve at a point must have a slope perpendicular to the slope of the tangent line. If

$f'(x) \neq 0$ then the equation for the normal line at a point (x_0, y_0) is

$$y - y_0 = \frac{-1}{f'(x_0)}(x - x_0).$$

PROBLEM

Find the equations of the tangent line and the normal to the curve: $y = x^2 - x + 3$, at the point (2, 5).

SOLUTION

Since the equation of a straight line passing through a given point can be expressed in the form: $y - y_1 = m(x - x_1)$, this is appropriate for finding the equations of the tangent and normal. Here $x_1 = 2$ and $y_1 = 5$. The slope, m, of the tangent line is found by taking the derivative, $\frac{dy}{dx}$, of the curve: $y = x^2 - x + 3$.

$$\frac{dy}{dx} = 2x - 1.$$

At (2, 5), $\frac{dy}{dx} = 2(2) - 1 = 3$, therefore the slope, m, of the tangent line is 3. Substituting x_1, y_1 and m into the equation $y - y_1 = m(x - x_1)$ we obtain:

$$y - 5 = 3(x - 2),$$

as the equation of the tangent line, or

$$3x - y - 1 = 0.$$

Since the slope of the normal is given by: $m' = -\frac{1}{m}$, and since $m = 3$, the slope of the normal is $m' = -\frac{1}{3}$. Substituting $x_1 = 2$, $y_1 = 5$

and the slope of the normal, $m' = -\frac{1}{3}$, into the equation: $y - y_1 = m'(x - x_1)$, we obtain:

$$y - 5 = -\frac{1}{3}(x - 2).$$

or

$$x + 3y - 17 = 0.$$

This is the equation of the normal.

Minimum and Maximum Values

If a function f is defined on an interval I, then

a) f is increasing on I if $f(x_1) < f(x_2)$ whenever x_1, x_2 are in I and $x_1 < x_2$.

b) f is decreasing on I if $f(x_1) > f(x_2)$ whenever $x_1 < x_2$ in I.

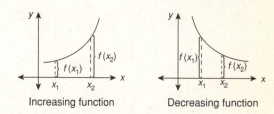

Increasing function   Decreasing function

c) f is constant if $f(x_1) = f(x_2)$ for every x_1, x_2 in I.

Suppose f is defined on an open interval I and c is a number in I then,

a) $f(c)$ is a local maximum value if $f(x) \leq f(c)$ for all x in I.

b) $f(c)$ is a local minimum value if $f(x) \geq f(c)$ for all x in I.

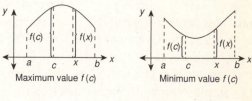

Maximum value $f(c)$ Minimum value $f(c)$

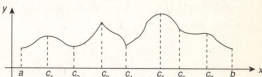

In the figure above in the interval $[a,b]$, the local maxima occur at c_1, c_3, c_5, with an absolute maximum at c_5 and local minima occur at c_2, c_4.

To find Absolute Extrema for functions, first calculate $f(c)$ for each critical number c, then calculate $f(a)$ and $f(b)$. The absolute extrema of f on $[a,b]$ will then be the largest and the smallest of these functional values. If $f(a)$ or $f(b)$ is an extremum we call it an endpoint extremum.

Viewing the derivative as the slope of a curve, there may be points (or critical values) where the curve has a zero derivative. At these values the tangent to the curve is horizontal.

Conversely, if the derivative at a point exists and is not zero, then the point is not a local extrema.

PROBLEM

> Find the maxima and minima of the function $f(x) = x^4$.

SOLUTION

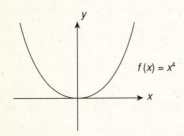

To determine maxima and minima we find $f'(x)$, set it equal to 0, and solve for x to obtain the critical points. We find: $f'(x) = 4x^3 = 0$, therefore $x = 0$ is the critical value. We must now determine whether $x = 0$ is a maximum or minimum value. In this example the Second Derivative Test fails because $f''(x) = 12x^2$ and $f''(0) = 0$. We must, therefore, use the First Derivative Test. We examine $f'(x)$ when $x < 0$, and when $x > 0$. We find that for $x < 0$, $f'(x)$ is negative, and for $x > 0$, $f'(x)$ is positive. Therefore there is a minimum at $(0, 0)$. (See figure.)

PROBLEM

> Locate the maxima and minima of $y = 2x^2 - 8x + 6$.

SOLUTION

To obtain the minima and maxima we find $\dfrac{dy}{dx}$, set it equal to 0 and solve for x. We find:

$$\frac{dy}{dx} = 4x - 8 = 0.$$

Therefore, $x = 2$ is the critical point. We now use the Second Derivative Test to determine whether $x = 2$ is a maximum or a minimum. We find:

$\dfrac{d^2 y}{dx^2} = 4$, (positive). The second derivative is positive, hence $x = 2$ is a minimum.

Now substitute this back into the original equation to get the corresponding ordinate.

$$y = 2x^2 - 8x + 6 = 2 \cdot 2^2 - 8 \cdot 2 + 6 = 8 - 16 + 6$$
$$= -2.$$

Therefore, the minimum is at $x = 2$, $y = -2$.

Solving Maxima and Minima Problems

Step 1. Determine which variable is to be maximized or minimized (i.e., the dependent variable y).

Step 2. Find the independent variable x.

Step 3. Write an equation involving x and y. All other variables can be eliminated by substitution.

Step 4. Differentiate with respect to the independent variable.

Step 5. Set the derivative equal to zero to obtain critical values.

Step 6. Determine maxima and minima.

PROBLEM

> Locate the maxima and minima of
> $$y = \frac{x^3}{3} - \frac{5x^2}{2} + 6x + 4.$$
>
>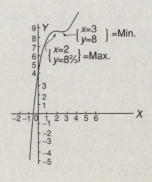

SOLUTION

To find the maxima and minima we find $\dfrac{dy}{dx}$, set it to 0, and solve for x, obtaining the critical points. Doing this we have:

$$\frac{dy}{dx} = x^2 - 5x + 6 = 0, \quad (x-2)(x-3) = 0$$

therefore,

$x = 3$ and 2.

We now use the Second Derivative Test to determine whether the critical values are maximum, minimum, or neither. We find:

$$\frac{d^2y}{dx^2} = 2x - 5.$$

For $x = 3$,

$$\frac{d^2y}{dx^2} = 2x - 5 = 2 \cdot 3 - 5 = +(positive),$$

which indicates a minimum.

For $x = 2$,

$$\frac{d^2y}{dx^2} = 2x - 5 = 2 \cdot 2 - 5 = -(negative),$$

which indicates a maximum.

Therefore, we have a minimum at $x = 3$ and a maximum at $x = 2$. We now wish to find the corresponding ordinates. Going back to the original equation, we have:

For $x = 3$,

$$y = \frac{x^3}{3} - \frac{5x^2}{2} + 6x + 4 = \frac{3^3}{3} - \frac{5 \cdot 3^2}{2} + 6 \cdot 3 + 4$$

$$= 9 - \frac{45}{2} + 18 + 4 = 8\frac{1}{2}.$$

For $x = 2$,

$$y = \frac{x^3}{3} - \frac{5x^2}{2} + 6x + 4 = \frac{2^3}{3} - \frac{5 \cdot 2^2}{2} + 6 \cdot 2 + 4$$

$$= \frac{8}{3} - 10 + 12 + 4 = 8\frac{2}{3}.$$

Therefore, minimum is at $x = 3$, $y = 8\dfrac{1}{2}$, and maximum is at $x = 2$, $y = 8\dfrac{2}{3}$.

Curve Sketching and the Derivative Tests

Using the knowledge we have about local extrema and the following properties of the first and second derivatives of a function, we can gain a better understanding of the graphs (and thereby the nature) of a given function.

A function is said to be smooth on an interval (a,b) if both f' and f'' exist for all $x \in (a,b)$.

The First Derivative Test

Suppose that c is a critical value of a function, f, in an interval (a,b), then if f is continuous and differentiable we can say that,

a) if $f'(x) > 0$ for all $a < x < c$ and $f'(x) < 0$ for all $c < x < b$, then $f(c)$ is a local maximum.

b) if $f'(x) < 0$ for $a < x < c$ and $f'(x) > 0$ for $c < x < b$, then $f(c)$ is a local minimum.

c) if $f'(x) > 0$ or if $f'(x) < 0$ for all $x \in (a,b)$ then $f(c)$ is not a local extrema.

PROBLEM

Find the maxima and minima of $f(x) = 3x^5 - 5x^3$.

SOLUTION

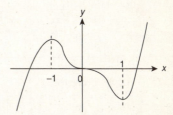

To determine maxima and minima we find $f'(x)$, set it equal to 0 and solve for x, obtaining the critical points. We find:

$$f'(x) = 15x^4 - 15x^2 = 15x^2(x^2 - 1).$$

Therefore, $x = 0, \pm 1$ are the critical points. We must now determine whether the function reaches a maximum, minimum or neither at each of these values. To do this we will use the second Derivative Test. Computing the second derivative f'', we have:

$$f''(x) = 60x^3 - 30x = 30(2x^2 - 1).$$

$f''(1) = 30 > 0$. Therefore, $x = 1$ is a relative minimum point and $x = -1$ is a relative maximum since $f''(-1) = -30 < 0$. Now, $f''(0) = 0$. Therefore the Second Derivative Test indicates a point which is neither maximum nor minimum. This is known as a point of inflection. For further study of the behavior of f at 0 we must use the First Derivative Test. We examine $f'(x)$ when $-1 < x < 0$ and when $0 < x < 1$. Let us select a representative value from each interval. We will use

$$x = -\frac{1}{2} \quad \text{and} \quad x = \frac{1}{2}. \quad \text{For } f'\left(-\frac{1}{2}\right) \text{ we obtain a}$$

negative value, and for $f'\left(\dfrac{1}{2}\right)$ we again obtain a negative value. Because there is no change in sign we conclude that at $x = 0$ there is neither a maximum nor a minimum, as can also be seen from the graph.

Concavity

If a function is differentiable on an open interval containing c, then the graph at this point is

a) concave upward (or convex) if $f''(c) > 0$;
b) concave downward if $f''(c) < 0$.

If a function is concave upward than f' is increasing as x increases. If the function is concave downward, f' is decreasing as x increases.

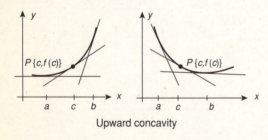

Upward concavity

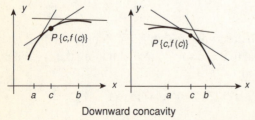

Downward concavity

PROBLEM

Find the intervals of x for which the curve

$$y = 2x^3 - 9x^2 + 12x - 3$$

is concave downward and concave upward,

SOLUTION

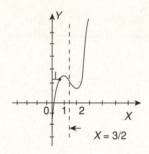

Differentiating twice,

$$\frac{dy}{dx} = 6(x^2 - 3x + 2)$$

and

$$\frac{d^2y}{dx^2} = 6(2x - 3)$$

By setting $\dfrac{d^2y}{dx^2} = 0$, we have $x = \dfrac{3}{2}$

y'' is positive or negative according to $x > \dfrac{3}{2}$ or $< \dfrac{3}{2}$. Hence the graph is concave downward to the left of $x = \dfrac{3}{2}$ and concave upward to the right of $x = \dfrac{3}{2}$.

Points of Inflection

Points which satisfy $f''(x) = 0$ may be positions where concavity changes. These points are called the points of inflection. It is the point at which the curve crosses its tangent line.

PROBLEM

Investigate the function $y = (x - a)^{\frac{1}{3}}$ $(2x - a)^{\frac{2}{3}}$ for maxima and minima.

SOLUTION

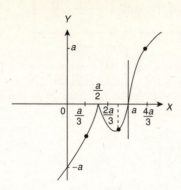

Differentiating

$$y' = \frac{(2x-a)^{\frac{2}{3}}}{3(x-a)^{\frac{2}{3}}} + \frac{4(x-a)^{\frac{1}{3}}}{3(2x-a)^{\frac{1}{3}}} = \frac{6x-5a}{3(x-a)^{\frac{2}{3}}(2x-a)^{\frac{1}{3}}}.$$

From $y' = 0$, and $\frac{1}{y'} = 0$, the critical points are

$$x = \frac{a}{2}, \ x = \frac{5a}{6}, \ x = a.$$

We must now determine whether each of these critical points is a maximum, minimum or neither. We choose a value of x less than and a value greater than each of the critical values and evaluate y' at these values. If the sign changes from positive to negative, we have a maximum. If it changes from negative to positive, we have a minimum. If the sign does not change there is neither one at that critical value.

Setting $x = \frac{a}{3}$ and $\frac{2a}{3}$ in turn, we have y' positive and negative respectively. Hence $x = \frac{a}{2}$ makes y a maximum.

Test $x = \frac{5a}{6}$, using values $\frac{2a}{3}$ and $\frac{9a}{10}$.

These show y' to be successively negative and positive, so the function has a minimum value at $x = \frac{5a}{6}$.

Apply the test to $x = a$, with the values $\frac{9a}{10}$ and $2a$. These show y' positive in both cases, therefore, at $x = a$ there is neither a maximum or a minimum. We observe that $y' = \frac{a}{0} = \infty$ at $x = a$, therefore the graph has a vertical tangent at this value. At $x = a$ there is a point of inflection as shown. The maximum point at $(\frac{a}{2}, 0)$ is called a cusp.

Graphing a Function Using the Derivative Tests

The following steps will help us gain a rapid understanding of a function's behavior.

A) Look for some basic properties such as oddness, evenness, periodicity, boundedness, etc.

B) Locate all the zeros by setting $f(x) = 0$.

C) Determine any singularities, $f(x) = \infty$.

D) Set $f'(x)$ equal to zero to find the critical values.

E) Find the points of inflection by setting $f''(x) = 0$.

F) Determine where the curve is concave, $f''(x) < 0$, and where it is convex $f''(x) > 0$.

G) Determine the limiting properties and approximations for large and small $|x|$.

H) Prepare a table of values $x, f(x), f'(x)$ which includes the critical values and the points of inflection.

I) Plot the points found in Step H and draw short tangent lines at each point.

J) Draw the curve making use of the knowledge of concavity and continuity.

PROBLEM

Find the maxima and minima of:
$$y = \frac{4}{x^2 - 4}, \text{ and trace the curve.}$$

SOLUTION

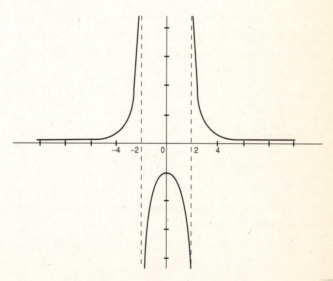

To find the maxima and minima we determine $\dfrac{dy}{dx}$, equate it to 0, and solve for x, obtaining the critical value. We find:

$$\frac{dy}{dx} = \frac{(x^2 - 4)(0) - 4(2x)}{(x^2 - 4)^2} = -\frac{8x}{(x^2 - 4)^2}.$$

$\dfrac{-8x}{(x^2 - 4)^2} = 0$, therefore $x = 0$. Substituting $x = 0$, into the original equation, $y = -1$, therefore the critical point is $(0, -1)$.

To determine whether a maximum, minimum, or neither occurs at this point, we use the First Derivative Test. We examine $\dfrac{dy}{dx}$ at a point less than 0, (use –1), and at a point greater than 0 (use 1). If $\dfrac{dy}{dx}$ changes sign from + to –, a maximum occurs at $x = 0$, from – to +, a minimum occurs, and if there is no change in sign, neither a maximum nor a minimum occurs. We find that at $x = -1$, $\dfrac{dy}{dx} = \dfrac{8}{9}$, a positive value, and at $x = 1$, $\dfrac{dy}{dx} = -\dfrac{8}{9}$, a negative value. Therefore, at the point $(0, -1)$, a maximum occurs.

Upon further investigation of the curve: $y = \dfrac{4}{x^2 - 4}$, we observe that for the values $x = 2, -2$, y is undefined or $y = \pm \infty$. Therefore, the graph of the curve has asymptotes at 2 and –2, as shown in the accompanying graph.

Rectilinear Motion

When an object moves along a straight line we call the motion rectilinear motion. Distance s, velocity v, and acceleration a, are the chief concerns of the study of motion.

Velocity is the proportion of distance over time.

$$\boxed{v = s/t}$$

$$\text{Average velocity} = \frac{s(t_2) - s(t_1)}{t_2 - t_1}$$

where t_1, t_2 are time instances and $s(t_2) - s(t_1)$ is the displacement of an object.

Instantaneous velocity at time t is defined as

$$\boxed{v = D\, s(t) = \lim_{h \to 0} \frac{s(t+h) - s(t)}{h}}$$

We usually write $\boxed{v(t) = \dfrac{ds}{dt}}$.

Acceleration, the rate of change of velocity with respect to time is

$$\boxed{a(t) = \frac{dv}{dt}}.$$

It follows clearly that

$$a(t) = v'(t) = s''(t).$$

When motion is due to gravitational effects, $g = 32.2$ ft/sec^2 or $g = 9.81$ m/sec^2 is usually substituted for acceleration.

Speed at time t is defined as $|v(t)|$. The speed indicates how fast an object is moving without specifying the direction of motion.

PROBLEM

A rope attached to a boat is being pulled in at a rate of 10 ft/sec. If the water is 20 ft below the level at which the rope is being drawn in, how fast is the boat approaching the wharf when 36 ft of rope are yet to be pulled in?

SOLUTION

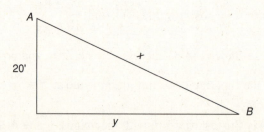

The length AB denotes the rope, and the position of the boat is at B. Since the rope is being drawn in at a rate of 10ft/sec.

$$\frac{dx}{dt} = 10.$$

To find how fast the boat is being towed in when 36 ft. of rope are left,

$\dfrac{dy}{dt}$ must be found at $x = 36$.

From the right triangle, $20^2 + y^2 = x^2$ or

$y = \sqrt{x^2 - 400}$. Differentiating with respect to t,

$$\frac{dy}{dt} = \frac{dy}{dx} \cdot \frac{dx}{dt} = \frac{1}{2}(x^2 - 400)^{-\frac{1}{2}}(2x)\frac{dx}{dt} = \frac{x\dfrac{dx}{dt}}{\sqrt{x^2 - 400}}.$$

Substituting the conditions that:

$$\frac{dx}{dt} = -10 \text{ and } x = 36,$$

$$\frac{dy}{dt} = \frac{-360}{\sqrt{896}} = -\frac{45}{\sqrt{14}}.$$

It has now been found that, when there are 36 ft of rope left, the boat is moving in at the rate of:

$$\frac{45}{\sqrt{14}} \text{ ft / sec}.$$

PROBLEM

A boat is being hauled toward a pier at a height of 20 ft above the water level. The rope is drawn in at a rate of 6ft/sec. Neglecting sag, how fast is the boat approaching the base of the pier when 25 ft of rope remain to be pulled in?

SOLUTION

Formulating the given data, we have:
$\dfrac{dz}{dt} = 6$, $z = 25$, and $\dfrac{dx}{dt}$ is to be found.
At any time t we have, from, the Pythagorean theorem,
$$20^2 + x^2 = z^2$$

By differentiation, we obtain:

$$x\frac{dx}{dt} = z\frac{dz}{dt}$$

When $z = 25$, $x = \sqrt{25^2 - 20^2} = 15$; therefore

$$15\frac{dx}{dt} = 25(-6)$$

$$\frac{dx}{dt} = -10 \text{ ft / sec}$$

(The boat approaches the base at 10 ft/sec).

Rate of Change and Related Rates

Rate of Change

In the last section we saw how functions of time can be expressed as velocity and acceleration. In general, we can speak about the rate of change of any function with respect to an arbitrary parameter (such as time in the previous section).

For linear functions $f(x) = mx + b$, the rate of change is simply the slope m.

For non-linear functions we define the

1) average rate of change between points c and d to be

$$\frac{f(d) - f(c)}{d - c}$$

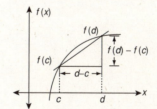

2) instantaneous rate of change of f at the point x to be

$$f'(x) = \lim_{h \to 0} \frac{f(x+h) - f(x)}{h}$$

If the limit does not exist, then the rate of change of f at x is not defined.

The form, common to all related rate problems, is as follows:

a) Two variables, x and y are given. They are functions of time, but the explicit functions are not given.

b) The variables, x and y are related to each other by some equation such as $x^2 + y^3 - 2x - 7y^2 + 2 = 0$.

c) An equation which involves the rate of change $\dfrac{dx}{dt}$ and $\dfrac{dy}{dt}$ is obtained by differentiating with respect to t and using the chain rule.

As an illustration, the previous equation leads to

$$2x\frac{dx}{dt} + 3y^2\frac{dy}{dt} - 2\frac{dx}{dt} - 14y\frac{dy}{dt} = 0$$

The derivatives $\dfrac{dx}{dt}$ and $\dfrac{dy}{dt}$ in this equation are called the related rates.

PROBLEM

Compute the average rate of change of $y = f(x) = x^2 - 2$ between $x = 3$ and $x = 4$.

SOLUTION

Average rate of change is defined as:

$\dfrac{\Delta y}{\Delta x}$ with $\Delta y = f(x + \Delta x) - f(x)$.

Given: $x = 3$, $\Delta x = 4 - 3 = 1$,

$y = f(x) = f(3) = 3^2 - 2 = 7$

For $x = 4$,

$y + \Delta y = f(x + \Delta x) = 4^2 - 2 = 14$

$\Delta y = f(x + \Delta x) - f(x) = f(4) - f(3)$

$\qquad = (4^2 - 2) - (3^2 - 2) = 14 - 7 = 7$

$\dfrac{\Delta y}{\Delta x} = \dfrac{7}{1} = 7$, the average rate of change.

PROBLEM

Find the rate of change of y with respect to x at the point $x = 5$, if $2y = x^2 + 3x - 1$.

SOLUTION

Rate of change is defined as

$\lim\limits_{\Delta x \to 0} \dfrac{\Delta y}{\Delta x}$, with

$\Delta y = f(x + \Delta x) - f(x)$.

We have:

$2\Delta y = (x + \Delta x)^2 + 3(x + \Delta x) - 1 - (x^2 + 3x - 1)$

$= x^2 + 2x \cdot \Delta x + (\Delta x)^2 + 3x + 3\Delta x - 1 - x^2 - 3x + 1$

$= 2x \cdot \Delta x + (\Delta x)^2 + 3\Delta x.$

Dividing by Δx,

$\dfrac{2\Delta y}{\Delta x} = \dfrac{2x \cdot \Delta x}{\Delta x} + \dfrac{(\Delta x)^2}{\Delta x} + \dfrac{3\Delta x}{\Delta x}$

$= 2x + \Delta x + 3$

and

$\dfrac{\Delta y}{\Delta x} = x + \dfrac{\Delta x}{2} + \dfrac{3}{2}.$

Now,

$\lim\limits_{\Delta x \to 0} \dfrac{\Delta y}{\Delta x} = \lim\limits_{\Delta x \to 0} x + \dfrac{\Delta x}{2} + \dfrac{3}{2} = x + \dfrac{3}{2}.$

For $x = 5$,

$\lim\limits_{\Delta x \to 0} \dfrac{\Delta y}{\Delta x} = 5 + \dfrac{3}{2} = 6\dfrac{1}{2}$

This means that the instantaneous rate of change of the function represented by the curve at the point $x = 5$ is $6\dfrac{1}{2}$.

The function, it is seen, changes $6\dfrac{1}{2}$ times as fast as the independent variable x at $x = 5$.

The slope of the tangent at $x = 5$ is $6\dfrac{1}{2}$.

The Definite Integral

Antiderivatives

Definition:

If $F(x)$ is a function whose derivative $F'(x) = f(x)$, then $F(x)$ is called the antiderivative of $f(x)$.

THEOREM:

If $F(x)$ and $G(x)$ are two antiderivatives of $f(x)$, then $F(x) = G(x) + c$, where c is a constant.

Power Rule for Antidifferentiation

Let "a" be any real number, "r" any rational number not equal to -1, and "c" an arbitrary constant.

$$\text{If } f(x) = ax^r, \text{ then } F(x) = \frac{a}{r+1}x^{r+1} + c.$$

THEOREM:

An antiderivative of a sum is the sum of the antiderivatives.

$$\frac{d}{dx}(F_1 + F_2) = \frac{d}{dx}(F_1) + \frac{d}{dx}(F_2) = f_1 + f_2$$

Area

To find the area under the graph of a function f from a to b, we divide the interval $[a,b]$ into n subintervals, all having the same length $(b-a)/n$. This is illustated in the figure.

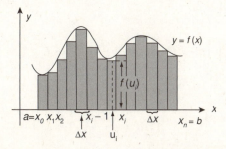

Since f is continuous on each subinterval, f takes on a minimum value at some number u_i in each subinterval.

We can construct a rectangle with one side of length $[x_{i-1}, x_i]$, and the other side of length equal to the minimum distance $f(u_i)$ from the x-axis to the graph of f.

The area of this rectangle is $f(u_i)\Delta x$. The boundary of the region formed by the sum of these rectangles is called the inscribed rectangular polygon.

The area (A) under the graph of f from a to b is

$$A = \lim_{\Delta x \to 0} \sum_{i=1} f(u_i)\Delta x.$$

The area A under the graph may also be obtained by means of circumscribed rectangular polygons.

In the case of the circumscribed rectangular polygons the maximum value of f on the interval $(x_{i-1}, x_i]$, v_i, is used.

Note that the area obtained using circumscribed rectangular polygons should always be larger than that obtained using inscribed rectangular polygons.

PROBLEM

Determine the area under the curve: $y = f(x) = x^2$ between $x = 2$ and $x = 3$.

SOLUTION

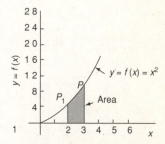

It is given that the area to be evaluated is between $x = 2$ and $x = 3$, therefore, these are the limits of the integral which gives us the required area. Area is equal to the integral of the upper function minus the lower function. From the diagram it is seen that the required area is between $y = x^2$ as the upper function and $y = 0$ (the x-axis) as the lower function. Therefore, we can write:

$$A = \int_2^3 (x^2 - 0)dx$$
$$= \int_2^3 x^2 dx$$
$$= \frac{x^3}{3}\Big]_2^3$$

$$A = \frac{3^3}{3} - \frac{2^3}{3} = \frac{19}{3}.$$

Definition of Definite Integral

A partition P of a closed interval $[a, b]$ is any decomposition of $[a, b]$ into subintervals of the form,

$$[x_0, x_1], [x_1, x_2], [x_2, x_3], \ldots, [x_{n-1}, x_n]$$

where n is a positive Integer and x_i are numbers, such that

$$a = x_0 < x_1 < x_2 < \ldots < x_{n-1} < x_n = b.$$

The length of the subinterval is $\Delta x_i = x_i - x_{i-1}$. The largest of the numbers $\Delta x_1, \Delta x_2 \ldots \Delta x_n$ is called the norm of the partition P and denoted by $\|P\|$.

$$\underbrace{\Delta x_1 = x_1 - x_0}\ \underbrace{\Delta x_2}\ \underbrace{\Delta x_3}\ \quad \underbrace{\Delta x_i}\ \quad \underbrace{\Delta x_n}$$
$$a = x_0 \quad x_1 \quad x_2 \quad x_3 \qquad\qquad b = xn$$

Definition:

Let f be a function that is defined on a closed interval $[a,b]$ and let P be a partition of $[a,b]$. A Riemann Sum of f for P is any expression R_p of the form,

$$R_p = \sum_{i=1}^{n} f(w_i)\Delta x_i,$$

where w_i is some number in $[x_{i-1}, x_i]$ for $i = 1, 2, \ldots, n$.

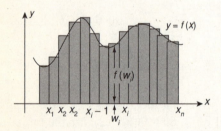

Definition:

Let f be a function that is defined on a closed interval $[a,b]$. The definite integral of f from a to b, denoted by

$$\int_a^b f(x)\,dx \text{ is given by}$$

$$\int_a^b f(x)\,dx = \lim_{\|P\| \to 0} \sum_i f(w_i)\Delta x_i$$

provided the limit exists.

THEOREM:

If f is continuous on $[a,b]$, then f is integrable on $[a,b]$ that is, the limit $\int_b^a f(x)\,dx$ exists.

THEOREM:

If $f(a)$ exists, then $\int_a^a f(x)\,dx = 0$.

PROBLEM

$$\frac{dy}{dx} = (a - bx)^n. \text{ What is } y = F(x)$$
$$\text{when } n = 2?$$

SOLUTION

$\frac{dy}{dx} = (a - bx)^n$ can be rewritten as $dy = (a - bx)^n dx$.

We can now write: $\int dy = \int (a - bx)^n dx$ or, $y = \int (a - bx)^n dx$. To integrate, we consider the formula: $\int u^n du = \frac{u^{n+1}}{n+1} + C$, with $u = (a - bx)$ and $du = -bdx$.

Applying the formula, we obtain:

$$y = \int (a - bx)^n \, dx = -\frac{1}{b} \cdot \frac{(a - bx)^{n+1}}{n+1}$$

$$= -\frac{(a - bx)^{n+1}}{b(n+1)} + C,$$

the integral in the general form.
For $n = 2$,

$$y = \int (a - bx)^2 \cdot dx = -\frac{(a - bx)^3}{3b} + C.$$

PROBLEM

$$\frac{dy}{dx} = (a + bx)^n. \text{ What is } y = F(x) \text{ when}$$
$$n = 1, n = 2, \text{ and } n = -2?$$

SOLUTION

In solving, we first find the integral in the general form and then substitute and find the integral for $n = 1$, $n = 2$, and $n = -2$.

$\dfrac{dy}{dx} = (a + bx)^n$ can be rewitten as

$dy = (a + bx)^n\, dx$. To find the integral, we write:

$\int dy = \int (a + bx)^n\, dx$ or, $y = \int (a + bx)^n\, dx$.

We now consider the formula:

$\int u^n du = \dfrac{u^{n+1}}{n+1} + C$, with $u = (a + bx)$ and $du = bdx$.

Applying the formula, we have:

$y = \int (a + bx)^n \cdot dx$

$= \dfrac{(a + bx)^{n+1}}{b(n+1)} + C,$

the integral in the general form.

For $n = 1$,

$\int (a + bx)^1\, dx = \dfrac{(a + bx)^{1+1}}{b(1+1)} = \dfrac{(a + bx)^2}{2b} + C.$

For $n = 2$,

$\int (a + bx)^2\, dx = \dfrac{(a + bx)^{2+1}}{b(2+1)} = \dfrac{(a + bx)^3}{3b} + C.$

For $n = -2$,

$\int \dfrac{dx}{(a + bx)^2} + \int (a + bx)^{-2} \cdot dx = \dfrac{(a + bx)^{-2+1}}{b(-2+1)}$

$= \dfrac{1}{b(a + bx)} + C.$

Properties of Definite Integral

A) If f is integrable on $[a,b]$, and k is any real number, then kf is integrable on $[a,b]$ and

$$\int_a^b kf(x)dx = k \int_a^b f(x)dx.$$

B) If f and g are integrable on $[a,b]$, then $f+g$ is integrable on $[a,b]$ and

$$\int_a^b [f(x) + g(x)]dx = \int_a^b f(x)dx + \int_a^b g(x)dx.$$

C) If $a < c < b$ and f is integrable on both $[a,c]$ and $[c,b]$ then f is integrable on $[a,b]$ and

$$\int_a^b f(x)dx = \int_a^c f(x)dx + \int_c^b f(x)dx.$$

D) If f is integrable on a closed interval and if a, b, and c are any three numbers in the interval, then

$$\int_a^b f(x)dx = \int_a^c f(x)dx + \int_c^b f(x)dx.$$

E) If f is integrable on $[a,b]$ and if $f(x) \geq 0$ for all x in $[a,b]$, then $\int_a^b f(x)dx \geq 0$.

PROBLEM

Evaluate the expression: $\displaystyle\int_2^3 \dfrac{(x+1)dx}{\sqrt{x^2 + 2x + 3}}\, dx$.

SOLUTION

We can rewrite the given integral as:

$\displaystyle\int_2^3 (x^2 + 2x + 3)^{-\frac{1}{2}} (x+1)dx,$

and make use of the formula: $\int u^n du = \dfrac{u^{n+1}}{n+1}$.

Let $u = x^2 + 2x + 3$. Then $du = (2x + 2)dx$, and $n = -\dfrac{1}{2}$. Applying the formula, we obtain:

$\displaystyle\int_2^3 \dfrac{(x+1)dx}{\sqrt{x^2 + 2x + 3}} = \dfrac{1}{2}\int_2^3 (x^2 + 2x + 3)^{-\frac{1}{2}} 2(x+1)dx$

$= \dfrac{1}{2}\left[\dfrac{(x^2 + 2x + 3)^{\frac{1}{2}}}{\frac{1}{2}} \right]_2^3 = \sqrt{x^2 + 2x + 3}\,\Big]_2^3.$

We now evaluate the definite integral between 3 and 2, obtaining:

$$\sqrt{3^2 + (2)(3) + 3} - \sqrt{2^2 + (2)(2) + 3} = \sqrt{18} - \sqrt{11}.$$

PROBLEM

Evaluate the expression: $\int_0^2 2x^2 \sqrt{x^3 + 1}\ dx$.

SOLUTION

We wish to convert the given integral into a form, to which we can apply the formula for $\int u^n du$, with $u = (x^3 + 1)$, $du = 3x^2$ and $n = \dfrac{1}{2}$. We obtain:

$$\int_0^2 2x^2 \sqrt{x^3 + 1}\ dx = \frac{2}{3} \int_0^2 (x^3 + 1)^{\frac{1}{2}} \left(\frac{3}{2} \cdot 2x^2 dx \right).$$

Applying the formula for $\int u^n du$, we obtain:

$$\frac{2}{3} \left[\frac{(x^3 + 1)^{\frac{3}{2}}}{\frac{3}{2}} \right]_0^2 = \frac{4}{9} (x^3 + 1)^{\frac{3}{2}} \Big]_0^2.$$

Evaluating between 2 and 0, we have:

$$\frac{4}{9}(8 + 1)^{\frac{3}{2}} - \frac{4}{9}(0 + 1)^{\frac{3}{2}}$$

$$= \frac{4}{9}(27 - 1)$$

$$= \frac{104}{9}.$$

The Fundamental Theorem of Calculus

The fundamental theorem of calculus establishes the relationship between the indefinite integrals and differentiation by use of the mean value theorem.

Mean Value Theorem for Integrals

If f is continuous on a closed interval $[a,b]$, then there is some number P in the open interval (a,b) such that

$$\int_a^b f(x)\, dx = f(P)(b - a).$$

To find $f(P)$ we divide both sides of the equation by $(b - a)$ obtaining

$$f(P) = \frac{1}{b - a} \int_a^b f(x)\, dx.$$

PROBLEM

What is the mean value or mean ordinate of the positive part of the curve $y = 2x - x^2$?

SOLUTION

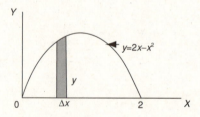

First determine the length of the base to fix the limits of integration for the area by setting y equal to zero, or:

$$0 = 2x - x^2 = x(2 - x).$$

Then, $x_1 = 0$, and $x_2 = 2$.

Now,

$$\bar{y}_x = \frac{1}{X_2 - X_1} \int y \cdot dx$$

$$= \frac{1}{2 - 0} \int_0^2 (2x - x^2)\, dx$$

$$= \int_0^2 \left(x - \frac{x^2}{2} \right) dx$$

$$= \left| \frac{x^2}{2} - \frac{x^3}{6} \right|_0^2 = \frac{4}{2} - \frac{8}{6} = \frac{2}{3},$$

the mean ordinate.

Definition of the Fundamental Theorem

Suppose f is continuous on a closed interval $[a,b]$, then

a) If the function G is defined by

$$G(x) = \int_a^x f(t)\,dt,$$

for all x in $[a,b]$, then G is an antiderivative of f on $[a,b]$.

b) If F is any antiderivative of f, then

$$\boxed{\int_a^b f(x)\,dx = F(b) - F(a)}$$

PROBLEM

Find the mean value of the ordinates of the circle $x^2 + y^2 = a^2$ in the first quadrant.

a) With respect to the radius along the x-axis

b) With respect to the arc-length.

SOLUTION

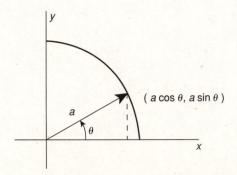

($a \cos \theta$, $a \sin \theta$)

a) Noting that the mean value is defined by:

$$f(x_o) = \frac{1}{b-a} \int_a^b f(x)\,dx, \text{ where } a < x_o < b,$$

we have:

$$f(x_o) = \frac{1}{a-o} \int_0^a \sqrt{a^2 - x^2}\,dx,$$

where $f(x) = y = \pm\sqrt{a^2 - x^2}$. We take $y = \sqrt{a^2 - x^2}$, because we are in the first quadrant. Also, noting that:

$$\int \sqrt{a^2 - x^2}\,dx = \frac{1}{2}\,x\sqrt{a^2 - x^2}$$

$$+ \frac{1}{2}\,a^2 \arcsin \frac{x}{a} + C,$$

we have:

$$f(x_o) = \frac{1}{4}\pi a.$$

b) The coordinates of any point on the circle can be expressed in terms of θ by the following method. For the point in question, drop a perpendicular line to the x-axis. We have a right triangle with hypotenuse of length a.

$$\cos(\theta) = \frac{x}{a},$$

or

$$x = a\cos(\theta). \qquad \sin(\theta) = \frac{y}{a},$$

or

$$y = a\sin(\theta).$$

Now an element of the arc length is $a\Delta\theta$. (Recall that the length of an arc of a circle is equal to $S = R\theta$ where R is the radius and θ the angle in radians.) Therefore the length of the arc of the circle in the first quadrant is $\frac{1}{2}\pi a$.

By taking the limit, $a\Delta\theta$ becomes $a\,d\theta$

$$f(\theta) = \frac{1}{\frac{1}{2}\pi a} \int_0^{\frac{\pi}{2}} a\sin\theta(a\,d\theta)$$

$$= \frac{2a}{\pi} \int_0^{\frac{\pi}{2}} \sin\theta\,d\theta = \frac{2a}{\pi} [\cos\theta]_0^{\frac{\pi}{2}}$$

$$= \frac{2a}{\pi}(1-0) = \frac{2a}{\pi}.$$

Indefinite Integral

The indefinite integral of $f(x)$, denoted by $\int f(x)\,dx$, is the most general integral of $f(x)$, that is

$$\int f(x)\,dx = F(x)+C.$$

$F(x)$ is any function such that $F'(x)=f(x)$. C is an arbitrary constant.

Integration of Formulas

1. $\int x^n dx = \dfrac{x^{n+1}}{n+1}+C,\ n \neq -1$

2. $\int \dfrac{dx}{x} = \ln|x|+C$

3. $\int \dfrac{dx}{x-a} = \ln|x-a|+C$

4. $\int \dfrac{x\,dx}{x^2+a^2} = \dfrac{1}{2}\ln|x^2+a^2|+C$

5. $\int \dfrac{dx}{x^2+a^2} = \dfrac{1}{a}\tan^{-1}\dfrac{x}{a}+C$

6. $\int \dfrac{dx}{(a^2-x^2)^{\frac{1}{2}}} = \sin^{-1}\dfrac{x}{a}+C$

7. $\int \sin ax\,dx = \dfrac{1}{a}\cos ax+C$

8. $\int \cos ax\,dx = \dfrac{1}{a}\sin ax+C$

9. $\int \sec^2 x\,dx = \tan x+C$

10. $\int e^{ax}\,dx = \dfrac{e^{ax}}{a}+C$

11. $\int \sinh ax\,dx = -\dfrac{1}{a}\cosh ax+C$

12. $\int \cosh ax\,dx = \dfrac{1}{a}\sinh ax+C$

$\ln x \equiv \log_e x$ is called the logarithm of base e where $e \equiv 2.7182818$ ---

PROBLEM

Integrate the expression: $\int \dfrac{dx}{1+e^x}$.

SOLUTION

We wish to convert the given integral into the form $\int \dfrac{du}{u}$. If we multiply $\dfrac{1}{1+e^x}$ by $\dfrac{e^{-x}}{e^{-x}}$ (which is equal to 1) we obtain:

$$\frac{e^{-x}(1)}{e^{-x}(1+e^x)} = \frac{e^{-x}}{e^{-x}+e^0} = \frac{e^{-x}}{e^{-x}+1}.$$

In integrating this, we apply the formula, $\int \dfrac{du}{u} = \ln|u|+C$, letting $u=e^{-x}+1$. Then $du=-e^x dx$. We obtain:

$$\int \frac{e^{-x}}{e^{-x}+1}\,dx = -\int \frac{-e^{-x}dx}{e^{-x}+1} = -\ln(1+e^{-x})+C.$$

Algebraic Simplification

Certain apparently complicated integrals can be made simple by simple algebraic manipulations.

Example: Find $\int \dfrac{x}{x+1}\,dx$

Write $\dfrac{x}{x+1} = \dfrac{x+1-1}{x+1} = 1-\dfrac{1}{x+1}$

$$\int \frac{x}{x+1}\,dx = \int dx - \int \frac{dx}{x+1} = x - \ln|x+1|+c$$

PROBLEM

Integrate: $\int \dfrac{2x}{x+1}\,dx$.

SOLUTION

To integrate the given expression we manipulate the integrand to obtain the form $\int \dfrac{du}{u}$. This can be done as follows:

$$\int \frac{2x}{x+1}\,dx = 2\int \frac{x}{x+1}\,dx$$

$$= 2\int \left(\frac{x+1}{x+1} - \frac{1}{x+1} \right) dx$$

$$= 2\int \left(1 - \frac{1}{x+1} \right) dx$$

$$= 2\int dx - 2\int \frac{dx}{x+1}.$$

Now, applying the formula $\int \frac{du}{u} = \ln u$, we obtain:

$$\int \frac{2x}{x+1}\,dx = 2x - 2\,\ln(x+1) + C.$$

Substitution of Variables

Suppose $F(x)$ is expressed as a composite function, $F(x)=f(u(x))$,

then $F'(x) = f'(u)\dfrac{du}{dx}$, and $F'(x)dx = f'(u)du$.

Therefore,

$$\int F'(x)\,dx = \int f'(u)\,du = f(u) + C$$
$$= f(u(x)) + C = F(x) + C.$$

THEOREM:

Let f and u be functions satisfying the following conditions:

a) f is continuous on a domain including the closed interval $\{x : a \le x \le b\}$.

b) For each point t in the closed interval $\{t : \alpha \le t \le \beta\}$, the value $u(t)$ is a point in $\{x : a \le x \le b\}$.

c) $u(\alpha) = a$, and $u(\beta) = b$.

d) u is continuous on $\{t : \alpha \le t \le \beta\}$.

The $\displaystyle\int_{a}^{b} f(x)\,dx = \int_{\alpha}^{\beta} f(u(t)) \cdot u'(t)\,dt.$

Example: Evaluate $\displaystyle\int \frac{x}{x^2 + a^2}\,dx$

Let $u = x^2 + a^2$

$$du = 2x\,dx$$
$$\frac{1}{2}du = x\,dx$$

$$\int \frac{x}{x^2 + a^2}\,dx = \frac{1}{2}\int \frac{du}{u} = \frac{1}{2}\ln|u| + C$$
$$= \frac{1}{2}\ln|x^2 + a^2| + C$$

PROBLEM

Evaluate the expression: $\displaystyle\int_{0}^{3} x\sqrt{1+x}\,dx.$

SOLUTION

We wish to convert the given integral into a form, to which we can apply the formula for $\int u^n du$. To evaluate the indefinite integral $\int x\,\sqrt{1+x}\,dx$, we let

$$u = \sqrt{1+x},\; u^2 = 1 + x,\; x = u^2 - 1,\; dx = 2u\,du$$

Substituting, we have:

$$\int x\sqrt{1+x}\,dx = \int (u^2 - 1)\,u\,(2u\,du)$$
$$= 2\int (u^4 - u^2)\,du.$$

We can now apply the formula for $\int u^n du$, and we obtain:

$$\frac{2}{5}u^5 - \frac{2}{3}u^3 + C = \frac{2}{5}(1+x)^{\frac{5}{2}} - \frac{2}{3}(1+x)^{\frac{3}{2}} + C,$$

by substitution. Therefore, the definite integral

$$\int_{0}^{3} x\sqrt{1+x}\,dx = \frac{2}{5}(1+x)^{\frac{5}{2}} - \frac{2}{3}(1+x)^{\frac{3}{2}} \Bigg]_{0}^{3}$$
$$= \frac{2}{5}(4)^{\frac{5}{2}} - \frac{2}{3}(4)^{\frac{3}{2}} - \frac{2}{5}(1)^{\frac{5}{2}} + \frac{2}{3}(1)^{\frac{3}{2}}$$
$$= \frac{64}{5} - \frac{16}{3} - \frac{2}{5} + \frac{2}{3}$$
$$= \frac{116}{15}.$$

Change of Variables

Example: Evaluate $\displaystyle\int_{0}^{1} x(1+x)^{\frac{1}{2}}dx$

Let $u = 1+x$, $du = dx$, $x = u - 1$

$$\int_0^1 x(1+x)^{\frac{1}{2}} = \int_1^2 (u-1)u^{\frac{1}{2}}\,du.$$

*Notice the change in the limits for $x=0$, $u=1$ and for $x=1$ $u=2$.

$$\int_1^2 (u-1)u^{\frac{1}{2}}\,du = \int_1^2 u^{3/2} - u^{\frac{1}{2}}\,du$$

$$= 2/5\,u^{5/2} - 2/3\,u^{3/2}\Big|_1^2$$

$$= [(2/5)\sqrt{32} - (2/3)\sqrt{8})] - \left(\frac{2}{5} - \frac{2}{3}\right)$$

$$= \frac{4\sqrt{2}}{15} - \frac{4}{15} = \frac{4}{15}(\sqrt{2} - 1).$$

PROBLEM

Evaluate the expression: $\int_1^2 \dfrac{x}{(1+2x)^3}\,dx$.

SOLUTION

This integral is difficult because of the expression: $1 + 2x$, in the denominator. Hence we choose our substitution to eliminate this expression. We let

$$u = 1 + 2x, \text{ then } x = \frac{u-1}{2} \text{ and } dx = \frac{1}{2}\,du.$$

Now

$u = 3$ when $x = 1$

$u = 5$ when $x = 2$,

giving us new limits. Using the substitution, we obtain:

$$\int_1^2 \frac{x}{(1+2x)^3}\,dx = \int_3^5 \left(\frac{\frac{u-1}{2}}{u^3}\right)\left(\frac{1}{2}\right)\,du$$

$$= \frac{1}{4}\int_3^5 \left(\frac{1}{u^2} - \frac{1}{u^3}\right)\,du.$$

We can now use the formula for $\int u^n\,du$ on both terms of the integrand, obtaining:

$$\frac{1}{4}\left[-\frac{1}{u} + \frac{1}{2u^2}\right]_3^5 = \frac{11}{450}.$$

Integration of Parts

This method is based on the formula

$$d(uv) = u\,dv + v\,du.$$

The corresponding integration formula,

$uv = \int u\,dv + \int v\,du$, is applied in the form

$$\boxed{\int u\,dv = uv - \int v\,du}$$

This procedure involves the identification of u and dv and their manipulation into the form of the latter equation. v must be easily determined. If a definite integral is

$$\int_a^b u\,\frac{dv}{dx}\,dx = uv\Big]_a^b - \int_a^b v\,\frac{du}{dx}\,dx.$$

Example: Evaluate $\int x\cos x\,dx$

$u = x \qquad dv = \cos x\,dx$

$du = dx \qquad v = \sin x$

$$\int x\cos x\,dx = x\sin x - \int \sin x\,dx$$

$$= x\sin x - (-\cos x) + C$$

$$= x\sin x + \cos x + C$$

PROBLEM

Integrate by parts the expression: $\dfrac{dy}{dx} = x^2 \ln x$.

SOLUTION

$dy = x^2 \ln x \cdot dx.$

$y = \int x^2 \ln x\,dx.$

To integrate by parts we use the equation:

$\int u\,dv = uv - \int v\,du.$

Now, let $u = \ln \cdot x$.

Then, $du = \dfrac{1}{x} \cdot dx.$

Let $dv = x^2 \cdot dx$.

Then, $v = \int dv = \int x^2 dx = \dfrac{x^3}{3}$,

by use of the formula for $\int u^n du$. Substituting into the above equation, we have:

$$y = \int \overset{u}{\ln x} \cdot \overset{dv}{x^2 \cdot dx} = \frac{x^3}{3} \ \ln x - \int \frac{x^3}{3} \cdot \frac{1}{x} \cdot dx.$$

We can now integrate

$$\int \frac{x^3}{3} \cdot \frac{1}{x} \cdot dx,$$

by using the formula for $\int u^n du$, with $u = x$, $du = dx$, and $n = 2$. Doing this, we obtain.

$$y = \frac{x^3}{3} \ln x - \frac{x^3}{9} + C.$$

Trigonometric Integrals

Integrals of the form $\int \sin^n x\, dx$ or $\int \cos^n x dx$ can be evaluated without resorting to integration by parts. This is done in the following manner;

We write $\int \sin^n x\, dx = \int \sin^{n-1} \sin x\, dx$, if n is odd.

Since the integer $n-1$ is even, we may then use the fact that $\sin^2 x = 1 - \cos^2 x$ to obtain a form which is easier to integrate.

Example: $\int \sin^5 x dx = \int \sin^4 x \sin x\, dx$

$$= \int (\sin^2 x)^2 \sin x\, dx$$

but $\sin^2 x = 1 - \cos^2 x$.

Hence, $\int \sin^5 x dx = \int (1 - \cos^2 x)^2 \sin x\, dx$

$$= \int (1 - 2\cos^2 x + \cos^4 x) \sin x\, dx$$

Substitute $u = \cos x$, $du = -\sin x\, dx$

$$= -\int (1 - 2u^2 + u^4) du = -u + \frac{2}{3}u^3 - \frac{u^5}{5}$$

$$= -\cos x + \frac{2}{3}\cos^3 x - \frac{1}{5}\cos^5 x + C.$$

A similar technique can be employed for odd powers of $\cos x$.

If the integrand is $\sin^n x$ or $\cos^n x$ and n is even, then the half angle formulas,

$$\boxed{\begin{array}{c} \sin^2 x = \dfrac{1 - \cos 2x}{2} \ \ or \\[2mm] \cos^2 x = \dfrac{1 + \cos 2x}{2} \end{array}}$$

may be used to simplify the integrand.

Example: $\int \cos^2 x\, dx = \frac{1}{2} \int (1 + \cos 2x)\, dx$

$$= \tfrac{1}{2} x + \tfrac{1}{4} \sin 2x + C$$

PROBLEM

Integrate the expression: $\int \cos^2 x \sin x\, dx$.

SOLUTION

In evaluating this integral we use the formula:

$$\int u^n du = \frac{u^{n+1}}{n+1}.$$

Let $u = \cos x$, $du = -\sin x\, dx$, and $n = 2$. Applying the formula, we obtain:

$$\int \cos^2 x \sin x\, dx = -\frac{\cos^3 x}{3} + C.$$

Applications of the Integral

Area

If f and g are two continuous functions on the closed interval $[a,b]$, then the area of the region bounded by the graphs of these two functions and the ordinates $x = a$ and $x = b$ is

$$A = \int\limits_a^b [f(x) - g(x)]\, dx.$$

where $f(x) \geq 0$ and $f(x) \geq g(x)$

$a \leq x \leq b$

This formula applies whether the curves are above or below the x-axis.

The area below $f(x)$ and above the x-axis is represented by $\int_a^b f(x)$. The area between $g(x)$ and the x-axis is represented by $\int g(x)$.

Example: Find the area of the region bounded by the curves $y = x^2$ and $y = \sqrt{x}$.

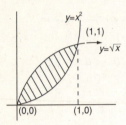

$$\text{Area} = A = \int_0^1 (\sqrt{x} - x^2)\,dx$$

$$= \int_0^1 \sqrt{x}\,dx - \int_0^1 x^2\,dx$$

$$= \left[\frac{2}{3} x^{\frac{3}{2}} - \frac{1}{3} x^3 \right]_0^1$$

$$A = \left[\frac{2}{3} - \frac{1}{3} \right] = \frac{1}{3}$$

It is generally advantageous to sketch the curve, since parts of the curve may have to be considered separately, particularly when positive and negative limits are given. The desired area is composed of the two parts: BOC and ODE. To find the total area, we can evaluate each area separately and then add. The area is the integral of the upper function minus the lower function. In the first quadrant, the upper function is the curve $y = x^3$, the lower function is $y = 0$, (the x-axis) and the limits are $x = 0$ and $x = 3$. In the third quadrant, the upper function is $y = 0$, the lower function is the curve $y = x^3$, and the limits are $x = -2$ and $x = 0$. Hence, we can write,

$$A_{\text{total}} = \int_0^3 (x^3 - 0)\,dx + \int_{-2}^0 (0 - x^3)\,dx$$

$$= \int_0^3 x^3\,dx + \int_{-2}^0 -x^3\,dx$$

$$= \left[\frac{x^4}{4} \right]_0^3 + \left[-\frac{x^4}{4} \right]_{-2}^0$$

$$= \frac{81}{4} + \frac{16}{4}$$

$$= 24\frac{1}{4}\ \text{sq. units.}$$

Note that refusal to consider this problem in two parts does <u>not</u> give area, but gives "net area" with one area considered positive and the other negative.

PROBLEM

Find the area between the curve: $y = x^3$, and the x-axis, from $x = -2$ to $x = 3$.

SOLUTION

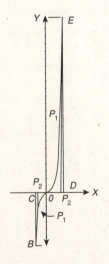

PROBLEM

Find the area of the region bounded by the x-axis, the curve: $y = 6x - x^2$ and the vertical lines: $x = 1$ and $x = 4$.

SOLUTION

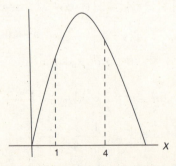

The limits of the integral which give the required area are $x = 1$ and $x = 4$. The function: $y = 6x - x^2$ is above the function $y = 0$ (the x-axis), therefore the area can be found by taking the integral of the upper function minus the lower function, or, $y = 6x - x^2$ minus $y = 0$, from $x = 1$ to $x = 4$. Therefore, we obtain:

$$A = \int_1^4 (6x - x^2) - 0 \; dx = \left[3x^2 - \frac{x^3}{3} \right]_1^4$$

$$= \frac{80}{3} - \frac{8}{3} = 24.$$

Volume of a Solid of Revolution

If a region is revolved about a line, a solid called a solid of revolution is formed. The solid is generated by the region. The axis of revolution is the line about which the revolution takes place.

There are several methods by which we may obtain the volume of a solid of revolution. We shall now discuss three such methods.

Disk Method

The volume of the solid generated by the revolution of a region about the x-axis is given by the formula

$$V = \pi \int_a^b [f(x)]^2 \, dx,$$

provided that f is a continuous, nonnegative function on the interval $[a,b]$.

PROBLEM

Find the volume of the solid generated by revolving about the y-axis the region bounded by the parabola: $y^2 = 4x$, the y-axis and the tine $y = 2$.

SOLUTION

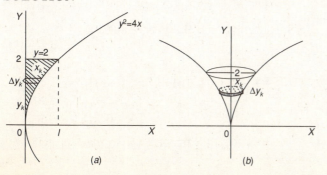

(a)   (b)

An element of volume is the disk generated by rotating a strip: x by dy, about the y-axis. The volume of the disk is: $dV = \pi x^2 dy$.

Hence,

$$V = \pi \int_0^2 x^2 \, dy$$

$$= \pi \int_0^2 \frac{1}{16} Y^4 \, dy = \frac{2}{5} \pi.$$

Shell Method

This method applies to cylindrical shells exemplified by

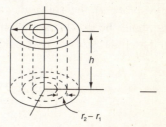

The volume of a cylindrical shell is

$$V = \pi r_2^2 h - \pi r_1^2 h$$
$$= \pi (r_2 + r_1)(r_2 - r_1)h$$
$$= 2\pi \left(\frac{r_2 + r_1}{2} \right)(r_2 - r_1)h$$

where r_1 = inner radius

r_2 = Outer radius

h = height.

Let $r = \dfrac{r_1 + r_2}{2}$ and $\Delta r = r_2 - r_1$, then the volume of a shell becomes

$$\boxed{V = 2\pi r h \Delta r}$$

The thickness of the shell is represented by Δr and the average radius of the shell by r.

Thus, $\boxed{V = 2\pi \int_a^b x f(x) \, dx}$

is the volume of a solid generated by revolving a region about the *y*-axis. This is illustrated by the figure below.

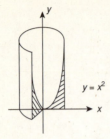

PROBLEM

Find the volume of the solid generated by revolving about the *y*-axis the region bounded by the parabola: $y = -x^2 + 6x - 8$, and the *x*-axis.

SOLUTION

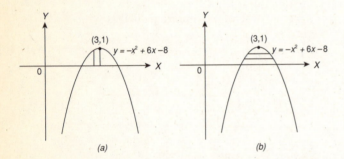

(a)   (b)

Method 1. We use the method of cylindrical shells. The curve:

$$y = -x^2 + 6x - 8,$$

cuts the *x*-axis at $x = 2$ and $x = 4$.

The cylindrical shells are generated by the strip formed by the two lines parallel to the *y*-axis, at distances *x* and $x + \Delta x$ from the *y*-axis, $2 \leq x \leq 4$, as shown in figure (a). When this strip is revolved about the *y*-axis, it generates a cylindrical shell of average height y^*, $y \leq y^* \leq y^* + \Delta y$, thickness Δx, and average radius x^*, $x < x^* \leq x + \Delta x$. The volume of this element is:

$$\Delta V = 2\pi x^* y^* \Delta x,$$

where $2\pi x^* y^*$ is the surface area. Expressing *y* in terms of *x* and passing to the limits, the sum of the volumes of all such cylindrical shells is the integral:

$$V = 2\pi \int_2^4 x(-x^2 + 6x - 8) \, dx$$

$$= 2\pi \int_2^4 (-x^3 + 6x^2 - 8x) \, dx$$

$$= 2\pi \left(-\frac{x^4}{4} + 2x^3 - 4x^2 \right) \Big|_2^4$$

$$= 2\pi \big((-64 + 128 - 64) - (-4 + 16 - 16) \big)$$

$$= 8\pi.$$

Method 2. This can also be thought of as the volume comprising a series of concentric washers with variable outer and inner radii, as sectionally shown in figure (b). The variable radii are as follows: Since

$$y = -x^2 + 6x - 8,$$

we solve for *x*.

To complete the square, we require a 9, so that

$$x^2 - 6x + 9$$

constitutes a perfect square. Rewriting the equation,

$$x^2 - 6x + 9 - 9 + 8 = -y.$$

$$x^2 - 6x + 9 = 1 - y.$$

$$(x - 3)^2 = 1 - y.$$

Therefore,

$$x = 3 \pm \sqrt{1 - y}$$

which shows the washers, *y* units from the *x*-axis, have an

inner radius: $x_{in} = 3 - \sqrt{1 - y}$, and an

outer radius: $x_o = 3 + \sqrt{1 - y}$.

(The particular one on the *x*-axis has $x_{in} = 2$ and $x_o = 4$.)

The volume of this washer with thickness *dy* is:

$$dV = \pi(x_o^2 - x_{in}^2) \, dy,$$

$$\text{or } dV = \pi \left[(x_o + x_{in})(x_o - x_{in}) \right] dy.$$

Substituting the values for x_o and x_{in},

$$dV = \pi \Big(\big((3 + \sqrt{1 - y}) + (3 - \sqrt{1 - y}) \big) \cdot$$

$$\big((3 + \sqrt{1 - y}) - (3 - \sqrt{1 - y}) \big) \Big) \, dy$$

$$= \pi(12 \sqrt{1 - y}) \, dy.$$

Since y varies from 0 to 1, the desired volume is:

$$V = 12\pi \int_0^1 (1-y)^{\frac{1}{2}} \, dy$$

$$= 12\pi \left(-\frac{2}{3}(1-y)^{\frac{3}{2}} \right) \Big|_0^1 = 8\pi.$$

Parallel Cross Sections

A cross section of a solid is a region formed by the intersection of a solid by a plane. This is illustrated by the figure.

If x is a continuous function on the interval $[a,b]$, then the volume of the cross sectional area $A(x)$ is

$$V = \int_a^b A(x) \, dx.$$

PROBLEM

Rotate the curve $y = 2x$ about the line $x = 4$ and find the volume produced by the rotation of the shaded portion.

SOLUTION

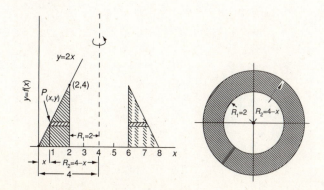

Area of washer $= \pi \left(R_2^{\,2} - R_1^{\,2} \right)$

Increment of volume, $dV = \pi \left(R_2^{\,2} - R_1^{\,2} \right) dy$.

$V = \int_a^b \pi \left(R_2^{\,2} - R_1^{\,2} \right) dy$, where a and b are limits of y.

$$V = \int_0^4 \pi \left((4-x)^2 - 2^2 \right) dy$$

$$= \int_0^4 \pi \left(16 - 8x + x^2 - 4 \right) dy$$

$$= \pi \int_0^4 \left(12 - 8x + x^2 \right) dy.$$

But the x terms must be in terms of y because of dy. We have: $x = \dfrac{y}{2}$, from the equation of the curve. Substituting,

$$V = \pi \int_0^4 \left(12 - 4y + \frac{y^2}{4} \right) dy$$

$$= \pi \left(12y - \frac{4y^2}{2} + \frac{y^3}{12} \right) \Big|_0^4$$

$$= \pi \left(48 - 32 + -\frac{16}{3} \right) = \frac{64\pi}{3}.$$

This is the washer method. The important point to remember is to obtain the radii from the center line of rotation.

SUBAREA IV:
Measurement and
Geometry

Points, Lines, and Angles

Geometry is built upon a series of undefined terms. These terms are those that we accept as known in order to define other undefined terms.

A) **Point:** Although we represent points on paper with small dots, a point has no size, thickness, or width.

B) **Line:** A line is a series of adjacent points that extends indefinitely. A line can be either curved or straight; however, unless otherwise stated, the term "line" refers to a straight line.

C) **Plane:** A plane is a collection of points lying on a flat surface that extends indefinitely in all directions.

Definitions

Definition 1

If A and B are two points on a line, then the **line segment** AB is the set of points on that line between A and B and including A and B, which are called the endpoints. The line segment is referred to as $\overline{AB}$.

Definition 2

A **half-line** is the set of all the points on a line on the same side of a dividing point, not including the dividing point, denoted by $\overleftrightarrow{AB}$.

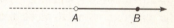

Definition 3

Let A be a dividing point on a line. Then, a **ray** is the set of all the points on a half-line and the dividing point itself. The dividing point is called the endpoint or the vertex of the ray. The ray AB shown below is denoted by $\overrightarrow{AB}$.

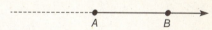

Definition 4

Three or more points are said to be collinear if and only if they lie on the same line.

Definition 5

Let X, Y, and Z be three collinear points. If Y is between X and Z, then $\overrightarrow{YX}$ and $\overrightarrow{YZ}$ are called **opposite rays**.

Definition 6

The **absolute value** of x, denoted by $|x|$, is defined as

$$|x| = \begin{cases} x & \text{if} \quad x > 0 \\ 0 & \text{if} \quad x = 0 \\ -x & \text{if} \quad x < 0 \end{cases}$$

Definition 7

The absolute value of the difference of the coordinates of any two points on the real number line is the **distance** between those two points.

Definition 8

The **length** of a line segment is the distance between its endpoints.

Definition 9

Congruent segments are segments that have the same length. The sign for congruent is $\cong$.

Definition 10

The **midpoint** of a segment is defined as the point of the segment that divides the segment into two congruent segments. (The midpoint is said to bisect the segment.)

PROBLEM

Solve for x when $|x - 7| = 3$.

SOLUTION

This equation, according to the definition of absolute value, expresses the conditions that $x - 7$ must be 3 or -3, since in either case the absolute value is 3. If $x - 7 = 3$, we have $x = 10$; and if $x - 7 = -3$, we have $x = 4$. We see that there are two values of x that solve the equation.

PROBLEM

Find point C between $\underline{A}$ and $\underline{B}$ in the figure below such that $AC \cong CB$.

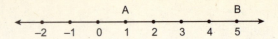

SOLUTION

We must determine point C in such a way that $\overline{AC} \cong \overline{CB}$, or $AC = CB$. We are first given that C is between A and B. Therefore, since the measure of the whole is equal to the sum of the measure of its parts:

(I) $AC + CB = AB$

Using these two facts, we can find the length of AC. From that we can find C.

First, since $AC = CB$, we substitute AC for CB in equation (I)

(II) $AC + AC = AB$

(III) $2(AC) = AB$

Dividing by 2 we have

(IV) $AC = (1/2) AB$

To find AC, we must know AB. We can find AB from the coordinates of A and B. They are 1 and 5, respectively. According,

(V) $AB = |5 - 1|$

(VI) $AB = 4$

We substitute 4 for AB in equation (IV)

(VII) $AC = (1/2) (4)$

(VIII) $AC = 2.$

Therefore, C is 2 units from A. Since C is between A and B, the coordinate of C must be 3.

Definition 11

The **bisector** of a line segment is a line that divides the line segment into two congruent segments.

Definition 12

An **angle** is a collection of points that is the union of two rays having the same endpoint. An angle such as the one illustrated the accompanying figure can be referred to in any of the following ways:

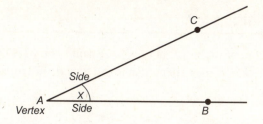

A) by a capital letter that names its vertex, ∡A;

B) by a lowercase letter or number placed inside the angle, ∡x;

C) by three capital letters, where the middle letter is the vertex and the other two letters are not on the same ray, i.e., ∡CAB or ∡BAC, both of which represent the angle illustrated in the above figure.

Definition 13

A set of points is **coplanar** if all the points lie in the same plane.

Definition 14

Two angles with a common vertex and a common side, but no common interior points, are called **adjacent angles.**

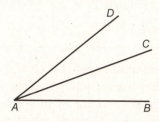

In the above figure, ∡DAC and ∡BAC are adjacent angles; ∡DAB and ∡BAC are not adjacent angles.

Definition 15

Vertical angles are two angles with a common vertex and with sides that are two pairs of opposite rays.

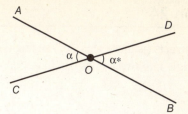

(∡α and ∡α* are vertical angles.)

Definition 16

An **acute angle** is an angle whose measure is larger that 0° but smaller than 90°.

Definition 17

An angle whose measure is 90° is called a **right angle**.

Definition 18

An **obtuse angle** is an angle whose measure is larger than 90° but less than 180°.

Definition 19

An angle whose measure is 180° is called a **straight angle**. Note: Such an angle is, in fact, a straight line.

Definition 20

An angle whose measure is greater than 180° but less than 360° is called a **reflex angle**.

Definition 21

Complementary angles are two angles, the sum of the measures of which equals 90°.

Definition 22

Supplementary angles are two angles, the sum of the measures of which equals 180°.

Definition 23

Congruent angles are angles of equal measure.

Definition 24

A ray **bisects** (is the bisector of) an angle if the ray divides the angle into two angles that have equal measure.

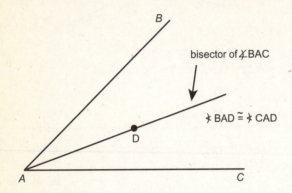

Definition 25

If the two non-common sides of adjacent angles form opposite rays, then the angles are called a **linear pair.** Note that α and β are supplementary.

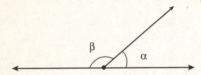

Definition 26

Two lines are said to be **perpendicular** if they intersect and form right angles. The symbol for perpendicular (or, is perpendicular to) is $\perp$; $\overleftrightarrow{AB}$ is perpendicular to $\overleftrightarrow{CD}$ is written as $\overleftrightarrow{AB} \perp \overleftrightarrow{CD}$.

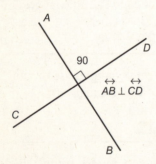

Definition 27

A line, a ray, or a line segment that bisects a line segment and is also perpendicular to that segment is called a **perpendicular bisector** of the line segment.

Definition 28

The **distance** from a point to a line is the measure of the perpendicular line segment from the point to that line. Note: This is the shortest possible distance from the point to the line.

Definition 29

Two or more distinct lines are said to be **parallel** ($\parallel$) if and only if they are coplanar and they do not intersect.

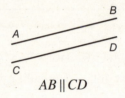

$$AB \parallel CD$$

Definition 30

The **projection of a given point** on a given line is the foot of the perpendicular drawn from the given point to the given line.

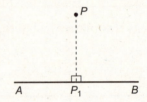

P_1 is the projection of P on $\overrightarrow{AB}$

The foot of a perpendicular from a point to a line is the point where the perpendicular meets the line.

Definition 31

The **projection of a segment** on a given line (when the segment is not perpendicular to the line) is a segment with endpoints that are the projections of the endpoints of the given line segment onto the given line.

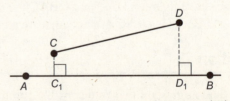

$\overline{C_1 D_1}$ is the projection of $\overline{CD}$ onto $\overleftrightarrow{AB}$

PROBLEM

> The measure of the complement of a given angle is four times the measure of the angle. Find the measure of the given angle.

SOLUTION

By the definition of complementary angles, the sum of the measures of the two complements must equal 90°.

Accordingly,

(1) Let x = the measure of the angle

(2) Then $4x$ = the measure of the complement of this angle.

Therefore, from the discussion above,

$$x + 4x = 90°$$
$$5x = 90°$$
$$x = 18°$$

Therefore, the measure of the given angle is 18°.

PROBLEM

> In the figure, we are given $\overleftrightarrow{AB}$ and triangle ABC. We are told that the measure of ∢1 is five times the measure of ∢2. Determine the measures of ∢1 and ∢2.

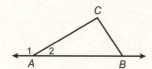

SOLUTION

Since ∢1 and ∢2 are adjacent angles whose non-common sides lie on a straight line, they are, by definition, supplementary. As supplements, their measures must sum to 180°.

If we let x = the measure of ∢1,

then $5x$ = the measure of ∢2.

To determine the respective angle measures, set $x + 5x = 180°$ and solve for x. $6x = 180°$. Therefore, $x = 30°$ and $5x = 150°$.

Therefore, the measure of ∢1 = 150° and the measure of ∢2 = 30°.

Postulates

Postulate 1 (The Point Uniqueness Postulate)

Let n be any positive number

Then there exists exactly one point N of $\overrightarrow{AB}$ such that $AN = n$. (AN is the length of n)

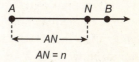

Postulate 2 (The Line Postulate)

Any two distinct points determine one and only one line that contains both points.

Postulate 3 (The Point Betweenness Postulate)

Let A and B be any two points. Then, there exists at least one point (and in fact an infinite number of such points) of $\overleftrightarrow{AB}$ such that P is between A and B, with $AP + PB = AB$.

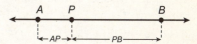

Postulate 4

Two distinct straight lines can intersect at most at only one point.

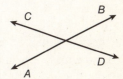

Postulate 5

The shortest line between any two points is a straight line.

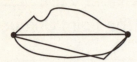

Postulate 6

There is a one-to-one correspondence between the real numbers and the points of a line. That is, to every real number there corresponds exactly one point of the line and to every point of the line there corresponds exactly one real number. (In other words, a line has an infinite number of points between any two distinct points.)

Postulate 7

One and only one perpendicular can be drawn to a given line through any point on that line. Given point O on line $\overleftrightarrow{AB}$, $\overrightarrow{OC}$ represents the only perpendicular to AB that passes through O.

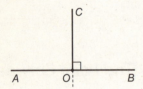

PROBLEM

In the accompanying figure, point B is between points A and C, and point E is between points D and F. Given that $\overline{AB} \cong \overline{DE}$ and $\overline{BC} \cong \overline{EF}$. Prove that $\overline{AC} \cong \overline{DF}$.

SOLUTION

Two important postulates will be employed in this proof. The Point Betweenness Postulate states that if point Y is between points X and Z, then $XY + YZ = XZ$.

Furthermore, the Postulate states that the converse is also true—that is, if $XY + YZ = XZ$, then point Y is between points X and Z.

The Addition Postulate states that equal quantities added to equal quantities yield equal quantities. Thus, if $a = b$ and $c = d$, then $a + c = b + d$.

Given: Point B is between A and C; point E is between points D and F; $\overline{AB} \cong \overline{DE}$; $\overline{BC} \cong \overline{EF}$

Prove: $\overline{AC} \cong \overline{DF}$.

Statement	Reason
1. (For the given, see above)	1. Given.
2. $AB = DE$ $BC = EF$	2. Congruent segments have equal lengths.
3. $AB + BC = DE + EF$	3. Addition Postulate.
4. $AC = DF$	4. Point Between Postulate.
5. $\overline{AC} \cong \overline{DF}$	5. Segments of equal length are congruent.

PROBLEM

Construct a line perpendicular to a given line through a given point on the given line.

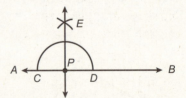

SOLUTION

Let line $\overleftrightarrow{AB}$ and point P be the given line and the given point, respectively.

We notice that $\angle APB$ is a straight angle. A line perpendicular to $\overleftrightarrow{AB}$ from point P will form adjacent congruent angles with $\overleftrightarrow{AB}$, by the definition of a perpendicular. Since $\angle APB$ is a straight angle, the adjacent angles will be right angles. As such, the required perpendicular is the angle bisector of $\angle APB$.

We can complete our construction by bisecting $\angle APB$.

1. Using *P* as the center and any convenient radius, construct an arc that intersects $\overleftrightarrow{AB}$ at points *C* and *D*.

2. With *C* and *D* as centers and with a radius greater in length than the one used in Step 1, construct arcs that intersect. The intersection point of these two arcs is point *E*.

3. Draw $\overleftrightarrow{EP}$.

    $\overleftrightarrow{EP}$ is the required angle bisector and, as such, $\overleftrightarrow{EP} \perp \overleftrightarrow{AB}$.

PROBLEM

> Present a formal proof of the following conditional statement:
>
> If $\overleftrightarrow{CE}$ bisects $\angle ADB$, and if $\overrightarrow{FDB}$ and $\overrightarrow{CDE}$ are straight lines, then $\angle a \cong \angle x$. (Refer to the accompanying figure).

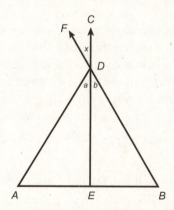

SOLUTION

In this problem, it will be necessary to recognize vertical angles and be knowledgeable of their key properties. Furthermore, we will need the definition of the bisector of an angle.

Vertical angles are two angles that have a common vertex, and whose sides are two pairs of opposite rays. Vertical angles are always congruent.

Lastly, the bisector of any angle divides the angle into two congruent angles.

Statement	Reason
1. $\overleftrightarrow{CE}$ bisects $\angle ADB$	1. Given.
2. $\angle a \cong \angle b$	2. A bisector of an angle divides the angle into two congruent angles.
3. $\overrightarrow{FDB}$ and $\overrightarrow{CDE}$ are straight lines	3. Given.
4. $\angle x$ and $\angle b$ are vertical angles	4. Definition of vertical angles.
5. $\angle b \cong \angle x$	5. Vertical angles are congruent.
6. $\angle a \cong \angle x$	6. Transitivity property of congruence of angles.

Note that step 3 is essential because without $\overrightarrow{FDB}$ and $\overrightarrow{CDE}$ being straight lines the definition of vertical angles would not be applicable to $\angle x$ and $\angle b$.

Postulate 8

The perpendicular bisector of a line segment is unique.

Postulate 9 (The Plane Postulate)

Any three non-collinear points determine one and only one plane that contains those three points.

Postulate 10 (The Points-in-a-Plane Postulate)

If two distinct points of a line lie in a given plane, then the line lies in that plane.

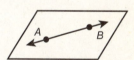

Postulate 11 (Plane Separation Postulate)

Any line in a plane separates the plane into two half planes.

Postulate 12

Given an angle, there exists one and only one real number between 0 and 180 corresponding to it. Note: $m\angle A$ refers to the measurement of angle *A*.

Postulate 13 (The Angle Sum Postulate)

If A is in the interior of $\sphericalangle XYZ$, then

$m\sphericalangle XYZ = m\sphericalangle XYA + m\sphericalangle AYZ$.

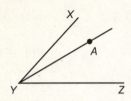

Postulate 14 (The Angle Difference Postulate)

If P is in the exterior of $\sphericalangle ABC$ and in the same half-plane (created by edge $\overleftrightarrow{BC}$) as A, then

$m\sphericalangle ABP = m\sphericalangle PBC - m\sphericalangle ABC$.

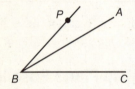

PROBLEM

In the accompanying figure $\overline{SM}$ is the perpendicular bisector of $\overline{QR}$, and $\overline{SN}$ is the perpendicular bisector of $\overline{QP}$. Prove that $SR = SP$.

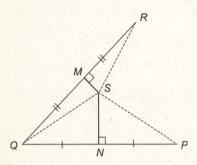

SOLUTION

Every point on the perpendicular bisector of a segment is equidistant from the endpoints of the segment.

Since point S is on the perpendicular bisector of $\overline{QR}$,

(I) $SR = SQ$

Also, since point S is on the perpendicular bisector of $\overline{QP}$,

(II) $SQ = SP$

By the transitive property (quantities equal to the same quantity are equal), we have:

(III) $SR = SP$.

PROBLEM

To construct an angle whose measure is equal to the sum of the measures of two given angles.

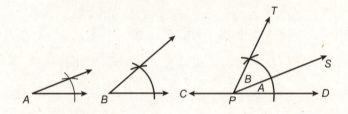

SOLUTION

To construct an angle equal to the sum of the measures of two given angles, we must invoke the theorem that states that the whole is equal to the sum of the parts. The construction, then, will duplicate the given angles in such a way as to form one larger angle equal in measure to the sum of the measures of the two given angles.

The two given angles, $\sphericalangle A$ and $\sphericalangle B$, are shown in the figure.

1. Construct any line $\overleftrightarrow{CD}$, and mark a point P on it.

2. At P, using $\overrightarrow{PD}$ as the base, construct $\sphericalangle DPS \cong \sphericalangle A$.

3. Now, using $\overrightarrow{PS}$ as the base, construct $\sphericalangle SPT \cong \sphericalangle B$ at point P.

4. $\sphericalangle DPT$ is the desired angle, equal in measure to $m\sphericalangle A + m\sphericalangle B$. This follows because the measure of the whole, $\sphericalangle DPT$, is equal to the sum of the measure of the parts, $\sphericalangle A$ and $\sphericalangle B$.

Theorems

Theorem 1

All right angles are equal.

Theorem 2

All straight angles are equal.

Theorem 3

Supplements of the same or equal angles are themselves equal.

Theorem 4

Complements of the same or equal angles are themselves equal.

Theorem 5

Vertical angles are equal.

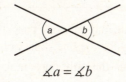

$$\measuredangle a = \measuredangle b$$

Theorem 6

Two supplementary angles are right angles if they have the same measure.

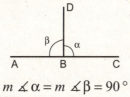

$$m \measuredangle \alpha = m \measuredangle \beta = 90°$$

Theorem 7

If two lines intersect and form one right angle, then the lines form four right angles.

PROBLEM

Find the measure of the angle whose measure is 40° more than the measure of its supplement.

SOLUTION

By the definition of supplementary angles, the sum of the measures of two supplements must equal 180°. Accordingly,

let x = the measure of the supplement of the angle.

Then $x + 40°$ = the measure of the angle.

Therefore, $x + (x + 40°) = 180°$

$$2x + 40° = 180°$$

$$2x = 140°$$

$$x = 70° \text{ and } x + 40° = 110°.$$

Therefore the measure of the angle is 110°.

PROBLEM

What is the measure of a given angle whose measure is half the measure of its complement?

SOLUTION

When two angles are said to be complementary we know that their measures must sum, by definition, to 90°.

If we let x = the measure of the given angle,

then $2x$ = the measure of its complement.

To determine the measure of the given angle, set the sum of the two angle measures equal to 90 and solve for x. Accordingly,

$$x + 2x = 90°$$

$$3x = 90°$$

$$x = 30°$$

Therefore, the measure of the given angle is 30° and its complement is 60°.

PROBLEM

Given that straight lines $\overleftrightarrow{AB}$ and $\overleftrightarrow{CD}$ intersect at point E, that $\measuredangle BEC$ has measure 20° greater than 5 times a fixed quantity, and that $\measuredangle AED$ has measure 60° greater than 3 times this same quantity: Find a) the unknown fixed quantity, b) the measure of $\measuredangle BEC$, and c) the measure of $\measuredangle CEA$. (For the actual angle placement, refer to the accompanying diagram.)

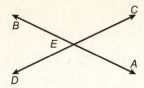

SOLUTION

a) Since $\overleftrightarrow{AB}$ and $\overleftrightarrow{CD}$ are straight lines intersecting at point E, $\angle BEC$ and $\angle AED$ are, by definition, vertical angles. As such, they are congruent and their measures are equal. Therefore, if we let x represent the fixed quantity, $\angle BEC = 5x + 20$ and $\angle AED = 3x + 60$; according to the information given. We can then set up the following equality, and solve for the unknown quantity.

$$5x + 20 = 3x + 60$$
$$5x - 3x = 60 - 20$$
$$2x = 40$$
$$x = 20$$

Therefore, the value of the unknown quantity is 20°.

b) From the information given about $\angle BEC$, we know that $m\angle BEC = (5x + 20)°$. By substitution, we have

$$m\angle BEC = 5(20°) + 20° = 100° + 20° = 120°.$$

Therefore, the measure of $\angle BEC$ is 120°.

c) We know that $\overleftrightarrow{AB}$ is a straight line; therefore, $\angle CEA$ is the supplement of $\angle BEC$. Since the sum of the measure of two supplements is 180°, the following calculation can be made:

$$m\angle CEA + m\angle BEC = 180°$$
$$m\angle CEA = 180° - m\angle BEC,$$

Substituting in our value for $m\angle BEC$, we obtain:

$$m\angle CEA = 180° - 120° = 60°$$

Therefore, the measure of $\angle CEA$ is 60°.

Theorem 8

Any point on the perpendicular bisector of a given line segment is equidistant from the ends of the segment.

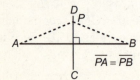

Theorem 9

If a point is equidistant from the ends of a line segment, this point must lie on the perpendicular bisector of the segment.

Theorem 10

If two points are equidistant from the ends of a line segment, these points determine the perpendicular bisector of the segment.

Theorem 11

Every line segment has exactly one midpoint.

Theorem 12

There exists one and only one perpendicular to a line through a point outside the line. Take point C outside line $\overleftrightarrow{AB}$. $\overleftrightarrow{OC}$ represents the only perpendicular to $\overleftrightarrow{AB}$ that passes through C.

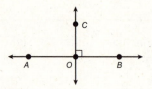

Theorem 13

If the exterior sides of adjacent angles are perpendicular to each other, then the adjacent angles are complementary.

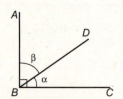

α and β are complementary

Theorem 14

Adjacent angles are supplementary if their exterior sides form a straight line.

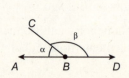

α and β are supplementary

Theorem 15

Two angles that are equal and supplementary to each other are right angles.

Congruent Angles and Congruent Line Segments

Definitions

Definition 1

Two or more geometric figures are congruent when they have the same shape and size. The symbol for congruence is $\cong$; hence, if triangle ABC is congruent to triangle DEF, we write $\triangle ABC \cong \triangle DEF$.

Definition 2

Two line segments are congruent if and only if they have the same measure.

Note: The expression "if and only if" can be used any time both a statement and the converse of that statement are true. Using definition 2, we can rewrite the statement as "two line segments have the same measure if and only if they are congruent." The two statements are identical.

Definition 3

Two angles are congruent if and only if they have the same measure.

PROBLEM

In the figure shown, $\triangle ABC$ is an isosceles triangle, such that $\overline{BA} \cong \overline{BC}$. Line segment $\overline{AD}$ bisects $\sphericalangle BAC$ and $\overline{CD}$ bisects $\sphericalangle BCA$. Prove that $\triangle ADC$ is an isosceles triangle.

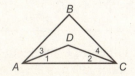

SOLUTION

In order to prove $\triangle ADC$ is isosceles, we must prove that two of its sides, $\overline{AD}$ and $\overline{CD}$, are congruent. To prove $\overline{AD} \cong \overline{CD}$ in $\triangle ADC$, we have to prove that the angles opposite $\overline{AD}$ and $\overline{CD}$, $\sphericalangle 1$ and $\sphericalangle 2$, are congruent.

Statement	Reason
1. $\overline{BA} \cong \overline{BC}$	1. Given.
2. $\sphericalangle BAC \cong \sphericalangle BCA$ or $m\sphericalangle BAC = m\sphericalangle BCA$	2. If two sides of a triangle are congruent, then the angles opposite them are congruent.
3. $\overline{AD}$ bisects $\sphericalangle BAC$ $\overline{CD}$ bisects $\sphericalangle BCA$	3. Given.
4. $m\sphericalangle 1 = (1/2)m\sphericalangle BAC$ $m\sphericalangle 2 = (1/2)m\sphericalangle BCA$	4. The bisector of an angle divides the angle into two angles whose measures are equal.
5. $m\sphericalangle 1 = m\sphericalangle 2$	5. Halves of equal quantities are equal.
6. $\sphericalangle 1 \cong \sphericalangle 2$	6. If the measure of two angles are equal, then the angles are congruent.
7. $\overline{CD} \cong \overline{AD}$	7. If two angles of a triangle are congruent, then the sides opposite these angles are congruent.
8. $\triangle ADC$ is an isosceles triangle.	8. If a triangle has two congruent sides, then it is an isosceles triangle.

Theorems

Theorem 1

Every line segment is congruent to itself.

Theorem 2

Every angle is congruent to itself.

Let R be a relation on a set A. Then:

    R is reflexive if aRa for every a in A.

    R is symmetric if aRb implies bRa.

    R is anti-symmetric if aRb and bRa imply $a = b$.

    R is transitive if aRb and bRc imply aRc.

Note: The term *aRa* means the relation *R* performed on *a* yields *a*. The term *aRb* means the relation *R* performed on *a* yields *b*.

Theorem 3

Given a line segment $\overline{AB}$ and a ray $\overrightarrow{XY}$, there exists one and only one point *O* on $\overrightarrow{XY}$ such that $\overline{AB} \cong \overline{XO}$.

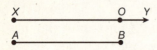

Theorem 4

If $\overline{AB} = \overline{CD}$, *Q* bisects $\overline{AB}$ and *P* bisects $\overline{CD}$, then $\overline{AQ} \cong \overline{CP}$ and $\overline{AQ} = \overline{CP}$.

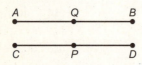

Theorem 5

If $m \angle ABC = m \angle DEF$, and $\overrightarrow{BX}$ and $\overrightarrow{EY}$ bisect $\angle ABC$ and $\angle DEF$, respectively, then $m \angle ABC = m \angle DEF$.

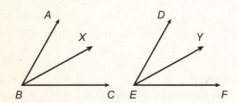

Theorem 6

Let *P* be in the interior of $\angle ABC$ and *Q* be in the interior of $\angle DEF$. If $m \angle ABP = m \angle DEQ$ and $m \angle PBC = m \angle QEF$, then $m \angle ABC = m \angle DEF$.

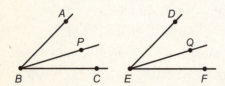

Theorem 7

Let *P* be in the interior of $\angle XYZ$ and *Q* be in the interior of $\angle ABC$. If $m \angle XYZ = m \angle ABC$ and $m \angle XYP = m \angle ABQ$ then $m \angle PYZ = m \angle QBC$.

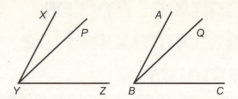

Postulates

By definition, a relation *R* is called an equivalence relation if relation *R* is reflexive, symmetric, and transitive.

Postulate 1

Congruence of segments is an equivalence relation.

(1) Congruence of segments is reflexive.
   If $\overline{AB} \cong \overline{AB}$, $\overline{AB}$ is congruent to itself.

(2) Congruence of segments is symmetric.
   If $\overline{AB} \cong \overline{CD}$, then $\overline{CD} \cong \overline{AB}$.

(3) Congruence of segments is transitive.
   If $\overline{AB} \cong \overline{CD}$ and $\overline{CD} \cong \overline{EF}$, then $\overline{AB} \cong \overline{EF}$.

Postulate 2

Congruence of angles is an equivalence relation, that is, it is reflexive, symmetric, and transitive.

Postulate 3

Any geometric figure is congruent to itself.

Postulate 4

A geometric congruence may be reversed.

Postulate 5

Two geometric figures congruent to the same geometric figure are congruent to each other.

PROBLEM

> Given triangle *RST* in the figure shown with $\overline{RT} \cong \overline{ST}$. Points *A* and *B* lie at the midpoint of $\overline{RT}$ and $\overline{ST}$, respectively. Prove that $\overline{RA} \cong \overline{SB}$.

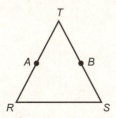

SOLUTION

This solution is best presented as a formal proof.

Statement	Reason
1. $\overline{RT} \cong \overline{ST}$ or $RT = ST$	1. Given.
2. *A* is the midpoint of $\overline{RT}$	2. Given.
3. $RA = (1/2)RT$	3. The midpoint of a line segment divides the line segment into two equal halves.
4. *B* is the midpoint of $\overline{ST}$	4. Given.
5. $\overline{SB} = (1/2)\overline{TS}$	5. The midpoint of a line segment divides the line segment into two equal halves.
6. $RA = SB$	6. Division Postulate: Halves of equal quantities are equal. Statements 3 and 5.
7. $\overline{RA} \cong \overline{SB}$	7. If two line segments are of equal length, then they are congruent.

Quiz: Method of Proof—Congruent Angles & Line Segments

Refer to the diagrams and find the appropriate solutions.

1. Find *a*.

   (A) 38°
   (B) 68°
   (C) 78°
   (D) 90°
   (E) 112°

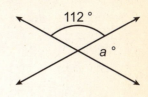

2. Find *c*.

   (A) 32°
   (B) 48°
   (C) 58°
   (D) 82°
   (E) 148°

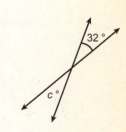

3. Determine *x*.

   (A) 21°
   (B) 23°
   (C) 51°
   (D) 102°
   (E) 153°

4. Find *z*.

   (A) 29°
   (B) 54°
   (C) 61°
   (D) 88°
   (E) 92°

5. In the figure shown, if $\overline{BD}$ is the bisector of angle *ABC*, and angle *ABD* is one-fourth the size of angle *XYZ*, what is the size of angle *ABC*?

   (A) 21°
   (B) 28°
   (C) 42°
   (D) 63°
   (E) 168°

6. $\overrightarrow{BA} \perp \overrightarrow{BC}$ and $m\angle DBC = 53°$.

   Find $m\angle ABD$.

   (A) 27°

   (B) 33°

   (C) 37°

   (D) 53°

   (E) 90°

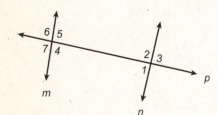

7. If $n \perp p$, which of the following statements is true?

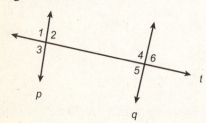

   (A) $\angle 1 \cong \angle 2$

   (B) $\angle 4 \cong \angle 5$

   (C) $m\angle 4 + m\angle 5 > m\angle 1 + m\angle 2$

   (D) $m\angle 3 > m\angle 2$

   (E) $m\angle 4 = 90°$

8. In the figure, if $p \perp t$ and $q \perp t$, which of the following statements is false?

   (A) $\angle 1 \cong \angle 4$

   (B) $\angle 2 \cong \angle 3$

   (C) $m\angle 2 + m\angle 3 = m\angle 4 + m\angle 6$

   (D) $m\angle 5 + m\angle 6 = 180°$

   (E) $m\angle 2 > m\angle 5$

9. If $a \parallel b$, find z.

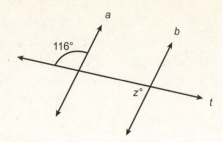

   (A) 26°   (C) 64°   (E) 116°

   (B) 32°   (D) 86°

10. If $m \parallel n$, which of the following statements is not necessarily true?

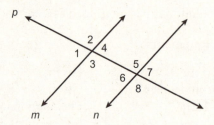

   (A) $\angle 2 \cong \angle 5$

   (B) $\angle 3 \cong \angle 6$

   (C) $m\angle 4 + m\angle 5 = 180°$

   (D) $\angle 1 \cong \angle 6$

   (E) $m\angle 7 + m\angle 3 = 180°$

ANSWER KEY

1.	(B)	6.	(C)
2.	(A)	7.	(A)
3.	(C)	8.	(E)
4.	(D)	9.	(C)
5.	(C)	10.	(B)

Regular Polygons (Convex)

A **polygon** is a figure with the same number of sides as angles.

An **equilateral polygon** is a polygon all of whose sides are of equal measure.

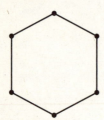

An **equiangular polygon** is a polygon all of whose angles are of equal measure.

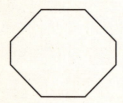

A **regular polygon** is a polygon that is both equilateral and equiangular.

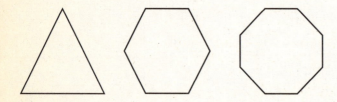

PROBLEM

Each interior angle of a regular polygon contains 120°. How many sides does the polygon have?

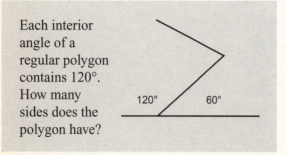
120°   60°

SOLUTION

At each vertex of a polygon, we can draw an exterior angle that is supplementary to the interior angle, as shown in the diagram.

Since we are told that the interior angle measures 120°, we can deduce that the exterior angle measures 60°.

Each exterior angle of a regular polygon of n sides measure $\dfrac{360°}{n}$ degrees. We know that each exterior angle measures 60°, and, therefore, by setting $\dfrac{360°}{n}$ equal to 60°, we can determine the number of sides in the polygon. The calculation is as follows:

$$\frac{360°}{n} = 60°$$

$$60°n = 360°$$

$$n = 6$$

Therefore, the regular polygon, with interior angles of 120°, has six sides and is called a hexagon.

The **perimeter** of a regular polygon is the product of the length of a side(s) and the number of sides (n) $P = ns$.

The area of a regular polygon can be determined by using the **apothem** and **radius** of the polygon. The apothem (a) of a regular polygon is the segment from the center of the polygon perpendicular to a side of the polygon. The radius (r) of a regular polygon is the segment joining any vertex of a regular polygon with the center of that polygon.

(1) All radii of a regular polygon are congruent.

(2) The radius of a regular polygon is congruent to a side.

(3) All apothems of a regular polygon are congruent.

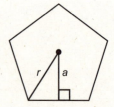
r a

The **area** of a regular polygon equals one-half the product of the length of the apothem and the perimeter.

$$\text{Area} = \frac{1}{2}a \times p$$

PROBLEM

Find the area of a regular hexagon if one side has length 6.

SOLUTION

Since the length of a side equals 6, the radius also equals 6 and the perimeter equals 36. The base of the right triangle, formed by the radius and apothem, is half the length of a side, or 3. You can find the length of the apothem by using the Pythagorean theorem.

$$a^2 + b^2 = c^2$$
$$a^2 + (3)^2 = (6)^2$$
$$a^2 = 36 - 9$$
$$a^2 = 27$$
$$a = 3\sqrt{3}$$

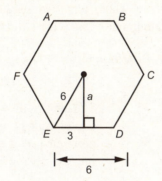

The apothem equals $3\sqrt{3}$. Therefore, the area of the hexagon

$$= \frac{1}{2} a \times p$$
$$= \frac{1}{2}(3\sqrt{3})(36)$$
$$= 54\sqrt{3}$$

Drill: Regular Polygons (Convex)

Angle Measures

DIRECTIONS: Find the appropriate solutions.

1. Find the measure of an interior angle of a regular pentagon.

   (A) 55°   (C) 90°

   (B) 72°   (D) 108°

2. Find the sum of the measures of the exterior angles of a regular triangle.

   (A) 90°   (C) 180°

   (B) 115°   (D) 360°

Area(s) and Perimeter(s)

DIRECTIONS: Find the appropriate solutions.

3. A regular triangle has sides of 24 mm. If the apothem is $4\sqrt{3}$ mm, find the area of the triangle.

   (A) 72 mm²   (C) 144 mm²

   (B) $96\sqrt{3}$ mm²   (D) $144\sqrt{3}$ mm²

4. Find the area of a regular hexagon with sides of 4 cm.

   (A) $12\sqrt{3}$ cm²   (C) $24\sqrt{3}$ cm²

   (B) 24 cm²   (D) 48 cm²

5. Find the area of a regular decagon with sides of length 6 cm and an apothem of length 9.2 cm.

   (A) 55.2 cm²   (C) 138 cm²

   (B) 60 cm²   (D) 276 cm²

Similar Polygons

Definition

Two polygons are similar if there is a one-to-one correspondence between their vertices such that all pairs of corresponding angles are congruent and the ratios of the measures of all pairs of corresponding sides are equal. Note that although they must have the same shape, they may have different sizes.

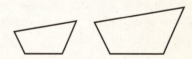

Theorem 1

The perimeters of two similar polygons have the same ratio as the measure of any pair of corresponding line segments of the polygons.

Theorem 2

The ratio of the lengths of two corresponding diagonals of two similar polygons is equal to the ratio of the lengths of any two corresponding sides of the polygons.

Theorem 3

The perimeters of two similar polygons have the same ratio as the measures of any pair of corresponding sides of the polygons.

Theorem 4

Two polygons composed of the same number of triangles similar each to each, and similarly placed, are similar.

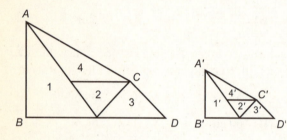

PROBLEM

Prove that any two regular polygons with the same number of sides are similar.

SOLUTION

For any two polygons to be similar, their corresponding angles must be congruent and their corresponding sides proportional. It is necessary to show that these conditions always exist between regular polygons with the same number of sides.

Let us examine the corresponding angles first. For a regular polygon with n sides, each vertex angle is $\frac{(n-2)180}{n}$. Therefore, two regular polygons with the same number of sides will have corresponding vertex angles that are all of the same measure and, hence, are all congruent. This fulfills our first condition for similarity.

We must now determine whether the corresponding sides are proportional. It will suffice to show that the ratios of the lengths of every pair of corresponding sides are the same.

Since the polygons are regular, the sides of each one will be equal. Call the length of the sides of one polygon ℓ_1 and the length of the sides of the other polygon ℓ_2. Hence, the ratio of the lengths of corresponding sides will be ℓ_1/ℓ_2. This will be a constant for any pair of corresponding sides and, hence, the corresponding sides are proportional.

Thus, any two regular polygons with the same number of sides are similar.

PROBLEM

The lengths of two corresponding sides of two similar polygons are 4 and 7. If the perimeter of the smaller polygon is 20, find the perimeter of the larger polygon.

SOLUTION

We know, by theorem, that the perimeters of two similar polygons have the same ratio as the measures of any pair of corresponding sides.

If we let s and p represent the side and perimeter of the smaller polygon and s' and p' represent the corresponding side and perimeter of the larger one, we can then write the proportion

$$p : p' = s : s'$$

By substituting the given values, we can solve for p'.

$$20 : p' = 4 : 7$$
$$4p' = 140$$
$$p' = 35.$$

Therefore, the perimeter of the larger polygon is 35.

Triangles

A closed three-sided geometric figure is called a **triangle**. The points of the intersection of the sides of a triangle are called the **vertices** of the triangle.

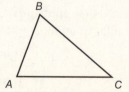

The **perimeter** of a triangle is the sum of the measures of the sides of the triangle.

A triangle with no equal sides is called a **scalene triangle**.

A triangle having at least two equal sides is called an **isosceles triangle**. The third side is called the **base** of the triangle, and the base angles (the angles opposite the equal sides) are equal.

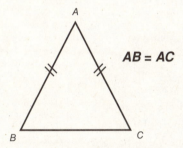

AB = AC

A side of a triangle is a line segment whose endpoints are the vertices of two angles of the triangle.

An **interior angle** of a triangle is an angle formed by two sides and includes the third side within its collection of points.

An **equilateral triangle** is a triangle having three equal sides. $\overline{AB} = \overline{AC} = \overline{BC}$. An equilateral, triangle is also **equiangular**, with each angle equaling 60°.

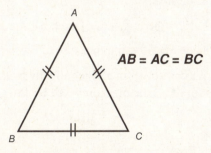

AB = AC = BC

The sum of the measures of the interior angles of a triangle is 180°.

A triangle with one obtuse angle (greater than 90°) is called an **obtuse triangle**.

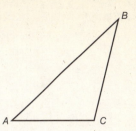

An **acute triangle** is a triangle with three acute angles (less than 90°).

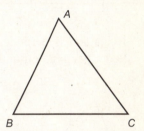

A triangle with a right angle is a **right triangle**. The side opposite the right angle in a right triangle is called the hypotenuse of the right triangle. The other two sides are called arms or legs of the right triangle. By the Pythagorean Theorem, the length of the three sides of a right triangle are related by the formula $c^2 = a^2 + b^2$ where c is the hypotenuse and a and b are the other sides (the legs).

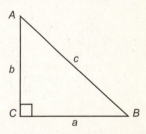

An **altitude** of a triangle is a line segment from a vertex of the triangle perpendicular to the opposite side.

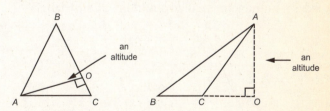

The **area** of a triangle is given by $A = \frac{1}{2}bh$ where h is the altitude and b is the base to which the altitude is drawn.

A line segment connecting a vertex of a triangle and the midpoint of the opposite side is called a **median** of the triangle.

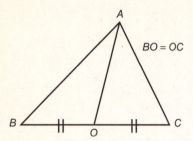

A line that bisects and is perpendicular to a side of a triangle is called a **perpendicular bisector** of that side.

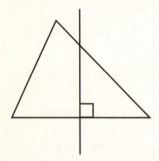

An **angle bisector** of a triangle is a line that bisects an angle and extends to the opposite side of the triangle.

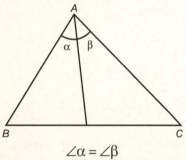

$$\angle \alpha = \angle \beta$$

The line segment that joins the midpoints of two sides of a triangle is called a **midline** of the triangle.

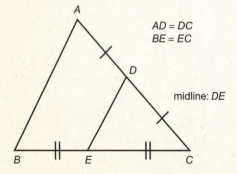

An **exterior angle** of a triangle is an angle formed outside a triangle by one side of the triangle and the extension of an adjacent side.

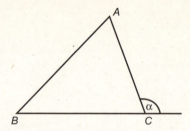

Three or more lines (or rays or segments) are **concurrent** if there exists one point common to all of them, that is, if they all intersect at the same point.

PROBLEM

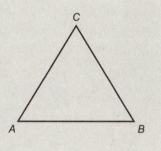

The measure of the vertex angle of an isosceles triangle exceeds the measurement of each base angles by 30°. Find the value of each angle of the triangle.

SOLUTION

We known that the sum of the values of the angles of a triangle is 180°. In an isosceles triangle, the angles opposite the congruent sides (the base angles) are, themselves, congruent and of equal value.

Therefore,

(1) Let x = the measure of each base angle.

(2) Then $x + 30$ = the measure of the vertex angle.

We can solve for x algebraically by keeping in mind the sum of all the measures will be 180°.

$$x + x + (x + 30) = 180$$
$$3x + 30 = 180$$
$$3x = 150$$
$$x = 50$$

Therefore, the base angles each measure 50°, and the vertex angle measures 80°.

Drill: Triangles

Angle Measures

DIRECTIONS: Refer to the diagram and find the appropriate solution.

1. In $\triangle PQR$, $\angle Q$ is a right angle. Find $m\angle R$.

    (A) 27°   (C) 54°

    (B) 33°   (D) 67°

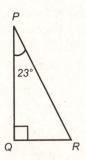

2. $\triangle MNO$ is isosceles. If the vertex angle, $\angle N$, has a measure of 96°, find the measure of $\angle M$.

    (A) 21°

    (B) 42°

    (C) 64°

    (D) 84°

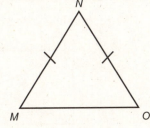

3. Find x.

    (A) 15°

    (B) 25°

    (C) 30°

    (D) 45°

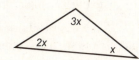

Similar Triangles

DIRECTIONS: Refer to the diagram and find the appropriate solution.

4. The two triangles shown are similar. Find b.

    (A) $2\frac{2}{3}$

    (B) 3

    (C) 4

    (D) 16

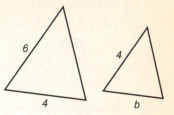

5. The two triangles shown are similar. Find a and b.

    (A) 5 and 10   (C) $4\frac{2}{3}$ and $7\frac{1}{3}$

    (B) 4 and 8   (D) $5\frac{1}{3}$ and 8

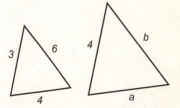

Area

DIRECTIONS: Refer to the diagram and find the appropriate solution.

6. Find the area of $\triangle MNO$.

    (A) 22

    (B) 49

    (C) 56

    (D) 84

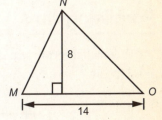

7. Find the area of $\triangle PQR$.

    (A) 31.5

    (B) 38.5

    (C) 53

    (D) 77

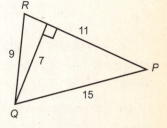

8.   Find the area of $\triangle STU$.

(A) $4\sqrt{2}$

(B) $8\sqrt{2}$

(C) $12\sqrt{2}$

(D) $16\sqrt{2}$

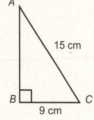

9.   Find the area of $\triangle ABC$.

(A)   54 cm²

(B)   81 cm²

(C)   108 cm²

(D)   135 cm²

10.   Find the area of $\triangle XYZ$.

(A)   20 cm²

(B)   50 cm²

(C) $50\sqrt{2}$ cm²

(D)   100 cm²

Quadrilaterals

A **quadrilateral** is a polygon with four sides.

Parallelograms

A **parallelogram** is a quadrilateral whose opposite sides are parallel.

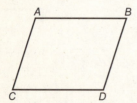

Two angles that have their vertices at the endpoints of the same side of a parallelogram are called consecutive angles.

The perpendicular segment connecting any point of a line containing one side of a parallelogram to the line containing the opposite side of the parallelogram is called the altitude of the parallelogram.

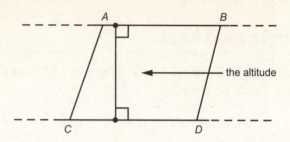

the altitude

A diagonal of a polygon is a line segment joining any two nonconsecutive vertices.

The area of a parallelogram is given by the formula $A = bh$, where b is the base and h is the height drawn perpendicular to that base. Note that the height equals the altitude of the parallelogram.

$A = bh$

$A = (10)(3)$

$A = 30$

Rectangles

A **rectangle** is a parallelogram with right angles.

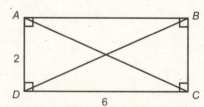

The diagonals of a rectangle are equal.

If the diagonals of a parallelogram are equal, the parallelogram is a rectangle.

If a quadrilateral has four right angles, then it is a rectangle.

The area of a rectangle is given by the formula $A = lw$, where l is the length and w is the width.

$A = lw$

$A = (3)(10)$

$A = 30$

Rhombi

A **rhombus** is a parallelogram that has two adjacent sides that are equal.

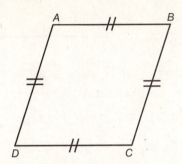

All sides of a rhombus are equal.

The diagonals of a rhombus are perpendicular to each other.

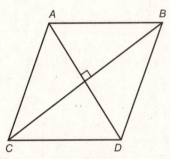

The area of a rhombus can be found by the formula $A = \frac{1}{2}(d_1 + d_2)$ where d_1 and d_2 are the diagonals.

The diagonals of a rhombus bisect the angles of the rhombus.

If the diagonals of a parallelogram are perpendicular, the parallelogram is a rhombus.

If a quadrilateral has four equal sides, then it is a rhombus.

A parallelogram is a rhombus if either diagonal of the parallelogram bisects the angles of the vertices it joins.

Squares

A **square** is a rhombus with a right angle.

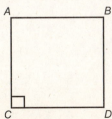

A square is an equilateral quadrilateral.

A square has all the properties of parallelograms and rectangles.

A rhombus is a square if one of its interior angles is a right angle.

In a square, the measure of either diagonal can be calculated by multiplying the length of any side by the square root of 2.

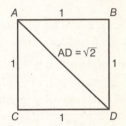

The area of a square is given by the formula $A = s^2$, where s is the side of the square. Since all sides of a square are equal, it does not matter which side is used.

$A = s^2$

$A = 6^2$

$A = 36$

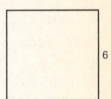

The area of a square can also be found by taking $\frac{1}{2}$ the product of the length of the diagonal squared.

$A = \frac{1}{2}d^2$

$A = \frac{1}{2}(8)^2$

$A = 32$

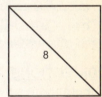

Trapezoids

A **trapezoid** is a quadrilateral with two and only two sides parallel. The parallel sides of a trapezoid are called **bases.**

The **median** of a trapezoid is the line joining the midpoints of the non-parallel sides.

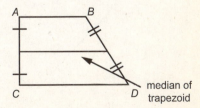

median of trapezoid

The perpendicular segment connecting any point in the line containing one base of the trapezoid to the line containing the other base is the **altitude** of the trapezoid.

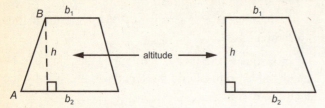

The area of a trapezoid equals one half the altitude times the sum of the bases, or $\frac{1}{2}h(b_1 + b_2)$.

An **isosceles trapezoid** is a trapezoid whose non-parallel sides are equal. A pair of angles including only one of the parallel sides is called a pair of base angles.

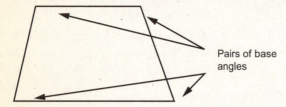

Pairs of base angles

The median of a trapezoid is parallel to the bases and equal to one-half their sum.

The base angles of an isosceles trapezoid are equal.

The diagonals of an isosceles trapezoid are equal.

The opposite angles of an isosceles trapezoid are supplementary.

Drill: Quadrilaterals

DIRECTIONS: Refer to the diagram and find the appropriate solution.

1. Quadrilateral *ABCD* is a parallelogram. If $m\angle B = (6x + 2)°$ and $m\angle D = 98°$, find *x*.

    (A) 12

    (B) 16

    (C) $16\frac{2}{3}$

    (D) 18

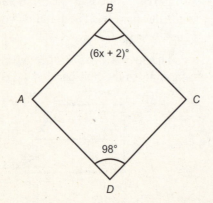

2. Find the area of parallelogram *STUV*.

    (A) 56

    (B) 90

    (C) 108

    (D) 162

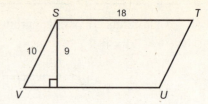

3. In rectangle *ABCD*, $\overline{AD} = 6$ cm and $\overline{DC} = 8$ cm. Find the length of the diagonal $\overline{AC}$.

    (A) 10 cm   (C) 20 cm

    (B) 12 cm   (D) 28 cm

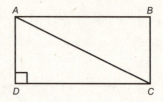

4. Find the area of rectangle *UVXY*.

    (A) 17 cm²

    (B) 34 cm²

    (C) 35 cm²

    (D) 70 cm²

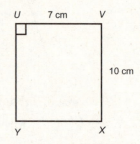

5. Find the length of $\overline{BO}$ in rectangle *BCDE* if the diagonal $\overline{EC}$ is 17 mm.

    (A) 6.55 mm

    (B) 8 mm

    (C) 8.5 mm

    (D) 17 mm

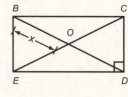

6. In rhombus *GHIJ*, $\overline{GI} = 6$ cm and $\overline{HJ} = 8$ cm. Find the length of $\overline{GH}$.

    (A) 3 cm

    (B) 4 cm

    (C) 5 cm

    (D) $4\sqrt{3}$ cm

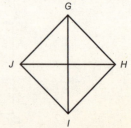

7. Find the area of the trapezoid *RSTU*.

    (A) 80 cm²

    (B) 87.5 cm²

    (C) 140 cm²

    (D) 175 cm²

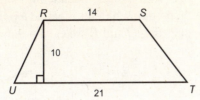

8. *ABCD* is an isosceles trapezoid. Find the perimeter.

    (A) 21 cm   (C) 30 cm

    (B) 27 cm   (D) 50 cm

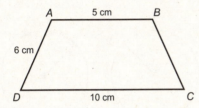

9. Find the area of trapezoid *MNOP*.

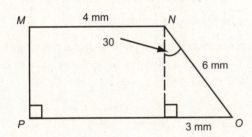

    (A) $(17 + 3\sqrt{3})$ mm²   (C) $\dfrac{33\sqrt{3}}{2}$ mm²

    (B) $\dfrac{33}{2}$ mm²   (D) 33 mm²

10. Trapezoid *XYZW* is isosceles. If $m\angle W = 58°$ and $m\angle Z = (4x - 6)°$, find x.

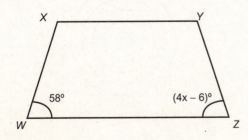

    (A) 8   (C) 13

    (B) 12   (D) 16

Circles

A **circle** is a set of points in the same plane equidistant from a fixed point, called its center. Circles are often named by their center point, circle *O*.

A **radius** of a circle is a line segment drawn from the center of the circle to any point on the circle.

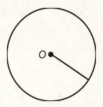

A portion of a circle is called an **arc** of the circle.

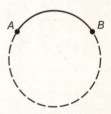

A line that intersects a circle in two points is called a **secant.**

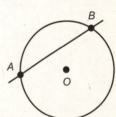

A line segment joining two points on a circle is called a **chord** of the circle.

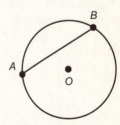

A chord that passes through the center of the circle is called a **diameter** of the circle.

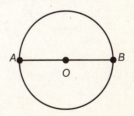

The line passing through the centers of two (or more) circles is called the **line of centers.**

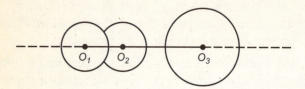

An angle whose vertex is on the circle and whose sides are chords of the circle is called an **inscribed angle** ($\angle$ BAC in the diagrams).

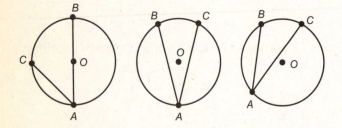

An angle whose vertex is at the center of a circle and whose sides are radii is called a **central angle.**

The measure of a minor arc is the measure of the central angle that intercepts that arc.

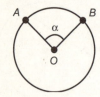

$$m\overset{\frown}{AB} = \alpha = m\angle AOB$$

The distance from a point P to a given circle is the distance from that point to the point where the circle intersects with a line segment with endpoints at the center of the circle and point P.

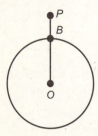

The distance of point P to the diagrammed circle with center O is the line segment $\overline{PB}$ of line segment $\overline{PO}$.

A line that has one and only one point of intersection with a circle is called a tangent to that circle, and their common point is called a **point of tangency.** In the diagram, Q and P are each points of tangency.

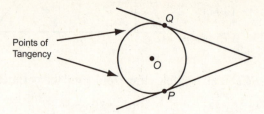

Congruent circles are circles whose radii are congruent.

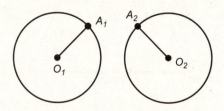

If $O_1A_1 \cong O_2A_2$, then $O_1 \cong O_2$.

The measure of a semicircle is 180°.

A **circumscribed circle** is a circle passing through all the vertices of a polygon. The polygon is said to be **inscribed** in the circle.

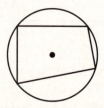

Circles that have the same center and unequal radii are called **concentric circles.**

Concentric Circles

The **circumference** of a circle is the length of its outer edge, given by $C = \pi d = 2\pi r$, where r is the radius, *d* is the diameter, and π(pi) is a mathematical constant approximately equal to 3.14.

The area of a circle is given by $A = 2\pi r^2$. A full circle is 360°. The length of arc intercepted by a central angle has the same ratio to the circle's circumference as the measure of the arc has to be 360°, the full circle. Therefore, arc length is given by $\frac{n}{360} \times 2\pi r$, where *n* = measure of the central angle. The measure of an arc in degrees, however, is the same as the measure of its central angle.

A sector is the portion of a circle between two radii. Its area is given by $A = \frac{n}{360}(\pi r^2)$ where *n* is the central angle formed by the radii.

PROBLEM

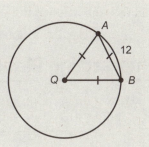

A and *B* are points on circle *Q* such that $\triangle AQB$ is equilateral. If the length of side $\overline{AB} = 12$, find the length of arc *AB*.

SOLUTION

To find the arc length of arc *AB*, we must find the measure of the central angle $\angle AQB$ and the measure of the radius $\overline{QA}$. $\angle AQB$ is an interior angle of the equilateral triangle $\triangle AQB$. Therefore,

$$m\angle AQB = 60°.$$

Similarly, in the equilateral $\triangle AQB$,

$$\overline{AQ} = \overline{AB} = \overline{QB} = 12.$$

Given the radius, *r*, and the central angle, *n*, the arc length is given by

$$\frac{n}{360} \times 2\pi r.$$

Therefore, by substitution,

$$\angle AQB = \frac{60}{360} \times 2\pi \times 12 = \frac{1}{6} \times 2\pi \times 12 = 4\pi.$$

Therefore, the length of arc $AB = 4\pi$.

Drill: Circles

DIRECTIONS: Determine the accurate measure.

1. Find the circumference of circle *A* if its radius is 3 mm.

    (A) 3π mm   (C) 9π mm

    (B) 6π mm   (D) 12π mm

2. Find the area of circle *I*.

    (A) 22 mm²

    (B) 121 mm²

    (C) 121π mm²

    (D) 132 mm²

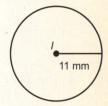

3. The diameter of circle *Z* is 27 mm. Find the area of the circle.

    (A) 91.125 mm²   (C) 191.5π mm²

    (B) 182.25 mm²   (D) 182.25π mm²

4. The area of circle *B* is 225π cm². Find the length of the diameter of the circle.

    (A) 15 cm   (C) 30 cm

    (B) 20 cm   (D) 20π cm

5. The area of circle *X* is 144π mm² while the area of circle *Y* is 81π mm². Write the ratio of the radius of circle *X* to that of circle *Y*.

    (A) 3 : 4   (C) 9 : 12

    (B) 4 : 3   (D) 27 : 12

6. The radius of the smaller of two concentric circles is 5 cm while the radius of the larger circle is 7 cm. Determine the area of the shaded region.

    (A) 7π cm²

    (B) 24π cm²

    (C) 25π cm²

    (D) 36π cm²

7. Find the measure of arc $\overset{\frown}{MN}$ if $m\angle MON = 62°$.

    (A) 16°

    (B) 32°

    (C) 59°

    (D) 62°

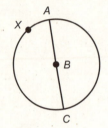

8. Find the measure of arc $\overset{\frown}{AXC}$.

    (A) 150°

    (B) 160°

    (C) 180°

    (D) 270°

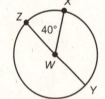

9. Find the measure of arc $\overset{\frown}{XY}$ in circle W.

    (A) 40°

    (B) 120°

    (C) 140°

    (D) 180°

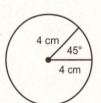

10. Find the area of the sector shown.

    (A) 4 cm²

    (B) 2π cm²

    (C) 16 cm²

    (D) 8π cm²

Solid Geometry

Cubes, Cylinders

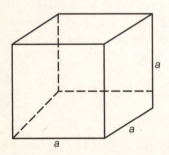

The volume of a cube with edge a is

$$V = a^3.$$

The surface area of a cube with edge a is

$$A = 6a^2.$$

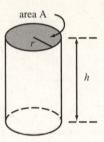

The volume of a right circular cylinder with radius r and height h is

$$V = \pi r^2 h.$$

The surface area of a right circular cylinder with radius r and height h is

$$A = 2\pi r^2 + 2\pi rh.$$

Intersecting Planes

If two different planes intersect, they intersect in a straight line.

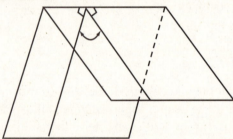

The angle between two planes is the angle between two rays on the two planes, each of which is perpendicular to the line of intersection of the planes.

Volume and Surface Area

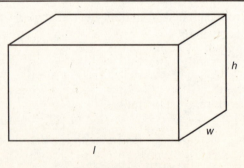

Rectangular solid

The volume of a rectangular solid with length *l*, width *w*, and height *h* is

$$V = lwh.$$

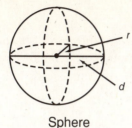

Sphere

The volume of a sphere with radius *r* is

$$V = \frac{4}{3}\pi r^3.$$

The surface area of a sphere with radius *r* is

$$A = 4\pi r^2.$$

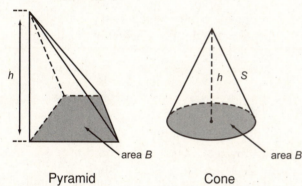

Pyramid   Cone

The volume of a pyramid or cone with base area *B* and height *h* is

$$V = \frac{1}{3}Bh.$$

If the base of the cone is a circle with radius *r*, then

$$A = \pi r^2,$$

so

$$V = \frac{1}{3}\pi r^2 h.$$

The total area of a cone is the sum of the surface area of the conical part (πrs), where *s* is the slant height, plus the area of the circular base, so $A = \pi rs + \pi r^2$.

PROBLEM

Calculate the circumference of a circle that has a radius of 12 inches.

SOLUTION

1. Write the formula for the circumference of a circle.

$$\text{circumference} = 2\pi r$$

2. Substitute the known values into the equation. Pi is approximately 3.14. The radius is 12.

$$\text{circumference} = 2(3.14)12$$

3. Solve the equation.

$$\text{circumference} = 75.4$$

The correct answer is that the circumference = 75.4 inches.

PROBLEM

Calculate the area of a circle that has a diameter of 10 meters.

SOLUTION

1. Write the formula for the area of a circle.

$$A = \pi r^2.$$

2. Substitute the known values into the equation. Pi is approximately 3.14. The diameter of the circle is 10 meters, so the radius is 5 meters.

$$A = \pi(5)^2$$

3. Solve the equation.

$$A = 78.5$$

The correct answer is that the area of the circle is 78.5 m².

PROBLEM

Calculate the volume of a sphere that has a radius of 2 meters.

SOLUTION

1. Write the formula for the volume of a sphere.

$$V = \frac{4}{3}\pi r^3$$

2. Substitute the known values into the equation. Pi is approximately 3.14 and the radius is 2 meters.

$$V = \frac{4}{3}\pi(2)^3$$

3. Solve the equation.

$$V = 33.49 \text{ or } \sim 33.5$$

The correct answer is that the volume of the sphere is 33.5 m³.

PROBLEM

Calculate the perimeter of the triangle below.

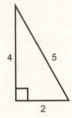

SOLUTION

1. Write the formula for the perimeter of a triangle.

perimeter = length of side 1 + length of side 2 + length of side 3

2. Substitute the known values into the formula.

perimeter = 4 + 2 + 5

3. Solve the equation.

perimeter = 11

The correct answer is that the perimeter of the triangle is 11.

PROBLEM

Calculate the area of the triangle below.

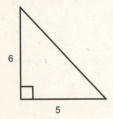

SOLUTION

1. Write the formula for the area of a triangle.

$$A = \frac{1}{2}bh$$

2. Substitute the known values into the formula. The base of the triangle is 5 and the height is 6.

$$A = \frac{1}{2}(5)(6)$$

3. Solve the equation.

$$A = 15$$

The correct answer is that the area of the triangle is 15.

PROBLEM

Calculate the volume of the cube that has a length of 5, a height of 1.5, and a width of 4.

SOLUTION

1. Write the formula for the volume of a cube.

$$V = l \times w \times h$$

2. Substitute the known values into the formula.

$$V = 5 \times 4 \times 1.5$$

3. Solve the equation.

$$V = 30$$

The correct answer is that the volume of the cube = 30.

PROBLEM

Calculate the volume of a pyramid that has a height of 3 feet. The area of the base of the pyramid was calculated to be 15 square feet.

SOLUTION

1. Write the formula for the volume of a pyramid.

$$V = \frac{1}{3}Bh,$$ where B is the area of the base of the pyramid.

2. Substitute the known values into the formula.

$$V = \frac{1}{3}(15)(3)$$

3. Solve the equation.

$$V = 15$$

The correct answer is that the volume of the pyramid is 15 cubic feet.

PROBLEM

Calculate the area of the triangle below.

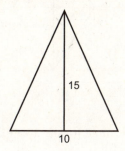

SOLUTION

1. Write the formula for the area of a triangle.

$$A = \frac{1}{2}bh$$

2. Substitute the known values into the formula. The base of the triangle is 10 and the height is 15.

$$A = \frac{1}{2}(10)(15)$$

3. Solve the equation.

$$A = 75$$

The correct answer is that the area of the triangle is 75.

PROBLEM

Calculate the volume of the cone below.

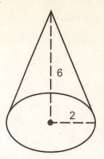

SOLUTION

1. Write the formula for the volume of a cone.

$$V = \frac{1}{3}\pi r^2 h$$

2. Substitute the known values into the equation.

$$V = \frac{1}{3}\pi(2)^2(6)$$

3. Solve the equation.

$$V = 25.12$$

The correct answer is that the volume of the cone is 25.12 cubic inches.

PROBLEM

Calculate the volume of the cylinder below.

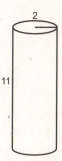

SOLUTION

1. Write the formula for the volume of a cylinder.

$$V = \pi r^2 h$$

2. Substitute the known values into the formula.

$$V = \pi(2)^2(11)$$

3. Solve the equation.

$$V = 138.16$$

The correct answer is that the volume is 138.16 m³.

PROBLEM

Calculate the total area of the cone below. Round to the nearest meter.

SOLUTION

1. Write the formula for the total area of a cone.

$A = \pi rs + \pi r^2$, where s is the slant height

2. Substitute the known values into the formula.

$$A = \pi(2)(5) + \pi(2)^2$$

3. Solve the equation.

$$A = 10\pi + 4\pi = \pi(10 + 4) = \pi(14)$$

$$A = 44$$

The correct answer is 44 m².

PROBLEM

Calculate the area of the trapezoid below.

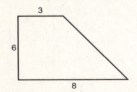

SOLUTION

1. Write the formula for the area of a trapezoid.

$A = \dfrac{1}{2}h(b_1 + b_2)$, where b_1 and b_2 are the bases

2. Substitute the known values into the formula.

$$A = \frac{1}{2}(6)(3 + 8)$$

3. Solve the equation.

$$A = 33$$

The correct answer is that the area of the trapezoid is 33 square feet.

PROBLEM

Calculate the area of the rhombus below.

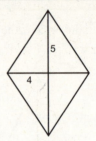

SOLUTION

1. Write the formula for the area of a rhombus.

$A = \dfrac{1}{2}(d_1 \text{ and } d_2)$, where d_1 and d_2 are the diagonals of the rhombus

2. Substitute the known values into the formula.

$$A = \frac{1}{2}(5)(4)$$

3. Solve the equation.

$$A = 10$$

The correct answer is that the area of the rhombus is 10 square feet.

PROBLEM

Calculate the area of the parallelogram below.

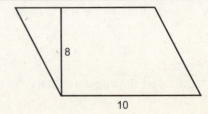

SOLUTION

1. Write the formula for the area of a parallelogram.

$A = bh$, where b is the base and h is the height

2. Substitute the known values into the formula.

$A = 10(8)$

3. Solve the equation.

$A = 80$

The correct answer is that the area of the parallelogram is 80.

Problem Solving with Triangles

PROBLEM

Using the Pythagorean theorem, calculate c in the figure below.

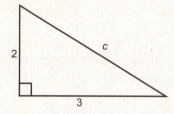

SOLUTION

1. Write the Pythagorean theorem.

$a^2 + b^2 = c^2$

2. Substitute the values of a and b into the equation.

$(3)^2 + (2)^2 = c^2$

3. Solve the left side of the equation.

$(3)^2 + (2)^2 = 13$

4. Rewrite the equation.

$13 = c^2$

5. Solve for c.

$\sqrt{13} = c$

The correct answer is $c = \sqrt{13}$.

PROBLEM

Using the Pythagorean theorem, calculate a in the figure below.

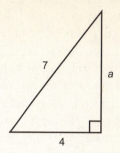

SOLUTION

1. Write the Pythagorean theorem.

$a^2 + b^2 = c^2$

2. Substitute the values of b and c into the equation.

$a^2 + (4)^2 = 7^2$

3. Simplify the equation.

$a^2 + 16 = 49$

4. Subtract 16 from both sides and rewrite the equation.

$a^2 = 33$

5. Solve for x.

$a = \sqrt{33}$

Coordinate Geometry

Coordinate geometry refers to the study of geometric figures using algebraic principles.

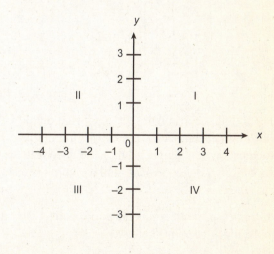

The graph shown is called the Cartesian coordinate plane. The graph consists of a pair of perpendicular lines called **coordinate axes.** The **vertical axis** is the *y*-axis and the **horizontal axis** is the *x*-axis. The point of intersection of these two axes is called the **origin;** it is the zero point of both axes. Furthermore, points to the right of the origin on the *x*-axis and above the origin on the *y*-axis represent positive real numbers. Points to the left of the origin on the *x*-axis or below the origin on the *y*-axis represent negative real numbers.

The four regions cut off by the coordinate axes are, in counterclockwise direction from the top right, called the first, second, third, and fourth quadrant, respectively. The first quadrant contains all points with two positive coordinates.

In the graph shown, two points *A* and *B* are shown. They can be identified by the ordered pair, (*x, y*) of numbers. The *x*-coordinate is the first number and the *y*-coordinate is the second number.

To plot a point on the graph when given the coordinates, draw perpendicular lines from the number-line coordinates to the point where the two lines intersect.

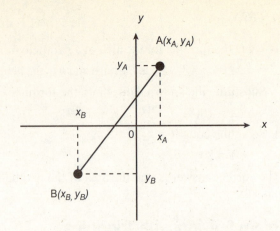

For any two points *A* and *B* with coordinates (x_A, y_A) and (x_B, y_B), respectively, the distance between *A* and *B* is represented by:

$$d = \sqrt{(x_A - x_B)^2 + (y_A - y_B)^2}$$

This is commonly known as the distance formula.

PROBLEM

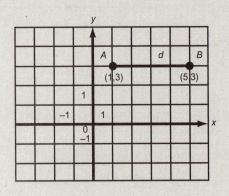

Find the distance between the point *A*(1, 3) and *B*(5, 3).

SOLUTION

In this case, where the ordinate of both points is the same, the distance between the two points is given by the absolute value of the difference between the two abscissas. In fact, this case reduces to merely counting boxes, as the figure shows.

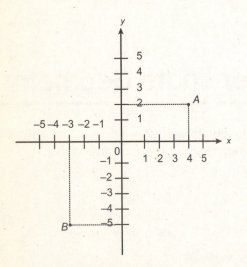

To find the coordinates of a given point on the graph, draw perpendicular lines from the point to the coordinates on the number line. The *x*-coordinate is written before the *y*-coordinate and a comma is used to separate the two.

In this case, point *A* has the coordinates (4, 2) and the coordinates of point *B* are (−3, −5).

Let, x_1 = abscissa of *A* y_1 = ordinate of *A*

x_2 = abscissa of *B* y_2 = ordinate of *B*

d = the distance

Therefore, $d = |x_1 - x_2|$. By substitution, $d = |1 - 5|$ $= |-4| = 4$. This answer can also be obtained by applying the general formula for distance between any two points.

$$d = \sqrt{(x_1 - x_2)^2 + (y_1 - y_2)^2}$$

By substitution,

$$d = \sqrt{(1-5)^2 + (3-3)^2}$$
$$= \sqrt{(-4)^2 + (0)^2}$$
$$= \sqrt{16}$$
$$= 4$$

The distance is 4.

To find the midpoint of a segment between the two given endpoints, use the formula

$$MP = \left(\frac{x_1 + x_2}{2}, \frac{y_1 + y_2}{2} \right)$$

where x_1 and y_1 are the coordinates of one point, and x_2 and y_2 are the coordinates of the other point.

Conic Sections

Conic sections are the curves formed when a plane intersects the surface of a right circular cone. As shown below, these curves are the circle, the ellipse, the parabola, and the hyperbola.

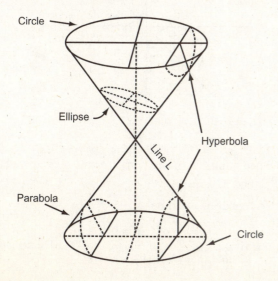

The Circle

As stated previously, a circle is defined to be the set of all points at a given distance from a given point. The given distance is called the radius, and the given point is called the center of the circle. Using the distance formula, it is easy to establish that an equation of a circle with center of (h,k) and radius of r is

$$(x - h)^2 + (y - k)^2 = r^2$$

An equation of this kind is said to be in standard form. Here are two examples that illustrate the practicality of the standard form.

•   **EXAMPLES**

1. Find an equation of the circle with center of $(2,-3)$ with radius of 6.

$$(x - 2)^2 + [y - (-3)]^2 = 6^2$$
$$(x - 2)^2 + (y + 3)^2 = 36$$

2. Graph the equation listed below.

$$x^2 + y^2 - 6x + 10y + 30 = 0$$
$$(x^2 - 6x) + (y^2 + 10y) = -30$$

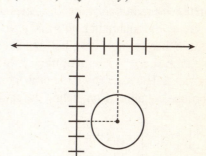

$$(x^2 - 6x + 9) + (y^2 + 10y + 25) = -30 + 34$$
$$(x - 3)^2 + (y + 5)^2 = 4$$

Notice, in the second example, how easy it is to graph

$$(x - 3)^2 + (y + 5)^2 = 4$$

and how difficult it would be to graph

$$x^2 + y^2 - 6x + 10y + 30 = 0$$

in that form.

Problem Solving Examples:

Write equations of the following circles:

(a) With center at $(-1,3)$ and radius 9.

(b) With center at (2,–3) and radius 5.

The equation of the circles with center at (a,b) and radius r is

$$(x - a)^2 + (y - b)^2 = r^2.$$

(a) Thus, the equation of the circle with center at $(–1,3)$ and radius 9 is

$$[x - (–1)]^2 + (y - 3)^2 = 9^2$$
$$(x + 1)^2 + (y - 3)^2 = 81$$

(b) Similarly the equation of the circle with center at $(2,–3)$ and radius 5 is

$$(x - 2)^2 + [y - (–3)]^2 = 5^2$$
$$(x - 2)^2 + (y + 3)^2 = 25$$

PROBLEM

Find the center and radius of the circle.

$$x^2 - 4x + y^2 + 8y - 5 = 0 \qquad (1)$$

SOLUTION

We can find the radius and the coordinates of the center by completing the square in both x and y. To complete the square in either variable, take half the coefficient of the variable term (i.e., the x term of the y term) and then square this value. The resulting number is then added to both sides of the equation. Completing the square in x:

$$\left[\frac{1}{2}(-4)\right]^2 = [-2]^2 = 4$$

Then equation (1) becomes:

$$(x^2 - 4x + 4) + y^2 + 8y - 5 = 0 + 4.$$

or

$$(x - 2)^2 + y^2 + 8y - 5 = 4 \qquad (2)$$

Before completing the square in y, add 5 to both sides of equation (2):

$$(x - 2)^2 + y^2 + 8y - \cancel{5} + \cancel{5} = 4 + 5$$
$$(x - 2)^2 + y^2 + 8y = 9 \qquad (3)$$

Now, completing the square in y:

$$\left[\frac{1}{2}(8)\right]^2 = [4]^2 = 16$$

Then equation (3) becomes:

$$(x - 2)^2 + (y^2 + 8y + 16) = 9 + 16,$$

or

$$(x - 2)^2 + (y + 4)^2 = 25 \qquad (4)$$

Note that the equation of a circle is:

$$(x - h)^2 + (y - k)^2 = r^2,$$

where (h,k) is the center of the circle and r is the radius of the circle. Equation (4) is in the form of the equation of a circle. Hence, equation (4) represents a circle with center $(2,–4)$ and radius = 5.

PROBLEM

Find the equation of the circle of radius $r = 9$, with center on $\ell : y = x$ and tangent to both coordinate axes.

SOLUTION

As seen in the figure, there are two such circles, O and O'. Let the centers of O and O' be (a,b) and (c,d), respectively.

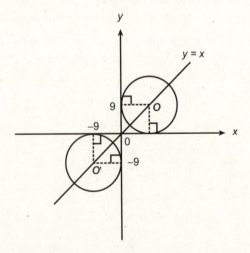

Since points (a,b) and (c,d) are on $\ell : y = x$, we have $a = b$ and $c = d$.

The equations will be

$$(x - a)^2 + (y - a)^2 = 9^2$$

and $(x - c)^2 + (y - c)^2 = 9^2$

Because the circles are tangent to both coordinate axes, we obtain $a = 9 = b$ and $c = -9 = d$ (see figure). Therefore, the equations are

$$(x - 9)^2 + (y - 9)^2 = 81 \text{ and}$$
$$(x + 9)^2 + (y + 9)^2 = 81$$

The Ellipse

An ellipse is defined to be the set of all points in a plane, the sum of whose distance from two fixed points is a constant. Each of the fixed points is called a focus. The plural of the word focus is foci. A simple method of constructing an ellipse comes directly from this definition. Mark two of the foci and call them F_1 and F_2, then insert a thumb tack at each focus. Next, take a string that is longer than the distance between F_1 and F_2 and tie one end at F_1 and the other end at F_2. Then, pull the string taut with a pencil and trace the ellipse. It will be oval shaped and will have two lines of symmetry and one point of symmetry.

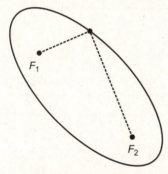

Using the distance formula, it is fairly easy to derive an equation of the ellipse with foci at $(c,0)$ and $(-c,0)$ with the sum of the distance of $2a$. The standard equation of such an ellipse is

$$\frac{x^2}{a^2} + \frac{y^2}{b^2} = 1,$$

where $b^2 = a^2 - c^2$. Obviously, $a^2 > b^2$. Here is a graph of such an ellipse.

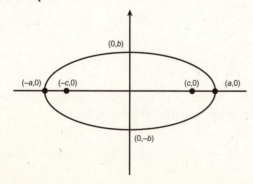

The center of the ellipse is the point midway between the foci. In this case, the center is at the origin. The segment from $(-a,0)$ to $(a,0)$ is called the major axis, and its length is $2a$. The segment from $(0,-b)$ to $(0,b)$ is called the minor axis, and its length is $2b$. In the ellipse, the x-axis and the y-axis are lines of symmetry, and the origin is a point of symmetry. The eccentricity e is defined to be $\frac{c}{a}$. When this ratio is close to 0, the ellipse resembles a circle, but when this ratio is close to 1, the ellipse is elongated.

It is very easy to graph an ellipse when the standard equation is given. In most cases, it is desirable to convert to that form. This process is illustrated in the example below.

•   **EXAMPLE**

Graph

$$9x^2 + 16y^2 = 144$$
$$\frac{9x^2}{144} + \frac{16y^2}{144} = \frac{144}{144}$$
$$\frac{x^2}{16} + \frac{y^2}{9} = 1$$
$$\frac{x^2}{4^2} + \frac{y^2}{3^2} = 1$$

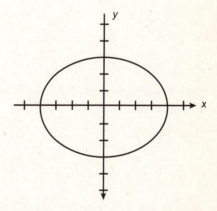

For an ellipse with foci at $(0,c)$ and $(0,-c)$, and with the sum of distances as $2a$, the standard equation is

$$\frac{y^2}{a^2} + \frac{x^2}{b^2} = 1$$

Here is a table that illustrates what happens when the center of the ellipse is not at the origin.

Center of ellipse	Sum of distance	Foci	Standard equation
(h,k)	$2a$	$(h+c,k)$ and $(h-c,k)$	$\dfrac{(x-h)^2}{a^2}+\dfrac{(y-k)^2}{b^2}=1$
(h,k)	$2a$	$(h,k+c)$ and $(h,k-c)$	$\dfrac{(y-k)^2}{a^2}+\dfrac{(x-h)^2}{b^2}=1$

In both cases, $b^2 = a^2 - c^2$.

Problem Solving Examples:

PROBLEM

Discuss the graph of $\dfrac{x^2}{25}+\dfrac{y^2}{9}=1$.

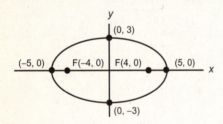

SOLUTION

Since this is an equation of the form $\dfrac{x^2}{a^2}+\dfrac{y^2}{b^2}=1$, with $a=5$ and $b=3$, it represents an ellipse. The simplest way to sketch the curve is to find its intercepts.

If we set $x = 0$, then

$$y=\sqrt{\left(1-\frac{x^2}{25}\right)9}=\sqrt{\left(1-\frac{0^2}{25}\right)9}=\pm 3$$

so that the y-intercepts are at $(0,3)$ and $(0,-3)$. Similarly the x-intercepts are found for $y = 0$:

$$x=\sqrt{\left(1-\frac{y^2}{9}\right)25}$$
$$=\sqrt{\left(1-\frac{0^2}{9}\right)25}$$
$$=\pm 5$$

to be at $(5,0)$ and $(-5,0)$ (see figure). To locate the foci we note that

$$c^2 = a^2 - b^2 = 5^2 - 3^2$$
$$c^2 = 25 - 9 = 16$$
$$c = \pm 4.$$

The foci lie on the major axis of the ellipse. In this case it is the x-axis since $a = 5$ is greater than $b = 3$. Therefore, the foci are $(\pm c,0)$, that is, at $(-4,0)$ and $(4,0)$. The sum of the distances from any point on the curve to the foci is $2a = 2(5) = 10$.

PROBLEM

In the equation of an ellipse,

$$4x^2 + 9y^2 - 16x + 18y - 11 = 0,$$

determine the standard form of the equation, and find the values of a, b, c, and e.

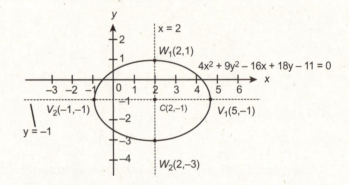

SOLUTION

By completing the squares, we can arrive at the standard form of the equation, from which the values of the parameters can be determined. Thus,

$$4(x^2 - 4x + 4) + 9(y^2 + 2y + 1) = 36.$$

or

$4(x-2)^2 + 9(y+1)^2 = 36$. Dividing by 36,

$$\frac{(x-2)^2}{9}+\frac{(y+1)^2}{4}=1.$$

Thus, the center of the ellipse is at $(2, -1)$. Comparing this equation with the general form,

$$\frac{x^2}{a^2}+\frac{y^2}{b^2}=1, \text{ where } a > b, \text{ we see that}$$

$a = 3$, $b = 2$, and

$$c = \sqrt{a^2 - b^2} = \sqrt{5}.$$

Finally, $e = \dfrac{c}{a} = \dfrac{\sqrt{5}}{3} \approx 0.745$.

PROBLEM

Find the equation of the ellipse that has vertices $V_1\,(-2,6)$, $V_2\,(-2,-4)$, and foci $F_1\,(-2,4)$, $F_2\,(-2,-2)$. (See figure.)

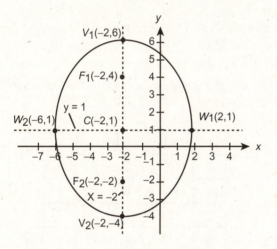

The Parabola

A parabola is defined to be the set of all points in a plane equally distant from a fixed line and a fixed point not on the line. The line is called the directrix and the point is called the focus. The axis of a parabola is the line that passes through the focus and is perpendicular to the directrix. The vertex of the parabola is at the point halfway between the focus and the directrix. A picture of a parabola is shown in the figure.

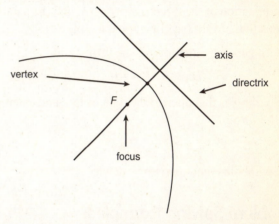

It is somewhat common for the undirected distance between the directrix and the focus to be labeled $2c$ (this means that $c > 0$.) The following table relates the standard equation to the position of the vertex, the position of the focus, and the equation of the directrix.

SOLUTION

Since the vertices and Foci are on the line $x = -2$, the major axis is on the line $x = -2$. The center has $x = -2$, the y value is half the difference between the vertices or $\frac{1}{2}(|6| - |-4|)$, or $\frac{1}{2}(10)$ or 5 units from either vertex, so the center is at $(-2,1)$. a, the length of the semimajor axis, equals the difference between the y-coordinates of V_1 (say) and the center, $a = 5$. From the coordinates of the foci, $c = 3$. Since $b^2 = a^2 - c^2$, $b = \sqrt{25 - 9} = 4$, and the ends of the minor axis, on $y = 1$, are at $W_1\,(2,1)$ and $W_2\,(-6,1)$. The equation can now be written, in the form

$$\frac{(y-k)^2}{a^2} + \frac{(x-h)^2}{b^2} = 1$$

$$\frac{(y-1)^2}{25} + \frac{(x+2)^2}{16} = 1.$$

Directrix	Focus	Vertex	Standard Equation	Direction Parabola Opens
$y = -c$	$(0,c)$	$(0,0)$	$x^2 = 4cy$	Up
$x = -c$	$(c,0)$	$(0,0)$	$y^2 = 4cx$	Right
$y = c$	$(0,-c)$	$(0,0)$	$x^2 = -4cx$	Down
$x = c$	$(-c,0)$	$(0,0)$	$y^2 = -4cx$	Left
$y = -c + k$	$(h, c + k)$	(h,k)	$(x-h)^2 = 4c(y-k)$	Up
$x = -c + h$	$(c + h, k)$	(h,k)	$(y-k)^2 = 4c(x-h)$	Right
$y = c + k$	$(h, -c + k)$	(h,k)	$(x-h)^2 = -4c(y-k)$	Down
$x = c + h$	$(-c + h, k)$	(h,k)	$(y-k)^2 = -4c(x-h)$	Left

This table illustrates that once an equation for a parabola is in standard form, it is easy to characterize the parabola. Consider the following:

$$y^2 - 6y - 6x + 39 = 0$$

$$y^2 - 6y = 6x - 39$$

$$y^2 - 6y + 9 = 6x - 30$$

$$(y - 3)^2 = 6(x - 5)$$

This is a parabola with a standard equation of $(y - k)^2 = 4c(x - h)$, with vertex at (5,3) and focus at $(6\frac{1}{2},3)$. The equation of the directrix is $x = 3\frac{1}{2}$, and the parabola opens to the right (see line 6 in the table).

In general, equations of the form

$$y^2 + Dx + Ey + F = 0$$

are parabolas that open to the right or left, and equations of the form

$$x^2 + Dx + Ey + F = 0$$

are parabolas that open up or down.

Problem Solving Examples:

PROBLEM

Construct the graph of the function defined by
$$y = x^2 - 6x + 10.$$

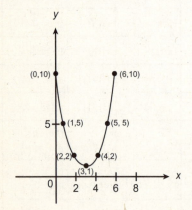

SOLUTION

We are given the function $y = x^2 - 6x + 10$.

The most general form of the quadratic function is $y = ax^2 + bx + c$ where a, b, and c are constants. If a is positive, the curve opens upward and it is U-shaped. If a is negative, the curve opens downward and it is inverted U-shaped.

Since $a = 1 > 0$ in the given equation, the graph is a parabola that opens upward. To determine the pairs of values (x,y) that satisfy this equation, express the quadratic function in terms of the square of a linear function of x.

$$y = x^2 - 6x + 10 = x^2 - 6x + 9 + 1$$

$$= (x - 3)^2 + 1$$

y is least when $x - 3 = 0$ This is true because the square of any number, be it positive or negative, is a positive number. Therefore y would always be greater than or equal to 1. Thus the minimum value of y is 1 when $x - 3 = 0$ or $x = 3$.

To plot the curve, select values for x and calculate the corresponding y values (see the table).

x	$x^2 - 6x + 10 =$	y
0	$(0)^2 - 6(0) + 10$	10
1	$(1)^2 - 6(1) + 10$	5
2	$(2)^2 - 6(2) + 10$	2
3	$(3)^2 - 6(3) + 10$	1
4	$(4)^2 - 6(4) + 10$	2
5	$(5)^2 - 6(5) + 10$	5
6	$(6)^2 - 6(6) + 10$	10

The points and graphs determined by the table are shown in the accompanying figure.

PROBLEM

Find the coordinates of the maximum point of the curve $y = -3x^2 - 12x + 5$, and locate the axis of symmetry.

SOLUTION

The curve is defined by a second degree equation $y = ax^2 + bx + c$. The coefficient of the x^2 term, a is negative. Hence, the graph of this curve is a parabola opening downward. The maximum point of the curve occurs at the vertex and has the x-coordinate:

$$-\frac{\text{coefficient of } x \text{ term}}{2\left(\text{coefficient of } x^2 \text{ term}\right)} = -\frac{b}{2a} = -\frac{-12}{2(-3)} = \frac{12}{-6} = -2.$$

For $x = -2$, $y = -3(-2)^2 - 12(-2) + 5 = 17$. Hence the coordinates of the vertex are $(-2,17)$. The curve is symmetric with respect to the vertical line through its vertex. The axis of symmetry of this curve is the vertical line through the point $(-2,17)$, or the line $x = -2$.

PROBLEM

Discuss the graph of the equation $y^2 = 12x$.

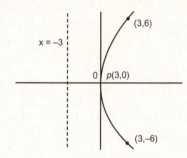

SOLUTION

The equation $y^2 = 12x$ is a quadratic equation of the form $y^2 = 4cx$ with the coefficient of the y^2 term positive. Therefore the graph is a parabola opening to the right. Since $f(x) = -f(x)$ the parabola is symmetric with respect to the x-axis. Point $(0,0)$ satisfies the equation and lies on the axis of symmetry. Hence the vertex of the parabola is at $(0,0)$ (see figure). The focus of the parabola lies on the axis of symmetry, $y = 0$, at the point $(c,0)$ where $4c =$ coefficient of x in the original equation: $4c = 12$, $c = 3$. Therefore the focus is at $(3,0)$. The directrix is the vertical line $x = -c = -3$. When $x = 3$, $y = \pm\sqrt{12x} = \pm\sqrt{12(3)} = \pm 6$. Therefore the points $(3,6)$ and $(3,-6)$ are points on the graph. The graph of this parabola is not the graph of a function, since for any given value of x there is more than one corresponding value of y.

PROBLEM

Write the equation of the parabola whose focus has coordinates $(0,2)$ and whose directrix has equation $y = -2$ (see figure).

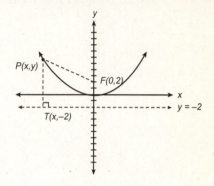

SOLUTION

Since, by definition, each point lying on a parabola is equidistant from both the focus and directrix of the parabola, the origin must lie on the specific parabola described in the statement of the problem (see figure).

To find the equation of the parabola, choose a point $P(x,y)$ lying on the parabola (see figure). By definition, then, the distance PT must equal the distance PF, where T lies on the directrix, directly below P. Since T also lies on $y = -2$, it has coordinates $(x,-2)$. Using the distance formula, we find for $PF = PT$:

$$\sqrt{(x-0)^2 + (y-2)^2} = \sqrt{(x-x)^2 + (y-(-2))^2}$$

$$\text{or } \sqrt{x^2 + (y-2)^2} = \sqrt{(y+2)^2}.$$

Squaring both sides of this equation, we obtain

$$x^2 + (y-2)^2 = (y+2)^2.$$

Expanding this,

$$x^2 + y^2 - 4y + 4 = y^2 + 4y + 4.$$

Subtracting y^2, $-4y$, and 4 from each side of this equation yields

$$x^2 = 8y.$$

Dividing both sides of this equation by 8 gives the equation of the parabola:

$$y = \frac{1}{8}x^2.$$

The Hyperbola

The hyperbola is defined to be the set of all points in a plane, the difference of whose distances from two fixed points is a constant. If the foci are at $(c,0)$ and $(-c,0)$, and if the difference of the distances is $2a$ with $0 < a < c$, then the standard equation for this hyperbola is

$$\frac{x^2}{a^2} - \frac{y^2}{b^2} = 1,$$

where $b^2 = c^2 - a^2$. A graph of the hyperbola follows.

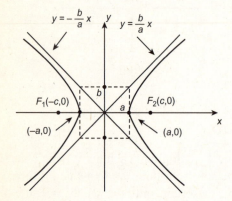

Notice that the hyperbola has two branches.

For the hyperbola, the focal axis is the line through the foci, the center is the point midway between the foci, and the conjugate axis is the line through the center, perpendicular to the focal axis. The hyperbola has symmetry with respect to those lines and that point. For the hyperbola in the figures, the focal axis is the x-axis, the conjugate axis is the y-axis, and the center is at the origin. Notice that, in this case, the lines

$$y = \frac{b}{a}x \quad \text{and} \quad y = \frac{-b}{a}x$$

are asymptotes for the hyperbola pictured, which means the hyperbola gets closer and closer to the lines but never crosses them. The fundamental rectangle is the dashed rectangle in the figure. The asymptotes are diagonal of this rectangle, which is bounded by the hyperbola.

If the foci are at $(0,c)$ and $(0,-c)$, and if the difference between the distances is still $2a$ with $0 < a < c$, then the standard equation for the hyperbola is

$$\frac{y^2}{a^2} - \frac{x^2}{b^2} = 1,$$

where $b^2 = c^2 - a^2$.

In this case, the center is at the origin, the focal axis is the y-axis, the conjugate axis is the x-axis, and the hyperbola has the lines

$$y = \frac{a}{b}x \quad \text{and} \quad y = \frac{-a}{b}x$$

as asymptotes. A graph of this hyperbola follows.

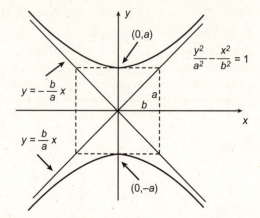

The standard form of the equation of the hyperbola with center at (h,k) and with focal axis parallel to the x-axis is

$$\frac{(x-h)^2}{a^2} - \frac{(y-k)^2}{b^2} = 1,$$

and the standard form for the equation of the hyperbola with center at (h,k) and with focal axis parallel to the y-axis is

$$\frac{(y-k)^2}{a^2} - \frac{(x-h)^2}{b^2} = 1.$$

Problem Solving Examples:

PROBLEM

Consider the equation
$$x^2 - 4y^2 + 4x + 8y + 4 = 0.$$

Express this equation in standard form, and determine the center, the vertices, the foci, and the eccentricity of this hyperbola. Describe the fundamental rectangle and find the equations of the two asymptotes.

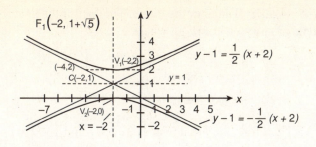

SOLUTION

Rewrite the equation by completing the squares:

$$(x^2 + 4x + 4) - 4(y^2 - 2y + 1) = -4$$

$$\text{or } (x + 2)^2 - 4(y - 1)^2 = -4$$

or, dividing by –4 and rearranging terms, gives

$$\frac{(y-1)^2}{1} - \frac{(x+2)^2}{4} = 1.$$

The center, located at (h, k) in the equation

$\dfrac{(y-k)^2}{a^2} - \dfrac{(x-h)^2}{b^2} = 1$ is, therefore, at $(-2,1)$.

Furthermore, $a = 1$ and $b = 2$. Thus,

$$c = \sqrt{1^2 + 2^2} = \sqrt{5} \text{ and } e = \frac{c}{a} = \sqrt{5}.$$

The vertices are displaced $\pm a$ from the center, while the foci are displaced $\pm c$ (along the transverse- or focal-axis). Therefore, the vertices are $(-2, 1 \pm 1)$ and the foci are $(-2, 1 \pm \sqrt{5})$.

By definition, the fundamental rectangle is the rectangle whose vertices are at $(h \pm b, k \pm a)$. Hence, in this example, the coordinates of the vertices of the rectangle are $(0,2)$, $(-4, 2)$, $(-4, 0)$, and $(0,0)$. The equations of the two asymptotes are determined by finding the slopes of the lines passing through the center of the hyperbola and two of the vertices of its fundamental rectangle (see figure). Then,

$$m = \frac{\Delta y}{\Delta x} = \pm \frac{1}{2}$$

gives the two slopes, and the point-slope form, choosing the point $(-2,1)$ which is common to both asymptotes, gives

$$y - 1 = \pm \frac{1}{2}(x + 2),$$

the equation of the asymptotes.

PROBLEM

Find the equation of the hyperbola with vertices $V_1(8,0)$, $V_2(2,0)$ and eccentricity $e = 2$.

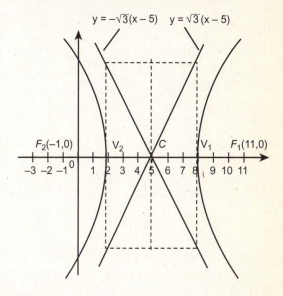

SOLUTION

There are two basic forms of the equation of a hyperbola that is not rotated with respect to the coordinate axes:

$$\frac{(x-h)^2}{a^2} - \frac{(y-k)^2}{b^2} = 1 \quad \text{and}$$

$$\frac{(y-k)^2}{a^2} - \frac{(x-h)^2}{b^2} = 1.$$

Which form is appropriate depends upon whether the transverse axis is parallel to the x-axis or to the y-axis, respectively. To determine the equation of a hyperbola, then, it is necessary to first discover which equation applies, then to determine the constants h, k, a, and c. The information about the vertices implies that the transverse axis is the x-axis.

Thus, the first form of the equation for a hyperbola applies. In this case, the center, which is the midpoint of the vertices is at $(5,0)$. The distance between the vertices is $2a = 6$; therefore, $a = 3$. In order to determine the value of b, we use the relation between eccentricity, e, c, and a: $e = c/a$. Thus, $c = e \times a = 2 \times 3 = 6$.

$$b = \sqrt{c^2 - a^2} = \sqrt{6^2 - 3^2} = \sqrt{27} \approx 5.2$$

Substituting for h, k, a, b, we have

$$\frac{(x-5)^2}{9} - \frac{y^2}{27} = 1,$$

or $3x^2 - y^2 - 30x + 48 = 0$.

PROBLEM

Discuss the graph of $\dfrac{x^2}{9} - \dfrac{y^2}{9} = 1$.

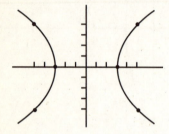

SOLUTION

$\dfrac{x^2}{9} - \dfrac{y^2}{9} = 1$ is an equation of the form $\dfrac{x^2}{a^2} - \dfrac{y^2}{b^2} = 1$ with $a = 3$ and $b = 3$. Therefore the graph is a hyperbola. The x-intercepts are found by setting $y = 0$:

$$\frac{x^2}{9} - \frac{y^2}{9} = 1$$
$$x^2 = 9$$
$$x = \pm 3.$$

Thus, the x-intercepts are at $(-3,0)$ and $(3,0)$. There are no y-intercepts since for $x = 0$, no real values of y satisfy the equation, that is, no real value of y satisfies

$$\frac{0^2}{9} - \frac{y^2}{9} = 1$$
$$y^2 = -9, \ y = \sqrt{-9}.$$

Solving the original equation for y:

$$y = \sqrt{\left(1 - \frac{x^2}{9}\right)(-9)} \ \text{ or } \ y = \sqrt{x^2 - 9}$$

shows that there will be no permissible values of x in the interval $-3 < x < 3$. Such values of x do not yield real values for y. For $x = 5$ and $x = -5$, use the equation for y to obtain the ordered pairs $(5,4)$, $(5,-4)$, $(-5,4)$, and

$(-5,-4)$ as indicated in the figure. The foci of the hyperbola are located at $(\pm c, 0)$, where

$$c^2 = a^2 + b^2$$
$$c^2 = 3^2 + 3^2 = 9 + 9 = 18$$
$$c = \pm\sqrt{18} = \pm 3\sqrt{2}.$$

Therefore, the foci are at $\left(-3\sqrt{2}, 0\right)$ and $\left(3\sqrt{2}, 0\right)$.

PROBLEM

Draw the graph of $xy = 6$.

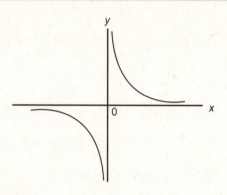

SOLUTION

Since the product is positive, the values of x and y must have the same sign, that is, when x is positive y must also be positive and when x is negative then y is also negative. Moreover, neither x nor y can be zero (or their product would be zero not 6), so that the graph never touches the coordinate axes. Solve for y and we obtain $y = \dfrac{6}{x}$. Substituting values of x into this equation, construct the following chart:

x:	−6	−3	−2	−1	1	2	3	6
y:	−1	−2	−3	−6	6	3	2	1

The graph is obtained by plotting the above points and then joining them with a smooth curve, remembering that the curve can never cross a coordinate axis. The graph of the equation, $xy = k$, is a hyperbola for all nonzero real values of k. If k is negative, then x and y must have opposite signs, and the graph is in the second and fourth quadrants as opposed to the first and third.

Quiz: Conic Sections

1. What is the center and radius of the circle given by $x^2 + y^2 + 6x - 10y = -32$?

   (A) center $(-3,5)$ radius: $\sqrt{2}$

   (B) center $(3,-5)$ radius: $\sqrt{2}$

   (C) center $(-3,5)$ radius: 2

   (D) center $(3,5)$ radius: 2

   (E) center $(5,3)$ radius: $\sqrt{2}$

2. A circle is centered at point $(3,4)$. The endpoints of a diameter are A and B. The coordinates of point A are $(-2,1)$. What are the coordinates of point B?

   (A) $(6,3)$.   (D) $(9,3)$.

   (B) $(8,7)$.   (E) $(5,8)$.

   (C) $(4,5)$.

3. An equation of a circle with center $\left(-\frac{2}{3}, \frac{1}{2}\right)$ and radius $\sqrt{7}$ is:

   (A) $3x^2 + 4x + 3y^2 = 3y = 227$

   (B) $36x^2 - 48x + 36y^2 + 36y = 259$

   (C) $36x^2 + 48x + 36y^2 - 36y = 227$

   (D) $3x^2 - 2x + y^2 + 2y = 7$

   (E) $48x^2 - 36x + 36y^2 + 36y = 227$

4. The equation $6x^2 - 24x + 4y^2 + 32y = -52$ represents which of the following?

   (A) circle   (D) ellipse

   (B) hyperbola   (E) none of these

   (C) parabola

5. The equation $x^2 - 2x + 2y^2 + 8y = -5$ is the equation of an ellipse. What are the coordinates of the foci of the ellipse?

   (A) $(3,-2)$ and $(-1,-2)$

   (B) $\left(1+\sqrt{2},-2\right)$ and $\left(1-\sqrt{2},-2\right)$

   (C) $\left(1-\sqrt{3},2\right)$ and $\left(1,-2-\sqrt{2}\right)$

   (D) $\left(1-\sqrt{3},2\right)$ and $\left(1+\sqrt{3},2\right)$

   (E) $\left(-1+\sqrt{2},2\right)$ and $\left(-1-\sqrt{2},2\right)$

6. What is the equation of a parabola which is symmetrical about the y-axis and passes through points $(0,-2)$ and $(2,0)$?

   (A) $y = x^2 - 2$ (D) $y = 2x^2 - 1$

   (B) $y = \frac{1}{2}x^2 - 2$ (E) $y = 2x^2 - \frac{1}{2}$

   (C) $y = \frac{3}{2}x^2 + \frac{1}{2}$

7. Find the center of the ellipse given by equation $x^2 + x + 3y + 2y^2 - 1 = 0$.

   (A) $\left(\frac{1}{2}, -\frac{3}{2}\right)$

   (B) $\left(\frac{1}{4}, \frac{3}{2}\right)$

   (C) $\left(\frac{1}{2}, -\frac{3}{4}\right)$ (D) $\left(-\frac{1}{2}, -\frac{3}{4}\right)$

   (E) $\left(1, -\frac{3}{4}\right)$

8. A parabola has the equation $y = \frac{-1}{2}x^2 + 3x - \frac{13}{2}$. What is the directrix of this parabola?

   (A) $y = \frac{-5}{2}$ (D) $y = \frac{-3}{2}$

   (B) $x = \frac{-3}{2}$ (E) $y = \frac{5}{2}$

   (C) $x = \frac{-5}{2}$

9. What are the equations of the asymptotes for the hyperbola given by $\frac{(x+1)^2}{9} - \frac{(y-2)^2}{4} = 1$?

   (A) $y = \frac{1}{3}x + \frac{2}{3}$ and $y = \frac{-1}{3}x - \frac{1}{3}$

(B) $y = \dfrac{2}{3}x + \dfrac{8}{3}$ and $y = \dfrac{-2}{3}x + \dfrac{4}{3}$

(C) $y = \dfrac{8}{3}x + \dfrac{-2}{3}$ and $y = \dfrac{-8}{3}x + \dfrac{4}{3}$

(D) $y = \dfrac{3}{3}x + 3$ and $y = \dfrac{-3}{2}x + \dfrac{1}{2}$

(E)   none of these

10.   Find a, b for the parabola

$y = ax^2 + bx + 3$

if the vertex is $(2, 4)$.

(A) $a = -\dfrac{1}{4},\ b = 2$

(B) $a = -1,\ b = -2$

(C) $a = 1,\ b = 2$

(D) $a = -\dfrac{1}{3},\ b = 1$

(E) $a = -\dfrac{1}{4},\ b = 1$

Quiz: Conic Sections

ANSWER KEY

1. (A)
2. (B)
3. (C)
4. (D)
5. (B)

6. (B)
7. (D)
8. (D)
9. (B)
10. (E)

Geometry Review

ANSWER KEY

Drill: Regular Polygons (Convex)

1. (D)
2. (D)
3. (D)
4. (C)
5. (D)

Drill: Triangles

1. (D)
2. (B)
3. (C)
4. (A)
5. (D)

6. (C)
7. (B)
8. (D)
9. (A)
10. (B)

Drill: Quadrilaterals

1. (B)
2. (D)
3. (A)
4. (D)
5. (C)

6. (C)
7. (D)
8. (B)
9. (C)
10. (D)

Drill: Circles

1. (B)
2. (C)
3. (D)
4. (C)
5. (B)

6. (B)
7. (D)
8. (C)
9. (C)
10. (B)

Detailed Explanations of Answers

Drill: Regular Polygons (Convex)

1. (D)

A regular pentagon is both equiangular and equilateral. A pentagon is five sided. Therefore,

$$360° \div 5 = 72° \qquad 180° - 72° = 108°$$

2. (D)

$$(3 \times 180°) - 180° = 360°$$

3. (D)

$$a = 4\sqrt{3} \qquad P = \text{perimeter} = 3(24) = 72$$

$$A = \frac{1}{2}ap = \frac{1}{2}(4\sqrt{3})(72) = 144\sqrt{3} \text{ mm}^2$$

4. (C)

$s = 4$ therefore, radius = 4 too, which makes the apothem

$$\sqrt{(4)^2 - (2)^2} = 2\sqrt{3}$$

$$A = \frac{1}{2}ap = \frac{1}{2}(2\sqrt{3})(6)(4) = 24\sqrt{3} \text{ cm}^2$$

5. (D)

$$A = \frac{1}{2}ap = \frac{1}{2}a(s)(10) = \frac{1}{2}(9.2)(6)(10) = 276 \text{ cm}^2$$

Drill: Triangles

1. (D)

Since $\angle Q$ is a right angle, $m\angle Q = 90°$. Therefore, $90° - 23° = 67°$

2. (B)

$$\frac{180° - 96°}{2} = \frac{84°}{2} = 42°$$

3. (C)

$$3x + 2x + x = 180°$$

$$6x = 180°$$

$$x = 30°$$

4. (A)

$$6 : 4 = 4 : b \Rightarrow \frac{6}{4} = \frac{4}{b} \Rightarrow 6b = 16$$

$$b = \frac{16}{6} = 2\frac{4}{6} = 2\frac{2}{3}$$

5. (D)

$$3 : 6 = 4 : b \qquad b = 8$$

$$3 : 4 = 4 : a$$

$$\frac{3}{4} = \frac{4}{a}$$

$$3a = 16 \quad a = 16\left(\frac{1}{3}\right) = 5\frac{1}{3}$$

6. (C)

$$A = \frac{1}{2}bh = \frac{1}{2}(14)(8) = 56$$

7. (B)

$$A = \frac{1}{2}bh = \frac{1}{2}(11)(7) = 38\frac{1}{2} \text{ or } 38.5$$

8. (D)

$$A = \frac{1}{2}bh = \frac{1}{2}(4)(8\sqrt{2}) = 16\sqrt{2}$$

9. (A)

Using the Pythagorean theorem,

$$\overline{AB} = \sqrt{(\overline{AC})^2 - (\overline{BC})^2} = \sqrt{(15)^2 - (9)^2} = \sqrt{144} = 12.$$

Then $A = \frac{1}{2}bh = \frac{1}{2}(9)(12) = 54 \text{ cm}^2$

10. (B)

This is an isosceles right triangle, so the legs are equal. Using the Pythagorean theorem,

$$(10\sqrt{2})^2 = a^2 + a^2$$
$$200 = 2a^2$$
$$a^2 = 100$$
$$a = 10$$

so the sides are 10 cm each.

$$A = \frac{1}{2}bh = \frac{1}{2}(10)(10) = 50 \text{ cm}^2$$

Drill: Quadrilaterals

1.   (B)

$\angle B$ and $\angle D$ are opposite angles in the parallelogram and are equal. Therefore,

$$6x + 2 = 98$$
$$6x = 96$$
$$x = 16$$

2. (D)

$$A = bh = (18)(9) = 162$$

3. (A)

Using the Pythagorean Theorem,

$$\overline{AC} = \sqrt{(\overline{AD})^2 + (\overline{DC})^2}$$
$$= \sqrt{(6)^2 + (8)^2}$$
$$= \sqrt{36 + 64}$$
$$= \sqrt{100}$$
$$= 10 \text{ cm}$$

4. (D)

$$A = bh = (7)(10) = 70 \text{ cm}^2$$

5. (C)

$$\overline{EC} = \overline{BD} = 17$$
$$\overline{BO} = \frac{1}{2}\overline{BD} = \frac{1}{2}(17) = 8.5$$

6. (C)

Using the Pythagorean theorem,

$$\overline{GH} = \sqrt{\left(\frac{1}{2}\overline{GI}\right)^2 + \left(\frac{1}{2}\overline{HJ}\right)^2}$$
$$= \sqrt{\left[\left(\frac{1}{2}\right)(6)\right]^2 + \left[\left(\frac{1}{2}\right)(8)\right]^2}$$
$$= \sqrt{(3)^2 + (4)^2}$$
$$= \sqrt{25} = 5$$

7. (D)

$$A = \frac{1}{2}(b_1 + b_2)h$$

$$= \frac{1}{2}(14 + 21)(10)$$
$$= \frac{1}{2}(35)(10)$$
$$= 175$$

8. (B)

$$\overline{BC} = \overline{AD} = 6$$
$$P = 6 + 6 + 5 + 10 = 27$$

9. (C)

Use the Pythagorean Theorem to find the height.

$b^2 = b^2 + 3^2$

$b^2 = 27$

$b = 3\sqrt{3}$.

The area of this trapezoid is the area of the rectangle plus the area of the triangle, or

$$A = \underset{\text{rectangle}}{bh} + \underset{\text{triangle}}{\frac{1}{2}bh} = (4)(3\sqrt{3}) + \frac{1}{2}(3\sqrt{3})(3)$$

$$= 12\sqrt{3} + \frac{9}{2}\sqrt{3} = \frac{33}{2}\sqrt{3}$$

10. (D)

The base angles of an isosceles trapezoid are equal.

Therefore, $\angle W = \angle Z$ so

$58 = 4x - 6$

$64 = 4x$

$16 = x$

Drill: Circles

1. (B)

$C = 2\pi r = 2(\pi)(3) = 6\pi$

2. (C)

$A = \pi r^2 = \pi(11)^2 = 121\pi$

3. (D)

$A = \pi r^2 \quad r = \frac{1}{2}d = \frac{1}{2}(27) = 13.5$

$A = \pi(13.5)^2 = 182.25\pi$

4. (C)

$A = 225\pi = \pi r^2$ so $r = \sqrt{225} = 15$

$d = 2r = 2(15) = 30$

5. (B)

$C_X = \pi r^2 = 144\pi \quad r_X = 12$

$C_Y = \pi r^2 = 81\pi \quad r_Y = 9$

$r_X : r_Y = 12 : 9 = 4 : 3$

6. (B)

Shaded Area = Larger Area – Smaller Area

$$= \pi r_1^2 - \pi r_2^2$$

$$= \pi(7)^2 - \pi(5)^5$$

$$= 49\pi - 25\pi$$

$$= 24\pi$$

7. (D)

Measure of arc = measure of central angle

8. (C)

The measure of a semicircle is 180º. Therefore, arc $\widearc{AXC} = 180º$.

9. (C)

Since $\widearc{XYZ}$ is semicircle, $180º - 40º = 140º$

10. (B)

$$\frac{45}{360}\pi r^2 = \frac{1}{8}\pi(4)^2 = \frac{16}{8}\pi = 2\pi$$

SUBAREA V:
Data Analysis, Probability, Statistics & Discrete Mathematics

Probability

Probability is defined as the likelihood of the occurrence of an event or as the chance that some particular event will occur.

- **EXAMPLE**

A weather report might indicate the chance of rain to be 70%, which could be interpreted as the probability of rain = .70.

a) Objective Probability (Calculated)

In most instances, the probability that an event will occur is determined by a mathematical formula and is based on empirical evidence.

$$P(X) = \frac{\text{No. of outcomes corresponding to event } X}{\text{Total no. of possible outcomes}}$$

- **EXAMPLE**

The probability of drawing a queen from a deck of cards is defined as:

$$P(\text{Queen}) = \frac{\text{No. of queens in the deck}}{\text{Total no. of cards in the deck}}$$

$$= \frac{4}{52} = \frac{1}{13} \text{ or } .077.$$

b) Subjective Probability

When the probability of an event occurring is based on the personal (or professional) judgment of an individual or group of individuals, the probability is referred to as "subjective."

- **EXAMPLE**

The probability that sales will increase by $500,000 next year if we increase our advertising expenditure by $10,000 is .25.

Properties of Probabilities

The following three properties are characteristics of all probabilities:

1. $0 \leq P(X) \leq 1$; every probability is contained within the range 0 to 1, inclusive, where 0 represents absolute certainty that the event will not occur and 1 represents absolute certainty that the event will occur.

- **EXAMPLE**

  P (Head on Coin) = 1/2

  P (6 on Die) = 1/6

  P (Ace of Spades) = 1/52

2. $\sum_{i=1}^{n} P_i(X) = 1$; the probabilities of all possible simple events that can occur within a given experiment will sum to 1.

- **EXAMPLE**

  coin: P(Head) + P(Tail) = 1/2 + 1/2 = 1

  die: P(1) + P(2) + P(3) + P(4) + P(5) + P(6) = 1/6 + 1/6 + 1/6 + 1/6 + 1/6 + 1/6 = 1

  cards: P(Club)+P(Heart)+P(Spade)+P(Diamond) = 1/4 + 1/4 + 1/4 + 1/4 = 1

3. $P(X) + P$ (Not X) = 1; the probability that event X occurs plus the probability that event X does not occur sums to 1.

- **EXAMPLE**

  coin: P (Head) + P (Not a Head) = 1/2 + 1/2 = 1

  die: P (6) + P (Not a 6) = 1/6 + 5/6 = 1

  cards: P (Spade) + P (Not a Spade) = 1/4 + 3/4 = 1 or 13/52 + 39/52 = 1

Methods of Computing Probabilities

a) Addition

1. Mutually Exclusive Events - those which cannot occur simultaneously. In order to determine the probability that either event X occurs or event Y occurs, the individual probabilities of event X and event Y are added.

   $P(X \text{ or } Y) = P(X) + P(Y)$

- **EXAMPLE**

  The probability that either a club or a spade is drawn from a deck of cards in a single draw is defined as:

  P (Club or Spade) = P (Club) + P (Spade)

  $\qquad = 13/52 + 13/52$

  $\qquad = 26/52$

  $\qquad = 1/2$ or .5

  Note: That this concept applies to three or more events as well.

2. Non-Mutually Exclusive Events - those which can occur simultaneously. In order to determine the probability that either event X occurs or event Y occurs, the individual probabilities of event X and event Y are added and the probability that the two occur simultaneously is subtracted from the total.

$$P(X \text{ or } Y) = P(X) = P(Y) - P(X \& Y)$$

- **EXAMPLE**

  The probability that either a Queen or a Spade is drawn from a deck of cards in a single draw is defined as:

  P (Queen or Spade) = P (Queen) + P (Spade) − P (Queen & Spade)

  $\qquad = 4/52 + 13/52 - 1/52$

  $\qquad = 16/52$

  $\qquad = 4/13.$

  Notice in this example that we must subtract 1/52 from the total since the Queen of Spades is counted in the total number of Queens and it is also counted in the total number of Spades. If we do not subtract P (Queen & Spade), we are counting that one card twice.

b) Multiplication

1. Independent Events

   Two (or more) events are independent if the occurrence of one event has no effect upon whether or not the other event occurs. In order to determine the probability that event X occurs and event Y occurs, the individual probability of event X and event Y are multiplied together.

$$P(X \text{ and } Y) = P(X) \times P(Y)$$

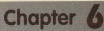

• **EXAMPLE**

1. The probability of tossing a 6 on a single die followed by the toss of a 3 is:

   P (6 and 3) $= P$ (6) $\times P$ (3)

   $= 1/6 \times 1/6$

   $= 1/36.$

2. The probability of tossing three heads in 3 tosses of a coin:

   P (H, H, H) $= P$ (H) $\times P$ (H) $\times P$ (H)

   $= 1/2 \times 1/2 \times 1/2$

   $= 1/8.$

3. The probability of drawing a heart from a deck of cards, replacing the first card, and drawing a club on the second draw:

   P (H and C) $= P$(H) $\times P$ (C)

   $= 13/52 \times 13/52$

   $= 1/4 \times 1/4$

   $= 1/16.$

2. Dependent Events

   Two (or more) events are dependent if the occurrence of one event has some effect upon whether or not the other event occurs. In order to determine the probability that event X occurs and event Y occurs, when X and Y are dependent, the formula is:

   $$P(X \text{ and } Y) = P(X) \times P(Y \mid X)$$

   or

   $$P(X \text{ and } Y) = P(Y) \times P(X \mid Y)$$

   where: $P(Y \mid X)$ is read as the probability that event Y will occur, given that event X has already occurred.

   And: $P(X \mid Y)$ is read as the probability that event X will occur given that event Y has already occurred.

• **EXAMPLE**

1. A box contains 6 red balls, 4 green balls, and 5 purple balls. What is the probability that a red ball is drawn on the first draw and a purple ball is drawn

on the second draw, if the first ball is not replaced prior to the second ball being drawn

P (Red and Purple) $= P(R) \times P(P \mid R)$

$= 6/15 \times 5/14$

$= 30/210$

$= 1/7$

2. Three cards are drawn from a deck. What is the probability that the first is a Queen, the second is a Queen, and the third is a King? Assume that each card is **not** replaced prior to the next one being drawn.

P ($Q1, Q2, K$) $= P$ ($Q1$) $\times P$ ($Q2 \mid Q1$) $\times$
$\qquad\qquad\qquad P$ ($K \mid Q1$ & $Q2$)

$= 4/52 \times 3/51 \times 4/50$

$= 48/132,600$

$= .0004$

Bayesian Decision Analysis

Sometimes the probability of an event occurring is influenced by the occurrence of a previous event. When this occurs, the probability is referred to as a conditional probability. Conditional probability is denoted by P ($X \mid Y$) and is read as "the probability of event X occurring given that event Y has already occurred." P ($X \mid Y$) may be calculated using the following formula:

$$P(X \mid Y) = \frac{P(X \text{ and } Y)}{P(Y)}$$

This formula is frequently "broken down" further and written this way:

$$P(Y \mid X) = \frac{P(X) \times P(Y \mid X)}{P(X) \times P(Y \mid X) + P(\text{Not } X) P(Y \mid \text{Not } X)}$$

This latter version is called **Bayes Theorem** and the use of it is called Bayesian Analysis.

• **EXAMPLE**

Two workers assemble parts from a production process. The probability that worker A makes a mistake in assembling a part is .02 and the probability that worker B makes a mistake is .03. However, worker A assembles 55% of the parts while worker B assembles the remaining 45%. If an assembled part is randomly selected from all of those produced during a given time period and it is determined to be defective, what is the probability that worker A assembled this part?

Let A = Assembled by worker A

B = Assembled by worker B (Same as "not A")

D = Defective

$$P(A\,|\,D) = $$
$$\frac{P(A)P(D\,|\,A)}{P(A)\times P(D\,|\,A) + P(B)\times P(D\,|\,B)} =$$
$$\frac{.55\times.02}{(.55)(.02)+(.45)(.03)} = \frac{.011}{.025} = .449$$

Probability Tables

A tabular approach is often easier to understand when calculating probabilities.

• **EXAMPLE**

For the previous example, the probability table looks as follows:

ASSEMBLED PARTS

		GOOD	DEFECTIVE	TOTAL
Worker	A	.5390	.0110	.55
	B	.4365	.0135	.45
TOTAL		.9755	.0245	1.00

The **cell** probabilities are referred to as **joint probabilities** which represent the combined probability of the two events (row and column) occurring; e.g., the probability that worker A assembled the part and it is good is .539. The **total** row and column probabilities are referred to as **marginal probabilities** which are the sums of the joint probabilities over the rows or columns.

For example, .45 is a marginal probability representing the probability that worker B assembled the part. It is the sum of .4365 (probability that worker B assembled it and it is good) plus .0135 (the probability that B assembled it and it is defective).

Counting Methods

Sampling and Counting

There are many instances in the application of probability theory where it is desirable and necessary to count the outcomes in the sample space and the outcomes in an event. For example, in the special instance of a uniform probability function, the probability of an event is known when the number of outcomes that comprises the event is known; that is, as soon as the number of outcomes in the subset that defines the event is known.

If a sample space $S = \{e_1, e_2, \ldots, e_n\}$ contains n simple events, $E_i = \{e_i\}$, $i = 1, 2, \ldots, n$, then using a uniform probability model, we assign probability $1/n$ for each point in S; that is, $P(E_i) = 1/n$. To determine the probability of an event A, we need,

1. The number of possible outcomes in S.

2. The number of outcomes in the event A.

   Then,

$$P(A) = \frac{\text{number of outcomes corresponding to } A}{\text{number of possible outcomes in } S}$$

Frequently, it may be possible to enumerate fully all the sample space points in S and then count how many of these correspond to the event A. For example, if a class consists of just three students, and the instructor always calls on each student once and only once during each class, then if we label the students 1, 2, and 3, we can easily enumerate the points in S as

$$S = \{(1, 2, 3), (1, 3, 2), (2, 1, 3), (2, 3, 1), (3, 1, 2), (3, 2, 1)\}$$

Assume that the instructor chooses a student at random, it would seem reasonable to adopt a uniform probability model and assign probability 1/6 to each point in S. If A is the event that John is selected last, then

John = B

$A = \{(1, 2, 3), (2, 1, 3)\}$

$P(A) = 2/6 = 1/3$

It would be most unusual for a class to consist of only three students. The total enumeration of the sample space becomes more complicated even if we increase the class size to 6 students. To deal with these situations in which the sample space contains a large number of points, we need to have an understanding of basic counting or combinatorial procedures.

The Fundamental Principle of Counting

Suppose a man has four ways to travel from New York to Chicago, three ways to travel from Chicago to Denver, and six ways to travel from Denver to San Francisco, how many ways can he go from New York to San Francisco via Chicago and Denver?

If we let A_1 be the event "going from New York to Chicago," A_2 be the event "going from Chicago to Denver," and A_3 be the event "going from Denver to San Francisco," then because there are four ways to accomplish A_1, 3 ways to accomplish A_2, and 6 ways to accomplish A_3, the number of routes the man can follow is

$(4) \times (3) \times (6) = 72$

We can now generalize these results and state them formally as the fundamental principle or multiplication rule of counting.

Fundamental Principle of Counting

If an operation consists of a sequence of k separate steps of which the first can be performed in n_1 ways, followed by the second in n_2 ways, and so on until the kth can be performed in n_k ways, then the operation consisting of k steps can be performed in

$n_1 \times n_2 \times n_3 \ldots .n_k$

ways.

Tree Diagrams

A tree diagram is a device that can be used to list all possible outcomes of a sequence of experiments where each experiment can occur only in a finite number of ways.

The following tree diagram list the different ways three different flavors of ice cream, chocolate (c), vanilla (v), and strawberry (s), can be arranged on a cone, with no flavor used more than once.

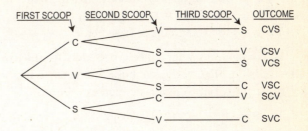

The tree starts with three branches in the first stage, representing the three possibilities for first stage. For each outcome at the first stage, there are two possibilities at the second stage. Then, for each outcome in the second stage, there is only one possibility at the third stage. Consequently, there are $3 \times 2 \times 1$, or 6, different arrangement.

Using a tree diagram, we can develop the sample space for an experiment consisting of tossing a fair coin and then rolling a die as follows:

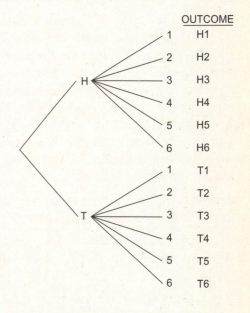

Factorial Notation

Consider how many ways the owner of an ice cream parlor can display ten ice cream flavors in a row along the front of the display case. The first position can be filled in ten ways, the second position in 9 ways, and the third position in 8 ways, and so on. By the fundamental counting principle, there are

$$(10) \times (9) \times (8) \times (7) \times \ldots \times (2) \times (1)$$

or 3,628,800 ways to display the flavor. If there are 16 flavors, there would be $(16) \times (15) \times (14) \times \ldots \times (3) \times (2) \times (1)$ ways to arrange them. In general

If n is a natural number, then the product from 1 to n inclusive is denoted by the symbol $n!$ (read as "n factorial" or as "factorial n" and is defined as

$$n! = n(n-1)(n-2) \ldots (3)(2)(1)$$

where n is a positive natural number.

There are two fundamental properties of factorials:

1. By definition, $0! = 1$
2. $n(n-1)! = n!$

For example, $(6)(5!) = 6!$

Counting Procedures Involving Order Restrictions (Permutations)

Suppose a class consists of 5 students. The instructor calls on exactly three students out of the 5 students during each class period to answer three different questions. To apply the uniform probability model, we need to know how many points there are in the sample space S. Note that each point in S is an ordered triplet; that is, the point $(3, 5, 1)$ is different from the point $(5, 3, 1)$. The same three people were called upon to respond, but the order of response is different. Such arrangement is referred to as a permutation.

A permutation of a number of objects is any arrangement of these objects in a definite order.

For example if a class consists of 3 students, then there are $3 \times 2 \times 1 = 6$ ways in which the students might be called upon.

In general, if the class had consisted of n students and all of them had been called upon, then the responses could have taken place in

$$n(n-1)(n-2) \ldots (3)(2)(1)$$

ways. Hence,

The number of permutations of a set of n distinct objects, taken all together, is $n!$

In our example of the class consisting of five students, only three students were to be called on to respond; that is, we are interested in an ordered subset.

An arrangement of r distinct objects taken from a set of n distinct objects, $r \leq n$, is called a permutation of n objects taken r at a time. The total number of such orderings is denoted by nPr, and defined as

$$nPr = \frac{n!}{(n-r)!}$$

In our example, $n = 5$, $r = 3$,

$$5P3 = \frac{5!}{(5-3)!} = 5 \times 4 \times 3 = 60$$

If we have n items with r objects alike, then the number of distinct permutations taking all n at a time is

$$\frac{n!}{r!}$$

In general,

In a set of n elements having r_1 elements of one type, r_2 elements of a second type and so on to r_k element of a kth type, then the number of distinct permutations of the n elements, taken all together, is given by

$$nPn = \frac{n!}{r_1! r_2! r_3! \ldots r_k!}$$

where $\sum_{i=1}^{k} r_i = n$

For example, the number of ways a group of 10 of which 6 are females and 4 are males can line up for theatre tickets, if we are interested only in distinguishing between sexes, is given by

$$10P10 = \frac{10!}{6! 4!} = 210$$

Counting Procedures Not Involving Order Restrictions (Combinations)

Suppose that a class of 12 students selects a committee of 3 to plan a party. A possible committee is John, Sally, and Joe. In this situation, the order of the three is not important because the committee of John, Sally, and Joe, is the same as the committee of Sally, Joe, and John.

When choosing committee members and in other cases of selection where order is not important, we are interested in combinations, not permutations.

A subset of r objects selected without regard to order from a set of n different objects, $r \leq n$, is called a combination of n objects taken r at a time. The total number of combinations of n things taken r at a time is denoted by nCr or $\binom{n}{r}$ and is defined as

$$nCr = \binom{n}{r} = \frac{n!}{r!(n-r)!}$$

In our example, the number of possible committees that could plan the party can be calculated by

$$12C3 = \binom{12}{3} = \frac{12!}{3!(12-3)!} = 220$$

PROBLEM

A deck of playing cards is thoroughly shuffled and a card is drawn from the deck. What is the probability that the card drawn is the ace of diamonds?

SOLUTION

The probability of an event occurring is

$$\frac{\text{the number of ways the event can occur}}{\text{the number of possible outcomes}}$$

In our case there is one way the event can occur, for there is only one ace of diamonds and there are 52 possible outcomes (for there are 52 cards in the deck). Hence, the probability that the card drawn is the ace of diamonds is 1/52.

PROBLEM

A bag contains four black and five blue marbles. A marble is drawn and then replaced, after which a second marble is drawn. What is the probability that the first is black and the second blue?

SOLUTION

Let C = event that the first marble drawn is black.

D = event that the second marble drawn is blue.

The probability that the first is black and the second is blue can be expressed symbolically:

$$P(C \text{ and } D) = P(CD).$$

We can apply the following theorem. If two events, A and B, are independent, then the probability that A and B will occur is

$$P(A \text{ and } B) = P(AB) = P(A) \times P(B).$$

Note that two or more events are said to be independent if the occurrence of one event has no effect upon the occurrence or non-occurrence of the other. In this case the occurrence of choosing a black marble has no effect on the selection of a blue marble and vice versa; since, when a marble is drawn it is then replaced before the next marble is drawn. Therefore, C and D are two independent events.

$$P(CD) = P(C) \times P(D)$$

$$P(C) = \frac{\text{number of ways to choose a black marble}}{\text{number of ways to choose a marble}}$$

$$= \frac{4}{9}$$

$$P(D) = \frac{\text{number of ways to choose a blue marble}}{\text{number of ways to choose a marble}}$$

$$= \frac{5}{9}$$

$$P(CD) = P(C) \times P(D) = \frac{4}{9} \times \frac{5}{9} = \frac{20}{81}$$

PROBLEM

A traffic count at a highway junction revealed that out of 5,000 cars that passed through the junction in one week, 3,000 turned to the right. Find the probability that a car will turn (A) to the right and (B) to the left. Assume that the cars cannot go straight or turn around.

SOLUTION

(A) If an event can happen in s ways and fail to happen in f ways, and if all these ways $(s + f)$ are assumed to be equally likely, then the probability (p) that the event will happen is

$$p = \frac{s}{s+f} = \frac{\text{successful ways}}{\text{total ways}}.$$

In this case $s = 3{,}000$ and $s + f = 5{,}000$. Hence,

$$p = \frac{3{,}000}{5{,}000} = \frac{3}{5}.$$

(B) If the probability that an event will happen is $\frac{a}{b}$, then the probability that this event will not happen is $1 - \frac{a}{b}$. Thus, the probability that a car will not turn right, but left, is $1 - \frac{3}{5} = \frac{2}{5}$. This same conclusion can also be arrived at using the following reasoning:

Since 3,000 cars turned to the right, $5{,}000 - 3{,}000 = 2{,}000$ cars turned to the left. Hence, the probability that a car will turn to the left is

$$\frac{2{,}000}{5{,}000} = \frac{2}{5}.$$

Drill: Permutations, Combinations, and Probability

1. How many games would it take a baseball coach to try every possible batting order with his nine players?

    (A) 9   (D) 362,880

    (B) 45   (E) 3.8742×10^8

    (C) 81

2. What is the probability of drawing an ace from a well-shuffled deck of 52 cards?

    (A) 0.0769   (D) 0.0385

    (B) 0.0192   (E) 0.5000

    (C) 0.0196

3. In how many different ways can the letters a, b, c, and d be arranged if they are selected three at a time?

    (A) 8   (D) 4

    (B) 12   (E) 48

    (C) 24

4. What is the probability that in a single throw of two dice the sum of 10 will appear?

    (A) $\frac{10}{36}$ (D) $\frac{2}{10}$

    (B) $\frac{1}{6}$ (E) $\frac{11}{12}$

    (C) $\frac{1}{12}$

5. A bag contains four white balls, six black balls, three red balls, and eight green balls. If one ball is drawn from the bag, find the probability that it will be either white or green.

    (A) $\frac{1}{3}$ (D) $\frac{4}{13}$

    (B) $\frac{2}{3}$ (E) $\frac{8}{21}$

    (C) $\frac{4}{7}$

6. A box contains 30 blue balls, 40 green balls, and 15 red balls. What is the probability of choosing a red ball first followed by a blue ball?

    (A) 0.3571   (D) 0.0620

    (B) 0.1765   (E) 0.0630

    (C) 0.3529

7. When rolling a six-sided die, what is the probability of getting either a four or five?

    (A) 0.5000   (D) 0.1670

    (B) 0.3333   (E) 3.0000

    (C) 0.2500

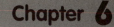
8. What is the probability of getting at most one head in three coin tosses?

    (A) 0

    (B) $\dfrac{1}{4}$

    (C) $\dfrac{1}{2}$

    (D) $\dfrac{3}{4}$

    (E) $\dfrac{7}{8}$

9. In how many ways can we arrange four letters (*a*, *b*, *c*, and *d*) in different orders?

    (A) 4

    (B) 8

    (C) 16

    (D) 24

    (E) 48

10. Six dice are thrown. What is the probability of getting six ones?

    (A) 0.0000214

    (B) 0.0278

    (C) 0.00001

    (D) 0.1667

    (E) 0.1

ANSWER KEY

1. (D)   6. (E)
2. (A)   7. (B)
3. (C)   8. (C)
4. (C)   9. (D)
5. (C)   10. (A)

Statistics

Data Description: Graphs

Repeated measurements yield data, which must be organized according to some principle. The data should be arranged in such a way that each observation can fall into one, and only one, category. A simple graphical method of presenting data is the pie chart, which is a circle divided into parts that represent categories.

• **EXAMPLE**

2006 Budget

38% came from individual income taxes

28% from social insurance receipts

13% from corporate income taxes

12% from borrowing

5% from excise taxes

4% other

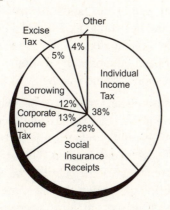

This data can also be presented in the form of a bar chart or bar graph.

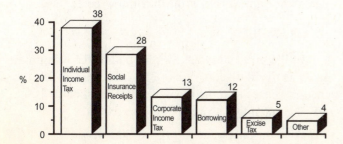

• **EXAMPLE**

The population of the United States for the years 1860 and 1960 is shown in the table below,

Year	Population in millions
1860	31.4
1870	39.8
1880	50.2
1890	62.9
1900	76.0
1910	92.0
1920	105.7
1930	122.8
1940	131.7
1950	151.1
1960	179.3

in this graph,

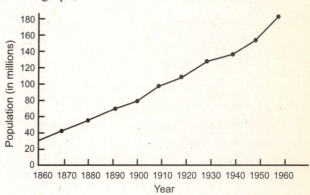

and in this bar chart.

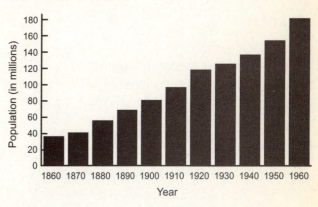

• **EXAMPLE**

A quadratic function is given by
$$y = x^2 + x - 2$$

We compute the values of y corresponding to various values of x.

x	-3	-2	-1	0	1	2	3
y	4	0	-2	-2	0	4	10

From this table, the points of the graph are obtained:

$(-3, 4)\ (-2, 0)\ (-1, -2)\ (0, -2)\ (1, 0)\ (2, 4)\ (3, 10)$

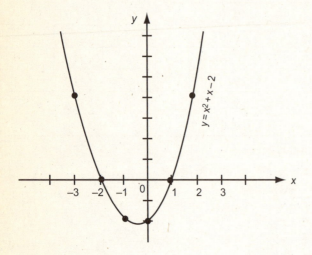

The curve shown is called a parabola. The general equation for a parabola is

$$y = ax^2 + bx + c, \, a \neq 0$$

where a, b, and c are constants.

PROBLEM

Twenty students are enrolled in the foreign language department, and their major fields are as follows: Spanish, Spanish, French, Italian, French, Spanish, German, German, Russian, Russian, French, German, German, German, Spanish, Russian, German, Italian, German, and Spanish.

(a) Make a frequency distribution table.

(b) Make a frequency bar graph.

SOLUTION

(a) The frequency distribution table is constructed by writing down the major field and next to it the number of students.

Major Field	Number of Students
German	7
Russian	3
Spanish	5
French	3
Italian	2
Total	20

(b) A bar graph follows:

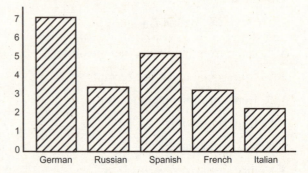

In the bar graph, the fields are listed and spaced evenly along the horizontal axis. Each specified field is represented by a rectangle, and all have the same width. The height of each, identified by a number on the vertical axis, corresponds to the frequency of that field.

A **box-and-whiskers** plot is a graph that displays five statistics. A minimum score, a maximum score, and three percentiles. A percentile value for a score tells you the percentage of scores lower than it. The beginning of the box is the score at the 25th percentile. The end of the box represents the 75th percentile. The score inside of the box is the median, or the score at the 50th percentile. Attached to the box you will find two whiskers. The score at the end of the left whisker is the minimum score. The score at the end of the right whisker is the maximum score.

• EXAMPLE

In the box-and-whiskers plot below, the minimum score is 70, the score at the 25th percentile is 78, the median score is 82, the score at the 75th percentile is 90, and the maximum score is 94.

Scores on a Test

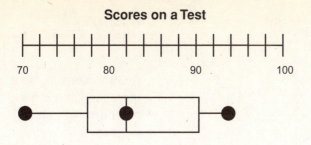

PROBLEM

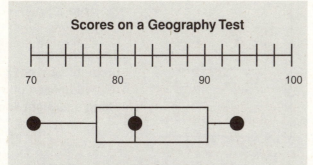

Scores on a Geography Test

Using the box-and-whiskers plot above, what was the median score on the geography test?

SOLUTION

The median score is 84. On a box-and-whiskers plot, the median score is the score on the inside of the box.

• EXAMPLE

A **stem-and-leaf plot** is a way of displaying scores in groups. A stem-and-leaf plot gives you a picture of the scores, as well as the actual numbers themselves in a compact form. In this type of plot, a score is broken into a stem and a leaf. The leaf consists of the smallest digit and the stem consists of the remaining larger digits.

Task: Create a stem and leaf plot using the following scores.

Scores: 64, 48, 61, 81, 63, 59, 70, 54, 76, 61, 55, 31

Solution: The first step is to take these scores and create a set of "ranked ordered scores," ordering the scores from smallest to largest. Notice that the minimum score is 31, while the maximum score is 81.

Ranked Ordered Scores: 31, 48, 54, 55, 59, 61, 61, 63, 64, 70, 76, 81

The second step is to list the range of scores for the stems in a column. The stem of our smallest score (31) is 3, and that of our largest score (81) is 8. List all of the whole numbers between 3 and 8.

The third step is to put the leaves on the stems. Take each score, one at a time and put the last digit in a column next to its stem. For example, the last digit of 31 is 1, so put a 1 next to its stem of 3. The last digit of 48 is 8, so put an 8 next to its stem of 4. Do this for the remaining scores.

Stems	Leaves
8	1
7	0 6
6	1 1 3 4
5	4 5 9
4	8
3	1

A stem-and-leaf plot gives you a picture of how the scores are grouped so that you can begin to understand their meaning. In this example, you can see that 4 people got a score in the 60s. You can also see that the high score was 81, and the low score war 31.

PROBLEM

Stems	Leaves
6	5
5	3 6
4	0 1 7
3	2 9
2	4

The stem-and-leaf plot above was created using what set of scores?

SOLUTION

In this stem-and-leaf plot, the stems are the first digit, and the leaves are the remaining digits. Starting from the bottom, the first score is 24, the second score is 32, then comes 39, 40, 41, 47, 53, 56, and 65.

• EXAMPLE

A **scatter-plot** is a graph that shows the relationship between two variables. A scatter-plot is a set of (*x*, *y*) coordinates. Each coordinate is a point on the graph. *x* represents a value of one variable, while *y* represents the value of another variable. Remember, a variable is just a measurement that can take on more than one value. A scatter-plot is useful because in one picture you can see if there is a relationship between two variables. It has been said mat, "A picture is worth a thousand words." Likewise, "A graph is worth a thousand numbers."

Given: Variable *x* represents Grade level. Variable *y* represents Hours of Homework each week.

Task: Using the data below, construct a scatter-plot.

Question: What is the relationship between these two variables?

x	**Grade Level**	1	2	3	4	5	6	7	8	9	10	11	12
y	**Hours of Homework**	2	3	3	6	4	10	7	10	12	9	14	15

Answer: You can think of these two variables as one set of (*x*, *y*) coordinates on a graph. Remember, a coordinate is just a point. Graph the following points: (1, 2), (2, 3), (3, 3), (4, 6), (5, 4), (6, 10), (7, 7), (8, 10), (9, 12), (10, 9), (11, 14), and (12, 15). This graph shows that as grade level increases, the number of homework hours per week tends to increase.

Scatterplot

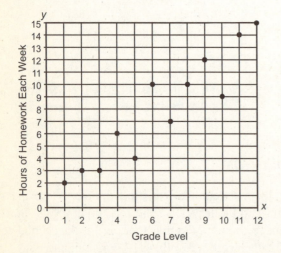

A statistic called **correlation** tells you if two measurements go together along a straight line. A scatter-plot is one way of looking at correlation. There are three different types of correlation.

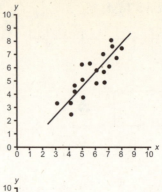

POSITIVE CORRELATION

As one measurement increases, the other measurement also increases.

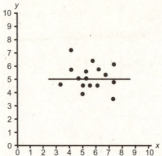

ZERO CORRELATION

The two measurements are not related to each other along a straight line.

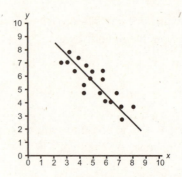

NEGATIVE CORRELATION

As one measurement increases, the other measurement decreases.

Types of Frequency Curves

In applications we find that most of the frequency curves fall within one of the categories listed.

1. One of the most popular is the bell-shaped or symmetrical frequency curve.

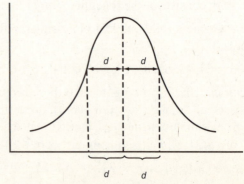

Bell-shaped or Symmetrical

Note that observations equally distant from the maximum have the same frequency. The normal curve has a symmetrical frequency curve.

2. The U-shaped curve has maxima at both ends.

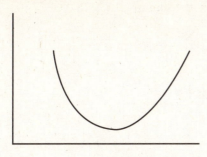

U-shaped

3. A curve can also be skewed to one side. A skew to the left is when the slope to the right of the maximum is steeper than the slope to the left. The opposite holds for the frequency curve skewed to the right.

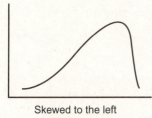

Skewed to the left   Skewed to the right
(negative skew)   (positive skew)

4. A J-shaped curve has a maximum at one end.

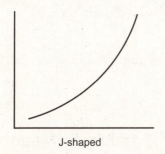

J-shaped

5. A multimodal (bimodal) frequency curve has two or more maxima.

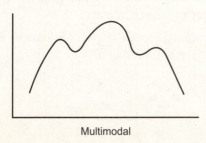

Multimodal

PROBLEM

What are two ways to describe the form of a frequency distribution? How would the following distributions be described?

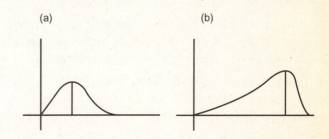

(a)   (b)

SOLUTION

The form of a frequency distribution can be described by its departure from symmetry or skewness and its degree of peakedness or kurtosis.

If the few extreme values are higher than most of the others, we say that the distribution is "positively skewed" or "skewed" to the right.

If the few extreme values are lower than most of the others, we say that the distribution is "negatively skewed" or "skewed" to the left.

(a) This distribution has extreme values in the upper half of the curve and is skewed to the right or positively skewed.

(b) The extreme values of this distribution are in the lower half of the curve. Thus, the distribution is negatively skewed or skewed to the left.

Numerical Methods of Describing Data

Introduction

Once we have a sufficient number of measurements, it is easy to find the frequency distribution. Graphic methods, however, are very often impractical or difficult to convey.

To remedy the situation, one can use a few numbers that describe the frequency distribution without drawing a real graph. Such numbers are called numerical descriptive measures, and each one describes a certain aspect of the frequency distribution. None of them yields the exact shape of the frequency distribution. Rather, they give us some notion of the general shape of the whole graph or parts of it.

For example, saying that somebody is 6'4" and weighs 250 lbs. does not describe the person in detail, but it does give us the general idea of a stout man.

It is important to describe the center of the distribution of measurements as well as how the measurements behave about the center of the distribution. For that purpose, we define central tendency and variability. In practical applications, we deal with one of two essentially different situations:

1. The measurements are gathered about the whole population.

   Numerical descriptive measures for a population are called **parameters.**

2. The measurements are gathered about the sample. Numerical descriptive measures for a sample are called **statistics.**

If we only have statistics, we are not able to calculate the values of parameters. But, using statistics, we can make reasonable estimates of parameters that describe the whole population. The most popular mathematical means of describing frequency distribution is an average. An **average** is a value that is representative or typical of a set of measurements.

Usually, averages are called measures of central tendency. We will be using different kinds of averages, such as the arithmetic mean, the geometric mean, and the harmonic mean. A different average should be applied depending on the data, the purpose, and the required accuracy.

Notation and Definitions of Means

By

$$x_1, x_2, \ldots, x_n$$

we denote the measurements observed in a sample of size n. The letter i in x_i is called a subscript or index. It stands for any of the numbers $1, 2, \ldots, n$.

We will be using the summation notation. The symbol

$$\sum_{i=1}^{n} x_i$$

denotes the sum of all x_i's, that is,

$$\sum_{i=1}^{n} x_i = x_1 + x_2 + \ldots + x_{n-1} + x_n$$

- **EXAMPLE**

$$\sum_{i=1}^{4} x_i y_i = x_1 y_1 + x_2 y_2 + x_3 y_3 + x_4 y_4$$

- **EXAMPLE**

Let a be a constant. Then

$$\sum_{k=1}^{n} ax_k = ax_1 + ax_2 + \ldots + ax_n$$
$$= a(x_1 + x_2 + \ldots + x_n)$$
$$= a\sum_{k=1}^{n} x_k$$

In general,

$$\sum ax_k = a\sum x_k$$

and

$$\sum (ax + by) = a\sum x + b\sum y$$

Often, when no confusion can arise, we write $\sum_{k} x_k$ instead of $\sum_{k=1}^{n} x_k$.

Definition of Arithmetic Mean

The arithmetic mean, or mean, of a set of measurements is the sum of the measurements divided by the total number of measurements.

The arithmetic mean of a set of numbers $x_1, x_2, \ldots, x_n$ is denoted by $\bar{x}$ (read "x bar").

$$\bar{x} = \frac{\sum_{i=1}^{n} x_1}{n} = \frac{x_1 + x_2 + \ldots + x_n}{n}$$

- **EXAMPLE**

The arithmetic mean of the numbers 3, 7, 1, 24, 11, and 32 is

$$\bar{x} = \frac{3+7+1+24+11+32}{6} = 13$$

- **EXAMPLE**

Let $f_1, f_2, \ldots, f_n$ be the frequencies of the numbers $x_1, x_2, \ldots, x_n$ (i.e., number x_i occurs f_i times). The arithmetic mean is

$$\bar{x} = \frac{f_1 x_1 + f_2 x_2 + \ldots + f_n x_n}{f_1 + f_2 + \ldots + f_n} = \frac{\sum_{i=1}^{n} f_i x_i}{\sum_{i=1}^{n} f_i}$$

$$= \frac{\sum fx}{\sum f}.$$

Note that the total frequency, that is, the total number of cases, is $\sum_{i=1}^{n} f_i$.

- **EXAMPLE**

If the measurements 3, 7, 2, 8, 0, and 4 occur with frequencies 3, 2, 1, 5, 10, and 6, respectively, then the arithmetic mean is

$$\bar{x} = \frac{3\times3+7\times2+2\times1+8\times5+0\times10+4\times6}{3+2+1+5+10+6} \approx 3.3$$

Keep in mind that the arithmetic mean is strongly affected by extreme values.

- **EXAMPLE**

Consider four workers whose annual salaries are $2,500, $3,200, $3,700, and $48,000. The arithmetic mean of their salaries is

$$\frac{\$57,400}{4} = \$14,350$$

The figure $14,350 can hardly represent the typical annual salary of the four workers.

- **EXAMPLE**

The deviation d_i of x_i from its mean $\bar{x}$ is defined to be

$$d_i = x_i - \bar{x}$$

The sum of the deviations of $x_1, x_2, \ldots, x_n$ from their mean $\bar{x}$ is equal to zero. Indeed,

$$\sum_{i=1}^{n} d_1 = \sum_{i=1}^{n} (x_i - \bar{x}) = 0$$

Thus,

$$\sum_{i=1}^{n}(x_i - \bar{x}) = \sum_{i=1}^{n} x_i - n\bar{x} = \sum x_i - n\frac{\sum x_i}{n}$$

$$= \sum x_i - \sum x_i = 0.$$

- **EXAMPLE**

If $z_1 = x_1 + y_1, \ldots, z_n = x_n + y_n$, then $\bar{z} = \bar{x} + \bar{y}$. Indeed,

$$\bar{x} = \frac{\sum x}{n}, \bar{y} = \frac{\sum y}{n}, \text{ and } \bar{z} + \frac{\sum z}{n}.$$

We have

$$\bar{z} = \frac{\sum z}{n} = \frac{\sum (x+y)}{n} = \frac{\sum x}{n} + \frac{\sum y}{n} = \bar{x} + \bar{y}.$$

The arithmetic mean plays an important role in statistical inference.

We will be using different symbols for the sample mean and the population mean. The population mean is denoted by μ, and the sample mean is denoted by $\bar{x}$. The sample mean $\bar{x}$ will be used to make inferences about the corresponding population mean μ.

- **EXAMPLE**

Suppose a bank has 500 savings accounts. We pick a sample of 12 accounts. The balance on each account in dollars is

657	284	51
215	73	327
65	412	218
539	225	195

The sample mean $\bar{x}$ is

$$\bar{x} = \frac{\sum_{i=1}^{12} x_i}{12} = \$271.75$$

The average amount of money for the of 12 sampled accounts is $271.75. Using this information, we estimate the total amount of money in the bank to be

$$\$271.25 \times 500 = \$135,875.$$

PROBLEM

The following measurements were taken by an antique dealer as he weighed to the nearest pound his prized collection of anvils. The weights were 84, 92, 37, 50, 50, 84, 40, and 98. What was the mean weight of the anvils?

SOLUTION

The average or mean weight of the anvils is

$$\bar{x} = \frac{\text{sum of observations}}{\text{number of observations}}$$

$$= \frac{84 + 92 + 37 + 50 + 50 + 84 + 40 + 98}{8}$$

$$= \frac{535}{8} = 66.88 \cong 67 \text{ pounds}$$

An alternate way to compute the sample mean is to rearrange the terms in the numerator, grouping the numbers that are the same. Thus,

$$\bar{x} = \frac{(84 + 84) + (50 + 50 + 37 + 40 + 90 + 98)}{8}$$

We see that we can express the mean in terms of the frequency of observations. The frequency of an observation is the number of times a number appears in a sample.

$$\bar{x} = \frac{2(84) + 2(50) + 37 + 40 + 90 + 98}{8}$$

The observations 84 and 50 appear in the sample twice, and thus each observation has frequency 2.

PROBLEM

The numbers 4, 2, 7, and 9 occur with frequencies 2, 3, 11, and 4, respectively. Find the arithmetic mean.

SOLUTION

To find the arithmetic mean, $\bar{x}$, multiply each different number by its associated frequency. Add these products, then divide by the total number of numbers.

$$\bar{x} = \left[(4)(2) + (2)(3) + (7)(11) + (9)(4) \right] \div 20$$
$$= (8 + 6 + 77 + 36) \div 20$$
$$= 127 \div 20 = 6.35$$

All means can also be computed for the grouped data, that is, when data are presented in a frequency distribution. Then, all values within a given class interval are considered to be equal to the class mark, or midpoint, of the interval.

Measures of Central Tendency

Definition of the Mode

The mode of a set of numbers is that value which occurs most often (with the highest frequency).

Observe that the mode may not exist. Also, if the mode exists, it may not be unique. For example, for the numbers 1, 1, 2, and 2, the mode is not unique.

• **EXAMPLE**

The set of numbers 2, 2, 4, 7, 9, 9, 13, 13, 13, 26, and 29 has mode 13.

The set of numbers that has two or more modes is called **bimodal**.

For grouped data – data presented in the form of a frequency table – we do not know the actual measurements, only how many measurements fall into each interval. In such a case, the mode is the midpoint of the class interval with the highest frequency.

Note that the mode can also measure popularity. In this sense, we can determine the most popular model of car or the most popular actor.

- **EXAMPLE**

One can compute the mode from a histogram or frequency distribution.

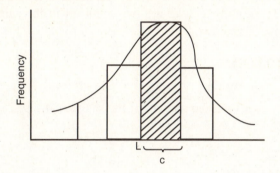

The shaded area indicates the modal class, that is, the class containing the mode.

$$Mode = L + c \left[\frac{\Delta_1}{\Delta_1 + \Delta_2} \right]$$

where

L is the lower class boundary of the modal class

c is the size of the modal class interval

Δ_1 is the excess of the modal frequency over the frequency of the next lower class

Δ_2 is the excess of the modal frequency over the frequency of the next higher class

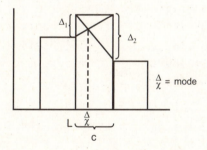

PROBLEM

Find the mode of the sample 14, 19, 16, 21, 18, 19, 24, 15, and 19.

SOLUTION

The mode is another measure of central tendency in a data set. It is the observation or observations that occur with the greatest frequency. The number 19 is observed three times in this sample, and no other observation appears as frequently. The mode of this sample is therefore 19.

PROBLEM

Find the mode or modes of the sample 6, 7, 7, 3, 8, 5, 3, and 9.

SOLUTION

In this sample the numbers 7 and 3 both appear twice. There are no other observations that appear as frequently as these two. Therefore, 3 and 7 are the modes of this sample. The sample is called "bimodal."

PROBLEM

Find the mode of the sample 14, 16, 21, 19, 18, 24, and 17.

SOLUTION

In this sample all the numbers occur with the same frequency. There is no single number that is observed more frequently than any other. Thus, there is no mode or all observations are modes. The mode is not a useful concept here.

Definition of Median

The median of a set of numbers is defined as the middle value when the numbers are arranged in order of magnitude.

Usually, the median is used to measure the midpoint of a large set of numbers. For example, we can talk about the median age of people getting married. Here, the median reflects the central value of the data for a large set of measurements. For small sets of numbers, we use the following conventions:

- For an odd number of measurements, the median is the middle value.

- For an even number of measurements, the median is the average of the two middle values.

In both cases, the numbers have to be arranged in order of magnitude.

• EXAMPLE

The scores of a test are 78, 79, 83, 83, 87, 92, and 95. Hence, the median is 83.

• EXAMPLE

The median of the set of numbers 21, 25, 29, 33, 44, and 47 is $\dfrac{29+33}{2} = 31$.

It is more difficult to compute the median for grouped data. The exact value of the measurements is not known; hence, we know only that the median is located in a particular class interval. The problem is where to place the median within this interval.

For grouped data, the median obtained by interpolation is given by

$$\text{Median} = L + \frac{c}{f_{\text{median}}}\left(\frac{n}{2} - \left(\sum f\right)_{\text{cum}}\right)$$

where

L = the lower class limit of the interval that contains the median

c = the size of the median class interval

f_{median} = frequency of the median class

n = the total frequency

$\left(\sum f\right)_{\text{cum}}$ = the sum of frequencies (cumulative frequency) for all classes before the median class

PROBLEM

Find the median of the sample 34, 29, 26, 37, and 31.

SOLUTION

The median, a measure of central tendency, is the middle number. The number of observations that lie above the median is the same as the number of observations that lie below it.

Arranged in order we have 26, 29, 31, 34, and 37. The number of observations is odd, and thus the median is 31. Note that there are two numbers in the sample above 31 and two below 31.

PROBLEM

Find the median of the sample 34, 29, 26, 37, 31, and 34.

SOLUTION

The sample arranged in order is 26, 29, 31, 34, 34, and 37. The number of observations is even and thus the median, or middle number, is chosen halfway between the third and fourth numbers. In this case, the median is

$$\frac{31+34}{2} = 32.5$$

• EXAMPLE

The weight of 50 men is depicted in the table below in the form of frequency distribution.

Weight	Frequency
115 – 121	2
122 – 128	3
129 – 135	13
136 – 142	15
143 – 149	9
150 – 156	5
157 – 163	3
TOTAL	50

Class 136 – 142 has the highest frequency.

The mode is the midpoint of the class interval with the highest frequency.

$$\text{Mode} = \frac{135.5+142.5}{2} = 139$$

We can also use the formula

$$\text{Mode} = L + c\left(\frac{\Delta_1}{\Delta_1 + \Delta_2}\right)$$

where $L = 135.5$

$c = 7$

$\Delta_1 = 2 \; (15 - 13 = 2)$

$\Delta_2 = 6 \; (15 - 9 = 6)$

$$\text{Mode} = 135.5 + 7 \times \frac{2}{2+6} = 137.25$$

The median is located in class $136 - 142$.

We have

$$\text{Median} = L + \frac{c}{f_{\text{median}}}\left[\frac{n}{2} - \left[\sum f\right]_{\text{cum}}\right]$$

where

$L = 135.5$

$c = 7$

$f_{\text{median}} = 15$

$n = 50$

$\left(\sum f\right)_{\text{cum}} = 2 + 3 + 13 = 18$

Hence,

$$\text{Median} = 135.5 + \frac{7}{15}\left[\frac{50}{2} - 18\right] = 138.77$$

To compute the arithmetic mean for grouped data, we compute midpoint x_i of each of the intervals and use the formula

$$\bar{x} = \frac{\displaystyle\sum_{i=1}^{n} f_i x_i}{\displaystyle\sum_{i=1}^{n} f_i}$$

We have

$\bar{x} =$

$$\frac{118 \times 2 + 125 \times 3 + 132 \times 13 + 139 \times 15 + 146 \times 9 + 153 \times 5 + 160 \times 3}{50}$$

$= 139.42$

For symmetrical curves, the mean, mode, and median all coincide.

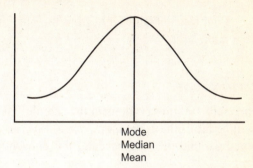

Mode
Median
Mean

For skewed distributions, we have the following.

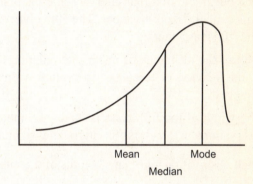

Mean   Mode
        Median

The distribution is skewed to the left

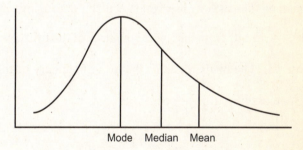

Mode   Median   Mean

The distribution is skewed to the right.

Class Boundaries	Class Weights	Frequencies
58.5 – 61.5	60	4
61.5 – 64.5	63	8
64.5 – 67.5	66	12
67.5 – 70.5	69	13
70.5 – 73.5	72	21
73.5 – 76.5	75	15
76.5 – 79.5	78	12
79.5 – 82.5	81	9
82.5 – 85.5	84	4
85.5 – 88.5	87	2

PROBLEM

Find the median weight from the previous table.

SOLUTION

There are 100 observations in the sample. The median will be the 50th observation. When using an even-numbered sample of grouped data, the convention is to call the $\frac{n}{2}$th observation the median. There are 37 observations in the first four intervals, and the first five intervals contain 58 observations. The 50th observation is in the fifth class interval.

We use the technique of linear interpolation to estimate the position of the 50th observation within the class interval.

The width of the fifth class is three, and there are 21 observations in the class. To interpolate we imagine that each observation takes up $\frac{3}{21}$ units of the interval. There are 37 observations in the first four intervals, and thus the 13th observation in the fifth class will be the median. This 13th observation will be approximately $13\left(\frac{3}{21}\right)$ units from the lower boundary of the fifth class interval. The median is thus the lower boundary of the fifth class plus $13\left(\frac{3}{21}\right)$ or

$$\text{median} = 70.5 + \frac{13}{7} = 72.36.$$

PROBLEM

A sample of drivers involved in motor vehicle accidents was categorized by age. The results appear as:

Age	Number of Accidents
16 – 25	28
26 – 35	13
36 – 45	12
46 – 55	8
56 – 65	19
66 – 75	20

What is the value of the median?

SOLUTION

We seek the $\frac{100}{2} = 50^{\text{th}}$ number, which appears in the third class (36 – 45).

The total number of accidents is 100. The median is the $\frac{100}{2} = 50^{\text{th}}$ number when the numbers are arranged in ascending order. (In this case, we have intervals of numbers instead of just numbers.) The two intervals 16 – 25 and 26 – 35 consist of 41 count. We need nine numbers from the interval 36 – 45. Use the lower boundary of this interval 36 – 45, which is 35.5, and add $\frac{9}{12}$ of the width of the interval (10).

Then

$$35.5 + \frac{9}{12}(10) = 43$$

Measures of Variability

Range and Percentiles

The degree to which numerical data tend to spread about an average value is called the **variation** or **dispersion** of the data. We shall define various measures of dispersion.

The simplest measure of data variation is the range.

Definition of Range

The **range** of a set of numbers is defined to be the difference between the largest and the smallest number of the set. For grouped data, the range is the difference between the upper limit of the last interval and the lower limit of the first interval.

• EXAMPLE

The range of the numbers 3, 6, 21, 24, and 38 is $38 - 3 = 35$.

Definition of Percentiles

The nth percentile of a set of numbers arranged in order of magnitude is that value which has $n\%$ of the numbers below it and $(100 - n)\%$ above it.

• EXAMPLE

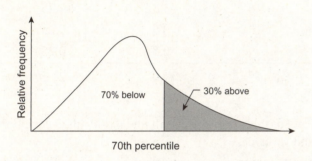

The 70th percentile of a set of numbers

Percentiles are often used to describe the results of achievement tests. For example, someone graduates in the top 10% of the class. Frequently used percentiles are the 25th, 50th and 75th percentiles, which are called the lower quartile, the middle quartile (median), and the upper quartile, respectively.

Definition of Interquartile Range

The interquartile range, abbreviated IQR, of a set of numbers is the difference between the upper and lower quartiles.

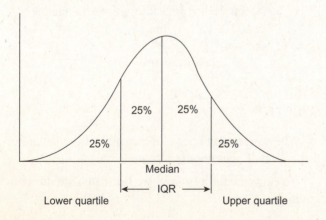

Now, we shall introduce an important concept of deviation.

The deviation of a number x from its mean $\bar{x}$ is defined to be

$$x - \bar{x}$$

Using deviations, we can construct many different measures of variability.

Observe that the mean deviation for any set of measurements is always zero. Indeed, let $x_1, x_2, \ldots, x_n$ be measurements. Their mean is given by

$$\bar{x} = \frac{\sum x_i}{n}$$

The deviations are $x_1 - \bar{x}, x_2 - \bar{x}, \ldots, x_n - \bar{x}$, and their mean is equal to

$$\frac{\sum_{i=1}^{n}(x_i - \bar{x})}{n} = \frac{\sum x_i}{n} - \bar{x} = 0$$

PROBLEM

Find the range of the sample composed of the observations 33, 53, 35, 37, and 49.

SOLUTION

The range is a measure of the dispersion of the sample and is defined to be the difference between the largest and smallest observations.

In our sample, the largest observation is 53 and the smallest is 33. The difference is $53 - 33 = 20$, and the range is 20.

The range is not a very satisfactory measure of dispersion as it involves only two of the observations in the sample.

PROBLEM

In a sample of data, the 75th percentile is the number 23. If the interquartile range is 10, what number represents the 25th percentile?

SOLUTION

The interquartile range = the difference between the 75th percentile and the 25th percentile. If $x = 25^{th}$ percentile, we have $23 - x = 10$, so $x = 13$.

Definition of Standard Deviation

The standard deviation of a set $x_1, x_2, \ldots, x_n$ of n numbers is defined by

$$s = \sqrt{\frac{\sum_{i=1}^{n}(x_i - \overline{x})^2}{n}} = \sqrt{\overline{(x - \overline{x})^2}}$$

The sample standard deviation is denoted by s, while the corresponding population standard deviation is denoted by σ.

For grouped data, we use the modified formula for standard deviation. Let the frequencies of the numbers $x_1, x_2, \ldots, x_n$ be $f_1, f_2, \ldots, f_n$, respectively. Then,

$$s = \sqrt{\frac{\sum f_i(x_i - \overline{x})^2}{\sum f_i}} = \sqrt{\frac{\sum f(x - \overline{x})^2}{\sum f}}$$

Often, in the definition of the standard deviation, the denominator is not n but $n - 1$. For large values of n, the difference between the two definitions is negligible.

Definition of Variance

The variance of a set of measurements is defined as the square of the standard deviation. Thus,

$$s^2 = \frac{\sum_{i=1}^{n}(x_i - \overline{x})^2}{n-1}$$

or

$$s^2 = \frac{\sum_{i=1}^{n} f_i(x_i - \overline{x})^2}{\sum_{i=1}^{n} f_i}$$

Usually, the variance of the sample is denoted by s^2, and the corresponding population variance is denoted by σ^2.

• EXAMPLE

A simple manual task was given to six children, and the time each child took to complete the task was measured. Results are shown in the table.

x_i	$x_i - \overline{x}$	$(x_i - \overline{x})^2$
12	2.5	6.25
9	−0.5	0.25
11	1.5	2.25
6	−3.5	12.25
10	0.5	0.25
9	−0.5	0.25
Total 57	0	21.5

For this sample, we shall find the standard deviation and variance.

The average $\overline{x}$ is 9.5.

$$\overline{x} = 9.5$$

The standard deviation is

$$s^2 = \sqrt{\frac{21.5}{5}} = 2.07$$

and the variance is

$$s^2 = 4.3$$

PROBLEM

A couple has six children whose ages are 6, 8, 10, 12, 14, and 16. Find the variance in ages.

SOLUTION

The variance in ages is a measure of the spread or dispersion of ages about the sample mean.

To compute the variance, we first calculate the sample mean.

$$\overline{X} = \frac{\sum X_i}{n} = \frac{\text{sum of observations}}{\text{number of observations}}$$

$$= \frac{6+8+10+12+14+16}{6} = \frac{66}{6} = 11$$

The variance is defined to be

$$s^2 = \frac{\sum_{i=1}^{n}(X_i - \overline{X})^2}{n-1}$$

$$= \frac{(6-11)^2 + (8-11)^2 + (10-11)^2 + (12-11)^2 + (14-11)^2 + (16-11)^2}{5}$$

$$= \frac{25+9+1+1+9+25}{5} = \frac{70}{5} = 14$$

Sampling

Sample quantities, such as sample mean, deviation, etc., are called **sample statistics** or **statistics**. Based on these quantities, we estimate the corresponding quantities for population, which are called **population parameters** or **parameters**. For two different samples, the difference between sample statistics can be due to chance variation or some significant factor. The latter case should be investigated, and possible mistakes corrected. The statistical inference is a study of inferences made concerning a population and based on the samples drawn from it.

Probability theory evaluates the accuracy of such inferences. The most important initial step is the choice of samples that are representative of a population. The methods of sampling are called the **design** of the experiment. One of the most widely used methods is random sampling.

Random Sampling

A sample of n measurements chosen from a population N $(N > n)$ is said to be a random sample if every different sample of the same size n from the population has an equal probability of being selected.

One way of obtaining a random sample is to assign a number to each member of the population. The population becomes a set of numbers. Then, using the random number table, we can choose a sample of desired size.

• EXAMPLE

Suppose 1,000 voters are registered and eligible to vote in an upcoming election. To conduct a poll, you need a sample of 50 persons, so to each voter you assign a number between one and 1,000. Then, using the random number table or a computer program, you choose at random 50 numbers, which are 50 voters. This is your required sample.

Sampling With and Without Replacement

From a bag containing ten numbers from 1 to 10, we have to draw three numbers. As the first step, we draw a number. Now, we have the choice of replacing or not replacing the number in the bag. If we replace the number, then this number can come up again. If the number is not replaced, then it can come up only once.

Sampling where each element of a population may be chosen more than once (i.e., where the chosen element is replaced) is called **sampling with replacement**. Sampling without replacement takes place when each element of a population can be chosen only once.

Remember that populations can be finite or infinite.

• EXAMPLE

A bag contains ten numbers. We choose two numbers without replacement. This is sampling from a finite population.

• EXAMPLE

A coin is tossed ten times and the number of tails is counted. This is sampling from an infinite population.

PROBLEM

The following sampling procedure is to be classified as producing a random sample or as producing a biased sample. Decide whether the procedure is random or biased.

In order to solve a particular problem, an investigator selects 100 people, each of which will provide 5 scores. The investigator will then take the average of each set of scores. This will yield 100 averages. Is this sample of average scores a random sample?

SOLUTION

A sample must meet the following conditions in order to be random:

(1) Equal Chance. A sample meets the condition of equal chance if it is selected in such a way that every observation in the entire population has an equal chance of being included in the sample.

(2) Independence. A sample meets this condition when the selection of any single observation does not affect the chances for selection of any other.

Samples that are not random are called biased.

The 100 elements are now independent. When repeated measures can be converted to a single score, so that each individual observed contributes just one summary observation (such as an average), the independence condition is met. Use of an average often helps to reduce the effects of chance variation within an individual's performance. Also, any observation would have an equal chance of being chosen. The sample is random.

PROBLEM

A wheat researcher is studying the yield of a certain variety of wheat in the state of Colorado. She has at her disposal five farms scattered throughout the state on which she can plant the wheat and observe the yield. Describe the sample and the target population. Under what conditions will this be a random sample?

SOLUTION

The sample consists of the wheat yields on the five farms. The target population consists of the yields of wheat on every farm in the state. This sample will be random if (1) every farm in the state has an equal chance of being selected and (2) the selection of any particular farm is independent of the selection of any other farm.

Sampling Distributions

A population is given from which we draw samples of size n, with or without replacement. For each sample, we compute a statistic, such as the mean, standard deviation, variance, etc. These numbers will depend on the sample, and they will vary from sample to sample. In this way, we obtain a distribution of the statistic which is called the **sampling distribution**.

For example, if for each sample we measure its mean, then the distribution obtained is the sampling distribution of means. We obtain the sampling distributions of variances, standard deviations, medians, etc. in the same way.

Correlation

Regression or estimation enables us to estimate one variable (the dependent variable) from one or more independent variables.

Correlation establishes the degree of relationship between variables. It answers the question: how well does a given equation describe or explain the relationship between independent and dependent variables?

Perfect Correlation

If all values of the variables fit the equation without errors, we say that the variables are perfectly correlated.

The area of a square S is in perfect correlation to its side d that

$$S = d^2.$$

Tossing two coins, we record the result for each coin. Assuming that the coins are fair, there is no relationship between the results for each coin, that is, they are uncorrelated.

Between perfectly correlated and uncorrelated situations, there are situations with some degree of correlation. The heights and weights of people show some correlation. We let x represent one variable (height) and let y represent the other variable (weight). We then try to determine the correlation between x and y.

Simple correlation and simple regression occur when only two variables are involved. When more than two variables are involved, we speak of multiple correlation.

Correlation Coefficient

The degree of relationship between two variables, x and y, is described by the correlation coefficient. If n observations are given

$$(x_i, y_i)\ i = 1, 2, \ldots, n$$

we can compute the sample correlation coefficient r.

$$r = \frac{\sum(x - \bar{x})(y - \bar{y})}{\sqrt{\sum(x - \bar{x})^2 \sum(y - \bar{y})^2}}$$

We shall list some properties of r:

1. $-1 \le r \le 1$

2. $r > 0$ indicates a positive linear relationship, and $r < 0$ indicates a negative linear relationship.

3. $r = 0$ indicates no linear relationship.

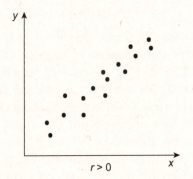

$r > 0$

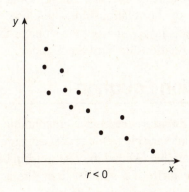

$r < 0$

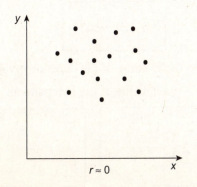

$r \approx 0$

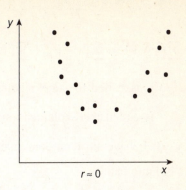

$r \approx 0$

If y tends to increase as x increases, the correlation is called positive.

Consider the linear model

$$y = a_0 + a_1 x + \varepsilon.$$

The total variability of the y's about their mean y can be expressed as

$$\sum(y - \bar{y})^2 = \sum(y - \hat{y})^2 + \sum(\hat{y} - \bar{y})^2$$

$\sum(\hat{y} - \bar{y})^2$ is that portion of the total variability that can be accounted for by the independent variable x. We have

$$\sum(y - \bar{y})^2 = \sum y^2 - \frac{\left(\sum \bar{y}\right)^2}{n}$$

$$\sum(y - \hat{y})^2 = \sum(y - \bar{y})^2 - \frac{\left(\sum(x - \bar{x})(y - \bar{y})\right)^2}{\sum(x - \bar{x})^2}$$

Hence,

$$\sum(\hat{y} - \bar{y})^2 = \frac{\left(\sum(x - \bar{x})(y - \bar{y})\right)^2}{\sum(x - \bar{x})^2}$$

and

$$\frac{\sum(y - \hat{y})^2}{\sum(y - \bar{y})^2} = 1 - r^2$$

$$\frac{\sum(\hat{y} - \bar{y})^2}{\sum(y - \bar{y})^2} = r^2$$

The total variation of y defined as

$$\sum(y - \bar{y})^2$$

225

is the sum of

$$\sum(y-\bar{y})^2 = \sum(y-\hat{y})^2 + \sum(\hat{y}-\bar{y})^2$$

where $\sum(y-\hat{y})^2$ is called the unexplained variation and $\sum(\hat{y}-\bar{y})^2$ is called the explained variation. The deviations $y-\hat{y}$ behave in a random manner, while $\hat{y}-\bar{y}$ have a definite pattern.

We define

$$\text{Coefficient of determination} = \frac{\text{explained variation}}{\text{total variation}}.$$

The value of coefficient of determination lies between zero and one. Note that

and $r^2 = $ coefficient of determination

$$r = \pm\sqrt{\frac{\text{explained variation}}{\text{total variation}}}.$$

Simple Linear Regression

Scatter Diagram

A *scatter diagram* is a graphic representation of the relationship between two variables. It consists of an *X*-axis for coding the *independent variable* and a *Y*-axis for coding the *dependent variable*. The data values are represented by points or dots within the grid and are plotted as they relate to both the *X* and *Y* variables.

- **EXAMPLE**

X = Speed of Machine (rpm)	Y = % Defectives Produced by Machine
50	1.5
75	1.9
60	2.0
65	1.5
90	3.0
70	2.5
55	1.0
45	1.2
80	1.7
70	2.0

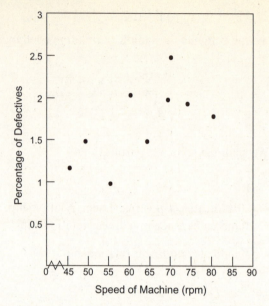

The purpose of a scatter diagram is to allow for the comparison of the independent variable (*X*) with the dependent variable (*Y*) so that we may get a feel for how they are related. We can observe both the direction of the relationship, i.e., whether they are both changing in the same direction or in opposite directions, as well as the apparent strength of the relationship between the two variables. If we imagine a straight line through the middle of the points and then look at how close the points are to this imaginary line, we can get some idea about the strength of the relationship. The closer the points are to the line, and the sharper the slope of the line, the stronger the relationship between *X* and *Y*.

Regression Equation

Simple linear regression is a technique by which one dependent variable (*Y*) is regressed against one independent variable (*X*) and the relationship between the two is in the form of a straight line. The equation for calculation of the regression line is:

$$Y_i = a + bX_i$$

where: $Y_i = $ the ith value of the dependent variable,

$X_i = $ the ith value of the independent variable.

$$b = \frac{\sum XY - n\bar{X}\bar{Y}}{\sum X^2 - n\bar{X}^2}$$

$$a = \frac{\sum Y - b\sum X}{n}$$

• **EXAMPLE**

Assume that we use the data from the previous example and compute the regression equation where X = speed of machine measured in revolutions per minute and Y = percentage of defective items produced by the machine at the specified rates.

X (rpm)	Y (%)	XY	X²
50	1.5	75.0	2,500
75	1.9	142.5	5,625
60	2.0	120.0	3,600
65	1.5	97.5	4,225
90	3.0	270.0	8,100
70	2.5	175.0	4,900
55	1.0	55.0	3,025
45	1.2	54.0	2,025
80	1.7	136.0	6,400
70	2.0	140.0	4,900
TOTAL 660	18.3	1,265.0	45,300

$$\bar{X} = \sum X / n \qquad \bar{Y} = \sum Y / n$$
$$= 660/10 \qquad\quad = 18.3/10$$
$$= 66 \qquad\qquad = 1.83$$

$$b = \frac{\sum XY - n\bar{X}\bar{Y}}{\sum X^2 - n\bar{X}^2}$$

$$= \frac{1265 - 10(66)(1.83)}{45,300 - 10(66)^2}$$

$$= \frac{1265 - 1207.8}{45,300 - 43,560}$$

$$= \frac{57.2}{1740}$$

$$= .033$$

$$a = \frac{\sum Y - b\sum X}{n}$$

$$= \frac{18.3 - .033(660)}{10}$$

$$= \frac{18.3 - 21.78}{10}$$

$$= \frac{-3.48}{10}$$

$$= -.348$$

Therefore: $Y = a + bX$, i.e.,

$$Y = -.348 + .033X.$$

The value of "b" is the slope of the line. In this equation, $b = .033$ tells us that for every unit increase in rpm, the percentage of defective units produced increases by .033 percent. This is an indication of a positive relationship between X and Y; i.e., as X increases, Y also increases, as evident as well from the scatter diagram. The value of "a", which is the y-intercept, indicates that at the point where $X = 0$, the regression line

SCATTER DIAGRAM WITH REGRESSION LINE

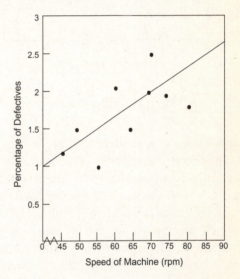

crosses the Y-axis at $-.348$. A strict interpretation of this value would be that if we operate the machine at 0 rpm, we would produce $-.348$ defectives. Obviously, if we were operating the machine at 0 rpm, it would not be producing any items and, consequently, the percentage of defectives would be 0 also. We must keep in mind that the regression equation is valid only for a relevant range of X values. Two possible modifications (which are beyond the scope of this text) which would resolve this problem are regression through the origin and (even better) logistic regression.

Once we have plotted the data in a scatter diagram and calculated the regression equation, it is generally useful to plot a regression line. Since we know that this will be a straight line, we may substitute two values for X into the equation solve for Y, and plot the straight line from these points. Using the previous example, we can illustrate this.

- **EXAMPLE**

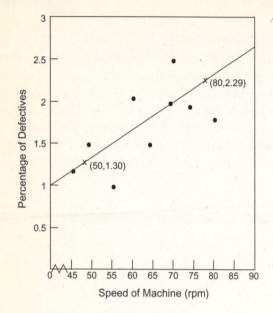

If $X = 50$; $Y = -.348 + .033(50) = 1.30$
If $X = 80$; $Y = -.348 + .033(80) = 2.29$

Now we have a "real" line through the data points and we can observe that the points fall "relatively" close to the line, which implies that the relationship between the speed at which the machine operates and the percentage of defectives it produces is "relatively" strong. Also, we note that the relationship is positive in that the line has an upward slope. If the relationship is inverse or negative, the sign of "b" will be negative and the regression line will therefore slope downward.

Once we have measured the relationship between X and Y, of what value is this knowledge? If we are satisfied that the relationship is strong enough, we may use the regression equation X to predict the value of Y from predetermined values of X. For example, what percentages of defective items should we expect if we set the rpm rate at some prespecified value? We can answer this question by substituting this prespecified value into the equation for X and solving for Y.

- **EXAMPLE**

What percentage of defectives would we expect if we set the rpm rate at 95?

$$Y = a + bX$$
$$Y = -.348 + .033(95)$$
$$Y = 2.787 \text{ or } 2.79\%$$

What percentage of defectives would we expect if we set the rpm rate at 40?

$$Y = -.348 + .033(40)$$
$$= .972 \text{ or } .97\%$$

Note that when we use a regression equation to predict values of Y from X, we should not use X values that are extremely different from those which were used to build the equation. That is, we cannot expect the same linear relationship to hold indefinitely over all values of X. Also, we must be sure when predicting that the assumptions of the regression model.

Experimental Design

Each design of an experiment consists of the following steps:

1. Statement of an objective. It usually consists of a description of the population and a description of the parameters of the population we have to estimate.

2. Statement of the amount of information required about the parameters.

3. Experimental design which consists of selection of the appropriate experimental plan.

4. Estimation of test procedure.

Suppose the objective is to find the parameter μ of the population. We have to decide how accurate μ should be. For that purpose we can apply a bound on the error of estimate of μ. That bound can be $\pm A$ units of μ from μ.

Note that A can assume any value we choose.

Suppose μ is a mean yearly income of a construction worker. Then we can choose $A = \$1.00$ and estimate μ to be within $\$1.00$.

Often the sample mean is used as a point estimate of μ; then, the bound on the error of estimate is

$$\frac{2\sigma}{\sqrt{n}}$$

Solving the equation

$$A = \frac{2\sigma}{\sqrt{n}}$$

for n

$$n = \frac{u\sigma^2}{A^2}$$

we find the sample size required to estimate μ to within A units.

Two terms are used frequently in descriptions of experimental design.

Experimental Unit

Any object or person on which a measurement is made is called an experimental unit.

Treatment

A treatment is a factor level, or combination of factor levels, applied to an experimental unit.

Suppose our experimental objective is to estimate the parameters μ and $\mu_1 - \mu_2$ or to test a hypothesis about them.

It is important to determine the quantity of information in an experiment relative to the parameter.

Often we estimate a parameter $\hat{\lambda}$, using a point estimate $\hat{\lambda}$. For the sampling distribution of the point estimates approximately normal with mean $\hat{\lambda}$, and standard deviation $\sigma_{\hat{\lambda}}$

the bound on the error of estimate $= 2\sigma_{\hat{\lambda}}$

If we are looking for a point estimate of λ then we can set the bound on the error of estimate, say A.

In general

$$\sigma_{\hat{\lambda}} = \sigma_{\hat{\lambda}}(n)$$

that is $\sigma_{\hat{\lambda}}$ depends on n. Hence solving the equation

$$A = 2\sigma_{\hat{\lambda}}$$

for n we find the sample size n necessary to achieve the bound on the error equal A.

We summarize the results concerning sample sizes in the table

λ	$\hat{\lambda}$	$\sigma_{\hat{\lambda}}$	Sample Size
μ	$\bar{y}_1$	$\dfrac{\sigma}{\sqrt{n}}$	$n = \dfrac{\mu\sigma^2}{A^2}$
$\mu_1 - \mu_2$	$\bar{y}_1 - \bar{y}_2$	$\sqrt{\dfrac{\sigma_1^2}{n} + \dfrac{\sigma_2^2}{n}}$	$n = \dfrac{\mu(\sigma_1^2 + \sigma_2^2)}{A^2}$

Note that in estimating

$$\mu_1 - \mu_2$$

we use

$$\bar{y}_1 - \bar{y}_2$$

and determine the sample size by solving the equation

$$A = 2\sqrt{\frac{\sigma_1^2}{n} + \frac{\sigma_2^2}{n}}$$

We want to estimate $\mu_1 - \mu_2$ to within A units.

• EXAMPLE

A chemist wants to estimate the difference in mean melting temperatures for two different alloys. From previous experiments he knows that the range in melting temperatures for each alloy is approximately $400°$. How many independent random samples of each kind of alloy must be checked to estimate

$$T_1 - T_2$$

within $50°$?

The range of melting temperatures for both alloys is the same, thus we can assume that the population variances σ_1^2 and σ_2^2 are approximately the same.

$$\sigma_1^2 = \sigma_2^2 = \sigma^2$$

The range estimate of σ is

$$\hat{\sigma} = \frac{\text{range}}{4} = \frac{400}{4} = 100$$

The sample size formula

$$n = \frac{4(\sigma_1^2 + \sigma_2^2)}{A^2}$$
$$= \frac{4(100^2 + 100^2)}{50^2} = 32$$

Thus we should examine 32 samples of alloy of each type to estimate $T_1 - T_2$ with a bound on the error of estimate

$$A = 50°$$

Observe that increasing the desired bound on the error of estimate we decrease the number of required samples, i.e., decrease the cost of conducting the experiment.

For example for

$$A = 75°$$

$$n = \frac{4(100^2 + 100^2)}{75^2} = 14$$

Now, suppose the objective is to find an interval estimate of the parameter λ. Let $\hat{\lambda}$ be a point estimate of the parameter λ. We assume that the sampling distribution of the point estimates is approximately normal, with mean λ and standard deviation $\sigma_{\hat{\lambda}}$.

For confidence coefficient

$$1 - \alpha$$

the confidence interval for λ is

$$\hat{\lambda} \pm Z_{\frac{\alpha}{2}} \sigma_{\hat{\lambda}}$$

One of the accepted measures of the amount of information important to the parameter λ is the half width $Z_{\frac{\alpha}{2}} \sigma_{\hat{\lambda}}$ of the confidence interval.

$$A = Z_{\frac{\alpha}{2}} \sigma_{\hat{\lambda}}$$

Solving this equation for n we find the sample size required to estimate a parameter λ by using confidence coefficient

$$1 - \alpha$$

and a confidence interval $\pm Z_{\frac{\alpha}{2}} \sigma_{\hat{\lambda}}$

The table below shows the results of interval estimates of the parameters μ and $\mu_1 - \mu_2$.

Suppose we want to test the research hypothesis

$$h_a : \lambda > \lambda_0$$

Then the null hypothesis is

$$h_0 : \lambda = \lambda_0$$

Assume that the distribution of $\hat{\lambda}$ is approximately normal with mean λ_0 and standard deviation $\sigma_{\hat{\lambda}}$ under the null hypothesis. We want the probability of a type 1 error to be α and the probability of a type II error to be β or less for the actual value of λ such that

$$\lambda - \lambda_0 \geq \Delta$$

i.e., λ lies a distance of Δ or more above λ_0.

λ	$\hat{\lambda}$	Confidence Interval	Sample Size
μ	$\bar{y}$	$\bar{y} \pm Z_{\frac{\alpha}{2}} \dfrac{\sigma}{\sqrt{n}}$	$n = \dfrac{Z_{\frac{\alpha}{2}}^2 \sigma^2}{A^2}$
$\mu_1 - \mu_2$	$\bar{y}_1 - \bar{y}_2$	$(\bar{y}_1 - \bar{y}_2) \pm Z_{\frac{\alpha}{2}} \sqrt{\dfrac{\sigma_1^2}{n} + \dfrac{\sigma_2^2}{n}}$	$n = \dfrac{Z_{\frac{\alpha}{2}}^2 (\sigma_1^2 + \sigma_2^2)}{A^2}$

λ	h_0	Δ	Test Statistic	Sample Size
μ	$\mu = \mu_0$	$|\mu - \mu_0|$	$Z = \dfrac{\bar{y} - \mu_0}{\sigma}\sqrt{n}$	$n = \dfrac{\sigma^2 (Z_\alpha + Z_\beta)^2}{\Delta^2}$
$\mu_1 - \mu_2$	$\mu_1 - \mu_2 = \delta$	$|\mu_1 - \mu_2 - \delta|$	$Z = \dfrac{(\bar{y}_1 - \bar{y}_2) - \delta}{\sqrt{\frac{\sigma_1^2}{n} + \frac{\sigma_2^2}{n}}}$	$n = \dfrac{(\sigma_1^2 + \sigma_2^2)(Z_\alpha + Z_\beta)^2}{\Delta^2}$

Discrete Mathematics

Sequences and Series

A sequence is a function whose domain is the set of all natural numbers. All the sequences described in this section will have a subset in the set of all real numbers as their range. It is common to let a_n represent the nth term of the sequence. For example, if

$$a_n = 10n$$

then the sequence is $10, 20, 30, 40 \ldots$

The sum of the first n terms of the sequence,

$$a_1, a_2, a_3, \ldots a_n,$$

is indicated by

$$a_1 + a_2 + a_3 + \ldots + a_n,$$

and the sum of these terms is called a series. The Greek letter Σ is used to represent this sum as indicated below.

$$\sum_{k=1}^{n} a_k = a_1 + a_2 + a_3 + \ldots + a_n$$

For a fixed number a and a fixed number d, the sequence

$$a, a + d, a + 2d, a + 3d, \ldots$$

is called an arithmetic sequence, and the nth term of this sequence is given by

$$a_n = a + (n-1)d$$

The number a is called the first term and d is called the common difference. The symbol S_n is used to represent the corresponding series and

$$\sum_{K=1}^{n} a + (K-1)d$$

or $S_n = n\left(\dfrac{a_1 + a_n}{2}\right)$

A sequence of the form

$$a, ar, ar^2, \ldots$$

is called a geometric sequence, where a is the first term and r is the common ratio. The nth term of such a sequence is

$$a_n = ar^{n-1}$$

The symbol S_n is used to represent the corresponding series and

$$S_n = \dfrac{a(1 - r^n)}{1 - r}.$$

Expressions of the form

$$a + ar + ar^2 \ldots$$

are called infinite geometric series. When $|r| < 1$, the sum S of the infinite geometric series exists and

$$S = \frac{a}{1-r}$$

PROBLEM

In an arithmetic sequence, $a_1 = 29$ and $a_8 = 78$. Find the common difference d and the sixth term a_6.

SOLUTION

The nth term in an arithmetic sequence is given by $a_n = a + (n-1)d$ where a is the initial term and d is the common difference. Using the given information we can first find d.

$$78 = 29 + (8-1)d$$
$$78 = 29 + 7d$$
$$49 = 7d$$
$$7 = d$$

Thus the common difference is 7. We may now use this information to obtain a_6.

$$a_6 = 29 + (6-1)(7)$$
$$= 29 + 35$$
$$= 64$$

thus the sixth term is 64.

Linear Equations and Matrices

A linear equation is an equation of the form $a_1x_1 + a_2x_2 + \ldots + a_nx_n = b$, where $a_1, \ldots, a_n$ and b are real constants.

- **EXAMPLES**

    a) $2x + 6y = 9$
    b) $x_1 + 3x_2 + 7x_3 = 5$
    c) $\alpha - 2 = 0$

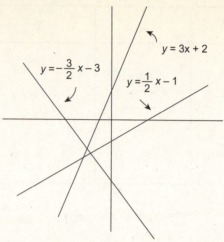

Linear equations in two variables are always straight lines.

A system of linear equations is a finite set of linear equations, all of which use the same set of variables.

- **EXAMPLES**

    a) $2x_1 + x_2 + 5x_3 = 4$
         $x_2 + 3x_3 = 0$
         $7x_1 + 3x_2 + x_3 = 9$
    b) $y - z = 5$
         $z = 1$

The solution of a system of linear equations is that set of real numbers which, when substituted into the set of variables, satisfies each equation in the system. The set of all solutions is called the solution set S of the system.

- **EXAMPLE**

    $y + z = 9$ $S = \{5, 4\}$
    $z = 4$

A consistent system of linear equations has at least one solution, while an inconsistent system has no solutions.

- **EXAMPLES**

    (a) $y + z = 9$ $S = \{5, 4\}$ (consistent system)
          $z = 4$

b) $x_1 + x_2 = 7$ $S = \emptyset$ (inconsistent system)
$\quad\quad x_1 = 3$
$\quad x_1 - x_2 = 7$

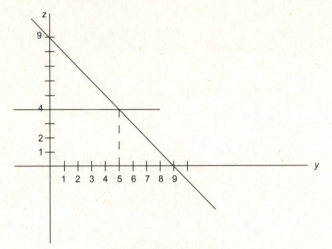

Consistent System

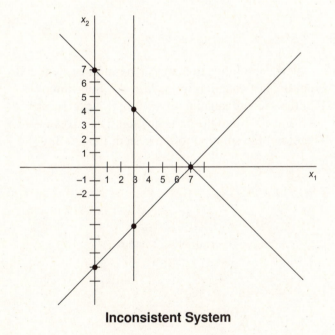

Inconsistent System

Every system of linear equations has either one solution, no solution, or infinitely many solutions.

A system of linear equations with infinitely many solutions is called a dependent system of linear equations.

The augmented matrix for a system of linear equations is the matrix of the form:

$$\begin{bmatrix} a_{11} & a_{12} \cdots & a_{1n} & b_1 \\ a_{21} & a_{22} \cdots & a_{2n} & b_2 \\ \vdots & & & \\ a_{m1} & a_{m2} \cdots & a_{mn} & b_m \end{bmatrix}$$

where a_{ij} represents each coefficient in the system and b_i represents each constant in the system.

• EXAMPLE

$$\begin{aligned} x_1 + 6x_2 - 2x_3 &= 4 \\ 3x_1 \quad\quad + x_3 &= 7 \\ 5x_1 - 3x_2 + x_3 &= 0 \end{aligned} \quad \begin{bmatrix} 1 & 6 & -2 & 4 \\ 3 & 0 & 1 & 7 \\ 5 & -3 & 1 & 0 \end{bmatrix}$$

Elementary row operations are operations on the rows of an augmented matrix, which are used to reduce that matrix to a more solvable form. These operations are the following:

a) Multiply a row by a non-zero constant.

b) Interchange two rows.

c) Add a multiple of one row to another row.

PROBLEM

By forming the augmented matrix and row reducing, determine the solutions of the following system:

$$\begin{aligned} 2x - y + 3z &= 4 \\ 3x \quad + 2z &= 5 \\ -2x + y + 4z &= 6 \end{aligned}$$

SOLUTION

The augmented matrix of the system is:

$$\begin{bmatrix} 2 & -1 & 3 & 4 \\ 3 & 0 & 2 & 5 \\ -2 & 1 & 4 & 6 \end{bmatrix}.$$

Add the first row to the third row:

$$\begin{bmatrix} 2 & -1 & 3 & | & 4 \\ 3 & 0 & 2 & | & 5 \\ 0 & 0 & 7 & | & 10 \end{bmatrix}$$

This is the augmented matrix of:

$$2x - y + 3z = 4$$
$$3x + 2z = 5$$
$$7z = 10$$

The system has been sufficiently simplified now so that the solution can be found.

From the last equation we have $z = {}^{10}\!/_7$. Substituting this value into the second equation and solving for x gives $x = {}^{5}\!/_7$. Substituting $x = {}^{5}\!/_7$ and $z = {}^{10}\!/_7$ into the first equation and solving for y yields $y = {}^{12}\!/_7$. The solution to the system is, therefore,

$$x = \frac{5}{7}, \quad y = \frac{12}{7}, \quad z = \frac{10}{7}.$$

PROBLEM

Solve the following linear system of equations:

$$2x + 3y - 4z = 5$$
$$-2x + z = 7$$
$$3x + 2y + 2z = 3$$

SOLUTION

The augmented matrix for the system is:

$$\begin{bmatrix} 2 & 3 & -4 & | & 5 \\ -2 & 0 & 1 & | & 7 \\ 3 & 2 & 2 & | & 3 \end{bmatrix}$$

which can be reduced by using the following sequence of row operations:

Add the first row to the second row.

$$\begin{bmatrix} 2 & 3 & -4 & | & 5 \\ 0 & 3 & -3 & | & 12 \\ 3 & 2 & 2 & | & 3 \end{bmatrix}$$

Divide the first row by 2 and the second row by 3.

$$\begin{bmatrix} 1 & \frac{3}{2} & -2 & | & \frac{5}{2} \\ 0 & 1 & -1 & | & 4 \\ 3 & 2 & 2 & | & 3 \end{bmatrix}$$

Add -3 times the first row to the third row.

$$\begin{bmatrix} 1 & \frac{3}{2} & -2 & | & \frac{5}{2} \\ 0 & 1 & -1 & | & 4 \\ 0 & -\frac{5}{2} & 8 & | & -\frac{9}{2} \end{bmatrix}$$

Add $\frac{5}{2}$ times the second row to the third row.

$$\begin{bmatrix} 1 & \frac{3}{2} & -2 & | & \frac{5}{2} \\ 0 & 1 & -1 & | & 4 \\ 0 & 0 & \frac{11}{2} & | & \frac{11}{2} \end{bmatrix}$$

This is the augmented matrix for the system:

$$x + {}^3\!/_2\, y - 2z = {}^5\!/_2$$
$$y - z = 4$$
$${}^{11}\!/_2\, z = {}^{11}\!/_2$$

Now the solution to this system can be easily found. From the last equation we have $z = 1$. Substituting $z = 1$ in the second equation gives $y = 5$. Next, substitute $y = 5$ and $z = 1$ into the first equation. This gives $x = -3$. Therefore, the solution to the system is $x = -3$, $y = 5$, $z = 1$.

PROBLEM

Solve the following system:

$$x + y + 2z = 9$$
$$2x + 4y - 3z = 1$$
$$3x + 6y - 5z = 0$$

SOLUTION

The augmented matrix for the system is:

$$\begin{bmatrix} 1 & 1 & 2 & | & 9 \\ 2 & 4 & -3 & | & 1 \\ 3 & 6 & -5 & | & 0 \end{bmatrix}.$$

It can be reduced by elementary row operations.

Add -2 times the first row to the second row and -3 times the first row to the third row.

$$\begin{bmatrix} 1 & 1 & 2 & 9 \\ 0 & 2 & -7 & -17 \\ 0 & 3 & -11 & -27 \end{bmatrix}$$

Multiply the second row by $\frac{1}{2}$.

$$\begin{bmatrix} 1 & 1 & 2 & 9 \\ 0 & 1 & -\frac{7}{2} & -\frac{17}{2} \\ 0 & 3 & -11 & -27 \end{bmatrix}$$

Add -3 times the second row to the third row.

$$\begin{bmatrix} 1 & 1 & 2 & 9 \\ 0 & 1 & -\frac{7}{2} & -\frac{17}{2} \\ 0 & 0 & -\frac{1}{2} & -\frac{3}{2} \end{bmatrix}$$

Multiply the third row by -2 to obtain

$$\begin{bmatrix} 1 & 1 & 2 & 9 \\ 0 & 1 & -\frac{7}{2} & -\frac{17}{2} \\ 0 & 0 & 1 & 3 \end{bmatrix}.$$

This is the augmented matrix for the system:

$$x + y + 2z = 9$$
$$y - \frac{7}{2}z = -\frac{17}{2}$$
$$z = 3$$

Solving this system gives $x = 1$, $y = 2$, and $z = 3$.

PROBLEM

For the following system, find the augmented matrix; then, by reducing, determine whether the system has a solution.

$$3x - y + z = 1$$
$$7x + y - z = 6 \qquad (1)$$
$$2x + y - z = 2$$

SOLUTION

The augmented matrix for the system is

$$\begin{bmatrix} 3 & -1 & 1 & 1 \\ 7 & 1 & -1 & 6 \\ 2 & 1 & -1 & 2 \end{bmatrix}.$$

This can be reduced by performing the following row operations. Divide the first row by 3.

$$\begin{bmatrix} 1 & -\frac{1}{3} & \frac{1}{3} & \frac{1}{3} \\ 7 & 1 & -1 & 6 \\ 2 & 1 & -1 & 2 \end{bmatrix}$$

Now add -7 times the first row to the second row and -2 times the first row to the third row.

$$\begin{bmatrix} 1 & -\frac{1}{3} & \frac{1}{3} & \frac{1}{3} \\ 0 & \frac{10}{3} & -\frac{10}{3} & \frac{11}{3} \\ 0 & \frac{5}{3} & -\frac{5}{3} & \frac{4}{3} \end{bmatrix}$$

Divide the second row by $^{10}\!/_3$, and add $-^5\!/_3$ times the second row to the third row.

Matrices

A matrix is a rectangular array of numbers, called entries.

• **EXAMPLES**

a) $\begin{bmatrix} 6 & 2 \\ 3 & 1 \\ 0 & 0 \end{bmatrix}$

b) $\begin{bmatrix} 3 \\ 1 \end{bmatrix}$

c) $\begin{bmatrix} 1 & 7 & 2 & 1 \end{bmatrix}$

A matrix with n rows and n columns is called a square matrix of order n.

• **EXAMPLE**

$\begin{bmatrix} 2 & 10 & 1 \\ 6 & 2 & 9 \\ 3 & 3 & 7 \end{bmatrix}$ is a square matrix of order 3.

Two matrices are called equal if they have the same size and entries in corresponding positions are the same.

Entries starting at the top left and proceeding to the bottom right of a square matrix are said to be on the main diagonal of that matrix.

• **EXAMPLE**

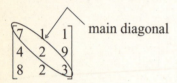

main diagonal

The sum $B + D$ is the matrix obtained when two matrices, B and D, are added together; they must both be of the same size. $B - D$ is obtained by subtracting the entries of D from the corresponding entries of B.

• **EXAMPLES**

a) $\begin{bmatrix} 1 & 2 \\ 2 & 6 \end{bmatrix} + \begin{bmatrix} -4 & 7 \\ 1 & 1 \end{bmatrix} = \begin{bmatrix} -3 & 9 \\ 3 & 7 \end{bmatrix}$

b) $\begin{bmatrix} 1 & 2 \\ 2 & 6 \end{bmatrix} - \begin{bmatrix} -4 & 7 \\ 1 & 1 \end{bmatrix} = \begin{bmatrix} 5 & -5 \\ 1 & 5 \end{bmatrix}$

The product of a matrix A by a scalar k is obtained by multiplying each entry of A by k.

• **EXAMPLE**

If $A = \begin{bmatrix} 4 & 7 \\ -1 & 2 \end{bmatrix}$ and $k = 3$, then $Ak = \begin{bmatrix} 12 & 21 \\ -3 & 6 \end{bmatrix}$.

When multiplying two matrices A and B, the matrices must be of the sizes $m \times n$ and $n \times p$ (the number of columns of A must equal the number of rows of B); to obtain the (ij) entry of AB, multiply the entries in row i of A by the corresponding entries in column j of B. Add up the resulting products; this sum is the (ij) entry of AB. If $AB = C$, then $C_{ij} = \sum_{k=1}^{n} a_{ik} b_{kj}$.

The size of C will be $m \times p$.

• **EXAMPLE**

If $A = \begin{bmatrix} 2 & 3 \\ 4 & 5 \end{bmatrix}$ and $B = \begin{bmatrix} 3 & 3 \\ 7 & 2 \end{bmatrix}$, then

$$AB = \begin{bmatrix} 27 & 12 \\ 47 & 22 \end{bmatrix}.$$

A matrix which contains entries corresponding to the coefficients of a system of linear equations, but excludes the constants of that system, is called a coefficient matrix.

• **EXAMPLE**

$$\begin{aligned} x_1 + 6x_2 - 2x_3 &= 4 \\ 3x_1 + x_3 &= 7 \\ 5x_1 - 3x_2 + x_3 &= 0 \end{aligned} \qquad \begin{bmatrix} 1 & 6 & -2 \\ 3 & 0 & 1 \\ 5 & -3 & 1 \end{bmatrix}$$

PROBLEM

Find $A + B$ where:

$$A = \begin{bmatrix} 1 & -2 & 4 \\ 2 & -1 & 3 \end{bmatrix}, \quad B = \begin{bmatrix} 0 & 2 & 4 \\ 1 & 3 & 1 \end{bmatrix}.$$

SOLUTION

Using the definition of matrix addition, add the (ij) entry of A to the (ij) entry of B. Thus,

$$A + B = \begin{bmatrix} 1+0 & -2+2 & 4-4 \\ 2+1 & -1+3 & 3+1 \end{bmatrix} = \begin{bmatrix} 1 & 0 & 0 \\ 3 & 2 & 4 \end{bmatrix}$$

PROBLEM

Let $A = \begin{bmatrix} 2 & 3 & 7 \\ 4 & m & \sqrt{3} \\ 1 & 5 & a \end{bmatrix}$, $B = \begin{bmatrix} \alpha & \beta & \delta \\ \sqrt{5} & 3 & 1 \\ p & q & 4 \end{bmatrix}$.

Find $A + B$.

SOLUTION

Using the definition of matrix addition, add the (ij) entry of A to the (ij) entry of B. Thus,

$$A + B = \begin{bmatrix} 2 & 3 & 7 \\ 4 & m & \sqrt{3} \\ 1 & 5 & a \end{bmatrix} + \begin{bmatrix} \alpha & \beta & \delta \\ \sqrt{5} & 3 & 1 \\ p & q & 4 \end{bmatrix}$$

$$= \begin{bmatrix} 2+\alpha & 3+\beta & 7+\delta \\ 4+\sqrt{5} & m+3 & \sqrt{3}+1 \\ 1+p & 5+q & a+4 \end{bmatrix}$$

PROBLEM

If $A = \begin{bmatrix} 2 & 3 & 4 \\ 1 & 2 & 1 \end{bmatrix}$ and $B = \begin{bmatrix} 0 & 2 & 7 \\ 1 & -3 & 5 \end{bmatrix}$, find $A - B$.

SOLUTION

$A - B$ is obtained by subtracting the entries of B from the corresponding entries of A.

$$A - B = \begin{bmatrix} 2 & 3 & 4 \\ 1 & 2 & 1 \end{bmatrix} - \begin{bmatrix} 0 & 2 & 7 \\ 1 & -3 & 5 \end{bmatrix}$$

$$= \begin{bmatrix} 2-0 & 3-2 & 4-7 \\ 1-1 & 2-(-3) & 1-5 \end{bmatrix}$$

$$= \begin{bmatrix} 2 & 1 & -3 \\ 0 & 5 & -4 \end{bmatrix}$$

PROBLEM

If $A = \begin{bmatrix} 2 & -2 & 4 \\ -1 & 1 & 1 \end{bmatrix}$ and $B = \begin{bmatrix} 0 & 1 & -3 \\ 1 & 3 & 1 \end{bmatrix}$, find $2A + B$.

SOLUTION

$$2A = 2\begin{bmatrix} 2 & -2 & 4 \\ -1 & 1 & 1 \end{bmatrix}$$

$$= \begin{bmatrix} 2\times2 & 2\times(-2) & 2\times4 \\ 2\times(-1) & 2\times1 & 2\times1 \end{bmatrix}$$

$$= \begin{bmatrix} 4 & -4 & 8 \\ -2 & 2 & 2 \end{bmatrix}$$

Then,

$$2A + B = \begin{bmatrix} 4 & -4 & 8 \\ -2 & 2 & 2 \end{bmatrix} + \begin{bmatrix} 0 & 1 & -3 \\ 1 & 3 & 1 \end{bmatrix}$$

$$= \begin{bmatrix} 4+0 & -4+1 & 8-3 \\ -2+1 & 2+3 & 2+1 \end{bmatrix}$$

$$2A + B = \begin{bmatrix} 4 & -3 & 5 \\ -1 & 5 & 3 \end{bmatrix}$$

PROBLEM

If $A = \begin{bmatrix} 1 & 2 & 4 \\ 2 & 6 & 0 \end{bmatrix}$ and $B = \begin{bmatrix} 4 & 1 & 4 & 3 \\ 0 & -1 & 3 & 1 \\ 2 & 7 & 5 & 2 \end{bmatrix}$, find AB.

SOLUTION

Since A is a 2×3 matrix and B is a 3×4 matrix, the product AB is a 2×4 matrix.

$$AB = \begin{bmatrix} 1 & 2 & 4 \\ 2 & 6 & 0 \end{bmatrix}\begin{bmatrix} 4 & 1 & 4 & 3 \\ 0 & -1 & 3 & 1 \\ 2 & 7 & 5 & 2 \end{bmatrix}$$

$$= \begin{bmatrix} 1\cdot4+2\cdot0+4\cdot2 & 1\cdot1+2\cdot(-1)+4\cdot7 & 1\cdot4+2\cdot3+4\cdot5 & 1\cdot3+2\cdot1+4\cdot2 \\ 2\cdot2+6\cdot0+0\cdot2 & 2\cdot1+6\cdot(-1)+0\cdot7 & 2\cdot4+6\cdot3+0\cdot5 & 2\cdot3+6\cdot1+0\cdot2 \end{bmatrix}$$

$$= \begin{bmatrix} 4+0+8 & 1-2+28 & 4+6+20 & 3+2+8 \\ 8+0+0 & 2-6+0 & 8+18+0 & 6+6+0 \end{bmatrix}$$

$$AB = \begin{bmatrix} 12 & 27 & 30 & 13 \\ 8 & -4 & 26 & 12 \end{bmatrix}$$

Matrix Arithmetic

Rules of Matrix Arithmetic

a) $A + B = B + A$ (Commutative Law of Addition)

b) $A + (B + C) = (A + B) + C$ (Associative Law of Addition)

c) $A(BC) = (AB)C$ (Associative Law of Multiplication)

d) $A(B \pm C) = AB \pm AC$ (Distributive Law)

e) $a(B + C) = aB + aC$

f) $(a \pm b)C = aC \pm bC$

g) $(ab)C = a(bC)$

h) $a(BC) = (aB)C = B(aC)$

A matrix whose entries are all zero is called a zero matrix, **0**.

• **EXAMPLES**

a) $\begin{bmatrix} 0 & 0 \\ 0 & 0 \end{bmatrix}$

b) $\begin{bmatrix} 0 \\ 0 \\ 0 \end{bmatrix}$

c) $\begin{bmatrix} 0 & 0 & 0 \\ 0 & 0 & 0 \\ 0 & 0 & 0 \end{bmatrix}$

Theorem

If the size of the matrices are such that the indicated operations can be performed, the following rules of matrix arithmetic are valid:

a) $A + 0 = 0 + A = A$

b) $A - A = 0$

c) $0 - A = -A$

d) $A0 = 0$

An identity matrix (I) is a square matrix with ones on the main diagonal and zeros everywhere else.

• **EXAMPLES**

a) $\begin{bmatrix} 1 & 0 \\ 0 & 1 \end{bmatrix}$

b) $\begin{bmatrix} 1 & 0 & 0 & 0 \\ 0 & 1 & 0 & 0 \\ 0 & 0 & 1 & 0 \\ 0 & 0 & 0 & 1 \end{bmatrix}$

If A is a square matrix and a matrix B exists such that $AB = BA = I$, then A is invertible and B is the inverse of A, (A^{-1}). An invertible matrix has one and only one inverse.

Theorem

If A and B are invertible matrices of the same size, then:

a) AB is invertible

b) $(AB)^{-1} = (B^{-1})(A^{-1})$

The formula for inverting a 2×2 matrix is

If $A = \begin{bmatrix} a & b \\ c & d \end{bmatrix}$, then $A^{-1} = \dfrac{1}{ad - bc} \begin{bmatrix} d & -b \\ -c & a \end{bmatrix}$.

• **EXAMPLE**

If $A = \begin{bmatrix} 1 & 2 \\ 3 & 4 \end{bmatrix}$, then $A^{-1} = \begin{bmatrix} -2 & 1 \\ \frac{3}{2} & -\frac{1}{2} \end{bmatrix}$.

Theorem

If A is an invertible matrix, then:

a) A^{-1} is invertible; $(A^{-1})^{-1} = A$

b) kA is invertible (where k is a non-zero scalar); $(kA)^{-1} = \dfrac{1}{k} A^{-1}$

c) A^n is invertible; $(A^n)^{-1} = (A^{-1})^n$

If A is a square matrix and x and y are positive integers, then:

a) $A^x A^y = A^{x+y}$

b) $(A^x)^y = A^{xy}$

PROBLEM

Show that

a) $A + B = B + A$ where:

$$A = \begin{bmatrix} 3 & 1 & 1 \\ 2 & -1 & 1 \end{bmatrix} \text{ and } B = \begin{bmatrix} 4 & 2 & -1 \\ 0 & 0 & 2 \end{bmatrix}.$$

b) $(A + B) + C = A + (B + C)$ where:

$$A = \begin{bmatrix} -2 & 6 \\ 2 & 1 \end{bmatrix}, B = \begin{bmatrix} 2 & 1 \\ 0 & 3 \end{bmatrix}, \text{ and } C = \begin{bmatrix} -1 & 0 \\ 7 & 2 \end{bmatrix}.$$

c) If A and the zero matrix have the same size, then $A + \mathbf{0} = A$ where:

$$A = \begin{bmatrix} 2 & 1 \\ 1 & 2 \end{bmatrix}.$$

d) $A + (-A) = \mathbf{0}$ where:

$$A = \begin{bmatrix} 2 & 1 \\ 1 & 2 \end{bmatrix}.$$

e) $(ab)A = a(bA)$ where $a = -5$, $b = 3$, and:

$$A = \begin{bmatrix} 6 & -1 & 0 \\ 1 & 2 & 1 \end{bmatrix}.$$

f) Find B if $2A - 3B + C = \mathbf{0}$ where:

$$A = \begin{bmatrix} -1 & 3 \\ 0 & 0 \end{bmatrix} \text{ and } C = \begin{bmatrix} -2 & -1 \\ -1 & 1 \end{bmatrix}.$$

SOLUTION

a) By the definition of matrix addition,

$$A + B = \begin{bmatrix} 3 & 1 & 1 \\ 2 & -1 & 1 \end{bmatrix} + \begin{bmatrix} 4 & 2 & -1 \\ 0 & 0 & 2 \end{bmatrix}$$

$$= \begin{bmatrix} 3+4 & 1+2 & 1+(-1) \\ 2+0 & -1+0 & 1+2 \end{bmatrix}$$

$$= \begin{bmatrix} 7 & 3 & 0 \\ 2 & -1 & 3 \end{bmatrix}$$

and

$$B + A = \begin{bmatrix} 4 & 2 & -1 \\ 0 & 0 & 2 \end{bmatrix} + \begin{bmatrix} 3 & 1 & 1 \\ 2 & -1 & 1 \end{bmatrix}$$

$$= \begin{bmatrix} 4+3 & 2+1 & -1+1 \\ 0+2 & 0+(-1) & 2+1 \end{bmatrix}$$

$$= \begin{bmatrix} 7 & 3 & 0 \\ 2 & -1 & 3 \end{bmatrix}$$

Thus, $A + B = B + A$.

b) $$A + B = \begin{bmatrix} -2 & 6 \\ 2 & 1 \end{bmatrix} + \begin{bmatrix} 2 & 1 \\ 0 & 3 \end{bmatrix}$$

$$= \begin{bmatrix} -2+2 & 6+1 \\ 2+0 & 1+3 \end{bmatrix}$$

$$= \begin{bmatrix} 0 & 7 \\ 2 & 4 \end{bmatrix}$$

and

$$(A + B) + C = \begin{bmatrix} 0 & 7 \\ 2 & 4 \end{bmatrix} + \begin{bmatrix} -1 & 0 \\ 7 & 2 \end{bmatrix}$$

$$= \begin{bmatrix} 0+(-1) & 7+0 \\ 2+7 & 4+2 \end{bmatrix}$$

$$= \begin{bmatrix} -1 & 7 \\ 9 & 6 \end{bmatrix}$$

$$B + C = \begin{bmatrix} 2 & 1 \\ 0 & 3 \end{bmatrix} + \begin{bmatrix} -1 & 0 \\ 7 & 2 \end{bmatrix}$$

$$= \begin{bmatrix} 2+(-1) & 1+0 \\ 0+7 & 3+2 \end{bmatrix}$$

$$= \begin{bmatrix} 1 & 1 \\ 7 & 5 \end{bmatrix}$$

and

$$A + (B + C) = \begin{bmatrix} -2 & 6 \\ 2 & 1 \end{bmatrix} + \begin{bmatrix} 1 & 1 \\ 7 & 5 \end{bmatrix}$$

$$= \begin{bmatrix} -2+1 & 6+1 \\ 2+7 & 1+5 \end{bmatrix}$$

$$= \begin{bmatrix} -1 & 7 \\ 9 & 6 \end{bmatrix}$$

Thus, $(A + B) + C = A + (B + C)$.

c) $A = \begin{bmatrix} 2 & 1 \\ 1 & 2 \end{bmatrix}$ $0 = \begin{bmatrix} 0 & 0 \\ 0 & 0 \end{bmatrix}$.

Thus,

$$A + 0 = \begin{bmatrix} 2 & 1 \\ 1 & 2 \end{bmatrix} + \begin{bmatrix} 0 & 0 \\ 0 & 0 \end{bmatrix}$$

$$= \begin{bmatrix} 2+0 & 1+0 \\ 1+0 & 2+0 \end{bmatrix}$$

$$= \begin{bmatrix} 2 & 1 \\ 1 & 2 \end{bmatrix}$$

Hence, $A + \mathbf{0} = A$.

d) $-A = -1 \times \begin{bmatrix} 2 & 1 \\ 1 & 2 \end{bmatrix}$

$$= \begin{bmatrix} -1 \times 2 & -1 \times 1 \\ -1 \times 1 & -1 \times 2 \end{bmatrix}$$

$$= \begin{bmatrix} -2 & -1 \\ -1 & -2 \end{bmatrix}$$

Thus,

$$A + (-A) = \begin{bmatrix} 2 & 1 \\ 1 & 2 \end{bmatrix} + \begin{bmatrix} -2 & -1 \\ -1 & -2 \end{bmatrix}$$

$$= \begin{bmatrix} 2+(-2) & 1+(-1) \\ 1+(-1) & 2+(-2) \end{bmatrix}$$

$$= \begin{bmatrix} 0 & 0 \\ 0 & 0 \end{bmatrix}$$

Therefore, $A + (-A) = \mathbf{0}$.

e) $bA = 3 \begin{bmatrix} 6 & -1 & 0 \\ 1 & 2 & 1 \end{bmatrix} = \begin{bmatrix} 3 \times 6 & 3 \times (-1) & 3 \times 0 \\ 3 \times 1 & 3 \times 2 & 3 \times 1 \end{bmatrix}$

$$= \begin{bmatrix} 18 & -3 & 0 \\ 3 & 6 & 3 \end{bmatrix}$$

and

$$a(bA) = -5 \begin{bmatrix} 18 & -3 & 0 \\ 3 & 6 & 3 \end{bmatrix}$$

$$= \begin{bmatrix} -90 & 15 & 0 \\ -15 & -30 & -15 \end{bmatrix}$$

$$(ab)A = ((-5)(3)) \begin{bmatrix} 6 & -1 & 0 \\ 1 & 2 & 1 \end{bmatrix}$$

$$= -15 \begin{bmatrix} 6 & -1 & 0 \\ 1 & 2 & 1 \end{bmatrix}$$

$$= \begin{bmatrix} -90 & 15 & 0 \\ -15 & -30 & -15 \end{bmatrix}$$

Thus, $(ab)A = a(bA)$.

f) $2A - 3B + C = 2A + C - 3B = 0$ since matrix addition is commutative.

Now, add $3B$ to both sides of the equation,

$$2A + C - 3B = 0,$$

to obtain $2A + C - 3B + 3B = 0 + 3B$.   (1)

Using the laws we exemplified in parts a) through d), (1) becomes $2A + C = 3B$. Now,

$$\frac{1}{3}(2A + C) = \frac{1}{3}(3B)$$

which implies

$$B = \frac{1}{3}(2A + C).$$

$$2A + C = \begin{bmatrix} 2(-1) & 2(3) \\ 2(0) & 2(0) \end{bmatrix} + \begin{bmatrix} -2 & -1 \\ -1 & 1 \end{bmatrix} = \begin{bmatrix} -4 & 5 \\ -1 & 1 \end{bmatrix}$$

Thus,

$$B = \frac{1}{3}(2A + C) = \frac{1}{3} \begin{bmatrix} -4 & 5 \\ -1 & 1 \end{bmatrix} = \begin{bmatrix} -\frac{4}{3} & \frac{5}{3} \\ -\frac{1}{3} & \frac{1}{3} \end{bmatrix}.$$

PROBLEM

Let $A = \begin{bmatrix} 1 & 1 \\ 3 & 7 \end{bmatrix}$ and $B = \begin{bmatrix} 2 & 5 \\ 4 & 0 \end{bmatrix}$. Show $AB \neq BA$.

SOLUTION

$$AB = \begin{bmatrix} 1 & 1 \\ 3 & 7 \end{bmatrix}\begin{bmatrix} 2 & 5 \\ 4 & 0 \end{bmatrix} = \begin{bmatrix} 1\cdot2+1\cdot4 & 1\cdot5+1\cdot0 \\ 3\cdot2+7\cdot4 & 3\cdot5+7\cdot0 \end{bmatrix}$$

$$= \begin{bmatrix} 2+4 & 5+0 \\ 6+28 & 15+0 \end{bmatrix}$$

$$= \begin{bmatrix} 6 & 5 \\ 34 & 15 \end{bmatrix}$$

$$BA = \begin{bmatrix} 2 & 5 \\ 4 & 0 \end{bmatrix}\begin{bmatrix} 1 & 1 \\ 3 & 7 \end{bmatrix} = \begin{bmatrix} 2\cdot1+5\cdot3 & 2\cdot1+5\cdot7 \\ 4\cdot1+0\cdot3 & 4\cdot1+0\cdot7 \end{bmatrix}$$

$$= \begin{bmatrix} 2+15 & 2+35 \\ 4+0 & 4+0 \end{bmatrix}$$

$$= \begin{bmatrix} 17 & 37 \\ 4 & 4 \end{bmatrix}$$

Therefore, $AB \neq BA$.

NYSTCE

New York State Teacher Certification Examinations

Mathematics CST (004)

Practice Test

Sample Mathematics Definitions and Formulas

Definitions and Formulas for Mathematics

LOGIC

$a \rightarrow b$	a implies b
$a \leftrightarrow b$	a if and only if b
$a \wedge b$	a and b
$a \vee b$	a or b
$\sim a$	not a
$A \cup B$	A union B
$A \cap B$	A intersect B
$\overline{A}$	complement of A
U	universal set
$\{\}$	empty set

ALGEBRA

$i = \sqrt{-1}$	imaginary unit
$\overline{z}$	complex conjugate of z
A^{-1}	inverse of matrix A
$\vec{v}$	vector v

GEOMETRY

surface area of a sphere	$S = 4\pi r^2$	$\sim$	is similar to
volume of a sphere	$V = \dfrac{4}{3}\pi r^3$	$\cong$	is congruent to

GEOMETRY *(Continued)*

Congruent Angles

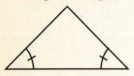

Parallel Lines

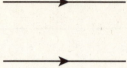

Ellipse

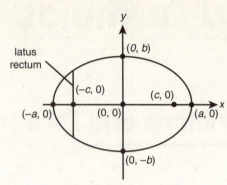

Congruent Sides

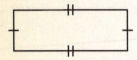

Heron's Formula

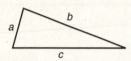

$$\text{Area} = \sqrt{s(s-a)(s-b)(s-c)}$$

$$\text{where } s = \frac{a+b+c}{2}$$

$$\frac{(x-h)^2}{a^2} + \frac{(y-k)^2}{b^2} = 1$$

$$\text{where } c^2 = a^2 - b^2$$

Parabola

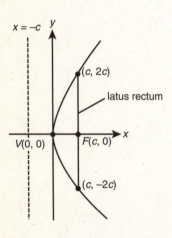

$$(y-k)^2 = 4c(x-h)$$

Hyperbola

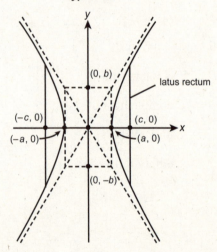

$$\frac{(x-h)^2}{a^2} - \frac{(y-k)^2}{b^2} = 1 \quad \text{where } b^2 = c^2 - a^2$$

Directrices of a Conic

$$x = \pm\frac{a}{e} = \pm\frac{a^2}{c}$$

Eccentricity of a Conic

$$e = \frac{c}{a}$$

TRIGONOMETRY

$$\sin(\theta_1 \pm \theta_2) = \sin\theta_1 \cos\theta_2 \pm \cos\theta_1 \sin\theta_2$$

$$\cos(\theta_1 \pm \theta_2) = \cos\theta_1 \cos\theta_2 \mp \sin\theta_1 \sin\theta_2$$

$$\tan(\theta_1 \pm \theta_2) = \frac{\tan\theta_1 \pm \tan\theta_2}{1 \mp \tan\theta_1 \tan\theta_2}$$

$$\sin\frac{\theta}{2} = \pm\sqrt{\frac{1-\cos\theta}{2}}$$

$$\cos\frac{\theta}{2} = \pm\sqrt{\frac{1+\cos\theta}{2}}$$

$$\tan\frac{\theta}{2} = \pm\sqrt{\frac{1-\cos\theta}{1+\cos\theta}}$$

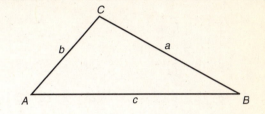

Law of Sines

$$\frac{\sin A}{a} = \frac{\sin B}{b} = \frac{\sin C}{c}$$

Law of Cosines

$$c^2 = a^2 + b^2 - 2ab\cos C$$

STATISTICS

$$\text{standard deviation of a sample mean} = \frac{\sigma}{\sqrt{N}}$$

NOTES FOR MATHEMATICS TEST

Assume all functions are real-valued functions unless otherwise noted.

Diagrams may not be drawn to scale.

Answer Sheet

1. Ⓐ Ⓑ Ⓒ Ⓓ	24. Ⓐ Ⓑ Ⓒ Ⓓ	47. Ⓐ Ⓑ Ⓒ Ⓓ	70. Ⓐ Ⓑ Ⓒ Ⓓ
2. Ⓐ Ⓑ Ⓒ Ⓓ	25. Ⓐ Ⓑ Ⓒ Ⓓ	48. Ⓐ Ⓑ Ⓒ Ⓓ	71. Ⓐ Ⓑ Ⓒ Ⓓ
3. Ⓐ Ⓑ Ⓒ Ⓓ	26. Ⓐ Ⓑ Ⓒ Ⓓ	49. Ⓐ Ⓑ Ⓒ Ⓓ	72. Ⓐ Ⓑ Ⓒ Ⓓ
4. Ⓐ Ⓑ Ⓒ Ⓓ	27. Ⓐ Ⓑ Ⓒ Ⓓ	50. Ⓐ Ⓑ Ⓒ Ⓓ	73. Ⓐ Ⓑ Ⓒ Ⓓ
5. Ⓐ Ⓑ Ⓒ Ⓓ	28. Ⓐ Ⓑ Ⓒ Ⓓ	51. Ⓐ Ⓑ Ⓒ Ⓓ	74. Ⓐ Ⓑ Ⓒ Ⓓ
6. Ⓐ Ⓑ Ⓒ Ⓓ	29. Ⓐ Ⓑ Ⓒ Ⓓ	52. Ⓐ Ⓑ Ⓒ Ⓓ	75. Ⓐ Ⓑ Ⓒ Ⓓ
7. Ⓐ Ⓑ Ⓒ Ⓓ	30. Ⓐ Ⓑ Ⓒ Ⓓ	53. Ⓐ Ⓑ Ⓒ Ⓓ	76. Ⓐ Ⓑ Ⓒ Ⓓ
8. Ⓐ Ⓑ Ⓒ Ⓓ	31. Ⓐ Ⓑ Ⓒ Ⓓ	54. Ⓐ Ⓑ Ⓒ Ⓓ	77. Ⓐ Ⓑ Ⓒ Ⓓ
9. Ⓐ Ⓑ Ⓒ Ⓓ	32. Ⓐ Ⓑ Ⓒ Ⓓ	55. Ⓐ Ⓑ Ⓒ Ⓓ	78. Ⓐ Ⓑ Ⓒ Ⓓ
10. Ⓐ Ⓑ Ⓒ Ⓓ	33. Ⓐ Ⓑ Ⓒ Ⓓ	56. Ⓐ Ⓑ Ⓒ Ⓓ	79. Ⓐ Ⓑ Ⓒ Ⓓ
11. Ⓐ Ⓑ Ⓒ Ⓓ	34. Ⓐ Ⓑ Ⓒ Ⓓ	57. Ⓐ Ⓑ Ⓒ Ⓓ	80. Ⓐ Ⓑ Ⓒ Ⓓ
12. Ⓐ Ⓑ Ⓒ Ⓓ	35. Ⓐ Ⓑ Ⓒ Ⓓ	58. Ⓐ Ⓑ Ⓒ Ⓓ	81. Ⓐ Ⓑ Ⓒ Ⓓ
13. Ⓐ Ⓑ Ⓒ Ⓓ	36. Ⓐ Ⓑ Ⓒ Ⓓ	59. Ⓐ Ⓑ Ⓒ Ⓓ	82. Ⓐ Ⓑ Ⓒ Ⓓ
14. Ⓐ Ⓑ Ⓒ Ⓓ	37. Ⓐ Ⓑ Ⓒ Ⓓ	60. Ⓐ Ⓑ Ⓒ Ⓓ	83. Ⓐ Ⓑ Ⓒ Ⓓ
15. Ⓐ Ⓑ Ⓒ Ⓓ	38. Ⓐ Ⓑ Ⓒ Ⓓ	61. Ⓐ Ⓑ Ⓒ Ⓓ	84. Ⓐ Ⓑ Ⓒ Ⓓ
16. Ⓐ Ⓑ Ⓒ Ⓓ	39. Ⓐ Ⓑ Ⓒ Ⓓ	62. Ⓐ Ⓑ Ⓒ Ⓓ	85. Ⓐ Ⓑ Ⓒ Ⓓ
17. Ⓐ Ⓑ Ⓒ Ⓓ	40. Ⓐ Ⓑ Ⓒ Ⓓ	63. Ⓐ Ⓑ Ⓒ Ⓓ	86. Ⓐ Ⓑ Ⓒ Ⓓ
18. Ⓐ Ⓑ Ⓒ Ⓓ	41. Ⓐ Ⓑ Ⓒ Ⓓ	64. Ⓐ Ⓑ Ⓒ Ⓓ	87. Ⓐ Ⓑ Ⓒ Ⓓ
19. Ⓐ Ⓑ Ⓒ Ⓓ	42. Ⓐ Ⓑ Ⓒ Ⓓ	65. Ⓐ Ⓑ Ⓒ Ⓓ	88. Ⓐ Ⓑ Ⓒ Ⓓ
20. Ⓐ Ⓑ Ⓒ Ⓓ	43. Ⓐ Ⓑ Ⓒ Ⓓ	66. Ⓐ Ⓑ Ⓒ Ⓓ	89. Ⓐ Ⓑ Ⓒ Ⓓ
21. Ⓐ Ⓑ Ⓒ Ⓓ	44. Ⓐ Ⓑ Ⓒ Ⓓ	67. Ⓐ Ⓑ Ⓒ Ⓓ	90. Ⓐ Ⓑ Ⓒ Ⓓ
22. Ⓐ Ⓑ Ⓒ Ⓓ	45. Ⓐ Ⓑ Ⓒ Ⓓ	68. Ⓐ Ⓑ Ⓒ Ⓓ	
23. Ⓐ Ⓑ Ⓒ Ⓓ	46. Ⓐ Ⓑ Ⓒ Ⓓ	69. Ⓐ Ⓑ Ⓒ Ⓓ	

91. Constructed Written Assignment

_____

_____

_____

_____

_____

_____

_____

_____

_____

_____

_____

_____

_____

_____

Continue on Next Page

Constructed Written Assignment *(Continued)*

NYSTCE Mathematics CST (004) Practice Test

TIME: **4 hours**
90 multiple-choice questions.
1 constructed-response assignment.

> **Directions:** Read each item and select the best answer.

1. To be eligible for the track team, a student must be able to run a mile in less than 10 minutes and throw a medicine ball at least 12 feet. The student must also have a grade point average (GPA) of at least 2.5 and be taking a minimum of three classes.

   The following students wish to try out for the team. Which ones, if any, are eligible?

   <u>Sam</u> is taking 4 classes and has a GPA of 3.2. He runs a mile in 10.3 minutes and throws the medicine ball 14 feet.

   <u>Lee Ann</u> is taking 3 classes and has a GPA of 3.8. She throws the medicine ball 12 feet and runs the mile in 9.9 minutes.

   <u>Ryan</u> is taking 5 classes and has a GPA of 2.6. He throws the medicine ball 12.1 feet and runs the mile in 8.8 minutes.

   (A) Sam and Ryan only

   (B) Lee Ann only

   (C) Lee Ann and Ryan only

   (D) All of the students are eligible.

2. In the triangle shown below, $\cos\omega$ is equal to

   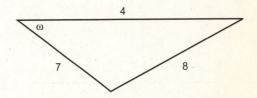

   (A) $\dfrac{1}{56}$.   (C) $\dfrac{1}{28}$.

   (B) $\dfrac{\sqrt{2}}{2}$.   (D) $\dfrac{\sqrt{3}}{3}$.

3. Of a freshman class, half of the students are enrolled in 15 class hours, most of the remaining freshmen are taking 12 hours with a few students taking 18 hours. Select the statement which is true about this distribution.

   (A) The mode is the same as the mean.

   (B) The median is less than the mean.

   (C) The mean is greater than the mode.

   (D) The mean is less than the median.

4. Which of the following triangles A' B' C' is the image of triangle ABC that results from reflecting the triangle ABC across the y-axis?

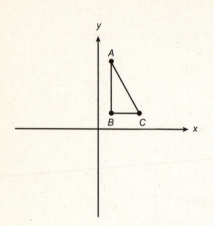

(A)

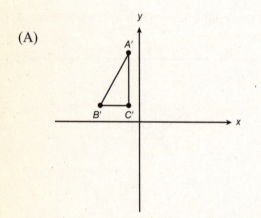

(B)

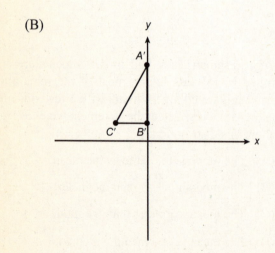

(C)

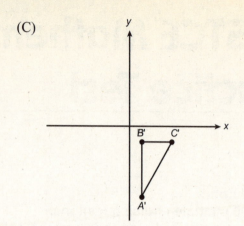

(D)

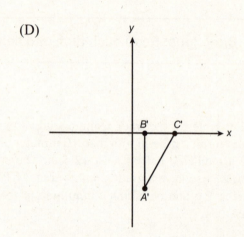

5. On a math quiz, Jim is asked to write down the mathematical expression for the words, "five more than three times a number." Jim incorrectly answers 8x. Which expression should he have used?

(A) $5x$ (C) $5x + 3$

(B) $5(3x)$ (D) $3x + 5$

6. The perimeter of the regular hexagon is 30 cm. The area of the shaded region is

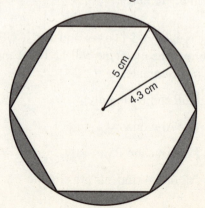

(A) 185 sq. cm. (C) 58 sq. cm.

(B) 69 sq. cm. (D) 14 sq. cm.

7. If $\log_8 3 = x\log_2 3$, then x equals

(A) $\dfrac{1}{3}$ (C) 3

(B) $\log_4 3$ (D) $\log_8 9$

8. How many games would it take a baseball coach to try every possible batting order with his nine players?

(A) 9 (C) 81

(B) 45 (D) 362,880

9. If $x = 3 + 2i$ and $y = 1 + 3i$, where $i^2 = -1$, then $\dfrac{x}{y} =$

(A) $\dfrac{9}{10} - \dfrac{2}{3}i$. (C) $\dfrac{9}{10} + \dfrac{2}{3}i$.

(B) $\dfrac{9}{10} - \dfrac{7}{10}i$. (D) $3 - \dfrac{7}{10}i$.

10. The sum of 3 angles of a triangle is 180°. The second angle is 11° less than the first angle. The third angle is twice the measure of the first angle increased by 3. If x represents the number of degrees in the first angle, which equation correctly represents the relationship among the three angles?

(A) $x + (11 - x) + (2x + 3) = 180$

(B) $x + (x - 11) + 2(x + 3) = 180$

(C) $x + (x - 11) + (2x + 3) = 180$

(D) $x + (x - 11) + (2x - 3) = 180$

11. If there exist positive integers a and b such that $8a + 12b = c$, then c must be divisible by

(A) 3. (C) 18.

(B) 4. (D) 24.

12. The slope of the line tangent to the curve $y^3 + x^2y^2 - 3x^3 = 9$ at $(1, 2)$ is approximately

(A) 0.0625 (C) −11.45

(B) 3.2 (D) −2.29

13. Point A has coordinates $(2, 5)$ and point B has coordinates $(-3, -3)$. What is the distance between point A and point B?

(A) 5.6 (C) 8.1

(B) 9.4 (D) 2.4

14. Read the statements below and answer the question.

1. All people who exercise have blue eyes.

2. Some of the people have brown eyes.

3. All people who have blue eyes enjoy movies.

4. People who have brown eyes like baseball.

5. Sarah has blue eyes.

Which must be true?

(A) Sarah has brown eyes.

(B) Sarah enjoys movies.

(C) Sarah exercises.

(D) Sarah likes baseball.

15. The sum of the first 50 terms of an arithmetic series is 100. If the common difference is 2, what is the first term?

(A) 47 (C) −48

(B) 48 (D) −47

16. For which of the following intervals is the graph of $y = x^4 - 2x^3 - 12x^2$ concave down?

(A) $(-2, 1)$ (C) $(-1, -2)$

(B) $(-1, 2)$ (D) $(-\infty, -1)$

17. Which functions(s) below is(are) symmetric with respect to the origin?

I. $f(x) = x^3 - x$

II. $f(x) = 2x + x^5$

III. $f(x) = 2x + 4$

(A) I and II. (C) I and III.

(B) I only. (D) II and III.

18. The area enclosed by the graphs of $y = x^2$ and $y = 2x + 3$ is

(A) $\dfrac{38}{3}$ (C) $\dfrac{32}{3}$

(B) $\dfrac{40}{3}$ (D) $\dfrac{16}{3}$

19. $\displaystyle\int_1^{e^2} \dfrac{\ln(x^2)}{x}\,dx$ is approximately

(A) $\dfrac{8}{3}$ (C) 0.805

(B) 2 (D) 4

20. If the probability of a certain team winning is ¾, what is the probability that this team will win its first 3 games and lose the fourth?

(A) $\dfrac{3}{256}$ (C) $\dfrac{27}{256}$

(B) $\dfrac{9}{256}$ (D) $\dfrac{81}{256}$

21. The first three terms of a progression are 3, 6, 12, ... What is the value of the tenth term?

(A) 1,200 (C) 188

(B) 2,468 (D) 1,536

22. A committee of 5 people is to be selected from a group of 6 men and 9 women. If the selection is made randomly, what is the probability that the committee consists of 3 men and 2 women?

(A) $\dfrac{1}{3}$ (C) $\dfrac{1}{9}$

(B) $\dfrac{240}{1001}$ (D) $\dfrac{1260}{3003}$

23. The base of a right prism, shown here, is an equilateral triangle, each of whose sides measure 4 units. The altitude of the prism is 5 units. Find the volume of the prism.

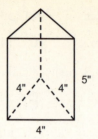

(A) $4\sqrt{3}$ (C) 60

(B) $20\sqrt{3}$ (D) 40

24. $\displaystyle\lim_{x \to 1} \dfrac{\dfrac{1}{x+1} - \dfrac{1}{2}}{x - 1} =$

(A) $-\dfrac{1}{4}$ (C) $\dfrac{1}{4}$

(B) -1 (D) 0

25. At what value of x does $f(x) = \dfrac{x^3}{3} - x^2 - 3x + 5$ have a relative minimum?

(A) -1 only (C) $+1$ only

(B) -1 and 3 (D) 3 only

26. Let T be a transformation function, $T(x, y) = (3.5x, 6.3y)$. Suppose the vertices of a rectangle of area 5 undergo the transformation $T(x, y)$. What is the area of the transformed rectangle?

(A) 49 (C) 110.25

(B) 4 (D) 259.7

27. A cube has its length, width, and height all equal to 5. The length of its diagonal is

(A) 11.2 (C) 8.66

(B) 5.22 (D) 9.1

28. An equation of the line normal to the graph of $y = x^4 - 3x^2 + 1$ at the point where $x = 1$ is

(A) $2x - y + 3 = 0$ (C) $2x - y - 3 = 0$

(B) $x - 2y + 3 = 0$ (D) $x - 2y - 3 = 0$

29. Let p, q represent statements in logic. Then $p \vee q$ is true under which one of the following circumstances?

    (A) At least one of p or q is true.

    (B) Only if both p and q are true.

    (C) Exactly one of p or q is true.

    (D) At least one of p or q is false.

30. If the graph of $px - 4y = 12$ is perpendicular to the graph of $5x + 6y = 24$, what is the value of p?

    (A) 5.4   (C) 3.75

    (B) 4.8   (D) 3.33

31. Suppose the points $(1, 6)$, $(2, 11)$, and $(3, 20)$ lie on the graph of a quadratic function $f(x) = ax^2 + bx + c$. What is the value of $a + b - c$?

    (A) −4   (C) 2

    (B) −2   (D) 6

32. Karen invests $2500 into a savings account which pays 8% interest compounded quarterly. To the nearest half-year, in how many years will she earn approximately $800 in interest?

    (A) 5.5   (C) 3.5

    (B) 4.5   (D) 2.5

33. Each point of the graph of $f(x) = (x + 3)^2 - 5$ is moved 4 units in a positive horizontal direction and 6 units in a negative vertical direction. If this new graph is called $g(x)$, which of the following describes $g(x)$?

    (A) $g(x) = (x - 1)^2 - 11$

    (B) $g(x) = (x - 1)^2 + 1$

    (C) $g(x) = (x + 7)^2 - 11$

    (D) $g(x) = (x + 7)^2 + 1$

34. The surface area of a cube is exactly the same as the lateral surface area of a cylinder with a radius of $6/\pi$ and a height of 15. What is the best approximation of the volume of the cube?

    (A) 135   (C) 165

    (B) 150   (D) 180

35. Given that $dy/dx + 2y = 3$, and $y(0) = 1$, which of the following is the correct equation?

    (A) $y = (2/3)(e^{2x}) + 1/3$

    (B) $y = (1/2)(e^{2x}) + 1/2$

    (C) $y = -1/2 + (3/2)(e^{-2x})$

    (D) $y = 3/2 - (1/2)(e^{-2x})$

36. From a group of 7 men and 10 women, how many different committees can be formed, where each committee consists of 2 men and 3 women?

    (A) 150   (C) 6188

    (B) 2520   (D) 30,240

37. In a linear programming problem involving ordered pairs (x, y), the restraints yield feasible solutions in a region where the corner points are $(0, 0)$, $(0, 10)$, $(16, 8)$, and $(40, 0)$. Which one of the following objective functions would <u>not</u> have a unique point on this region that corresponds to a maximum P value?

    (A) $P = 20x + 70y$ (C) $P = 40x + 100y$

    (B) $P = 30x + 90y$ (D) $P = 30x + 350y$

38. The height of an object is given by the equation $z = -16t^2 + 144t$, where z is the distance in feet and t is the time in seconds. After how many seconds will this object reach its maximum height?

    (A) 3   (C) 7.5

    (B) 4.5   (D) 9

39. According to the Fundamental Theorem of Calculus, if f is a continuous function on the closed interval $[c, d]$, then $F(x) = \int_{c}^{x} f(t)\, dt$ has what property at every point x in $[c, d]$?

    (A) It may not be defined nor differentiable at a finite number of values of x.

    (B) It is differentiable but may not be defined at each x.

    (C) It is defined and differentiable at each x.

    (D) It is defined but may not be differentiable at each x.

40. Given triangle PQR, where points P, Q, and R are located at $(-4, 0)$, $(1, 6)$, and $(3, 0)$, respectively, what is the slope of the median from Q to $\overline{PR}$?

(A) 4

(B) 4.5

(C) 7.5

(D) 9

41. Which one of the following statements is true for the series $\sum_{n=a}^{\infty} \dfrac{x^n}{n!}$?

(A) It converges for each x value except zero.

(B) It diverges for each x value.

(C) It converges for each x value.

(D) It diverges for each x value except zero

42. At the ACE Security Company, each ID badge has 3 letters which appear consecutively and alphabetically in order, followed by 3 digits from 1 through 7 with no repetition and in any order. How many different ID badges are possible?

(A) 8918

(B) 8232

(C) 5460

(D) 5040

43. Let a_i, i = 1, 2, 3, ... represent a recursive sequence so that $a_1 = 3$, $a_i = a_{i-1}^2 + 5$. What is the value of $a_3 + a_4$?

(A) 40,205

(B) 40,406

(C) 40,607

(D) 40,808

44. Which one of the following matrices represents the product of $\begin{bmatrix} 2 & 3 & -1 \\ -2 & 1 & 2 \end{bmatrix}$ and $\begin{bmatrix} 1 & 3 \\ 2 & 0 \\ -1 & 2 \end{bmatrix}$

(A) $\begin{bmatrix} 9 & -2 \\ 4 & -2 \end{bmatrix}$

(B) $\begin{bmatrix} -9 & -4 \\ 2 & 2 \end{bmatrix}$

(C) $\begin{bmatrix} 9 & 4 \\ -2 & -2 \end{bmatrix}$

(D) $\begin{bmatrix} -9 & 2 \\ -4 & 2 \end{bmatrix}$

45. Consider $f(x) = 10 - x$, where x is defined on the closed interval $[2, 8]$. For what value of x will $f(x)$ achieve its average (mean) value on this interval?

(A) 8

(B) 6

(C) 4

(D) 2

46. An ice cream parlor claims that 40% of its customers prefer chocolate, 35% prefer vanilla, 15% prefer strawberry, and the remaining 10% prefer other flavors. In an actual survey of 100 people, 49 preferred chocolate, 29 preferred vanilla, 17 preferred strawberry, and the remaining people preferred other flavors. Using the 5% level of significance with the chi-square goodness of fit test, which of the following is completely correct?

(A) The test chi-square value is 8.13 and the claim should be rejected.

(B) The test chi-square value is 8.13 and the claim should not be rejected.

(C) The test chi-square value is 5.82 and the claim should be rejected.

(D) The test chi-square value is 5.82 and the claim should not be rejected.

47. Which one of the following functions has a domain of all real numbers except 2 and –2?

(A) $f(x) = (x + 2) / (x - 2)$

(B) $f(x) = 2x / (x^2 - 4)$

(C) $f(x) = (x + 4) / (x + 2)$

(D) $f(x) = (x + 4) / 2x$

48. What is the smallest positive even number that is the product of five different prime numbers?

(A) 15,015

(B) 10,395

(C) 2310

(D) 1890

49. In a shipment of two boxes, Box I has 5 radios and Box II has 4 radios. Box I contains 1 defective radio and Box II contains 2 defective radios. After emptying the contents of both boxes into a bin, a radio is randomly selected. If the selected radio is defective, what is the probability that it came from Box I?

(A) 1/2

(B) 2/5

(C) 1/3

(D) 2/7

50. Look at the following figure:

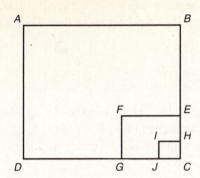

ABCD is a square with area 9. EFGC is a square in which EC = (1/3)(BC). HIJC is a square in which HC = (1/3)(EC). If this pattern is continued so that there are a total of ten squares with a common vertex at C, and in which each square lies inside its predecessor, what is the area of the tenth square?

(A) 9^{-12}

(C) 9^{-9}

(B) 9^{-10}

(D) 9^{-8}

51. Let $Y = Cp^x$ represent an exponential model for the points (1, 8) and (3, 18). Given that C and p are positive numbers, what is the best approximation to the sum of C and p?

(A) 5.33

(C) 6.83

(B) 5.83

(D) 7.33

52. The graph of which one of the following equations has no x-intercept?

(A) $5y = 10$

(C) $2x + 5y = 10$

(B) $2x = 10$

(D) $5x - 2y = 10$

53. What is the period of the function $f(x) = (1/2)(\sin 2x/3) + 1/4$?

(A) 3π

(C) $4\pi/3$

(B) $3\pi/2$

(D) $2\pi/3$

54. In order to be accepted into a program at West Point, a person must score in the top 2% of a standardized test on general knowledge. Historically, the mean score for this test is 70, with a standard deviation of 3. What would be the <u>minimum</u> integer score on this test in order for a person to be accepted into this program?

(A) 83

(C) 79

(B) 81

(D) 77

55.

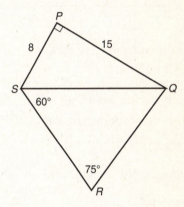

Note: Figure not drawn to scale.

In the figure shown above, what is the length of $\overline{QR}$? Your answer should be to the nearest tenth.

(A) 16.2

(C) 15.2

(B) 15.7

(D) 14.7

56. How many distinct arrangements of the word PARALLEL are possible if each arrangement must begin with the letter P? Assume that like letters are indistinguishable.

(A) 420

(C) 3360

(B) 840

(D) 5040

57. The graph of $y = x^2 + 12x + 35$ is reflected about the x-axis. What is the location of the vertex after the reflection?

(A) (−6, −1)

(C) (1, 6)

(B) (−6, 1)

(D) (1, −6)

58. Given vectors $v = 2i - 4j$ and $w = i + 2j$, what is the value of $|v| - |w|$?

(A) $\sqrt{5}$

(C) $2\sqrt{5}$

(B) $2\sqrt{3}$

(D) $\sqrt{15}$

59.

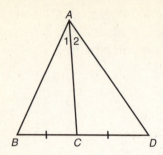

Note: Figure not drawn to scale.

In the figure shown above, $BC = CD$. Which additional information would not be sufficient to conclude that $\overline{AC}$ is perpendicular to $\overline{BD}$?

(A) $\angle B \cong \angle D$

(B) Triangle ABC is equilateral

(C) $AB = AD$

(D) $\angle 1 \cong \angle 2$

60. In a certain geometric sequence, the third term is 8 and the sixth term is 125. What is the first term?

(A) .064   (C) 1.28

(B) .512   (D) 3.2

61. Given a group of n data arranged in order, where n is even, the position of the first quartile is given by $(n + 2)/4$. The position of the third quartile is given by $(3n + 2)/4$. What is the sum of the first and third quartiles of the following group of data? 3, 5, 6, 9, 10, 15, 18, 22, 24, 30, 36, 40

(A) 46.5   (C) 24

(B) 34.5   (D) 13

62. Given points A, B, C, D, which are located at (0, 5), (4, −1), (−2, 7), and (−8, 3), respectively, what is the distance between the midpoint of $\overline{AB}$ and the midpoint of $\overline{CD}$?

(A) $\sqrt{18}$ (C) $\sqrt{58}$

(B) $\sqrt{38}$ (D) $\sqrt{78}$

63. The mean number of hours per week that a teenager uses the computer is 10, with a standard deviation of 1.5 hours. Assuming a Normal Distribution, what is the best approximation to the percent of teenagers who use the computer more than 7.6 hours?

(A) 94.5   (C) 64.5

(B) 75.5   (D) 55.5

64. Triangle ABC is situated in the xy-plane so that the coordinates of A, B, C, are (−3, 4), (0, 0), and (8, 0), respectively. To the nearest degree, what is the measure of $\angle B$?

(A) 97°   (C) 117°

(B) 107°   (D) 127°

65. Which principle is commonly used in proving a statement that uses mathematical induction?

(A) A rule that only applies to specific cases should not be applied to more general cases

(B) A rule that applies to general cases can also be applied to more specific cases.

(C) A rule that applies to specific cases can be extended to apply to more general cases.

(D) A rule that applies to general cases should not be applied to specific cases.

66. A sequence of P values is defined as follows: $P_1 = 1, P_2 = 2, P_i = (2)(P_{i-1})$ if i is even, and $P_i = P_{i-1} + 1$ if i is odd. What is the value of $P_5 + P_6$?

(A) 11   (C) 17

(B) 15   (D) 21

67. What is the maximum number of positive real zeros for $f(x) = Ax^{10} + Bx^9 + Cx^8 + Dx^7 + E$, if exactly four of these coefficients are negative?

(A) 4   (C) 2

(B) 3   (D) 1

68. Which one of the following equations has no solution in real numbers?

(A) $\sqrt{x-3} \leq 0$ (C) $\sqrt{-x-3} > 0$

(B) $\sqrt{x+7} < 0$ (D) $\sqrt{-x+7} \geq 0$

69. A geometric figure containing the point (10, 2) is rotated 90° in a counterclockwise direction about the origin. What will be the location of this point after the rotation?

    (A) (–10, 2)   (C) (–2, –10)

    (B) (–2,10)   (D) (10, –2)

70. A function contains the points (8, 3), (–1, –3), (–2, 6), and (7, 6). Which one of the following <u>must</u> be a point belonging to the inverse of this function?

    (A) (3, –8)   (C) (–2, 7)

    (B) (1, 3)   (D) (6, 7)

71. A job placement counselor claims that at the 5% level of significance, the mean entry-level salary of an accountant is $30,000 per year. In a sample of 8 entry-level accountants, it is discovered that their mean salary is $28,000 per year with a standard deviation of $1500. Assuming a Normal Distribution and using the small sample t-test for means, which of the following is completely correct?

    (A) The critical t-test value is –3.77 and the claim should be rejected.

    (B) The critical t-test value is –3.77 and the claim should not be rejected.

    (C) The critical t-test value is –1.33 and the claim should be rejected.

    (D) The critical t-test value is –1.33 and the claim should not be rejected.

72. The corresponding angles of two geometric figures may be congruent but the sides may not be in proportion.

    The above statement could apply to which one of the following?

    (A) Two squares   (C) Two rhombuses

    (B) Two rectangles   (D) Two triangles

73. If the second-order difference of terms of a particular sequence is 3, which one of the following could be such a sequence?

    (A) 3, 9, 27, 81, 243, ...

    (B) 3, 6, 9, 12, 15, ...

    (C) 2, 6, 13, 23, 36, ...

    (D) 1, 5, 14, 31, 56, ...

74.

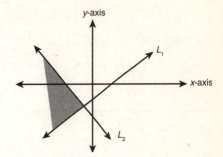

The shaded region could represent the graphical solution to which pair of inequalities?

(A) $2x + 3y \geq -6$ (C) $2x + 3y \leq -6$

    $x - y \leq -1$ $x - y \leq 1$

(B) $2x - 3y \geq 6$ (D) $2x - 3y \leq 6$

    $x + y \geq -1$ $x + y \geq 1$

75. For a regular polygon of five sides with a perimeter of n, each side measures $n/5$. Suppose you added one side of each of a regular polygon of 6 sides, 7 sides, 8 sides, ..., 59 sides, where each polygon has a perimeter of n. By what amount would this sum decrease if you replaced the regular 6-sided figure with a regular 60-sided figure?

    (A) $59n/60$ (C) $2n/59$

    (B) $9n/60$ (D) $n/59$

76.

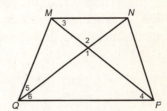

Note: Figure not drawn to scale.

In the figure shown above, *MNPQ* is an isosceles trapezoid, with $\overline{MN} \parallel \overline{QP}$. Which of the following is <u>not</u> necessarily true?

(A) $\angle 3 \cong \angle 4$ (C) $\angle 1 \cong \angle 2$

(B) $\angle 5 \cong \angle 6$ (D) $\angle 4 \cong \angle 6$

77. If $0° < x < 180°$, what values of x, to the nearest degree, are the solutions to the equation $2\tan^2 x + 5\tan x - 12 = 0$?

   (A) 56° and 104°   (C) 56° and 166°

   (B) 34° and 104°   (D) 34° and 166°

78.

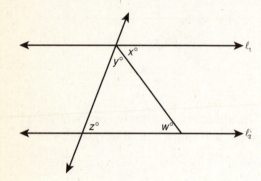

In the figure shown above, $x° = y°$. Which additional information would be sufficient to conclude that line ℓ_1 is parallel to line ℓ_2?

   (A) $z = 180 - 2x$ (C) $z = 90 - w$

   (B) $w = 180 - y - z$ (D) $w = z - x$

79. In the equation $T(x) = T_2 + (T_1 - T_2)\,e^{-kx}$, an object with an initial temperature T_1 is placed in an environment with temperature T_2, so that the object will either cool or warm to temperature $T(x)$ after x minutes (k is a constant). Suppose a cup of coffee with an initial temperature of 100° F is placed in a refrigerator with a temperature of 25° F. After 5 minutes, the temperature of the coffee is 70° F. If the coffee is left in the refrigerator, what will be its temperature after a total of 8 minutes? (Nearest degree)

   (A) 50° F   (C) 55° F

   (B) 53° F   (D) 58° F

80. What is the range of the function $f(x) = -x^2 - 3x + 4$?

   (A) All numbers less than or equal to –1.5

   (B) All numbers between –1 and 4, inclusive

   (C) All numbers less than or equal to 6.25

   (D) All numbers between –4 and 1, inclusive

81. Lisa and Mike work at night as security guards for the *WXYZ* company. Lisa is off work once every 12 nights and Mike is off work once every 14 nights. If both of them are off work on April 15th, when is the next date on which both of them will be off work?

   (A) September 15th   (C) June 24th

   (B) July 8th   (D) May 11th

82. In a certain apartment complex of 144 units, 16 units have electric heating and the remaining units have gas heating. The builder wishes to build 26 new units so that the ratio of those with electric heating to those with gas heating doubles. How many of these new units will have electric heating?

   (A) 42   (C) 18

   (B) 34   (D) 8

83. Look at the following table.

x	–2	–1	1	2
y	19	7	–5	–17

Which of the following equations best fits this data?

   (A) $y = -x^3 + 5x + 1$

   (B) $y = x^3 - 5x + 1$

   (C) $y = x^3 + 5x - 1$

   (D) $y = -x^3 - 5x + 1$

84. A circle has a diameter of 8 inches. What is the length, in inches, of an arc formed by a central angle of 135°?

   (A) 2π (C) 4π

   (B) 3π (D) 5π

85. Note: Figure is not drawn to scale.

In the figure shown, $m\angle A = 130°$, $m\angle B = 95°$, and $m\angle C = 90°$. Point O is the center of a circle with a radius of 12. The area bounded by the polygon

ABCO is 30% larger than the shaded area. What is the value of the shaded area?

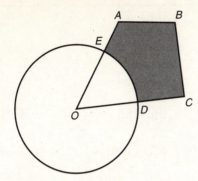

(A) 18π

(C) 42π

(B) 24π

(D) 60π

86. Suppose a rational function is expressed as $f(x) = p(x)/q(x)$, where $p(x)$ and $q(x)$ are polynomial functions. If the slant asymptote of $f(x)$ is given by $y = (2/3)x$, which one of the following could be the expression for $f(x)$?

(A) $(2x^3 + x - 1)/ (3x^4 + 2x - 1)$

(B) $(2x^4 - 2x + 1)/ (3x^4 + x - 2)$

(C) $(2x^4 - x + 3)/ (3x^3 - 2x + 1)$

(D) $(2x^5 + 2x - 1)/ (3x^3 - x + 2)$

87. The mean weight of 20 people in a room is 130 pounds. Bob and Diane are among these 20 people. If both of them leave the room, the mean weight will decrease by 3%. What is the mean weight, in pounds, for Bob and Diane?

(A) 162

(C) 168

(B) 165

(D) 171

88. What is the solution for x in the inequality $2x^2 - x - 3 < 0$?

(A) $-1 < x < 3/2$

(B) $x > 3/2$ or $x < -1$

(C) $-3/2 < x < 1$

(D) $x > 1$ or $x < -3/2$

89. Given parallelogram *KLMN*, where points *K*, *L*, *M*, *N* are located at (2, 5), (*b*, *c*), (7, 1), (0, 1) respectively, which of the following is equivalent to *c*?

(A) $b - 12$

(C) $2b - 13$

(B) $b + 5$

(D) $2b + 4$

90. In a large survey, it was discovered that 1 out of every 5 adults visits Disney World every year. If 30 adults are randomly selected, what is the probability that exactly 7 of them will visit Disney World this year?

(A) .233

(C) .154

(B) .167

(D) .125

91. **Constructed Written Assignment**

Directions: Prepare a legibly written response of one to two pages on the problem below. Plan, write, review, and edit your response. Your response will not be judged on writing ability, but must be communicated clearly and will be scored on a scale of 1 to 4. It will be evaluated on the following:

Purpose: Fulfill the charge of the assignment.

Application of Content: Accurately and effectively apply the relevant knowledge and skills.

Support: Support the response with appropriate examples and/or sound reasoning reflecting an understanding of the relevant knowledge and skills.

In the town of Moneyville, a wage tax is imposed on individuals who work there. If a person is a resident of Moneyville, the tax is $2 for the first $200 of the gross amount of the paycheck, and 0.6% for any gross amount over $200. For a non-resident, the tax is $5 for the first $100 of the gross amount of the paycheck, and 1.2% for any gross amount over $100.

- If James lives and works in Moneyville, how much tax will he pay per week if his weekly gross salary is $800?

- If Marianne works in Moneyville but is not a resident, how much tax will she pay per week if her weekly gross salary is $600?

- Linda is a new employee for one of the companies in Moneyville. Currently, she is a non-resident. If her weekly gross salary will be $1000, how much less tax will she pay for an entire year if she becomes a resident of Moneyville? (Assume that her weekly gross salary will remain $1000)

1. (C)	19. (D)	37. (B)	55. (C)	73. (C)
2. (A)	20. (C)	38. (B)	56. (C)	74. (C)
3. (D)	21. (D)	39. (C)	57. (B)	75. (B)
4. (A)	22. (B)	40. (A)	58. (A)	76. (B)
5. (D)	23. (B)	41. (C)	59. (D)	77. (A)
6. (D)	24. (A)	42. (D)	60. (C)	78. (A)
7. (A)	25. (D)	43. (C)	61. (B)	79. (D)
8. (D)	26. (C)	44. (C)	62. (C)	80. (C)
9. (B)	27. (C)	45. (B)	63. (A)	81. (B)
10. (C)	28. (D)	46. (D)	64. (D)	82. (C)
11. (B)	29. (A)	47. (B)	65. (C)	83. (D)
12. (A)	30. (B)	48. (C)	66. (D)	84. (B)
13. (B)	31. (A)	49. (D)	67. (C)	85. (D)
14. (B)	32. (C)	50. (D)	68. (B)	86. (C)
15. (D)	33. (A)	51. (C)	69. (B)	87. (B)
16. (B)	34. (C)	52. (A)	70. (D)	88. (A)
17. (A)	35. (D)	53. (A)	71. (A)	89. (C)
18. (C)	36. (B)	54. (D)	72. (B)	90. (C)

Practice Test

Detailed Explanations of Answers

1. (C)

Sam is ineligible because he requires more than 10 minutes to run the mile. Both Lee Ann and Ryan are eligible as they meet every requirement listed.

2. (A)

To solve, we use the law of cosines:

$$c^2 = a^2 + b^2 - 2ab\cos(\text{included angle}).$$

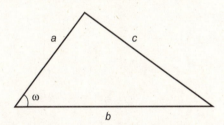

In the figure given, $a = 4$, $b = 7$, $c = 8$, and ω is the included angle.

We solve the law of cosine relation for $\cos\omega$:

$$c^2 = a^2 + b^2 - 2ab\cos\omega.$$

Transposing a^2 and b^2 and dividing through by $-2ab$, we obtain:

$$\frac{c^2 - a^2 - b^2}{-2ab} = \cos\omega.$$

Substituting for a, b, and c we obtain

$$\cos\omega = \frac{8^2 - 4^2 - 7^2}{-2(4)(7)} = \frac{64 - 16 - 49}{-56} = \frac{-1}{-56} = \frac{1}{56}.$$

3. (D)

From the information given, the mode and median would be 15, and the mean would be less than 15. So, the mean is less than the median. (A) is incorrect because the mode is not the same as the mean. (B) is incorrect because the median is greater than the mean. (C) is incorrect because the mean is less than the mode.

4. (A)

Find the y-axis. Find the side of the figure closest to the y-axis and measure the distance that this side is from the y-axis. A reflection of the figure will put this side the same distance from the y-axis, but on the other side.

Also, notice the point labeled C. A reflection of this point across the y-axis will also be the same distance from the y-axis, but on the other side.

5. (D)

Convert the words "five more than three times a number" into an expression. The term "five more" means to add five, and the term "three times a number" means multiply by three. Therefore, the expression $3x + 5$ is correct.

6. (D)

Shaded area = area of the circle – area of the hexagon

Area of the circle = πr^2

Area of hexagon = 6 × area of each triangle

$$= 6 \times \frac{1}{2}bh$$

$$= 6 \times \frac{1}{2} \times 5 \times 4.3$$

Shaded area = $\pi \times 5^2 - 6 \times 0.5 \times 5 \times 4.3$

7. **(A)**

Let $y = \log_8 3 = x \log_2 3$.

Then $8^y = 3 \Rightarrow 2^{3y} = 3$ (1)

and $y = x\log_2 3 \Rightarrow 2^y = 3^x$ (2)

Substituting the expression for 2^y in (2) into (1) we obtain

$$3 = (2^y)^3 = (3^x)^3 = 3^{3x}.$$

Hence $3x = 1 \Rightarrow x = \dfrac{1}{3}$.

8. **(D)**

This is the possible number of combinations of nine items which is $n!$ (n-factorial). Most scientific calculators have an $x!$ button. Otherwise, the factorial formula is $9 \times 8 \times 7 \times 6 \times 5 \times 4 \times 3 \times 2 \times 1 = 362,880$.

9. **(B)**

$$\frac{x}{y} = \frac{3+2i}{1+3i}$$
$$= \frac{3+2i}{1+3i} \times \frac{1-3i}{1-3i}$$
$$= \frac{3-9i+2i-6i^2}{1^2-3^2 i^2}$$
$$= \frac{9-7i}{1+9}$$
$$= \frac{9}{10} - \frac{7}{10}i$$

10. **(C)**

x = number of degrees in the first angle. The second angle is $11°$ less than the **first angle**; so the second angle $= x - 11$, where less than signifies subtraction (switching around), and the first angle (x) is the first term and $11°$ (11) is the second term.

The third angle is twice **the measure of the first angle** increased by 3; so the third angle $= 2x + 3$, where twice represents multiplication by 2 and increased by means addition.

Since the **sum** of the angles of a triangle equals $180°$, then

first angle $+$ second angle $+$ third angle $= 180°$

$\downarrow$ and$\downarrow$

$x \quad + \quad (x-11) \quad + \quad (2x+3) = 180°$

Answer choice (A) is wrong because of an error in interpretation of 11 less than x.

$$\angle 2 = (11-x)$$

Answer choice (B) is wrong because of an error in interpretation of twice x increased by 3.

$$\angle 3 = 2(x+3)$$

Answer choice (D) is wrong because of an error in interpretation of twice x increased by 3.

$$\angle 3 = (2x-3)$$

11. **(B)**

$$8a + 12b = c$$
$$4(2a + 3b) = c$$

Only 4 can be factored out.

12. **(A)**

$$\frac{d}{dx}(y^3 + x^2 y^2 - 3x^3) = \frac{d}{dx}(9)$$
$$3y^2 y' + 2xy^2 + 2yy'x^2 - 9x^2 = 0$$

Note: the product rule must be used when differentiating $x^2 y^2$. Factor y' from the first and third terms.

$$y'(3y^2 + 2yx^2) = 9x^2 - 2xy^2$$
$$y' = \frac{9x^2 - 2xy^2}{3y^2 + 2x^2 y}$$

$\dfrac{dy}{dx}$ at $(1.5, 2)$ is $\dfrac{9(1)^2 - 2(1)(2)^2}{3(2)^2 + 2(1)^2(2)} = \dfrac{1}{16} = 0.0625$

13. **(B)**

Distance d between any two points (x_1, y_1), (x_2, x_2) in the two-dimensional coordinate system is

$$d = \sqrt{(x_1 - x_2)^2 + (y_1 - y_2)^2}$$

The problem can be calculated as:

$$d = \sqrt{(2-(-3))^2 + (5-(-3))^2} = \sqrt{89} = 9.434$$

14. (B)

Statement 1 implies people who exercise have blue eyes. Statement 3 implies people who have blue eyes enjoy movies. If Sarah has blue eyes, then Sarah enjoys movies.

Answer (A) is wrong because it contradicts statement 5. Answer (C) is wrong because statement 1 says "All people who exercise have blue eyes," not "All people with blue eyes exercise." Answer (D) is wrong because "People who have brown eyes like baseball," so this has no bearing on Sarah.

15. (D)

The sum of n terms in arithmetic series with first term t_1, and common difference d is given by

$$S_n = \frac{n}{2}[2t_1 + (n-1)d]$$

In this problem $S_n = 100$, $n = 50$, $d = 2$, thus,

$$100 = \frac{50}{2}(2t_1 + (50-1)2)$$
$$100 = 25(2t_1 + 98)$$
$$\frac{100}{25} = 2t_1 + 98$$
$$4 = 2t_1 + 98$$
$$2t_1 = 4 - 98 = -94$$
$$t_1 = -\frac{94}{2} = -47$$

16. (B)

$$y = x^4 - 2x^3 - 12x^2$$
$$y' = 4x^3 - 6x^2 - 24x$$
$$y'' = 12x^2 - 12x - 24$$
$$= 12(x-2)(x+1)$$

$$+ + + + + 0 - - - - - - - - - - - - 0 + + +$$
$$\text{(concave down)}$$

17. (A)

A function is symmetric with respect to the origin if replacing x by $-x$ and y by $-y$ produces an equivalent function.

(I)
$$y = f(x) = x^3 - x$$
$$(-y) = (-x)^3 - (-x)$$
$$-y = -x^3 + x$$
$$y = x^3 - x$$

(I) is symmetric.

(II)
$$y = f(x) = 2x + x^5$$
$$-y = 2(-x) + (-x)^5$$
$$-y = -2x - x^5$$
$$y = 2x + x^5$$

(II) is symmetric.

(III)
$$y = f(x) = 2x + 4$$
$$-y = 2(-x) + 4$$
$$-y = -2x + 4$$
$$y = 2x - 4$$

(III) is not symmetric.

18. (C)

First determine where the graphs $y = x^2$ and $y = 2x + 3$ intersect.

$$x^2 = 2x + 3$$
$$x^2 - 2x - 3 = 0$$
$$(x-3)(x+1) = 0$$
$$x = 3, -1$$

$$A = \int_{-1}^{3} (2x + 3 - x^2)\, dx$$
$$= \int_{-1}^{3} \{(2x+3) - x^2\}\, dx$$
$$= \left(x^2 + 3x - \frac{1}{3}x^3 \right)\Bigg|_{-1}^{3}$$
$$= 3^2 - (-1)^2 + 3(3 - (-1)) - \frac{1}{3}(3^3 - (-1)^3)$$
$$= 9 - 1 + 3(4) - \frac{1}{3}(27 + 1)$$
$$= 20 - \frac{28}{3}$$
$$= \frac{32}{3}$$

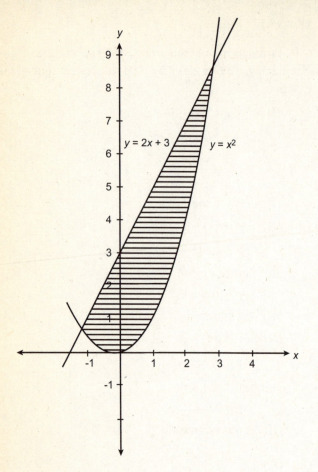

$y = 2x + 3$ $y = x^2$

19. (D)

Since $\ln (x^2) = 2 \ln x$, we have

$$\int_1^{e^2} \frac{\ln(x^2)}{x} dx = 2\int_1^{e^2} \frac{\ln x}{x} dx.$$

This integral can be evaluated by using the substitution $u = \ln x$. The integrand becomes, u, with $du = \dfrac{dx}{x}$, and the limits of integration change to

$$u(1) = \ln 1 = 0$$
$$u(e^2) = \ln(e^2) = 2.$$

We get

$$2\int_0^2 u \, du = u^2 \Big|_0^2$$
$$= 2^2 - 0 = 4$$

20. (C)

Let's call the event winning A and not winning $\overline{A}$. We want the probability P given by the following expression:

$$P = P(A) \times P(A) \times P(A) \times P(\overline{A})$$
$$= \frac{3}{4} \times \frac{3}{4} \times \frac{3}{4} \times \frac{1}{4} = \frac{27}{256}$$

21. (D)

The progression given is a geometric progression. The expression for the nth term of a geometric progression is:

$$L_n = a_1 r^{n-1}$$

where a_1 is the first term and r is the common ratio between terms.

In the given sequence, the first term is 3. The common ratio is found to be $\dfrac{6}{3} = \dfrac{12}{6} = 2$.

Therefore, letting $n = 10$ (for the tenth term), we have:

$$L_{10} = 3(2)^{10-1} = 3(2)^9.$$
Since $2^9 = 512$:
$$L_{10} = 3(512) = 1,536$$

22. (B)

There are 5 members to be selected from a group of 15 people. Therefore the total number of possible ways is

$$\binom{15}{5} = 3003.$$

We have to select 3 men out of 6 men, so the number of possible ways is

$$\binom{6}{3} = 20.$$

Two women have to be selected from 9 women. The total number of possible ways is

$$\binom{9}{2} = 36.$$

Hence the desired probability

$$= \frac{20 \times 36}{3003} = \frac{240}{1001}$$

Calculator: 15 INV nCr 5 = 3003

6 INV nCr 3 = 20

9 INV nCr 2 = 36.

23. (B)

We imagine the prism as a stack of equilateral triangles, congruent to the base of the prism. Let each of these triangles be one unit of measure thick. We can then calculate the area of the base, B, and multiply it by the number of bases needed to complete the height of the prism, h, to obtain the volume of the prism. Therefore,

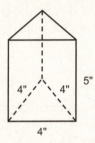

$$V = Bh.$$

All prism volumes can be thought of in this way.

In this particular problem, the base is an equilateral triangle. Therefore

$$B = \frac{s^2\sqrt{3}}{4},$$

where s is the length of a side of the base. By substitution,

$$B = \frac{(4)^2\sqrt{3}}{4} = 4\sqrt{3}.$$

Since the prism is 5 units high,

$$V = Bh = (4\sqrt{3})5 = 20\sqrt{3}.$$

Therefore, the volume of the prism is $20\sqrt{3}$ cu. units.

24. (A)

$$\lim_{x \to 1} \frac{\dfrac{1}{x+1} - \dfrac{1}{2}}{x-1}$$

Obtain a common denominator in the main numerator.

$$\lim_{x \to 1} \frac{\dfrac{2-(x+1)}{2(x+1)}}{x-1} = \lim_{x \to 1} \frac{1-x}{2(x+1)(x-1)}$$

$$= \lim_{x \to 1} \frac{-1}{2(x+1)}$$

$$= \frac{-1}{2(1+1)} = -\frac{1}{4}$$

Note: $\dfrac{1-x}{x-1} = -1$ for $x \neq 1$

25. (D)

$$f'(x) = x^2 - 2x - 3 = (x+1)(x-3)$$

$(x+1)(x-3) = 0 \Rightarrow x = -1$ and 3 are critical values.

The numbers -1 and 3 divide the x-axis into 3 intervals, from $-\infty$ to -1, -1 to 3, and 3 to $-\infty$.

$f(x)$ has a relative minimum value at $x = x_1$, if and only if $f'(x_1) = 0$ and the sign of $f'(x)$ changes from $-$ to $+$ as x increases through x_1.

If $-1 < x < 3$, then $f'(x) = -$

If $x = 3$, then $f'(x) = 0$

If $x > 3$, then $f'(x) = +$

Therefore, $f(3)$ is a relative minimum.

Note that when $x < -1$, $f'(x) = +$. If $x = -1$, $f'(x) = 0$. If $-1 < x < 3$, $f'(x) = -$.

Thus, $f(-1)$ is a relative maximum, not minimum.

26. (C)

The width will be multiplied by 3.5 and the length by 6.3, so the area will be $3.5 \times 6.3 = 22.05$ times the original area $= 22.05 \times 5 = 110.25$.

27. (C)

As shown in the figure, the diagonal on each side of the cube is

$$\sqrt{5^2 + 5^2} = 7.07$$

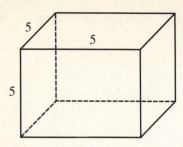

The diagonal of the cube lies in the rectangle whose height is 5 and width is 7.07, as shown in the figure. Therefore, it can be easily found that the length of the diagonal is

$$\sqrt{5^2 + 7.07^2} = 8.66$$

28. **(D)**

The normal line is the line that is perpendicular to the curve at the given point. Its equation is $y = y_0 + m(x - x_0)$ where (x_0, y_0) is the given point and m is the slope. At the point where $x = 1$,

$$y = x^4 - 3x^2 + 1$$
$$= (1)^4 - 3(1)^2 + 1$$
$$= -1$$

Thus, $(x_0, y_0) = (1, -1)$. The slope m of the normal line is the negative reciprocal of the slope of the tangent line, which is the value of the derivative at the given point;

i.e., $m = \dfrac{-1}{\dfrac{dy}{dx}\Big|_{x=1}}$

$$\frac{dy}{dx} = \frac{d}{dx}\left(x^4 - 3x^2 + 1\right)$$

$$= 4x^3 - 6x,$$

$$m = \frac{-1}{\left(4x^3 - 6x\right)\big|_{x=1}}$$

$$= \frac{-1}{(4-6)}$$

$$= \frac{-1}{-2}$$

$$= \frac{1}{2}$$

Thus, the equation of the normal line is:

$$y = y_0 + m\left(x - x_0\right)$$
$$y = -1 + \frac{1}{2}(x - 1)$$
$$2y = -2 + (x - 1)$$
$$2y = x - 3$$
$$x - 2y - 3 = 0$$

29. **(A)**

The symbol "$\vee$" represents the word "or." If at least one of two statements is true, the compound statement of these statements with the word "or" is also true.

30. **(B)**

The slope of the graph of $5x + 6y = 24$ is $-5/6$, so the slope of the graph of $px - 4y = 12$ must be $6/5$. Then $6/5 = p/4$. Solving, $p = 24/5 = 4.8$

31. **(A)**

Substituting $(1, 6)$ into $f(x)$, we get $6 = a + b + c$. Substituting $(2, 11)$ into $f(x)$, we get $11 = 4a + 2b + c$. Substituting $(3, 20)$ into $f(x)$, we get $20 = 9a + 3b + c$. Solving these simultaneous equations, $a = 2$, $b = -1$, and $c = 5$. Then $a + b - c = -4$.

32. **(C)**

The appropriate formula is $A = P(1 + R)^x$, where A = Amount, P = Principal, R = Rate per interest period, and x = Number of interest periods. In this example, A = \$2500 + \$800 = \$3300, P = \$2500, R = .08/4 = .02, and x is unknown. The equation will read as follows: $3300 = 2500(1.02)^x$. Then $\log 3300 = \log 2500 + (x)(\log 1.02)$. Solving, $x \approx 14$ periods, which corresponds to 3.5 years.

33. **(A)**

For a parabolic function $f(x) = A(x - h)^2 + k$, the vertex is located at (h, k). When this function is moved in a positive horizontal direction, the value of h increases;

when the function is moved in a negative vertical direction, the value of k decreases. In this example, the original values of h and k are -3 and -5, respectively. The new value of h is $-3 + 4 = 1$, and the new value of k is $-5 - 6 = -11$. So, the function $g(x) = (x - 1)^2 - 11$.

34. (C)

The surface area of a cube is given by the expression $6s^2$, where s is the length of one side. The lateral surface area of a cylinder is given by the expression $2\pi rh$, where r is the radius and h is the height. Equating these expressions, we get $6s^2 = (2)(\pi)(6/\pi)(15)$. Simplifying, we get $6s^2 = 180$, so $s = \sqrt{30} \approx 5.48$ This means that the volume of the cube is $(5.48)^3 \approx 165$.

35. (D)

In the standard form $dy/dx + [P(x)]\,[y] = Q(x)$. In this example, $P(x) = 2$ and $Q(x) = 3$. The solution will be given by $y = 1/v(x) \cdot \int [v(x)][Q(x)]\,dx$, $v(x) = e^{\int 2\,dx} = e^{2x}$. Then $y = 1/2e^{2x} \cdot \int (e^{2x})(3)\,dx = (1/e^{2x})[(3/2)e^{2x} + C] = 3/2 + Ce^{-2x}$ where C is a constant. Since $y(0) = 1$, we can write $1 = 3/2 + Ce^{\circ}$. Since $e^{\circ} = 1$, $C = -1/2$.

36. (B)

The number of committees is given by $({}_7C_2)({}_{10}C_3) = (21)(120) = 2520$. The meaning of ${}_nC_r$ is the number of combinations of n items taken r at a time, which is mathematically equivalent to $(n)(n-1)(n-2)(\ldots)(n-r+1)$ divided by $r!$ So ${}_{10}C_3 = (10)(9)(8)/3!$ and ${}_7C_2 = (7)(6)/2!$

37. (B)

In order for an objective function not to have a unique point that corresponds to a maximum P value, the slope of this function must be the same as one of the lines that form the boundary of this region. The slope of the x-axis is zero and that of the y-axis is undefined. The slope of the line containing $(0, 10)$ and $(16, 8)$ is $-1/8$; the slope of the line containing $(40, 0)$ and $(16, 8)$ is $-1/3$. The only

objective function among these four answer choices with either of these slope values is $P = 30x + 90y$. This objective function has a slope of $-30/90 = -1/3$.

38. (B)

The maximum height of any parabola given in the form $y = Ax^2 + Bx + C$, where A is negative, is given by the y value of the vertex. In this example, z replaces y, and t replaces x. The x value of the vertex is given by $-B/2A = 144/-32 = 4.5$, and this is the required time in seconds.

39. (C)

By definition, since $f(x)$ is continuous on the closed interval $[c, d]$, the integral of $f(x)$ over some interval within $[c, d]$, which is denoted by $F(x)$, must be defined and differentiable at each x.

40. (A)

By definition, the median from Q contains the midpoint of $\overline{PR}$ which is $(-.5, 0)$. The slope of this median is $(6 - 0)/(1 + .5) = 4$.

41. (C)

Using the Ratio Test, $|u_{n+1}/u_n| = [x^{n+1}/(n+1)!][n!/x^n] = |x|/(n+1)$, which approaches zero for every value of x.

42. (D)

The first letter can be any of 24 letters from A through X. Once the first letter is selected, there is only one choice for each of the second letter and the third letter. The reason is because each of the second and third letters must follow the first letter, both alphabetically and in order. For example, if Q is the first letter, then R must be the second letter and S must be the third letter. There are 7 choices for the first digit, 6 choices for the second digit, and 5 choices for the third digit. The number of different ID badges is $(24)(1)(1)(7)(6)(5) = 5040$.

43. (C)

$a_2 = (a_1)^2 + 5 = 9 + 5 = 14$, $a_3 = (14)^2 + 5 = 201$, $a_4 = (201)^2 + 5 = 40,406$. Then $a_3 + a_4 = 201 + 40,406 = 40,607$.

44. (C)

The entry in the upper left is $(2)(1) + (3)(2) + (-1)(-1) = 9$. The entry in the upper right is $(2)(3) + (3)(0) + (-1)(2) = 4$. The entry in the lower left is $(-2)(1) + (1)(2) + (2)(-1) = -2$. The entry in the lower right is $(-2)(3) + (1)(0) + (2)(2) = -2$.

45. (B)

The average value of $f(x) = 1/(10-2)\int_2^{10}(10-x)\,dx$

$= (1/8)[10x - x^2/2]_2^{10} = (1/8)[100 - 50 - 20 + 2]$

$= (1/8)(32) = 4$. Then $4 = 10 - x$, so $x = 6$.

46. (D)

The observed values of the 4 flavors are: 49, 29, 17, and 5.

The expected values of the 4 flavors are: 40, 35, 15, and 10.

Note that the expected values are simply the percents multiplied by the actual number of people, which is 100.

The chi-square value is calculated by the formula $\sum \dfrac{(O_i - E_i)^2}{E_i}$, where each O_i is an observed value and each E_i is an expected value. Then, the chi-square value $= 81/40 + 36/35 + 4/15 + 25/10 \approx 5.82$

The next step is to locate the critical chi-square value in a table. Here, the number of degrees of freedom is 3. (One less than the number of pairs of data). At the 5% level of significance, the critical chi-square value is 7.815. Since $5.82 < 7.815$, the claim should not be rejected.

47. (B)

For a rational function in the form of $p(x)/q(x)$, where each of $p(x)$ and $q(x)$ are polynomial functions, the domain is found by solving $q(x) = 0$. So, $x - 4 = 0$ becomes $(x - 2)(x + 2) = 0$. This implies that $x = 2$ and $x = -2$.

48. (C)

The required number is $(2)(3)(5)(7)(11) = 2310$.

49. (D)

Using Bayes' Theorem, let $P(A \mid B)$ mean the probability of event A occurring, given that event B has already occurred. Then $P(\text{Box I} \mid \text{a defective box is selected}) = [P(\text{Box I}) \cdot P(\text{Defective box} \mid \text{Box I is selected}) / \{[P(\text{Box I}) \cdot P(\text{Defective box} \mid \text{Box I is selected}] + P(\text{Box II}) \cdot P(\text{Defective box} \mid \text{Box II is selected})\} = (1/2)(1/5) / [(1/2)(1/5) + (1/2)(2/4)] = (1/10)/(7/20) = 2/7$.

50. (D)

The area of the first square $= 9$, the area of the second square $= (1/9)(9) = 1$. Each subsequent square will have an area equal to 1/9 of its predecessor. The tenth term is given by $(9)(1/9)^9 = 9^{-8}$.

51. (C)

By substitution, $8 = Cp$ and $18 = Cp^3$. Dividing the second equation by the first equation, $p^2 = 2.25$, so $p = 1.5$ Now, $y = (C)(1.5)^x$. Using the point $(1,8)$, $8 = (C)(1.5)$, so $C = 5.33$. Finally, $C + p = 6.83$.

52. (A)

If a graph of a line has no x-intercept, it must be parallel to the x-axis. This means that the general form of the equation is $y = k$, where k is a constant. The equation $5y = 10$ can be reduced to $y = 2$, so it represents a line which is parallel to the x-axis.

53. (A)

The period of a function given by $y = A \sin Bx + C$, where A, B, C are constants is $2\pi / B = 2\pi / (2/3) = 3\pi$.

54. (D)

Using the Normal Distribution, the critical z value is 2.05. The corresponding raw score is $(3)(2.05) + 70 = 76.15$ Since we need a minimum integer score, the correct answer is 77.

55. (C)

Using the Pythagorean Theorem, $QS = \sqrt{8^2 + 15^2} = \sqrt{289} = 17$. Using the Law of Sines on triangle QRS, $17/\sin 75° = QR/\sin 60°$. Then, $QR = 17 \sin 60°/\sin 75° \approx 15.2$

56. (C)

There are a total of 8 letters, with two A's and 3 L's. The number of arrangements is given by $8!/[(2!)(3!)] = 3360$. Note that the exclamation point means "factorial" and is defined as: $n! = (n)(n-1)(n-2)(\dots)(1)$ for any non-negative integer. Also, $0!$ is defined as 1.

57. (B)

For the parabola given by $y = Ax^2 + Bx + C$, the x value of the vertex is given by $-B/2A$. In this example, $-B/2A = -12/2 = -6$. The corresponding y value is $(-6)^2 + (12)(-6) + 35 = -1$. So the original vertex is $(-6, -1)$. When reflected about the x-axis, the x value remains the same, but the y value changes sign. Thus, the reflected point becomes $(-6, 1)$.

58. (A)

$v = \sqrt{2^2 + 4^2} = \sqrt{20}$ and $w = \sqrt{1^2 + 2^2} = \sqrt{5}$. Since $\sqrt{20} = 2 \cdot \sqrt{5}$, then $\sqrt{20} - \sqrt{5} = 2\sqrt{5} - \sqrt{5} = \sqrt{5}$.

59. (D)

If $\angle 1 \cong \angle 2$, the triangles ABC and ACD would have two pairs of congruent sides and a pair of non-inclusive congruent angles. This would be insufficient to prove that these triangles are congruent, which means that we cannot conclude that $\angle ACB \cong \angle ACD$. Thus, we cannot conclude that $\overline{AC}$ is perpendicular to $\overline{BD}$. Answer choice (A) would imply that triangles ABC and ACD are congruent by side-angle-angle, so $\angle ACB \cong \angle ACD$ by corresponding parts. This would imply that $\overline{AC}$ is perpendicular to $\overline{BD}$. Answer choice (B) would already establish that since $\angle B \cong \angle D$, $\angle ACB \cong \angle ACD$. Thus we would conclude that $\overline{AC}$ is perpendicular to $\overline{BD}$. Answer choice (C) would imply that triangles ABC and ACD are congruent by side-side-side, so $\angle ACB \cong \angle ACD$ by corresponding parts. This would imply that $\overline{AC}$ is perpendicular to $\overline{BD}$.

60. (C)

The general formula is $L = (a)(r)^{n-1}$ where L is the nth term, a is the first term, and r is the common ratio between terms. We can then write $8 = (a)(r)^2$ and $125 = (a)(r)^5$. Dividing the second equation by the first equation, we get $r^3 = 15.625$, so $r = 2.5$ The first term can be found by the equation $8 = (a)(2.5)^2 = 6.25a$. Thus $a = 8/6.25 = 1.28$

61. (B)

Since there are 12 data, the position of the first quartile is $(12 + 2)/4 = 3.5$; the 3.5th number is the mean of the 3rd and 4th numbers $= (6 + 9)/2 = 7.5$ The position of the third quartile is $(36 + 2)/4 = 9.5$; the 9.5th number is the mean of the 9th and 10th numbers $= (24 + 30)/2 = 27$. Finally $7.5 + 27 = 34.5$.

62. (C)

The midpoint of $\overline{AB}$ is $(2, 2)$ and the midpoint of $\overline{CD}$ is $(-5, 5)$. The distance between these midpoints is $\sqrt{(-5-2)^2 + (5-2)^2} = \sqrt{58}$.

63. (A)

The standard score, denoted by z, is found by the formula $z = (x - \mu)/\sigma$, where μ is the mean and σ is the standard deviation. Then $z = (7.6 - 10)/1.5 = -1.6$. In the chart of Normal Distribution values of z, the probability that a z score is greater than -1.6 is $.9452$, which is approximately 94.5%.

64. (D)

Using the Distance Formula, $AB = \sqrt{(4-0)^2 + (-3-0)^2} = \sqrt{25} = 5$. Clearly, $BC = 8$. Drop a perpendicular segment from point A to the x-axis. Call this point D which is located at $(-3, 0)$; we can see that $AD = 4$ and $DB = 3$. In right triangle ADC, $AD = 4$, $DC = DB + BC = 11$. Using the Pythagorean Theorem, $AC^2 = 4^2 + 11^2 = 137$. Now, using the Law of Cosines in triangle ABC, $AC = AB + BC - (2)(AB)(BC) (\cos \angle B)$. By substitution, $137 = 25 + 64 - (2)(5)(8)(\cos \angle B)$. This simplifies to $137 = 89 - 80 \cos \angle B$, so $\cos \angle B = -0.6$ This means $\angle B \approx 127°$.

65. (C)

By definition, mathematical induction is the process of using the results of either one case or a particular group of cases to formulate a theory about the results in all cases.

66. (D)

$P_3 = P_2 + 1 = 3$. $P_4 = (2)(P_3) = 6$, $P_5 = P_4 + 1 = 7$, $P_6 = (2)(P_5) = 14$. Then $P_5 + P_6 = 7 + 14 = 21$.

67. (C)

Using Descartes' rule of signs, the maximum number of positive zeros for a polynomial function corresponds to the number of sign changes for the function $f(x)$. If four of the given five coefficients are negative, there is one positive coefficient. If either A or E is positive, there will be only one change of signs; however, if either B, C, or D is positive, there will be two changes of signs. So, two is the maximum number of positive zeros.

68. (B)

A square root of any quantity must have a value of at least zero. The solution for answer choice (A) is $x = 3$. The solution for answer choice (C) is $x < -3$. The solution for answer choice (D) is $x \leq 7$.

69. (B)

When any point (x, y) is rotated $90°$ counter-clockwise, the new point changes to $(-y, x)$. Notice that the slope of the line connecting $(0, 0)$ with (x, y) is y/x and the slope of the line connecting $(0, 0)$ with $(-y, x)$ is $-x/y$. These two lines must be perpendicular to each other due to the $90°$ rotation. Recall that two lines are perpendicular to each other if their slopes are negative reciprocals of each other. Thus, when the point $(10, 2)$ is rotated $90°$ counter-clockwise, the new point is $(-2, 10)$.

70. (D)

The inverse of the graph of any function is found by reflecting the graph across the line $y = x$. This means that for any point (x, y) on the original graph, the point (y, x) must be on the inverse graph. The point $(6, 7)$ is a point on the graph of the inverse since $(7, 6)$ is on the graph of the original function.

71. (A)

Using a table of t values, where the number of degrees of freedom is 7. The critical t values are 2.365. The test value of t is given by the formula $t = (\bar{x} - \mu)/(s/\sqrt{n})$, where $\bar{x}$ is the sample mean, μ is the population mean, s is the sample standard deviation, and n is the size of the sample. By substitution, $t = (28,000 - 30,000)/(1500/\sqrt{8}) \approx -3.77$. Since $-3.77 < -2.65$, the claim should be rejected.

72. (B)

The only requirement about the sides of a rectangle is that they must be parallel in pairs and that four right angles must be present. For two squares, two rhombuses, or two triangles, if the corresponding angles are equal, the corresponding sides must be in proportion. Specifically, for any two rhombuses or squares, all sides of any one figure are equal.

73. (C)

The quickest way to solve this would be to test each sequence. For choice (A), the first-order difference is given by 6, 18, 54, 162, … , so its second-order difference is given by 12, 36, 108, … . Choice (A) is wrong. For choice (B), the first-order difference is given by 3, 3, 3, 3, … , so its second-order difference is given by 0, 0 , 0, … . Choice (B) is wrong. For choice (C), the first-order difference is given by 4, 7, 10, 13, . . . , so its second-order difference is given by 3, 3, 3, ... Choice (C) is correct. We should also check choice (D). Here, the first-order difference is given by 4, 9, 17, 25, . . . , so the second-order difference is given by 5, 8, 8, ... Choice (D) is wrong.

74. (C)

The equation $2x + 3y = 6$ has a slope of $-2/3$, so it must be represented by L_2. Similarly, the equation $x - y = 1$ has a slope of 1, so it must be represented by L_1. The inequality $2x + 3y \leq -6$ can be rewritten as $y \leq (-2/3)x - 2$, so we are looking for a region below L_2. Likewise, the inequality $x - y \leq 1$ can be rewritten as $y \geq x - 1$, so we are also looking for a region above L_1. The given shaded region satisfies both of these requirements.

75. (B)

The sum of the perimeters of all regular polygons from 6 sides through 59 sides $= n/6 + n/7 + n/8 + … + n/59$. By replacing the 6-sided polygon with a 60-sided polygon, the new sum $= n/7 + n/8 + n/9 + … + n/60$.

Subtracting the new sum from the original sum, we get $n/6 - n/60 = 9n/60$.

76. (B)

$\angle 5$ and $\angle 6$ together form the base angle at point Q, but they need not be congruent. $\angle 3 \cong \angle 4$, since they are alternate interior angles of parallel lines. $\angle 1 \cong \angle 2$, since they are vertical angles. Triangles MPQ and NQP can be shown to be congruent by side-side-side. (Note that the diagonals of an isosceles trapezoid are congruent.) Then $\angle 4 \cong \angle 6$, since they are corresponding parts of congruent triangles.

77. (A)

Factoring the left side of the equation, we get $(2\tan x - 3)(\tan x + 4) = 0$. If $2\tan x - 3 = 0$, $x = $ Arctan $(3/2) \approx 56°$. If $\tan x + 4 = 0$, $x = $ Arctan $(-4) \approx 104°$.

78. (A)

If $z = 180 - (x + y)$, we would have parallel lines, since interior angles of the same side of the transversal would be supplementary. Since $x = y$, the expression $180 - (x + y)$ is equivalent to $180 - 2x$. The statement in answer choice (B) would always be true, since the sum of the angles of any triangle is 180°. The statement in answer choice (C) would be impossible since this would mean that each of x and y equals 90, and the transversal would coincide with line ℓ_1. The statement in answer choice (D) would imply that since $z = w + x = w + y$, $z = 90$. Each of x and y would be the same value less than 90, but would not imply that $\ell_1 \parallel \ell_2$.

79. (D)

By direct substitution, $70 = 25 + (100 - 25) e^{-5k}$. Simplifying this equation, we get $.6 = e^{-5k}$. Then $\ln .6 = -5k$ and so $k \approx .102$. Now $T(8) = 25 + (100 - 25) e^{(-.102)(8)} = 25 + 75 e^{-.816} \approx 58$.

80. (C)

The x-value of the vertex of this parabola is given by $-(-3)/[(2)(-1)] = -1.5$. The corresponding y-value $= -(-1.5)^2 - 3(-1.5) + 4 = 6.25$. Since the coefficient of x^2 is negative, this parabola will have its highest point at the vertex, which is $(-1.5, 6.25)$. Thus, the range will be all numbers less than or equal to the y-value of the vertex, which is 6.25.

81. (B)

The least common multiple of 12 and 14 is 84. We need to count 84 days from April 15th. There are 15 days left for April, so 84 − 15 = 69. The month of May has 31 days, so 69 − 31 = 38. The month of June has 30 days, so 38 − 30 = 8. Thus, the required date is the 8th day of July.

82. (C)

Let x = the number of new units with electric heating and $26 - x$ = the number of new units with gas heating. Currently, the ratio of units with electric heating to those with gas heating is 16/128 = 1/8. After the new units are built, the number of units with electric heating will be $16 + x$ and the number of units with gas heating will be $128 + 26 - x = 154 - x$. Since the required ratio will double, we can write $(16 + x)/(154 - x) = 1/4$. Cross-multiplying, we get $64 + 4x = 154 - x$. Finally, $x = 18$.

83. (D)

The quickest way to find the correct answer is to substitute the given values to verify which equation contains all four pairs. The pair (−2, 19) does not belong to answers (B), nor (C), so we can conclude that only (A) or (D) can be correct. However, the pair (−1, 7) does not belong to (A), so we are left with answer choice (D) as the correct answer. Note that by substitution, we can check each pair. $19 = -(-2)^3 - (5)(-2) + 1$, $7 = -(-1)^3 - (5)(-1) + 1$, $-5 = -(1)^3 - (5)(1) + 1$, and $-17 = -(2)^3 - (5)(2) + 1$.

84. (B)

The circumference of the circle = $(\pi)(d) = 8\pi$. The length of the required arc = $(8\pi)(135/360) = 3\pi$.

85. (D)

The central angle of sector $EOD = 360° - 130° - 95° - 90° = 45°$. Then the area of sector $EOD =$

$(45°/360°)(\pi)(12)^2 = 18\pi$. Let x = shaded area. The area of polygon $ABCO = 1.30x$. So $1.30x - x = 18\pi$. Solving, $x = 60\pi$.

86. (C)

If a rational function has a slant asymptote, the degree of its numerator must be one higher than the degree of its denominator. Only answer choice (C) satisfies this requirement. Also, the equation for the slant asymptote is given by $y = (A/B)x$, where A/B represents the ratio of the leading coefficient of the numerator divided by the leading coefficient of the denominator. In choice (C), this ratio is 2/3, which matches $y = (2/3)(x)$.

87. (B)

The original total weight of all the people in the room is (20)(130) = 2600 pounds. After Bob and Diane leave the room, the mean weight of the remaining 18 people will be (130)(.97) = 126.1 pounds. This means that the total weight for these 18 people is (18)(126.1) ≈ 2270 pounds. Then 2600 − 2270 = 330 pounds is the total weight for Bob and Diane. Finally, the mean weight for Bob and Diane is 330 / 2 = 165 pounds.

88. (A)

Factor the left side of the inequality to get $(2x - 3)(x + 1) < 0$. If $2x - 3 > 0$ and $x + 1 < 0$, we get $x > 3/2$ and $x < -1$, which is impossible. If $2x - 3 < 0$ and $x + 1 > 0$, we have the actual solution of $-1 < x < 3/2$.

89. (C)

The slope of the line segment connecting (2, 5) and (0, 1), which is 2, must equal the slope of the line segment connecting (7, 1) and (b, c). Thus, $2 = (c - 1)/(b - 7)$. This becomes $2b - 14 = c - 1$, so $c = 2b - 13$. Another approach would be to realize that the segment connecting (0, 1) and (7, 1) has a distance of 7 and a slope of zero. This would mean that point (b, c) is really (2 + 7, 5) = (9, 5). This would match the relationship shown in answer choice (C), since $5 = (2)(9) - 13$.

90. (C)

Use the Binomial Distribution, which states Probability of x successes in n trials $= (_nC_x)(p^x)(1 - p)^{n - x}$. In this formula, $_nC_x =$ the number of combinations of x successes in n trials $= (n)(n - 1)(n - 2) (...)(n - x + 1)/x!$, and $p =$ probability of success on any single trial. Here, $n = 30$, $x = 7$, $p = .2$, and $_{30}C_7 = (30)29(28) (...)(24)/7! = 2,035,800$. Thus, the required probability $= (2,035,000)(.2)^7 (.8)^{23} \approx .154$.

91.

- James' weekly tax will be $\$2 + (.006)(\$800 - \$200) = \$5.60$

- Marianne's weekly tax will be $\$5 + (.012)(\$600 - \$100) = \$11.00$

- If Linda were to remain as a non-resident of Moneyville, her weekly tax would be $\$5 + (.012)(\$1000 - \$100) = \$15.80$. If she were to become a resident of Moneyville, her weekly tax would become $\$2 + (.006)(\$1000 - \$200) = \$6.80$. Thus, she would pay $\$9$ less per week. Her tax savings for an entire year would be $(\$9)(52) = \$468$.

See Next Page for Scoring Guidelines for Constructed Written Assignment

Scoring Guidelines for Constructed Written Assignment

Performance Characteristics

The following characteristics guide the scoring of responses to the written assignment.

Purpose:	Fulfill the charge of the assignment.
Application of Content:	Accurately and effectively apply the relevant knowledge and skills.
Support:	Support the response with appropriate examples and/or sound reasoning reflecting an understanding of the relevant knowledge and skills.

Scoring Scale

Scores will be assigned to each response to the written assignment according to the following scoring scale.

Score Point	Score Point Description
4	**The "4" response reflects a thorough command of the relevant knowledge and skills.** • The response completely fulfills the purpose of the assignment by responding fully to the given task. • The response demonstrates an accurate and highly effective application of the relevant knowledge and skills. • The response provides strong support with high-quality, relevant examples and/or sound reasoning.
3	**The "3" response reflects a general command of the relevant knowledge and skills.** • The response generally fulfills the purpose of the assignment by responding to the given task. • The response demonstrates a generally accurate and effective application of the relevant knowledge and skills. • The response provides support with some relevant examples and/or generally sound reasoning.

2	**The "2" response reflects a partial command of the relevant knowledge and skills.** • The response partially fulfills the purpose of the assignment by responding in a limited way to the given task. • The response demonstrates a limited, partially accurate and partially effective application of the relevant knowledge and skills. • The response provides limited support with few examples and/or some flawed reasoning.
1	**The "1" response reflects little or no command of the relevant knowledge and skills.** • The response fails to fulfill the purpose of the assignment. • The response demonstrates a largely inaccurate and/or ineffective application of the relevant knowledge and skills. • The response provides little or no support with few, if any, examples and/or seriously flawed reasoning.

INDEX

Index

Δ-method, 112, 113

A

abscissa, 98, 180
absolute value, definition of, 72, 148
absolute value equations, 72
acute angle, 149
acute triangle, 165
addition postulate, 152
adjacent angles, 149, 156
algebra terms, 51
algebraic expressions
    factors of, 53
    simplifying, 53–55
angle difference postulate, 154
angles, 97–104, 149
    theorems related to, 154–156
    types of, 149
angle sum postulate, 154
antiderivatives, 133
antidifferentiation, power rule for, 133
application of the derivative, 120–132
applications of the integral, 141–145
    area calculation, 141–143
    volume of a solid of revolution, 143
area under a graph, 133
arguments, 33
    evaluating, 33–34
arithmetic mean, 214–215
arithmetic operations, representations of, 44
associative property of addition, 46
associative property of multiplication, 46
averages, *see* measures of central tendency
axioms, postulates, and assumptions, 39–40

B

bar chart (or bar graph), 209
basic principles, laws, and theorems, 37
Bayes theorem, 201

Bayesian decision analysis, 201–202
binomial, 51
box-and-whiskers plot, 210

C

calculus, 97, 107–112
    the fundamental theorem of, 136
Cartesian coordinate plane, 180, *see also* coordinate
    plane
Cartesian coordinate system, 90–91, 98
chord of a circle, 171
circles, 171, 181
    arc, 171
    area, 173
    central angle, 172
    circumference, 172
    equation, 182
    inscribed angle, 172
    point of tangency, 172
    radius, 171
circumscribed circle, 172
closed interval, 111, 112, 120, 121, 134, 136, 139, 141
closure property of addition, 46
closure property of multiplication, 46
coefficient of a variable, 51
collinear points, 147
combinations, 204–206
complementary angles, 149
complex numbers, 47–48
    imaginary part, 47
    real part, 47
composite function, 88
concavity, 128
conclusion-indicator words, 33
conditional statement, 36, 153
confidence interval, 230
congruent angles, 149, 157–159
    method of proof, 159–160
congruent segments, 148, 157–159
    method of proof, 159–160

conic sections, 181–190
  circle, 181
  ellipse, 181, 183
  hyperbola, 181, 188
  parabola, 181, 185
consistency, 35
constant, 51
continuity, 110
  theorems of, 111–112
continuous function, *see* continuity
coordinate geometry, 179–181
coordinate plane, 90, 91, *see also* Cartesian coordinate plane
  quadrants in, 91, 180
coplanar points, 149
corollary, 39–40
correlation, 212, 224
  perfect, 224
correlation coefficient, 224–225
cosecant, 98
cosine, 97
cotangent, 97
counting, 202
  fundamental principle of, 203
counting methods, 202–205
counting procedures
  involving order restrictions, *see* permutations
  not involving order restrictions, *see* combinations
cross-multiplication, 55
cubes, 174
cumulative property of addition, 46
cumulative property of multiplication, 46
curve sketching and the derivative tests, 127–129
cylinders, 174

D

data analysis, 199
data description
  graphs, 209–213
  numerical methods, 213–220
deductive reasoning, 37
deductive validity and invalidity, 34
definite integral, 133–141
  definition, 134
  properties of, 135–136
degrees, 98, *see also* radian
dependent equations, 58
derivative
  application of the, 120–132
  definition, 112
  high order, 119
  notations for, 112

derivative at a point, 114
deviation, 221, *see also* standard deviation
directrix, 185
discrete mathematics, 199, 231–232
disk method, 143
dispersion, *see* variation
distributive property, 46–47
domain of a function, 87

E

elementary functions, 87–89
ellipse, 181, 183
  eccentricity, 183
  focus, 183
equiangular polygon, 162
equilateral polygon, 162
equilateral triangle, 165
equivalence relation, 158
equivalent inequalities, 73
equivalent representations, 43
experimental design, 228–230
  treatment, 229
experimental unit, 229
exponential differentiation, 118
exponential function, 88, 118, *see also* logarithmic function
expression, 51

F

factorial notation, 203–204
first derivative test, 127–128
formulas for factoring of polynomials, 54
frequency curves, types of, 212–213
frequency distribution, 210, 213, 214, 216, 217
function, 87
  absolute extrema for a, 125
  derivative of a, 112
  inverse of a, 88
  properties of a, 89–90
  rate of change of a, *see* derivative
fundamental theorem, definition, 137

G

geometric mean, 214
geometry, 147
graph, drawing, 91
graphing a function, 90–93
  using the derivative tests, 129–130
greatest common factor (GCF), 54

H

half-line, 147
harmonic mean, 214
high order derivatives, 119
histogram, 217
horizontal asymptote, 94
hyperbola, 181, 188, 189
    eccentricity, 188, 189

I

identity matrix, 238
identity property of addition, 46
identity property of multiplication, 46
implicit differentiation, 116
indefinite integral, 138
    algebraic simplification, 138
indirect proof, 37
inductive reasoning, 38–39
inductive strength and weakness, 34
inequalities, 72–74
    properties of, 73
integration of formulas, 138
integration by parts, 140–141
intermediate value theorem, 111
interquartile range, 221
intersecting planes, 174
invalid arguments, 34
inverse of a function, 88
inverse property of addition, 46
inverse property of multiplication, 46
inverse trigonometric differentiation, 117
inverse trigonometric functions, 101–102
invertible matrix, 238
"is inversely proportional to", 78
"is proportional to", 78
isosceles triangle, 157, 165

J

joint probabilities, 202

L

least common denominator (LCD), 55
least common multiple (LCM), 54
L'Hôpital's rule, 123, 124
limits
    definition, 107
    nonexistent, 109
    one-sided, 108
    special, 109
    theorems on, 107–108
line, 39, 147
line postulate, 151
line segment, 147, 156
    bisector of a, 148
    length of a, 148
linear equations, 55–56, 92, 232
    augmented matrix for a system of, 233
    intercept form of, 56
    point-slope form of, 56
    slope-intercept form of, 56, 57
    two-point form of, 56
    with two unknown variables, 57
    methods for solving systems of, 58
linear regression, simple, 226–228
logarithm properties, 89
logarithmic differentiation, 118
    steps in, 119
logarithmic function, 88, *see also* exponential function
logic
    basic concepts of, 33–35
    definitions, 35–36
logical falsity, 35
logical indeterminacy (contingency), 35
logical truth, 35

M

marginal probabilities, 202
mathematical connections, 42–43
mathematical topics, relationships between, 43–44
mathematics
    as communication, 41
    defining objects and concepts in, 41
    language of, 42
    teaching, 42–43
matrices (sing. matrix), 232, 235–237
matrix arithmetic, rules of, 238–241
maxima, 125–127
means, notations and definitions of, 214
mean value theorem, 120, 121, 123
    consequences of the, 122
    extended, 122
    for integrals, 136
measurement, 147
measures of central tendency, 214, 216–220
measures of variability, 220–223
median, definition, 217
method of proof, 35–41
minima, 125–127
minimum and maximum values, *see* minima, maxima

mode, definition, 216
monomial, 51
mutually exclusive events, 200

N

National Council of Teachers of Mathematics, 41
New York schools, 1
New York State Education Department, 1, 3
New York State Teacher Certification Examination
      (NYSTCE), 1
  about the test, 1
  format, 3–4
  mathematics CST, subareas, 1, 2
  retaking the test, 2
  scoring the mathematics CST, 4
  studying for the mathematics CST, 3
  test-taking tips, 5
  website, 2
  when to take the NYSTCE, 2
non-mutually exclusive events, 200
normals, 124–125

O

objective probability, 199
obtuse angle, 149
obtuse triangle, 165
one-sided limits, 108
open interval, 107, 108, 111, 112, 114, 120, 121, 125, 128,
      136
operations with polynomials, 51–53
ordinate, 98, 180

P

parabola, 65, 181, 185, 210
parallel cross sections, 145
parallel lines, definition, 150
parallelograms, 168
  area, 168
  consecutive angles, 168
  diagonal, 168
percentiles, 220
  definition, 221
periodicity of a function, 102
permutations, 204
perpendicular bisector, 150, 156
perpendicular lines, 150
pie chart, 209
plane, 39, 147
plane postulate, 153

plane separation postulate, 153
point, 39, 147
point betweenness postulate, 151, 152
point uniqueness postulate, 151
points of inflection, 128–129
points-in-a-plane postulate, 153
polygon, 162
polynomials, 51
  operations with, 51–53
  factoring of, 54
polynomial functions, 93–95
premises and conclusion, evidential strength
      between, 34
premise-indicator words, 33
prime factors, 54
probability, 199
  conditional, 201
  methods of computing, 200–201
  properties of, 199–200
probability tables, 202
projection of a given point, 150
projection of a segment, 150
pyramid, 176
Pythagorean theorem, 131, 163, 165, 179, 196

Q

quadrant angle, 98
quadratic equations, 61–70
  methods of solving, 61
  roots of, 61, 62
  in two unknowns, 66
quadratic formula, 62–64
quadratic functions, 65–66
quadrilaterals, 168–170

R

radian, 98, *see also* degrees
radical equation, 64–65
random sampling, 223
range, 220
range of a function, 87
rate of change, 131–132
ratio, proportion, and variation, 76–80
rational functions, graphs, 94
ray, 147
  vertex of a, 147
real number operations, 46
real numbers, 45
  and points of a line, 152
  properties of equality, 45–46

rectangles, 168
   area, 168
rectilinear motion, 130–131
reflex angle, 149
reflexive property of equality, 45
regular polygon, 162
   apothem, 162
   area of a, 162, 163
   perimeter of a, 162, 163
relation, 158
rhombus (pl. rhombi), 169
   area, 169
Riemann sum, 134
right angle, 149
Rolle's theorem, 120, 121

S

sampling, 202, 223–226
sampling distributions, 224
scalar, 74, *see also* vector
scalar (DOT) product, 75
scalene triangle, 165
scatter diagram, 226, 227
scatter-plot, 211–212
secant (trigonometry), 97
secant (circle), 171
semicircle, 172, 197
sentences, 33
   logical equivalence of, 35
   logical properties of, 35
sequences and series, 231–232
set, 39
shell method, 143–144
similar polygons, 163–164
sine, 97
sines and cosines, product formulas of, 100
slope of a line, 56–58
solid geometry, 174–179
solving minima and maxima problems, 126–127
special functions, graphs, 94–95
special limits, 109
sphere, 175
squares, 169
standard deviation, 222, *see also* deviation
statistics, 199, 209
stem-and-leaf plot, 211
straight angle, 149
subjective probability, 199
supplementary angles, 149
syllogism, 37

symmetric property of equality, 45
systems of equations, 66–69

T

tangent (trigonometry), 97
tangents, 124
terms, defined and undefined, 39–40
theorems, 39–40
transitive property of equality, 46
trapezoids, 169
   altitude, 170
   median, 169
   isosceles, 170
tree diagrams, 203
triangles, 164–166
   altitude, 165
   angle bisector, 166
   area, 165
   exterior angle, 166
   median, 166
   midline, 166
   perimeter, 165
trigonometric differentiation, 116–117
trigonometric functions, 97–104
   addition and subtraction formulas, 100
   basic identities, 99
   double-angle formulas, 100
   half-angle formulas, 100
   inverse, 101–102
   properties and graphs of, 101
   sum and difference formulas, 100
trigonometric integrals, 141
trigonometry, 97
   and right-triangle problems, 102–104
trinomial, 51
truth values, 33
   of premises and conclusion, 34

U

unit circle, 98

V

variable, 51
variance, 222
variation, 77–78, 220
vector, 74–76, *see also* scalar
vertical angles, 149, 153
vertical asymptote, 91

NOTES

NOTES

NOTES

NOTES

NOTES